THE SOVIET PARADOX

Seweryn Bialer

THE SOVIET PARADOX

External Expansion,
Internal Decline

VINTAGE BOOKS
A Division of Random House
New York

This book is dedicated to
W. Averell Harriman
to whom the world owes so much

FIRST VINTAGE BOOKS EDITION, August 1987

Library of Congress Cataloging-in-Publication Data
Bialer, Seweryn.
The Soviet paradox.
Reprint. Originally published:
New York: Knopf, 1986.
Bibliography: p.
Includes index.
1. Soviet Union—Politics and
government 1953 2. Soviet
Union—Foreign relations—1975- .
3. Soviet Union—Economic
conditions—1976- . 4. Soviet
Union—Social conditions—1970- .
I. Title.
DK288.B53   1987   327.47073   86-40477
ISBN 0-394-75288-0 (pbk.)

Manufactured in the United States of America
10 9 8 7 6 5 4 3 2 1

Contents

Preface

This book has been written for the interested reader in politics, government, business, journalism, and academia. It is based not only on thirty years of research and writing on twentieth-century Soviet history and politics, but also on many hours of conversation with people active in international relations in the Soviet Union, the United States, Eastern Europe, China, and other countries. My major goal has been to make the book comprehensive rather than to pursue in depth various points of interest to the specialist but esoteric to the general reader. For this reason I have reduced the scholarly "scaffolding" to a minimum. The reader will find a fair selection of sources and additional explanations concerning the Soviet Union in the bibliographical essay at the end of the book.

The writing of this book has been facilitated by a grant from the National Council of Soviet and East European Studies and, of course, by the award of the MacArthur Fellowship Prize. I am extremely grateful to my friend Michael Mandelbaum, whose constructive criticism and editorial advice have been invaluable. In preparation of the manuscript I benefited from many recommendations by Ashbel Green of Knopf, who remains for me a model of the perfect editor. I owe a debt of gratitude to my students and research assistants Peter Charow, Scott Monje, and Thomas Sherlock, all of whom at one time or another were extremely helpful in my work on this book. Finally, I would like to thank my secretary, Ellen Zbinovsky, and Audrey McInerney and the staff of the Research Institute on International Change for their patience and perseverance in the many typings, revisions, and proofreadings of the manuscript. Peter Biesada assisted in compiling the index.

S.B.

I

RUSSIA IN TRANSITION

> What is at stake is the ability of the Soviet Union to enter
> the new millennium in a manner worthy of a great and
> prosperous power. . . . Without the hard work and complete
> dedication of each and every one it is not even possible to
> preserve what has been achieved.
>
> Mikhail Gorbachev,
> General Secretary of the Soviet Communist Party

When Stalin died in March 1953, the leaders of the Soviet Communist Party and government appealed to the population not to panic. These were men who had made a demigod of Stalin and who had devoted their careers to trying to win his approval. Their appeal thus reflected their own uncertainty about what life would be like without the capricious, cruel, but always infallible leader. No one knew.

When Brezhnev died in November 1982, the leaders who survived him had no reason to issue such an appeal. This was not just because of the collegial character of the Brezhnev regime. It was also a result of the fact that during the last years of his rule, with the general secretary seriously ill and sometimes entirely inactive, the decision-making apparatus was almost paralyzed. His passing brought a sense of relief to both the Party and the general population. Stalin's death threatened chaos; Brezhnev's promised a return to efficiency and order.

Yet the death of Brezhnev may prove to have been as important to the future of the Soviet Union—and the United States—as the death of Stalin. And this may be so not only if the new leaders bring major changes to Russia, but also in the more likely event that the forces of inertia and continuity remain dominant. Both Western observers and members of the Soviet establishment are coming increasingly to the conclusion that the domestic system reached its peak under Brezhnev, and that without sweeping changes it will decline in its effectiveness in serving the goals of the Politburo.

The troubles that the Soviets face at home constitute a crisis of the system. The crisis can be eased by various measures, but can be solved only by changing the system. Such changes are, however, extremely difficult. The new leadership and political elite seem unprepared to engage in reforms that go beyond the boundaries of the existing system. The requirements of growth and technological progress clash with the leadership's and political elite's determination to preserve their immense power. The conditions of growth and progress are in contradiction with the imperative for central control and direct planning. The goal of leadership stability is inconsistent with the need for innovation.

On the domestic scene, the Soviet paradox is expressed in the following dilemmas: First, military growth is one of the chief sources of the internal problems besetting the Soviet Union and makes more difficult their resolution; at the same time, military growth is regarded by the leadership as a supreme value to which the economy and the society must be subordinated. Second, economic revitalization of the system would require a devolution of political power; yet the paramount goal of the leadership, from the regime's inception, has been the centralization and concentration of political power.

To deal with the Soviet Union in the years ahead, we will have to understand where the regime and the society now stand and how both are likely to evolve.

1

Stalinism and Anti-Stalinism in Historical Perspective

Over thirty years after his death, the ghost of Joseph Stalin still haunts Russia. It was he who elevated to power the core of the leadership that ruled Russia until 1985. Key institutions are still recognizably his creations. He is cast in literature and historical writings in a more positive light today than he was in the 1960s. The bulwark of his power, the secret police, has been fully rehabilitated and provided the springboard for Yuri Andropov's short tenure in the top Party post. During Leonid Brezhnev's last years, many working people longingly recalled an idealized version of the Stalinist era, when there was a boss who imposed order on the country. The fact that the entire period since Stalin's death is still characterized, both in the Soviet Union and in the West, as post-Stalinist, testifies to the deep imprint of his rule.

The revolution of October 1917 and the three years of civil war that followed are generally viewed as major turning points in Russian history—indeed, the crucible from which the Soviet Union emerged. They were, to be sure, crucial political events, which firmly established the Bolshevik party in power. But the decade spanning the Revolution, the civil war and the New Economic Policy (1921–28) was primarily a time of preparation, clearing the way for the real revolution, which was yet to occur. This first decade of Soviet power can be considered a continuation of the disintegration of Russian society that began in the last decades of tsarist rule. The Civil War of 1918–20 provided a preview of the real Soviet attitude toward the peasantry, which was one of deeply rooted animosity. This attitude was suspended temporarily during the period of the New Economic Policy in favor of coexistence with small landholders; but the Civil War and the policy of War Communism pur-

3

sued in this period also persuaded the core of the Bolshevik party of the need for extreme measures to effect social change. These attitudes were translated into practice during the next decade. The real Soviet revolution, the transformation of Russian society, took place from 1929 to 1939. It was directed by Stalin.

When Leon Trotsky, a central figure of the October Revolution, condemned the Stalinist revolution for betraying the original Bolshevik goals, his judgment was both correct and irrelevant. Those original goals were utopian, and could not be realized. The Bolsheviks promised egalitarianism and freedom. The objectives of swift modernization, however, required harsh authority, glaring inequality, and ruthless mobilization of resources. Stalin's historical role was to use the Bolsheviks' political power to reshape the main elements of the system that he had inherited—social, economic, cultural, military—and in so doing, to change the nature of Soviet political power itself. The industrialization that began in the late 1920s, the collectivization of the early 1930s, the militarization of society and, finally, the Great Purge of 1936–38 were all crucial steps in Stalin's revolution from above. In retrospect, Stalinism can be viewed as an extremely brutal and cruel, albeit successful, attempt to reverse the process of disintegration that characterized early twentieth-century Russia and to bridle the spontaneity of the Bolshevik revolution itself.

In several important respects both the Stalinist period and the early post-Stalinist decades were the functional equivalents in Russia of revitalization movements in other countries, such as the Meiji restoration in Japan or the Bismarckian revolution from above in Germany in 1870–80. Several major tasks were accomplished: the reintegration of society through a mixture of the familiar principle of nationalism with the new and specifically Soviet practices of mass terror, thought control, collective responsibility, and secularization of values; the acceleration of the industrial modernization of the society which had begun under the tsars; the transformation of the social structure; the radical improvement of the military competitiveness of the state in the international arena. All this was achieved, however, not by overcoming but rather by reinforcing the traditional Russian subjugation of the individual to the state and without creating a civil society of the Western type with its division between public and private sectors. The Soviet Union under Stalin became a modern but not a Western state. It came to have industry but not democracy.

The Stalinist revolution from above constituted, however, only one aspect of Stalinism—the dynamic one. Others were embodied in the system that he shaped through several decades of turmoil. The original pure Stalinist system featured mass terror directed against both the population and various elites; a highly developed police state, the central activities of which were imposed on all areas of society (the police were not only concerned with preserving public order and eradicating enemies of the state, but were in charge of the millions of slave laborers in the Archipelag Gulag, directly controlled many ministries in extracting industries, and supervised atomic research); a decision-making process based on personal dictatorship; an unbridled, all-pervasive cult of the supreme leader who embodied the source of authority; the transformation of the Party from a political movement into a political machine lorded over by the professional Party bureaucracy; the lack of any permanent rank order among the various bureaucracies—political, military, police, economic, administrative; the utter dependence of various elite groups and factions on the access of their leaders to Stalin, and on Stalin's benevolence; the dominance of Moscow over the Russian and non-Russian peripheries in all areas of activity; the total control of the political over the economic order, with Party and state bureaucrats making all the major economic decisions and an extreme centralization and concentration of economic decision-making (the command economy); the achievement of economic growth by a mobilization of resources aimed permanently in favor of military and heavy industries and by ever-increasing investments of labor, land, and capital; the elevation of the goal of enhanced military power to permanent priority, far more important than the objectives of economic growth, or public education and welfare; the establishment of a highly stratified status system in which one's position was determined directly by political power or through service provided to the holders of political power; a cultural rigidity and uniformity geared to produce an artificial cultural optimism. (The key formula of Stalinist culture, "socialist realism," was to present life in the Soviet Union not as it was, but as it should be); the fusion of Leninist messianism with Russian great-power nationalism as the basis of an ideology that proclaimed the uniqueness of the Soviet state; a high level of autarky in economic planning and an extreme effort to isolate the Soviet population from foreign influences; and, in the last decade of Stalin's rule, the end of the revolutionary impulse to change society and the emergence of a conservative attitude towards existing and sometimes prerevolutionary institutions and modes of behavior.

The elements of the mature Stalinist system depicted above convey its basic structural characteristics. Obviously, Stalinism is also associated with numerous policies aimed at the reinforcement of these characteristics, such as the consistent neglect of the peasantry and the agricultural sector, or the harsh Russification of non-Russian ethnic groups. While the policy elements of Stalinism can be altered without destroying the integrity of the system, many of its structural characteristics show an amazing resistance to change. There has, it is true, been *some* change.

The Stalinist system has ceased to exist, and a return to the old pattern in its pure form is almost impossible. The various elites have certainly learned that Stalinist terror strikes the powerful official as well as the rank-and-file citizen. As long as the memories of Stalinism linger, these elites will unify in opposition to any attempt by the top leader to amass too much power (as they did in the fall of 1964 when they ousted Khrushchev). The Soviet professional military, who were almost destroyed by the Great Purge of 1938, will not permit the secret police to gain control over them. Yet the system still contains many Stalinist characteristics at its core. Indeed, those characteristics are so important, and the continuity of the political culture is so pronounced, that one is justified in considering the transition of the Soviet Union from Stalinism to post-Stalinism as a change in the form of rule, not in its basic substance.

Continued existence of specific characteristics of the Stalinist system is inevitable. The survival of the police state, the permanent priority assigned to military growth, and the fusion of Leninist messianism with Great Russian nationalism are the most obvious Stalinist features of the contemporary Soviet Union. Yet in the long term the command economy, with its fusion of the political and economic spheres, with the political dominant, is probably the most persistent and significant legacy of Stalinism.

The command economy and the model of economic growth associated with it have the following main features:

• The state, which ultimately means the Communist Party leadership, owns and controls the economy. Land, mineral resources, factories, banks, commerce, foreign trade are all nationalized; each is controlled by a state monopoly.

• The Communist leadership is committed to economic growth as its major aim. Growth is oriented by goals, which are dictated not by the invisible hand of the market but by the visible hand of the state.

• While economic growth is an ambition of the Communist leadership, economic criteria for growth are a low-ranking consideration. What should grow, how fast and at what cost are all decided according to political criteria—that is to say, in response to the goals of the leadership.

• The operation of the economy is highly centralized, and is supervised by a giant bureaucracy organized along vertical lines of authority. The management of the primary units of production and services have very little freedom to decide what to do and how to do it. This, of course, is in complete contrast to Western market economies.

• The specific objectives of economic development are selective; the aim is not balanced growth. A relatively narrow range of high-priority tasks, such as military goals, are supplied with the necessary resources. Production and distribution of consumer goods must make do with the leftovers. Thus the Soviet Union is a major military power, but its people have a standard of living inferior to that in the West.

• The command planning of economic growth is extremely taut. Overambitious goals are calculated to bring forth the maximum expenditure of effort and energy. The economic reserves left for the element of the unexpected in planning for the future are very limited.

• Economic growth in the command economy depends primarily on massive and steadily increasing inputs of labor and capital—that is to say, on extensive growth. The rise of labor productivity, innovations and diffusion of new technology—that is to say, intensive development, which has been crucial to the West—has been of distinctly secondary importance in expanding the command economy.

• The directors of the command economy attach critical importance to quantitative indices of achievement. Their incentive system is geared largely to promote higher outputs, far more than higher quality or lower costs. The managers of microeconomic units know that they will be severely punished for not fulfilling their quotas. They and their workers also realize that they will get away with shortcomings in quality, diversity and costs. They obviously draw appropriate conclusions from this state of affairs. The incentive is to produce more but not better products.

• The money supply, price mechanism, and credit—the financial instruments that stimulate lower costs and higher productivity, quality and diversity of products in market economies—are absent or feeble. At best they perform an imperfect and artificial accounting function for the directors of the economy. And of course there is no such thing as consumer sovereignty. Russians cannot choose among competing brands. They must take what the state offers or do without.

• The Stalinist model of growth and the command economy were designed to be operated in virtual isolation from the outside world. After Stalin's death this total isolation was pierced. But even now Soviet dependence on the world market is marginal.

Stalinism could not survive in Russia in an undiluted form. At the time of Stalin's death, this was much more clearly understood by the Soviet political elite than by Western analysts. However, after the liquidation of secret police chief Lavrenti Beria in time-honored Stalinist fashion, the consensus among the leadership was quite narrow on the question of how much of the Stalinist legacy was to be preserved and how much should be eradicated. All, probably even senior secret police officials, were agreed on the abolition of mass terror. Self-serving instincts dictated the retention of the police state, but henceforth as a rational police state.

The Soviet elites were also determined not to permit the development of another uninhibited personal dictatorship. Their image of what type of leadership would be right, just, and effective was that of a ruling oligarchy, benevolent to elite members and strictly authoritarian to the society.

The consensus also included, though not without debate and struggle, the elevation of the Party apparatus to unquestioned leadership as the first among equals of the bureaucratic hierarchies. This elevation was not, as is sometimes portrayed, simply a Khrushchevian device to curry favor with the most powerful bloc of votes in the Central Committee. More importantly, it signaled the recognition by the leadership that the charismatic foundation of authority had to be replaced.

The only sources of post-Stalin authority that the elites believed could be effective, while at the same time preserving their authoritarian rule, were the myths of the Revolution, the Party, and Lenin—the triad that under Stalin had been immensely weakened—and the force of Russian great-power nationalism that they inherited from Stalin. In addition to the consensus on these structural changes, the leadership and the various elites shared the belief that many of Stalin's policies had become anachronistic, and had to be replaced, without undermining the structural pillars of rule.

They agreed that Stalin's policy of squeezing the peasant and letting the agricultural sector be starved for substantial investment had outlived its usefulness. Without mass terror, the urban population required more food and consumer goods as a condition of its tranquillity and political compliance. The leaders gradually became convinced that national strength and economic growth required the separation of science and ideology. Scientists had to have more freedom to pursue knowledge unhindered by ideological commissars. The ridiculous verdicts of Stalin's time that, for example, Einstein's theories of relativity and the modern science of genetics were anticommunist, had to be abandoned. In the interest of stability, the leaders were in favor of milder policies towards the country's non-Russian nationalities. Cultural self-definition of non-Russians was to be given more leeway. Moscow would put greater stress on co-opting local ethnic elites.

This was the extent of the post-Stalin consensus. Khrushchev himself wanted to go further. In the course of his anti-Stalin campaign—beginning in 1955 and lasting until his fall nine years later—he tried to tell at least some of the truth about the criminal nature of Stalin's rule; he attempted to shake the bureaucratic hierarchies out of their slumber; and he sought to foster greater participation by rank-and-file Party members in the process of government. While the campaign aroused opposition among his fellow heirs to Stalin's power, the majority of the Politburo involuntarily retired in the 1956–63 period, and their replacements, Khrushchev's creatures, were either in no position to voice their opposition to him or only later became frightened of the potential negative consequences of anti-Stalinism.

To the new Khrushchevian group, and the political and military elites, the anti-Stalin campaign had the advantage of denigrating the dead dictator and so elevating their own role in Soviet accomplishments during and after the Second World War. Khrushchev, for instance, described in some detail the constant fear in which the Party elite had lived under Stalin, citing the example of a car ride to Stalin's office during which he and Bulganin shared the thought: Will we return from this trip alive? The main direction of Khrushchev's attacks was reserved, however, for Stalin's wartime performance. He demonstrated that, far from winning the war singlehandedly, as propaganda had once asserted, Stalin bore the entire responsibility for the country's lack of preparation for the Nazi invasion and for the initial catastrophic defeats of the Red Army. Khrushchev went on to assert that it was the commanders in the field who developed and executed the plans for victory and the middle-level Party leaders on the home front who, in very difficult circumstances, kept supplies flowing to the troops. It subsequently became apparent, however, that the leaders would have preferred to build a conspiracy of silence around Stalin, to consign their old master to oblivion without registering his crimes and misdeeds, in which, after all, they had also participated.

Khrushchev seems to have had more far-reaching designs for the anti-Stalin campaign. It appears likely that at the outset his goal was simply to aggregate and consolidate his power by implicating his old Stalinist colleagues, and to preempt their possible use of an anti-Stalin campaign against *him*. However, once his old comrades had lost a mathematical majority in the Politburo in 1957 and he had attained unquestioned dominance within the group, he pursued his anti-Stalin campaign beyond its initial rationale. The height of the anti-Stalin campaign was not Khrushchev's secret speech at the Twentieth Party Congress in 1956, but rather the period from the Twenty-second Party Congress in 1961 to October 1964, when he was ousted.

With his solid victory in the Politburo in 1957, Khrushchev began to pursue a more open and forceful anti-Stalin campaign directed towards three parallel goals: the revival of the spirit of the Party in order to restore it as a mass movement; the mobilization of authentic support outside the Party in order to "get Russia moving again"; and the preparation of organizational-administrative changes.

The restoration of the Party as a mass movement was a necessary element of Khrushchev's design to build authority in the void left by Stalin's death. Through an intensive and protracted ideological campaign built around the slogan "Back to Leninism," Khrushchev attempted to revitalize the Party ideologically and to replace the personal charisma of Stalin with that of a vital and infallible institution, the Leninist Party. Through a number of initiatives intended to increase the amount of direct contact between the leadership and the Party masses and to expand the participation of rank-and-file Party members in social and political activities, Khrushchev hoped to transform the Party, guided by the precedent of the 1920s and the first five-year plan, into a powerful machine capable of spurring Russia on to its own version of a "Great Leap Forward."

Recognizing the working class's political apathy and indifference to Party goals, particularly in the economic realm, Khrushchev attempted to bind them once again to the Party. He hoped to accomplish this by presenting to the population grandiose visions of the Soviet Union overtaking the United States in production and consumption by the late 1970s or early 1980s, and by promising that the "present generation of Soviet citizens will live under full communism." (In Marxist-Leninist mythology, full communism describes a utopia in which human nature itself is transformed. It is a time of total abundance, when money is abolished, when everyone works only at the job he likes, and when everybody is rewarded "according to his needs.") In the nearer term, he proposed to increase immediately the material incentives for higher labor productivity, sometimes even at the cost of military expenditures. This curious mixture of an ideological communist vision and "goulash communism"—that is, pay incentives—was to be combined with efforts at enhancing popular participation in communal affairs in order to give the working classes a greater stake in economic progress. This was to be accomplished through the organs of the local government, the Soviets, the creation of institutions of popular participation such as the people's courts, and by such ideological innovations as the proclamation that the Soviet Union is "the state of the whole people."

His seemingly sincere belief that "full communism" was within reach if the popular spirit was freed from the yoke of Stalinist oppression and stagnation (coupled with his collectivist proclivities) led Khrushchev to proclaim that elements of this future society should immediately, if perhaps gradually, be introduced into Soviet life.

Most important, however, and most ominous for Khrushchev's own fate, were his attempts to use the anti-Stalin campaign to shake up the stagnant bureaucracies. During his rule, he engaged in almost continuous and often chaotic efforts to change the way the Stalinist system was organized. In the countryside, he abolished the machine-tractor stations, under Stalin a symbol of the exploitation of the peasants; he increased the size of the collective farms and introduced a policy of gradual transformation of farmers' cooperatives, the *kolkhozy,* into state farms; he stressed the collective work of the farmers and tried to curtail the cultivation of private plots. In industry, Khrushchev created regional economic coordinating bodies, the *sovnarkhozy,* in place of centralized ministerial controls. He attempted to reorganize the Party apparatus for the first time since the early thirties by splitting the apparatus into two types of organization—industrial and agricultural. While the *sovnarkhoz* reform challenged the power of the central state economic bureaucracy, the division of the Party apparatus diluted its overall power and tried to reorient it from political to economic activities.

Neither Khrushchev's anti-Stalin campaign nor his administrative changes could by any stretch of the imagination be considered radical. Yet they were responsible for his ouster—something unprecedented in Soviet history—by his comrades in October 1964. It was the product of unanimous agreement among his Politburo colleagues and among the bureaucratic elite. The unanimity of anti-Khrushchev feeling was demonstrated by the fact that after his removal only a small number of second-rank officials were dismissed from their positions.

Khrushchev failed in his effort to shift from Stalinism because both his anti-Stalin campaign and his limited administrative reforms were considered dangerous by his colleagues. The anti-Stalin campaign raised questions about the basic legitimacy of the regime. The leadership and political elite had wanted to make some changes in the Stalinist regime. They wished to do so, however, without denigrating the dictator whom they had served faithfully, lest some of the mud they threw at him should stick to them. This group was not interested in comprehensively reevaluating Stalin's place in Soviet history. They simply wanted to forget him.

There had been even less interest in constant administrative and organizational reforms, which could lead to changes in the structural elements of the system established by Stalin. Aside from a determination to abolish the mass terror, which endangered the elites' lives, and the extreme personal dictatorship, which drastically limited their power, they were unwilling to countenance further structural reforms. There was no desire to bring into question the foundations of authoritarianism in the Soviet Union.

Ironically, the most immediate cause of the Politburo's conspiracy to oust Khrushchev was his attempt to be independent of the bureaucratic elites that had brought him to power, and particularly of the Party apparatus. Khrushchev wanted to fight Stalinism in a partly Stalinist way, by establishing a personal power base. Paradoxically, while he concluded that the only effective way to fight Stalinism was to follow Stalin's example, his colleagues, in defense of the Stalinist structural principles, deposed him.

Khrushchev's example showed that without the terror that paralyzed the bureaucratic elites in the 1930s and 1940s, attempts to effect major structural changes in the Soviet system are unlikely to succeed. Despite the widespread image of Khrushchev as the proponent of "goulash communism"—that is to say, pragmatic communist rule oriented to popular welfare—in reality he represented primarily an attempt to revitalize the Party and the regime ideologically. In all probability, his was the final such attempt, and he will pass into the annals of Soviet history as the last true believer in the ideals of the original Bolsheviks to hold a leadership position. His successors care about their own and their country's power, not about communism.

It is also possible that Khrushchev's whirlwind reform activities will be judged in historical perspective as premature anti-Stalinism. His attempts to convert the political descendants of Stalin into anti-Stalinists were condemned to failure because they encroached on basic power interests. Moreover, by demonstrating to the bureaucracy the destabilizing side effects of the anti-Stalin campaign, he compromised the cause of anti-Stalinism for a whole generation of Soviet leaders. The elites that might have embraced Khrushchev's moderately anti-Stalinist goals were, at the time, still two decades away from positions of power. Yet now, when a new generation of Soviet leaders is assuming high positions in increasing numbers, the memory of Khrushchev's failure will serve as a warning about the dangers of the anti-Stalin campaign and anti-Stalinist programs.

Khrushchev's anti-Stalin and anti-Stalinist campaigns were not, of course, the only instances of backlash following the dictator's death. After the abolition of mass terror, and encouraged initially by the official anti-Stalin campaign, there developed in the Soviet Union a heterogeneous dissident movement that went far beyond the timid anti-Stalinism of Khrushchev himself. The appearance, growth, and international repercussions of this dissent, ranging from the Leninist revisionism of Roy Medvedev to Alexander Solzhenitsyn's religious and nationalistic anti-Sovietism, served to reinforce the conviction of the political elite that Khrushchev's course was dangerous. His replacement by a leadership group headed by Brezhnev in October 1964 signified the end of the period during which the sources and main features of Stalin's rule were openly and officially questioned.

The Brezhnev years were characterized by an initially successful attempt to cut off both the official and the underground critique of Stalin and the institutions of his rule. An effort was also made to solidify the traditional Stalinist power structure—with the exception of mass terror and the personal dictatorship—while at the same time quietly changing some of the policies associated with the dictator. Whereas Khrushchev had sought to replace the charismatic authority of Stalin with that of a revitalized mass Party, Brezhnev and his colleagues proposed to replace it with the corporate authority of the bureaucratic elite. Whereas Khrushchev's manner of building authority was populist and personalized, Brezhnev's was corporatist and initially faceless.

Brezhnev's approach did not neglect the Leninist, revolutionary sources of Soviet authority. As a matter of fact, the veneration of the founding father culminated in the ideological bacchanalia of Lenin's hundredth birthday, which was celebrated in 1970 before a largely indifferent or amused public. Brezhnev's claim to legitimacy, however, was much more solidly based on the promise of the effective performance of the existing bureaucratic hierarchies, and particularly the Party bureaucracy. His claim to power rested on his success at raising the standard of living, not his fidelity to Lenin's ideals, such as they were.

The question "Why is it so difficult for the Soviet Union to sever its connections with its Stalinist origins?" then is easy to answer in light of Khrushchev's experience. While all the bureaucratic elites agree in their rejection of Stalin's personalized arrangements and extreme methods of rule, they have developed an overwhelming vested interest in the preservation of the basic components of the system. The essence of the Brezhnev regime was the substitution of a stable and conservative corporate entity for the personal dictatorship of Stalin, and of strong, efficient, nationalist authoritarian rule for the extremes of Stalin's terror. The Party wishes to hold on to its monopoly of power. That is the heart, the essence, of the Soviet system.

The opportunity to shape a new political elite was closed to Khrushchev. His desire to break out of the confining conditions of his leadership—the fact that his colleagues and lieutenants were inherited from the Stalin era and firmly imbued with Stalinist values—goes far in explaining his effort after 1962 to break with his power base—the Party apparatus—and establish a personal dominion over the system and its elites.

The popularity of Brezhnev's rule within the political elite showed quite clearly the continuing vitality of Stalinist modes of thinking and management among the rulers and within bureaucratic strata of their elite supporters. There were of course many ways in which Brezhnev's rule departed from the model established by Stalin. For example, his enormous investments in agriculture, compared with Stalin's ruthless neglect. Yet, for all those departures, central elements of Stalinism dominated the Brezhnev era. In some instances, this was the result of the inertia of accustomed actions, but mostly it represented a conscious choice to preserve the bureaucratic balance of vested interests against structural changes and unconventional ideas. Brezhnev's rule, at least in its first decade, presented to the establishment the best of both worlds: It continued the commitment to eradicate mass terror and to avoid personal dictatorship, while at the same time it restabilized the system after Khrushchev's experimentation and pursued pragmatic policies within the limits of the institutional arrangements inherited from Stalin.

The most important hallmark of Brezhnev's rule was the preservation of political dominance over the economy. Yet for a while the system that maintained its priorities for political reasons brought economic benefits. During Brezhnev's first decade, the Soviet Union enjoyed not only impressive overall growth but also a major increase in consumption. Then growth slowed to its lowest level in Soviet history. This slowdown is not cyclical but represents a long-range trend and constitutes the central problem of the Soviet Union in the 1980s. Yet when it became clear that the system was not effectively serving even the goals of the Soviet rulers, Brezhnev and his supporters successfully resisted changes in the established order of political-economic decision-making and in the Stalinist system of economic management.

Is there anti-Stalinism in contemporary Russia? If so, who represents it, and how strong is it? The answer to these questions must, of course, be tentative. Yet it seems that the core of the Soviet governing establishment is Stalinist in the sense of its attachment to and defense of the existing system, and particularly the command economy. This is true even if one assumes, with justification, that many members of this establishment remember Stalin's rule with revulsion.

The reason is simple: The Stalinist institutions provide the rationale for the Party functionaries' power. This is equally true for the planners and economic officials in Moscow, in the republics and in the provinces. The economic managers of factories, farms, and service units, contrary to the picture so often presented in the West, are not proponents of anti-Stalinist reforms. They have learned to live with the existing system. More than that, they have learned how to take advantage of it. They are not prepared, professionally or personally, for a radical transformation. The military elite sees in the survival of Stalinist institutions the precondition for strict social discipline, the preservation of the priority of military tasks, and the continuation of the military-industrial complex as a separate and favored entity in the Soviet economic order. The cultural commissars who rule the unions of writers, painters and actors, as well as most of the union members, are committed to the present system, in which talent, creativity, and artistic integrity are not required for high status and economic rewards. For the KGB, the secret police, anti-Stalinism is associated with the derision, decline, and political isolation that became their lot in the Khrushchev years.

Yet, of course, anti-Stalinism is present in the Soviet Union. Its primary and most vocal representatives are the dissenters, who have been the most novel addition to the political scene. The dissent movement, like any free movement anywhere, is inevitably heterogeneous. Its range is very broad. There is a rigid authoritarian right which is Slavophile and deeply religious and would like to see the restoration of a modified traditional Russian system as it existed under the tsars. The most famous of exiled Russian writers, Alexander Solzhenitsyn, is close to this view. Another strain, represented by Roy Medvedev, takes a "true" Bolshevik view, considers everything that happened in post-Lenin Russia as a heretical departure from Leninist teachings, and longs for the restoration of a true Leninist democracy in the party and society. A strong branch of the dissent is the democratic center, represented by men like Andrei Sakharov and Valery Chalidze. Nonmessianic, pragmatic, and Westernizing, this current traces its roots back to the traditions and values of the old Russian democratic intelligentsia. The dissent movement also includes a social democratic left (for example, the writer Lev Kopelev, now in exile in West Germany), which looks upon Bolshevism as a cardinal departure from Marxian democratic socialism and has as its model for a changed Russia something resembling present-day Sweden. Finally, there are various shades of ethnocentric and separatist groups who identify with the variety of non-Russian nations in the Soviet Union, such as the Ukrainian Moroz. As for Soviet Jews, while they are overwhelmingly anti-Stalinist and a substantial element is overtly anti-Soviet, they can hardly be identified as part of the dissent movement in the sense in which this term is used here. Most Jewish opponents of the regime are not committed to efforts to change the system, but wish rather to leave it.

As in the 1920s, when Bolshevik opponents of Stalin's drive for absolute power represented, in Robert V. Daniel's phrase, the "conscience of the revolution," now the dissenters represent the conscience of anti-Stalinism. But the fate of the Bolshevik dissenters in the 1920s foreshadowed the present and likely future fate of today's anti-Stalinist dissenters. Their individual heroism, strong faith, and commitment mask their weakness as a movement. They have no significant mass support. Those who have not emigrated have been decimated by official re-

pression and have little influence. Open anti-Stalinist dissent in today's
Russia is unlikely to become, in the short or intermediate term, a meaningful political force.

They do not even provide a clear alternative to the present regime in
Russia. As Edward L. Keenan has written:

... with a few remarkable exceptions, these [dissenting] individuals remain
within the traditional political culture, i.e., their dissent, like that of their predecessors and forebears, is personal, principled, philosophical, and ineffective.
They reject the state as it is, but offer no alternative. They decry the lack of liberty, but have grave doubts about democratic institutions, doubts that flow from
their low estimate of man and from their pessimistic expectations of the working
classes. There is little evidence that this group might provide, either as leaders or
as gadflies, the analytical tools and policy devices that could permit the present
political culture successfully to "transcribe" itself the more effectively to meet
the political needs of a modern mass society.*

The dissident movement in the contemporary Soviet Union cannot by
itself provide the spark that would ignite the various streams of existing
social dissatisfaction or overcome the political apathy of the working
classes.

It is the tragedy of today's Russia that one cannot find evidence for the
existence of any meaningful anti-Stalinist forces either in the establishment itself or in the various strata of Soviet society. Perhaps such forces
exist but are dormant and no outside observer is capable of penetrating
the system deeply enough to establish their existence and evaluate their
scope. But this is not likely. Soviet dissenters in exile do not convey an
image of broad-based anti-Stalinist feelings and aspirations in Russia,
but rather one of isolation, fear, and preoccupation with private rather
than public concerns. Moreover, a dormant anti-Stalinism has no active
influence on the course of Soviet development. This fallow undercurrent
may play an important role if the stability of the regime is undermined.
Yet so long as the stability of the system is not in question, anti-Stalinism will not provide a focus for existing dissatisfactions in the society.
Moreover, precisely because of its quiescence, this sentiment cannot
serve as a catalyst to bring about the destabilization of Soviet power.
Those who study the Soviet Union are struck by the atrophy of public
interest that the society exhibits. The industrial working class seems to
be anti-intellectual and politically apathetic. The peasants are fragmented and politically isolated. Soviet youth is cynical and career-
oriented. Despite its fascination with Western mass culture, it experienced none of the political enthusiasm that absorbed young people in

* From an unpublished paper by Professor Edward L. Keenan on Russian political
culture.

Western democratic societies in the 1960s and 1970s. The professional class is on the whole both materialistic and preoccupied with professional concerns. It does not bear any resemblance to the old Russian intelligentsia. Of course there are many within the professional class who are clearly anti-Stalinist, but for their own and their families' sake they accommodate themselves to the existing system. There are many whose longings and instincts are anti-Stalinist, but the anti-Stalinism they practice is private, confined to their families and close friends. As a whole, the behavior of the professional class confirms for the Soviet Union the Marxist-Leninist proposition that the intelligentsia is a servant of the leadership.

Yet Stalinism is in one respect on the defensive. The command economy has survived because it has served well the interests of the leadership and political elite. It is on the defensive not because the leadership and the political elite have had a change of heart about its intrinsic values, but because its effectiveness in attaining the goals posed by the political leadership and elite is visibly declining. There is no reason to believe that this decline can be arrested without fundamental change in the organization of the economy. Indeed, the question of basic reforms, capable of countering the slide in growth and stimulating rapid technological progress, is at the center of Soviet politics and policy-making in the 1980s. Yet there is no evidence to suggest that the leadership or the elites are convinced that the system has outlived its economic usefulness to the extent that it endangers its political rationale. In all probability, the view shared by the establishment is that the restoration of social discipline and some extensive patching up of the economic system will serve to arrest its decline.

Anti-Stalinism, particularly in regard to this crucial facet of the surviving Stalinist system, may be victorious only through another revolution from above by a strong leader in the historical mold of other Russian leader-reformers. But the elite seems capable of mustering enough power and determination to prevent the appearance of a strong leader committed to radical reforms, or at least to nullify his attempts at reform in the very process of their implementation.

In the absence of such a leader, the necessary consensus for drastic reforms will crystallize within the ruling establishment only when the political price of sweeping change is recognized as being lower than that of muddling through. Such an eventuality, one may speculate, will arise if and when powerful social tensions and unrest from below erupt, fed by rising expectations that cannot be fulfilled by the command system. Another possible cause of drastic reform could be economic stagnation that threatened to render the military establishment backward and feeble in comparison with that of the West. Still another potential stimulus for change, and at present the one most likely to be effective, is the growing technological gap between the Soviet Union and not only the West or Japan, but also the newly industrializing countries like Taiwan, South Korea, and Singapore. It is quite possible that in the not-too-distant future this list might be expanded to include China, which would be the most telling blow to Russia's pride and security.

For many years, under Stalin and under his successors, the Soviet Union was gradually closing the economic gap between its production and that of the capitalist industrial countries. With the exception of postwar Japan, the Soviet GNP grew faster than that of other countries. Russia became the world's largest producer of grain, oil, steel, chemical fertilizers, iron ore, and many other basic commodities. Yet in the late 1970s and in the 1980s the growth rate of the economy declined very substantially. The gap between the Soviet Union and the West in modern technology is visibly and dramatically increasing, with clear signs that the trend will continue.

In one of his last works, Lenin concluded that in the final analysis the global competition between the socialist and capitalist systems would be resolved in favor of that system which manages to secure the higher long-range level of economic productivity. By Lenin's standards, the verdict of history is in: The Soviet Union and its Stalinist command economy are the losers. This truth is visible to outsiders, but it was not recognized openly by the old-guard Soviet leaders and elites—because of both their vested interests and their ideological blinders. If, as suggested above, the Bolshevik Revolution and the Stalinist dictatorship that followed can be understood as a revitalization cycle in Russian history, then in the domestic arena its dynamism and therefore its usefulness have clearly come to an end. A society that has not come to terms with its past cannot help living in the shadow of that past.

2

Sources of Stability

The events following Stalin's death in 1953 could have been destabilizing to the Soviet regime. The abolishment of mass terror and elimination of police methods from intra-elite struggles, the release of political prisoners from concentration camps, the anti-Stalin campaign of Khrushchev and his administrative reforms, the emergence of a dissent movement—all these had the potential for disillusion, unrest, and disorder. Similarly, the economic difficulties of the 1970s and 1980s and the pronounced loss of the system's vitality have the potential to upset the system now. Yet hopes for a radical change in the Soviet Union represent wishful thinking of liberals, and expectations of the destabilization of the regime are the wishful thinking of conservatives.

The Soviet Union is presently in the throes of a crisis of effectiveness. There is little reason to believe that the situation will change in the foreseeable future. But it is unlikely that the state is now, or will be in the late 1980s, in danger of social or political disintegration. Thus, we must study the factors which made the regime stable in the post-Stalin era and are still at work at the present.

The system has existed for most of a century—a period sufficiently long to demonstrate its ability to adapt to its internal and international environments. It also has roots in Russian history. There is little in the system today inconsistent with the national and imperialist tradition from which it developed. In fact, as Zbigniew Brzezinski remarked in his article "From the Future to the Past?"* the character of Soviet socio-

* Zbigniew Brzezinski, "Soviet Politics: From the Future to the Past?" in Paul Cocks, Robert V. Daniels, and Nancy Heer, eds., *The Dynamics of Soviet Politics* (Cambridge: Harvard University Press, 1976).

political-economic development is now much closer to its Russian past than to the original scheme of the founders of the Soviet state.

Without doubt, the key to stability has been the high visibility of the coercive apparatus and policies. During Stalin's rule, both the society as a whole and the elites were virtually paralyzed by a terror that was both massive and unpredictable. The social order was that of a cemetery. After Stalin died and Beria, the secret-police chief, was eliminated, the KGB apparatus was purged and placed firmly under the control of the Party. Could the system survive without mass terror?

Actually, aside from the experience of the Second World War, this abolition of terror was the greatest test of the stability of the system. There are three main reasons why the Soviet system survived: First, for the generations brought up under Stalin and their children, the memory of the Great Terror served for many years—and still serves today—as a restraint on unorthodox behavior. People feel in their bones that mass terror could once again become a reality. I have encountered this attitude often enough to conclude that it will diminish in intensity only over a very long period of time.

Secondly, while the policy of mass terror was abolished in post-Stalin Russia, the apparatus was simply purged, not dismantled. The Soviet Union is still an authoritarian and intimidating police state. The character of the political system differs from what it was in Stalin's day. There is less coercion. It is more predictable—one is tempted to say rational. Punishments are now commensurate, by Soviet standards, with the nature and degree of the behavior being punished.

The unpredictability and extreme harshness of Stalin's terror can best be seen in a prison-camp joke of those times, in which one prisoner asks another, "What is your sentence?" The other prisoner replies, "Twenty years." The first prisoner asks, "What did you do?" to which the answer is "Nothing." The first prisoner replies, "That is impossible. For nothing you get only ten years." A real example concerns a Soviet Jew whose name was Gitler (the Russian pronunciation of Hitler): he was arrested during the war on suspicion of being Hitler's relative. Another example is of a soldier who rolled a cigarette with a piece of newspaper and was arrested for defaming the Great Leader, as the piece of newspaper contained a picture of Stalin. Members of a philatelist club were arrested because the collection of foreign postage stamps was considered dangerous exposure to alien propaganda and a sign of potential disloyalty. Nowadays people are usually punished for something real: anti-Soviet views, antiregime propaganda, contact with foreigners, publication abroad, etc. The punishment is still harsh, but it is rarely the death penalty. In the case of well-known dissenters, it is more often exile abroad and deprivation of citizenship than disappearance forever in the labor-camp system.

The network of informers that blankets the Soviet Union precludes the formation of independent groups that could challenge Soviet power. Moreover, after Khrushchev's ouster, the police apparatus was gradually rehabilitated and assumed a growing role in everyday life. While during the Khrushchev period the visibility and prerogatives of the police were limited, the Andropov succession marked the final stage of the KGB's rehabilitation as junior partner of the Party in ruling the Soviet Union. What still remains unchanged is the exclusion of police methods from leadership competition: Party officials do not have their rivals shot. Molotov, Bulganin, Malenkov, and Voroshilov when purged by Khrushchev; Shelepin, Semichastny, and Ilichev when fired or demoted by Brezhnev; Romanov when dropped by Gorbachev, simply disappeared from public view to live on substantial pensions.

The elimination of Stalinist terror and the substitution of a coercive police state diminished the risks of deviant economic behavior while preserving the dangers of deviant political behavior. Deviant economic behavior, while costly in economic terms, is not politically dangerous. It acts as a substitute for political aspirations and to some extent performs the function of a safety valve for the pent-up dissatisfactions in Soviet society. The energies of the working classes, middle class and official-dom have thus been channeled not into political activities and spiritual aspirations, but into bribery, corruption, and economic crimes.

Of course many citizens and numerous managers and high-ranking officials are caught stealing and using their positions for personal profit. They are prosecuted and jailed, especially in periods when a new leader assumes power and a new broom is trying to cleanse Russia. Yet stealing, corruption and profiteering have become a way of life. Short-lived campaigns against these abuses by new leaders are doomed to failure as long as the economic system does not change. A Russian anecdote provides a sense of the atmosphere where stealing is the norm rather than the exception. In a wood factory, the employees are permitted to take home sawdust to use for heating. A worker with an enormous sack on a wheelbarrow approaches the gate of the factory. The plant policeman says, "Tell me, what do you have in the sack? What items did you hide there?" The worker assures him that he is only taking out sawdust, as permitted. After a close inspection of the sack, the policeman, surprised by the worker's honesty, lets him go. This scene is repeated day after day for many months. Finally, one day the policeman says to the worker, "Look, I am retiring tomorrow and I still cannot understand your method of stealing. Please tell me—I will not disclose it to anyone." The worker answers, "It is very simple. I don't steal things by hiding them in the sawdust sack. I steal wheelbarrows."

Finally, the limited impact of the abolition of terror on the stability of the system indicates that stability—both now and even in the Stalinist period—also depends on factors other than mass terror and a police state that have come to play a larger role in the post-Stalin era.

Aside from coercive measures, the stability of regimes depends on economic performance and on the ability to satisfy the material needs of society. What is important here is not the absolute level of economic performance, but rather its relation to the expectations of the population. In these terms, the system has worked well. Economic performance was not radically outdistanced by the rising expectations of the workers, the peasants, and the professional and middle classes. No revolution of rising expectations has occurred in the Soviet Union. Probably because of their past experiences and their cynicism regarding the promises of the government, the people's expectations have remained quite low.

It is important to remember that the standard of living and the quality of life rose quite substantially during the sixties and seventies. In the case of the peasantry, this improvement reflected a significant change in leadership attitudes that began under Khrushchev and was accelerated under Brezhnev. While the rural standard of living is still considerably lower than the urban standard, it is now commensurate, at least in terms of manufactured consumer products, with the urban living standard of ten to twelve years ago. During the last twenty-five years, the peasantry has been transformed from the internal colony it was under Stalin into an integrated part of society. The peasant has, in short, become a full-fledged citizen of the Soviet Union.

A number of benefits have accrued to the peasants as a result. For the first time in Soviet history, they received internal passports, which enabled them to travel within the country without a special permit. For the first time since collectivization, they began to receive social-security benefits. Also, their pay was tied to a minimum wage guaranteed by the government. The *kolkhoz* itself was included in the net of government insurance, which, at least in part, lifted the burden of a bad harvest. In addition, state budgetary investments in agriculture rose dramatically and made possible a much higher level of mechanization in the *kolkhozy* and much more fertilization and irrigation of farmland.

Yet, regardless of the progress in the countryside, the main avenue of improvement for the peasant remained migration to the cities, which accelerated significantly in the late 1960s and 1970s. In urban areas, the peasant enjoys not only a higher standard of living, which is enhanced by government food subsidies, but also greater access to better education and cultural amenities. The migration from the *kolkhoz* has also resulted in a badly skewed demographic profile in the rural areas. The rural population is now either old or very young, and the work force is dominated by women. Such a peasantry is not likely to be a source of instability. If the countryside is to be the spawning ground of unrest in the near future, it will much more likely be the result of poor agricultural performance, and its effects on industrial workers, than peasant discontent.

The urban working class has also enjoyed a major improvement in its living conditions over the last twenty years. The industrial worker was the main beneficiary of Brezhnev's wage policy, receiving a significant increase in the minimum wage. Better supplies of meat, milk, and butter were made available to the cities. Consumer goods, and especially consumer durables, became much more readily available. There was also a substantial increase in expenditures for social welfare. While the housing situation remains bad and the quality of housing very low, between 1960 and 1983 about 53 million apartments were built in the Soviet Union. As of 1983, the year after Brezhnev died, 60.5 million apartments had gas fuel, 84 percent of the population had radios, 83 percent had television sets, 71 percent had refrigerators, 58 percent had washing machines, and 70 percent had sewing machines.

The middle and professional classes gained the least in material terms during Brezhnev's tenure. During the 1970s and 1980s, their real salaries have remained almost constant, even as the industrial workers' wages rose considerably. This was partly the result of a conscious policy of *uravnilovka*, or wage-leveling, meant to decrease the range of income differentiation. However, the level of wages of these groups is still much higher than that of the working classes; their standard of living is not much different from the one prevailing in the West at the beginning of the era of mass consumption—for example, of urban Italy in the 1950s.

For a significant and influential part of this group, the size of their salaries does not reflect adequately their standard of living relative to the rest of Soviet society. They get many nonmonetary rewards: They can purchase items that are in short supply from special stores. They are selected from time to time to travel abroad. They can acquire hard currency. Moreover, as will be discussed below, this segment of society has made very real gains of other kinds.

Of course, the standard of living today for every class is much lower than that of its Western counterparts, or even its Eastern European counterparts. However, what is salient for the Soviet citizen—and hence crucial for the stability of the system—is not how this level of material well-being compares with Western society, which he has never seen, or even how it compares to that of the political elite, since their conspicuous consumption is not reported in the media. The benchmark by which the citizen assesses his standard of living is that of his parents and of his own past. The leadership has thus been able to avoid a widening of the gap between economic performance and popular expectations. The widest divergence between standard of living and expectations in society today is probably within the middle and professional classes. In their case, however, the threat to the stability of the regime, for reasons which will be outlined later, is probably the lowest.

In material terms, therefore, the regime was able in the entire post-Stalin era to neutralize potential dissatisfaction and unrest by a combination of low popular expectations with marked improvements in the overall standard of living.

Another moderating mechanism, mentioned previously, is the system of corruption. Virtually everyone has participated in and gained from unofficial economic activities. The entire *na levo* network—the stealing, the bribery and barter—operated throughout the 1970s with limited risks, and came to function as a means of national income redistribution. By providing a means for the realization of material expectations outside the official system, this subeconomy offered its participants the trappings, if not the formal recognition, of a higher status. It also served to maintain the overall standard of living above its official level.

Aside from various forms of bribery, Gregory Grossman, the foremost American expert on the "second economy," describes diverse types of activity *na levo*: The single artisan, such as tailor, plumber, or painter, who works with stolen tools and materials; the teacher, doctor, or dentist engaged in private practice; the merchant-entrepreneur who engages a number of people who work at home, supplying them with materials and selling the products (jeans, for example) through an agent; private production on the job, using state materials on "company time" for the black market; private underground manufacturing without any official pretext; and private construction teams.

Some studies of the second economy estimate it as comprising 10 to 20 percent of the Soviet GNP.

Another factor promoting stability is the predominantly lower-class origin of the upper political strata in the Soviet Union. Since the working class and the political elite share the same tradition and come from similar socioeconomic backgrounds, there results a symmetry of cultural attitudes and tastes cutting across the rulers and the working classes. This is reflected in the official culture and language of the society.

The Soviet Union is one of the few societies where the cultures of the mass and the elite are almost inseparable. The vocabulary, the idiom, the accent in which officials address one another and the public are identical to those used by the public. The Soviet-Russian language as spoken by a Khrushchev, Brezhnev, or Chernenko represents its lowest common denominator. In cultural terms, the political elite and the public share anti-intellectualism and a preference for highly traditional art forms and for "low-brow" literature, art, theater, and movies. Both display intolerance toward cultural experimentation and a lack of cultural imagination. And they share as well the traditional Russian sentimentality and a definition of the good life based on the model of the nineteenth-century Russian merchant class.

The leaders do, to be sure, feel obliged to pay their respects to the traditional landmarks of high Russian culture—Petipa's ballet, Stanislavsky's theater, Repin's paintings, Tolstoy's novels, Pushkin's poetry, Mussorgsky's operas, Tchaikovsky's operas and symphonies. The Stalinist leadership generation, those who comprised the politburos of Stalin, Khrushchev, and Brezhnev, knew that a great nation and superpower requires of its leaders a certain attention to its classics. To appear cultivated, many of them attended *Swan Lake* and *Boris Godunov* twenty or thirty times, with or without high-level foreign visitors. Yet they and their successors regard this rich prerevolutionary cultural heritage chiefly as an adornment of their ruling status, and they seek to preserve it totally unchanged. At the same time, they promote a new Soviet culture which, aside from flagrant propaganda, is a hybrid of entertainment and morality play and which is attractive both to them and to the common citizen. Its closest counterpart in the United States would be a highly politicized soap opera.

It is only a narrow and very isolated stratum of intellectuals, together with some middle-level experts and members of the bureaucracy, that is genuinely interested in the classical heritage for its own sake, and in actively carrying on the great tradition.

Still another support for stability during the 1960s and early 1970s was the high level of mobility from the working class into the middle and professional classes, and particularly into the political class. (*Political class*, a term unknown in the West, denotes the professional functionaries of the Communist Party.) This mobility was partly a result of rapid economic development and the expansion of educational institutions, the major conduit for it; partly a result of self-selection, whereby the offspring of professional-class parents tend to follow in their footsteps, while children of the lower classes are much more prone to enter the political class; and partly a result of deliberate policy aimed at equalizing the educational chances of individuals of middle- and lower-class origin. All these factors have made upward mobility in the Soviet Union quite high. This is demonstrated by the difficulty one has in finding an extended family in the Soviet Union with no members who belong to the official class.

Finally, while the low standard of living may cause economic inequality to seem more obnoxious than in the West, the range of economic stratification is in fact relatively narrow. This was particularly true during the Brezhnev regime. No citizen found that his neighbor had much more than he did. (Those elite and subelite members who did live much better than they did were simply not their neighbors. One element of the *Soviet* stratification system is segregation of housing, which puts people of similar status, and often even the same profession, together in apartment houses.)

Instability, however, can often result from unfulfilled political and spiritual aspirations. No doubt the rise of nonmaterial expectations would present dangers to stability. The most explosive combination would be the merging of the unfulfilled material expectations of the workers or peasants and the spiritual and political aspirations of the intelligentsia. (This was exactly what happened in Poland in 1980, as well as in other major political upheavals in the Eastern bloc since 1945.) It seems clear that nonmaterial expectations and aspirations of various Soviet groups and the population at large differ today in many respects from what they were twenty or twenty-five years ago. All Soviet citizens now expect a secure life, free from capricious harassment and from terror. All aspire to live in a state that preserves a modicum of legality in its day-to-day contacts with citizens.

The regime is highly repressive toward any political and spiritual aspirations that depart from established norms. Such behavior is for the most part rare and rather timid. The working and middle classes of society are permeated by a deep sense of resignation toward the existing state of affairs and an extraordinary apathy toward "high" politics. The workers in particular exhibit very little in terms of political, cultural, or spiritual aspirations, and in those occasional instances they conform closely to the preferences of the leadership and the political elite. This in itself is an important source of stability, and it would take a major shock to change such attitudes. Moreover, if such a shock did occur, it would most likely be of local origin—a specific intolerable injustice—and the reaction to it would not take the form of organized and directed action, but rather of blind fury, the unleashing of a pent-up proclivity for violence. (Indeed, in the late 1960s and in the 1970s there were instances of violent strikes in Rostov, Chernigov and Riga which were brutally put down by security forces.) In any event, there is no reason to believe that the values of the working classes are any less authoritarian, anti-intellectual, or traditional than those of their political overlords, so such a scenario is highly unlikely.

There is little more to be expected in this regard from the intelligentsia, which includes anybody who is not engaged in physical labor. At the outset, it should be pointed out that this group has little in common with the two variants of educated classes of nineteenth- and early twentieth-century Russia that bore the same name, the first being the democratic intelligentsia of 1840–60, the other the revolutionary intelligentsia of the post-1860s. Then the term connoted not only educational attainments but also, and most importantly, a critical spiritual and political attitude, an alienation from the contemporary social and political system and an adherence to the idea of "the good of the people," which it was felt should inform one's activities. The intelligentsia explicitly rejected the existing sociopolitical structure and propounded radical, utopian solutions to the shortcomings they perceived.

Nothing could be further from this traditional Russian class than the present Soviet intelligentsia. With some exceptions, the group is only a statistical category. It is basically integrated into the system. It does not selflessly champion the cause of the people, nor, for the most part, do its members advocate radical alternatives to the status quo. In addition, the intelligentsia is rather isolated from the simple people. More often than not, workers have only thinly disguised anti-intellectual attitudes, while the intelligentsia has an only thinly disguised contempt for the workers. This intelligentsia is highly materialistic and primarily interested in pursuing careers.

Of course, some individuals and small groups do resemble the old intelligentsia, particularly within the "creative" intelligentsia—writers, poets, actors, painters, scientists, etc. Yet this is a small, unorganized layer or, more likely, a collection of individuals. The material improvements of the intelligentsia's position, the higher degree of professional autonomy bestowed on them during the Brezhnev era, the disappearance of mass terror and the commensurate increase in private freedoms have only strengthened their inbred conformist attitude. This is a class from which the regime has little to fear.

Most of the creative intelligentsia has much more narrowly defined expectations. They aspire to greater but not unlimited artistic freedom. They expect to continue to enjoy the advantage of "opting out," of engaging safely in artistic pursuits that do not affect the goals of the regime.

More broadly speaking, the members of the professional class believe that they will never again be isolated from the mainstream of nonsocialist world culture. Professional groups expect a greater degree of autonomy and aspire to expand still further their limits, to gain greater access to information and data about their own and other societies, and to be able to address the areas of their expertise more freely, if only in closed discussions and publications of limited circulation. (This is certainly true of scientists, scholars in international relations, physicians, and, to some extent, economists.)

These, however, are largely conformist attitudes and they have been significantly reinforced by the gains these groups have made. Today the professionals exert a considerable influence on the administrative structure. The era of the political dilettante lording it over an uneducated, developing society and a structure of semiprofessional, self-taught administrators is over. Under Brezhnev, for the first time in Soviet postwar history, the professional who was not an integral part of the political bureaucracy became a growing and important factor in Soviet decision-making. The leap here can be seen to a very limited degree in the "soft" professions of social science, but it is especially evident in economics, managerial sciences, communication, information and processing sciences, and, of course, in applied technology. Most importantly, professionals who are not a part of the public administration have come to serve as consultants and experts in the formulation of the goals and especially the means of Soviet policies in all spheres. This is true not only for the central authorities but also in local administration. The professionals perform their role through direct participation in the decision-making bodies, consultative positions with executive organizations, preparation of position papers and participation in permanent and *ad hoc* advisory councils.

The broader background and underpinning of the evolving professionalization of society are provided by the theorists of two new concepts in Soviet ideology: the scientific-technological revolution and the scientific management of society. During the Brezhnev period, these concepts assumed a central place in Soviet ideology. The literature on them is already large and growing by leaps. The old cult of technology centered on the means of production. The new concepts supplement this focus with the cult of scientism in shaping and managing socioeconomic and political relations. They proclaim that the optimally effective and profitable ways of managing society should not simply be equated with the existence of a socialist economic system. Such a system is said to provide only propitious potential conditions for achieving optimal growth and profitability. Its realization, however, requires profound understanding, training, and effort, which necessitate the upgrading of the role of science, the management of technology, the development of "scientific methods" and the placement of professionals in all spheres of leadership and management. To put it simply, progress requires not just ideological fervor but professional expertise as well. The Brezhnev era signified a major step in the transition from the revolutionary spirit of Leninism, the stress on leadership of Stalinism, and the populist attitudes of Khrushchevism to a professional-administrative ethos.

While the new professionalism reflects a desire for, and the attainment of, a higher degree of autonomy for professional pursuits, it does not constitute a challenge to the existing system. The professionals are dis-satisfied with many of the regime's policies and features, but are com-mitted to their careers and advancement within the system.

That the professional groups try to influence official policy is amply documented. That they are sometimes successful can also be demon-strated. What policies do they try to influence and when are they suc-cessful? First, as a rule, the closer their profession is to technology and the more removed from ideology, the less likely their interests and pressures are to be ignored. Writers, on the one extreme, and scientists, on the other, represent the two poles of permissible freedom and influ-ence. (The gravitation of economists from identification with cultural to scientific spheres is significant here.) Second, the main pressures emanating from these groups concern the status of their professions, their share in the allocation of state resources, and their right to a measure of professional autonomy and integrity. In these concerns, scientific and technological groups were very successful during the Brezhnev period. Yet the importance to the Soviet system and society of science and scientists (let alone other professional groups), their suc-cess in developing professional integrity and autonomy in basic re-search, and their proximity to men of power do not mean that they have significant political influence. While respecting their expertise and responding to their needs, the Soviet politician is unlikely to attrib-ute to them superior insight and wisdom in more broadly defined areas. Since 1969, under the impact of Andrei Sakharov's manifesto *Peace, Coexistence and Intellectual Freedom* and the subsequent defense of his person and position by a number of scientists, the Party has shown in-creasing anxiety about the political and social attitudes of scientists and has moved to tighten its supervision of personnel policy in the scientific establishment and to denigrate the expertise of scientists in social and political matters.

Even without the Party's efforts, the Soviet professional communities are politically fragile. Each group—the sociologists, the computer spe-cialists, and particularly the economists—displays a very broad range of views and opinions concerning the matters on which it advises the politi-cal authorities. It is composed of individuals of different generations with different training, institutional associations, and career orientations. The choice among conflicting advice and pressures remains with the pol-iticians. To what extent this choice will gravitate from one option to an-other (market-oriented economic reforms versus mathematization and computerization of centralized planning, civilian versus military em-phasis in scientific research, or a restriction versus the free flow of scien-tific information across institutional and national borders) may have very important consequences. But this choice depends only marginally on what goes on within the professional groups. It depends decisively on elite goals, elite perceptions of internal and international opportunities, and the elites' quest for self-preservation.

But what of that segment of the intelligentsia that is not satisfied with its advancement within the system and does not have limited aspirations and conformist attitudes? The émigré dissident Valery Chalidze has contended that active dissent in the Soviet Union represents only a tip of the iceberg: that behind each active dissenter there are scores of hidden dissenters among the intelligentsia and even within the elites who share their ideas but lack the courage, opportunity, ability, or desire to act openly. We cannot know whether Chalidze is correct. In all probability, he accurately describes those groups of dissenters who hold the most moderate views. Even if Chalidze were right, however, from the point of view of the regime's stability a crucial distinction must be made between a dissident movement that is small and active and one that is large and inactive. The active dissent can be defeated with relative ease: It can be fragmented, isolated, neutralized. Inactive dissent does not produce instability; its danger to the regime lies in the possibility of its activation under conditions of instability.

Chalidze may exaggerate the extent of inactive dissent by incorrectly identifying widely shared sentiments as dissent. In light of the raised nonmaterial expectations and aspirations of various groups in Soviet society, it is more probable that what he has observed is the partial coincidence of aspirations of dissenters and professionals. Yet these aspirations, especially in their scope and intensity, represent only a small part of the program of the dissenters. Moreover, they hope to achieve their goals through systemic change. In contrast, the various professional groups aspire to realize their limited goals within the system by means of political pressure that results in policy relaxation.

The nondissident groups do not expect basic changes in the system, but rather seek accommodation within it. Moreover, their expectations and, within limits, their aspirations are not neglected. Their expectations are based on changes that have already taken place with the willing or grudging support of the leadership. These changes—towards greater professional autonomy, greater freedom of expression, greater contact with the nonsocialist world—did not endanger the regime's stability. Indeed, by co-opting large parts of the professional classes, they diminish the likelihood of broader political demands by these groups in the near future. Besides, their implementation may have owed less to pressure from professional groups than to the coincidence of those pressures with interests of the leadership itself. The leadership slowly became convinced that the changes the intelligentsia wanted could buttress the effectiveness of the system. But the professionals will make no headway with aspirations, like writing a true Soviet history, that infringe on issues which the regime considers essential to its survival.

Thus these groups do not pose a threat to the system as long as they do not share the dissidents' broader goals and selection of means for their attainment. As Walter Connor has put it:

> The political culture links the bureaucratic elite and the "masses" more closely than it links the dissidents to either. The institutional framework that emerged in the Stalin era fitted rather well with the antecedent political culture of Tsarist Russia at the most critical points, and to all appearances the contemporary Soviet political culture still "fits" this relatively unchanged institutional pattern quite well.*

The degree of private freedom today would have been unimaginable in the Stalin era. Under Stalin, even the family did not provide a sanctuary from thought control and from the necessity to express actively one's support for the regime. During that time, the model hero of the youth was a peasant boy, Pavlik Morozov, whose claim to fame consisted in his denunciation of his father's anti-Soviet views to the authorities. Morozov is still the official hero of the Communist youth organizations. Thousands of monuments to his "achievement" are still preserved or built in cities, towns, and villages. Nevertheless, freedom of expression within the family and parental authority over offspring constitute today a gray area which, while not wholly free of state control, is a place where that control is marginal and muted.

Yet there is another category of great salience to the question of stability: the national composition of society and its relation to the political regime. Only about 50 percent of the Soviet Union's population is composed of Great Russians. Of the remainder, about one-half is not even Slavic. The whole southern and western tiers are inhabited by non-Russian nations—many of them with a recorded history and traditions that go back centuries or even millennia before the emergence of Russia itself, as, for example, the Georgians, the Abkhazians, and the Armenians. In all, the Soviet Union includes over a hundred distinct nationalities. Of these, however, only twenty-two comprise more than a million people, and of these twenty-two only fifteen, including the Great Russians, live in their own large administrative units, the so-called Union Republics, and are of real political importance.

In the modern world, one of the major sources of instability is multinational or multiracial populations. The Soviet Union today is by any

---

* Walter D. Connor, "Dissent in a Complex Society: The Soviet Case," *Problems of Communism,* Vol. 22, No. 1 (March/April 1973), p. 50.

standard the largest such state, and in its system of government, with its political, economic, and partly cultural supercentralization, the relations between the Great Russian center and the non-Russian peripheries can fairly be characterized as imperial. The internal empire (together with its external empire in Eastern Europe) makes the Soviet Union and Russia the world's largest and last colonial or semicolonial power.

The main colonial characteristics of this empire are the centralization of the Party and state bureaucracy, with control exercised by Moscow. Moscow makes budgetary decisions and distributes key resources for the entire country. There is no ethnic influence on military and foreign policies. Moscow controls the *nomenklatura* appointments within the non-Russian republics (that is, the right to hire, promote, or fire the local Party and state officials). The Supreme Soviet, the parliament, in which representation is proportional, has no real power. Upward career mobility for non-Russian officials is limited, with the partial exception of Ukrainians and Byelorussians, to the bounds of their own republics. Russian, or other Slavic, officials are appointed to state and Party positions within the republics as overseers and controllers, most often as seconds-in-command. Thus the second Party secretary of the republic is always a Slav, as are most of the second secretaries of the provinces, the deputy heads of republican central committee departments, and the deputy ministers of all important ministries. The Russian language, moreover, is preferred in official business, and knowledge of Russian is a prerequisite for advancement.

The potential for instability due to ethnic or racial divisions and conflicts is, as noted above, enormous. The national problem is the most difficult one to resolve without a drastic alteration of the system. It is highly probable that ethnic issues will become in the future the single most important cause of sweeping change or even disintegration. Yet even in the present age of global anticolonialism, which has witnessed the dissolution of all other large-scale colonial systems and the reassertion of ethnic interests and broad political participation, the Soviet state is certainly in no immediate danger of such disintegration. How can this enduring imperial stability be explained?

Empires do not generally disintegrate when the ruling metropolis is at the peak of its military power, as in Russia today. More specifically, Moscow keeps tight control over the military forces deployed inside the Soviet Union by making sure that the officer corps is predominantly Russian, that conscripts of any non-Russian nationality for the most part do not serve in their own republics, and that the troops deployed in the republics are clearly visible to the population.

An essential stabilizing force among the ethnic populations is the tight

net of KGB supervision. The secret police are attuned to any manifestation of local nationalism. Dissidence in non-Russian areas has an even
lower threshold of intervention than in Russia proper. The local KGB
apparatus is also under the strict control and supervision of Russian representatives.

Another major stabilizing element is the continuing duality of Soviet
nationality policies toward the republican administrations and cultures.
The most important elements of political, economic, and social-cultural
power are concentrated in Moscow and in the hands of Russian officials,
but some symbols of nationhood, a high degree of local cultural autonomy, and partial bureaucratic independence are granted to the republics.

The symbols and realities of cultural autonomy—the preservation and
utilization of the native language, native literature, and native folk-
lore—do much to make the reality of Russian political domination palatable to the native population. Recent censuses have shown either an
increase or at least stability in the number of people in the non-Russian
republics who consider their own language as their primary language. Of
course, upwardly mobile professionals or bureaucrats must possess a
good knowledge of Russian and of the Russian life-style and patterns of
behavior, but even they are not forced to abandon their own customs,
language, or cultural heritage. This heritage is of course strongly "adjusted" to exclude any anti-Russian traditions, but nevertheless provides
the lower and middle classes with an important outlet for ethnocentric
feelings.

Governmentally, the goodly number of official posts held by Russians
or other Slavs notwithstanding, it is with few exceptions native bureaucrats who administer the republics on a day-to-day basis—especially at
the top level, where positions are visible and symbolic, and at the lowest
levels, where the bureaucracy comes into daily contact with the population. (In this respect, different republics enjoy different degrees of administrative nativization with Georgia and Armenia on the high end of
the spectrum and Kazakhstan on the low end.)

There also occurred during the Brezhnev era a major change in the
type of Russian political and economic officials who serve in the Union
Republics. Previously they were, most often, specialists in ideology and
propaganda and they came without any background in the local customs, problems, and culture. Now in most cases they either are descendants of Russian settlers in the area or have at least made their way to
high positions in the republican bureaucracy after serving for a prolonged period on lower levels. Moreover, they are mostly specialists in
industrial or agricultural management, rather than ideological supervisors.

This trend has been paralleled by a process of Russian co-optation of the native elites. The pattern of their careers within their republics, the rewards for their service, and their socialization through secular and Party education are similar to that of the Russian elites. The native political and administrative elites usually stay in office longer than their Russian counterparts. In most cases, they are sufficiently Russified to satisfy the Russians, and yet retain sufficient ties with the local culture and customs to be seen by the native population as their "own" leaders. The most important thing denied by Moscow to these native elites is (as noted above) the chance of advancement to the central apparatus: for the overwhelming majority of the native bureaucrats, their careers begin and end within the borders of their own republics. (This, incidentally, is the reason they display greater horizontal mobility than the Russian and Ukrainian elites—that is, they move more often from one job to another at the same level, and from one bureaucratic hierarchy—political, economic, administrative, police—to another.) The natives, of course, desire greater autonomy from the decision-making and supervision imposed by Moscow. They are truly proud of their cultural heritages. In contrast to the common Western tendency to equate the terms *Soviet* and *Russian*, they find many ways to stress their ethnic identities. For instance, a group of United Nations delegates from the Ukraine once preferred to speak with me in English rather than in Russian. Yet these high-level republican officials hardly seem committed to the idea of separatism or independence.

The participation of the non-Russian republics in the process of economic modernization has also served to mitigate the ethnic centrifugal forces. Industrial and agricultural development in the politically important non-Russian regions, the Caucasus and Central Asia, keeps pace with the rest of the Soviet Union.

After noting that labor productivity in the European part of the Soviet Union is growing faster than in the "colonies," Martin C. Spechler remarks:

On the other hand, income and welfare have not become more unequal over time and this indicates substantial and growing transfers (even if nonbudgetary) of goods and services to the "colonies." In consequence, by the standards of semi-developed dictatorships and fraternal Communist countries more developed than itself, the Soviet Union is rather egalitarian, although the modern USA is more so.*

* Martin C. Spechler, "Regional Developments in the USSR, 1958–78," in *The Soviet Economy in a Time of Change,* Vol. I. A compendium of papers submitted to the U.S. Congress, Joint Economic Committee (Washington, D.C.: Government Printing Office, 1979), p. 161.

Under the impact of economic growth and political modernization, the traditional national patterns of authority have declined radically, while at the same time the familial and communal patterns have been preserved to a surprising degree, allowing a safety valve for the ethnic identity and aspirations of the native population in these regions.

The stability of the republics has been further supported by the benefits accruing from more recent economic policy. There has been an increased commitment to the general development of the non-Russian republics; to higher wages, particularly in the agricultural sector, in the Caucasus and Central Asia; and to a greater tolerance for the activities of the second economy and private initiative generally in the republics as compared to Russia proper. As a result, the indigenous populations in these areas enjoy a higher standard of living than does the Russian peasantry. The relatively greater accessibility to a wide variety of low-cost food is also explained by the better climatic conditions in those areas than in Russia proper, and the lack of necessary transportation, storage, and refrigeration that would make the native produce more accessible to the northern regions of the Soviet Union. They cannot sell in Moscow what they grow in the provinces, so they keep it.

In maintaining its dominance over the internal empire, Moscow is aided by the traditional divisions and animosity among the non-Russian republics. Conflict over and competition for resources exacerbate these differences. The Russians often deliberately foster the ethnic animosities through budgetary procedures, forced migration, and appointments to political and economic offices. The upshot of this is a lack of unified pressure on the central government. The only recent substantial ethnic unrest in the south of the Soviet Union occurred in 1978, and, ironically, it was directed not against the Russians but against the Georgians. The Abkhazian Autonomous Republic, which is under the jurisdiction of the Georgian party and government, appealed to Moscow with the complaint that the Georgians were discriminating against it with respect to economic investment and development. To mollify the Abkhazians, Moscow reportedly promised them 750 million rubles in industrial, transportation, agricultural, and educational investment.

The Soviet nations are not equal in their importance for the preservation of the Soviet internal empire or in their potential effect on nationalism. Because of their size—about a quarter of the total population—their location on the western borders, and their contribution to the country's economic and military might, the non-Russian Slavs, the Ukrainians and Byelorussians, are a decisive factor in the maintenance of the internal empire. Fortunately for Moscow, it is the Slavs of the Soviet Union that are most Russified. In addition, the Slavs are treated differently than other nationalities, with the partial exception of the

Armenians. They are often elevated to the central elite in Moscow (in 1985 the Ukrainian trade minister Grigorii Vatchenko was appointed Minister of Trade of the USSR), and they are well represented in many central hierarchies, including Gosplan, the Army, and the KGB. Moreover, Slavs in part perform the supervisory role of controlling the non-Slavic elites in their own republics. As long as the junior partnership of the Ukrainians and the Byelorussians with the Russian establishment survives intact, the sheer weight and power of such a coalition is sufficient to squelch any irredentist aspirations among the non-Slavs.

The prominence of an Azerbaidzhani, Geidar A. Aliyev, who was appointed first deputy prime minister of the Soviet Union in late 1982, and a Georgian, Eduard A. Shevardnadze, who was picked as foreign minister in 1985, is unprecedented in the post-Stalin period. Their appointments probably do not signify a change in the general situation. The first secretaries of non-Russian republics who are full Politburo members, such as Dinmukhamed Kunayev, the chief of Kazakhstan, do not belong to the Politburo's inner circle, and do not even attend all the meetings. The chiefs of the republics who are alternate members of the Politburo seldom advance, as Aliyev and Shevardnadze did, to full membership. Neither under Khrushchev nor under Brezhnev nor under Gorbachev has the top executive body of the Party, the Central Committee Secretariat in Moscow, had even a single member who was not of Slavic origin. The basic proposition that the career of a non-Slavic member of the elite has its ceiling within his own republic remains largely in force.

In the final analysis, stability depends on the strength of a regime's legitimacy as perceived by the population at large and the elites. Stability hinges on the extent and intensity of support for the structure, goals, and policies of the regime. A government may lose its legitimacy in a crisis situation such as war, or through a gradual process of erosion and decline. The question of legitimacy is especially important for revolutionary regimes that have ostensibly broken with traditional patterns of authority and, as in the case of the Soviet Union, still draw on the revolution itself as a key source of legitimacy.

The term *legitimacy* most often conveys the extent of the regime's popular support. Despite the probably accurate impression that popular support for the Soviet regime has declined, especially in the 1980s, the Kremlin still enjoys both significant popular backing and, as important, the absence of strong opposition. There are a number of factors that both explain and illustrate this situation.

The regime benefits from the lack of any democratic tradition in its own and its tsarist past. Authoritarianism remains the only model of rule with which the population as a whole has had any experience. As a matter of fact, there are many indications that the erosion of legitimacy in recent years is connected not with any democratic yearning but with the lack of strong rule and order. The desire for a visible and decisive boss in the last years of Brezhnev's rule was unmistakable. To a foreigner this desire finds expression in conversations with ordinary citizens, in the photos of Stalin on the visors of many taxis and buses, and in the thriving business of privately produced tokens with Stalin's picture. And this attitude is by no means limited to the lower classes but is prevalent as well among the professional groups and especially in the bureaucratic hierarchies. The more authoritarian the rule of the man at the top, the broader are the prerogatives of bureaucrats with regard to their subordinates.

Implicit, and sometimes even explicit, in the views of the professionals (including even parts of the dissident movement at home and abroad) are a contempt for and isolation from the working classes, a fear that democracy would give license to the worst instincts of the public, and a belief that the disintegration of the regime in its present form would set the stage for the sort of widespread violence that has flared up so often in Russian history. There is, in short, a widely shared conviction that Russia is not ready for democracy—often based on or coupled with a principled antipathy toward democracy in general.

Where the legitimacy of a regime is concerned, all citizens are not equal. Even in Western democracies, legitimacy rests on the active support of a part of the population and the political apathy of the rest. In the Soviet Union, active support for the regime also comes only from that part of the population which participates in the political process within the central bureaucracy or in the political, economic, and cultural institutions at the local level. This segment is not small. It is concentrated in the Communist Party, which includes almost one-third of the adult male urban population with higher education, and the activists of numerous intermediary associations and organizations such as the local Soviets, the Komsomol (Young Communist League), and the trade unions.

Despite its revolutionary origins, the Soviet Union began relatively early to utilize and promote the symbols of traditional Russian authority: Russian nationalism, Russian international ambitions, and Russian messianic views of their national and international mission. To a very large extent, the official Soviet world view is a result of the fusion of Marxist-Leninist ideology with Russian nationalism and messianism. The official outlook also reconciles the Slavophile and Westernizing streams in Russian political thought. It stresses the uniqueness of Russia and the unacceptability of Western political institutions and culture, and at the same time the need, indeed the imperative, for scientific, technological, and economic modernization. Because of its traditional Russian sources, popular legitimacy is strongest among the Russian population and weaker among non-Russians. The attempt to identify specifically Russian nationalism with Soviet patriotism is only moderately successful.

The political acquiescence of the population is also based on the overwhelming sense of a lack of alternatives. Moreover, the authoritarian system requires much less support than democratic systems, and can function and survive with only limited active backing. The foundations of the system rest on both power and authority, but their mix is different from that in democratic societies, being skewed in favor of power.

Finally, the strength of popular legitimacy, while not tested through many major crises or traumatic events, has nevertheless survived a few: the death of Stalin and the end of personal dictatorship and mass terror, Khrushchev's anti-Stalin campaign, and, last but not least, the emergence and development of political dissent. The continuity of power after Stalin's death has been uninterrupted.

Nonetheless, it would be a mistake to exaggerate the strength of Soviet popular legitimacy, which is without doubt much weaker than in traditional or modernized democratic societies. In the only real, practical test of that legitimacy—the Nazi-Soviet war—the Russians largely supported their national government. Considering the nature of the Nazi plans for Slavs, however, this was not so much backing of the regime as a desire for survival as a nation.

It is also important to note that a regime's legitimacy defines not only the extent of its popular support, but also the ability of its leaders to rule when popular support is low. The relative thinness of Soviet legitimacy is counterbalanced by the enormous powers of coercion, control, and manipulation at the disposal of the regime. In a future time of major trouble or protracted crisis, the limitations of popular legitimacy may pose a serious threat to the regime's survival. However, in the face of the normal challenges of everyday life, as long as the will to rule of the leadership and political elite remains as strong as it is today, the continuation of authoritarianism is assured.

One must also recognize that the legitimacy of regimes has another important dimension—that of the sense of legitimacy among the system's elites. From the time of the writings of the great sociologists of the nineteenth and early twentieth centuries, especially Vilfredo Pareto, it has been recognized that conditions of stability are to a large extent also a function of the situation within a society's elite. While Pareto stressed particularly the elite's will for power as a key indicator of legitimacy, Karl Marx and Max Weber stressed the unity of the various functional elites. The insight of these classic writers has been confirmed by the entire experience of communist regimes. It is now an accepted axiom that

in almost all cases of instability in Eastern European communist countries, the decline of the will to rule, and internal divisions and conflict
within the elite, were the condition and the harbinger of the unrest.

Soviet legitimacy has been solidified by the longevity of the regime's
existence, its victory in World War II, the rulers' ability to fuse its revolutionary doctrine with great-power nationalism to form a domestically
conservative ideology to which all subscribe, the cohesion of the elites
against the outside world, and their commitment to the preservation of
their empire and the advancement of their global ambitions. Despite the
obvious differences of particular interests among the rulers, all these
factors make it very unlikely that there will be long-lasting divisions that
undermine the system or that prevent the elites from providing mutual
support should a popular threat arise.

Divisions between such elite groups as the military and the top Party
bureaucracy do emerge. They were very clear during the time of Khrushchev and have reappeared in the last few years. These differences,
however, did not concern disputes about the nature of the system and
the future of its major institutions but were primarily questions of resource allocation. In the early 1960s Khrushchev reduced the size of the
armed forces by about 15 percent. (At that time erstwhile army officers
drove Moscow taxis.) Obviously the army high command opposed such
a move. Khrushchev ridiculed the need to build aircraft carriers, and the
navy disagreed with his decision. The chief of the general staff, Nikolai
Ogarkov, citing the dangerous state of Soviet-American relations,
stressed the necessity of continuing growth of military expenditures, particularly in conventional weapons, and was demoted. Some Party leaders, however, such as Andropov in his time, or even the "political"
(civilian) Defense Minister Ustinov, have been concerned with reconciling the requirements of the military with increases in industrial investments and keeping at least unchanged the popular consumption levels.
But these and other disputes and conflicts have not called into question
the basic authoritarian and Party-dominated formula of the Soviet system.

It seems clear that the leaders' will to power and the commitment to
the existing system have remained unshaken. When speaking about the
diverse groups and interests in society, we tend to concentrate on conflict
among different groups. Conflict, after all, gives them their uniqueness
and variety. But when we consider the interaction of elite groups in the
Soviet Union, we must note that those groups accept the system fundamentally while competing for advantages within it. The difference on
this score between the Soviet political elite and that of Eastern Europe is
as striking as the difference between the Soviet and Eastern European
societies.

Still, despite all the factors that argue for the survivability of the Soviet system, its stability is in some areas narrowly based. It relies heavily
on the visible hand of political control, administrative organization, and
conscious manipulation and intervention, and depends far less than
Western governments on the invisible processes of socialization, tradition, and internalized controls. It cannot rely extensively on the forces of
tradition at a time when the country is being rapidly modernized. It
cannot rely on charismatic authority, which dissipated with the death of
Stalin. It cannot rely on legal authority when the political and constitutional laws are so clearly rigged in favor of the rulers. The Soviet Union
is no longer a totalitarian nation, but it does not yet have a traditional
authoritarian regime. And it has not come any closer in the post-Stalin
years to being a *rechtsstaat*, a legal-rational democratic regime. The kind
of stability on which the government is based may be severely tested in
the decade to come.

3

Brezhnev's Legacy

Brezhnev's rule was both a source and an example of unprecedented stability and a major contributing factor to the prospects of destabilization and trouble which the regime faces now. The Brezhnev era spanned a period of eighteen years, during which the general secretary was the dominant figure on the political scene. His tenure was almost as long as Stalin's, and considerably longer than that of such dominant Western figures as Roosevelt, Churchill, Adenauer, or de Gaulle.

In the Soviet system it makes a great difference who the top leader is. This fact alone would mark the two decades of Brezhnev's rule as a distinctive and important period in Soviet history. Its distinctiveness is also the result of discontinuities between Brezhnev's rule on the one hand and that of Khrushchev and Stalin on the other.

In addition to Khrushchev's previously mentioned achievements, he can also be credited with abolishing Stalin's most ignorant and irrational economic policies and improving the standard of living of the ordinary Soviet citizen. He opposed Stalin's formulation that in a socialist economy demand should always run ahead of supply, a pure justification of permanent shortages of consumer goods; he eliminated the irrationally high taxation of collectivized peasants' private orchards, which, at a time when little fruit was available to the cities, actually motivated the farmers to keep their orchards very small. He turned over agricultural machinery—which was owned by the state and had previously been controlled by the machine-tractor stations—to the peasants themselves, to be used in accordance with their local needs.

In the event, however, Khrushchev's genuinely felt optimism about what the Soviet Union, freed from the shackles of Stalinism, could achieve both at home and abroad turned out to be naïve. He left behind him exaggerated popular expectations of domestic economic growth, political liberalization, and international power and influence.

Khrushchev's colleagues feared that his anti-Stalin campaign was promoting a critical spirit among the population and within the Party that would undermine the discipline and intellectual conformity that the system required. They were dissatisfied with his highly charged ideological experimentation and the increased influence of ideology on policies. His fellow "Politbureaucrats" were wary of the destabilizing effects of any attempt to rebuild the Party as a mass movement and to heighten the element of self-administration in the local and municipal Soviets through participation of the rank and file in the making and implementation of policy. His colleagues were also unhappy with Khrushchev's jarringly sudden essays at organizational reforms and his short-term campaigns. He contributed immensely to their preference for gradualism. The elites, who under him attained security of life, were yearning by the end of his rule for security of office. Professional and specialists' groups desired greater autonomy.

During Khrushchev's rule the Party apparatus gained permanent dominance among the various elites and escaped from the uncertain and changing rank order of the bureaucracies of the Stalin era. The last two years of Khrushchev's rule also showed the determined opposition of the Party to any shift in its responsibilities from political decision-making to economic management. Finally, Khrushchev's ouster demonstrated that once the top leader has relinquished the instrument of terror, he must preserve a consensus within the leadership group and among the heads of the major bureaucracies in order to survive. He must therefore be able to forge compromises among their competing interests.

Brezhnev was elected by his colleagues to the position of Party leader at a time when virtually all of the bureaucratic hierarchies were disaffected with Khrushchev's leadership. He received a clear mandate to restabilize the system and to revamp his predecessor's domestic policies. The first steps of the Brezhnev regime were to end the anti-Stalin campaign, to reaffirm the elites' acceptance of and devotion to their past traditions, and to restore the procedures that had been shaken by Khrushchev's innovations and his impulsive and haphazard reorganizations. Throughout its existence, the Brezhnev regime put the utmost premium on the stability of the system, continuity of elite rule, and compromise resolution of conflicts. Brezhnev's corporate and conservative leadership was nowhere as noticeable as in the structure of politics and decision-making.

Meanwhile, KGB influence increased. The more distant the crimes of the Stalin era became, the more political visibility the KGB attained.

One example is the highly favorable, even heroic portrayal, in the press, books, and films, of the KGB and of its predecessors, the Cheka, OGPU, NKVD, MVD, and MGB. Another sign of the KGB's renewed political importance was the elevation of its leader, Yuri Andropov, to full membership in the Politburo in April 1973. A further example was the inclusion under Brezhnev, for the first time since Stalin's rule, of all republic KGB chairmen in the republican Party bureaus, and of all KGB chairmen in the provinces (*oblasty*) of Russia, in the *obkom* bureaus. By Brezhnev's death the KGB, which under Khrushchev was depicted as the accessory to Stalin's crimes, was once again portrayed as the sword and shield of the revolution and of the state. Andropov's KGB became once again a model organization to be emulated by youth, and an important participant in politics.

The most important feature of the political system under Brezhnev was its transformation from the personal dictatorship of Stalin and the highly personalized and confrontational leadership of Khrushchev into a relatively stable oligarchy. The top leadership that developed in the Brezhnev era was to a large degree collective; almost all of the major bureaucratic interests were represented. No single bureaucratic group or personal machine dominated. Although the role of the Party general secretary and his supporters within the Politburo clearly increased from 1972 onward, the latitude the leader enjoyed was still more limited than in the past.

The important differences between Brezhnev's and Khrushchev's leadership styles cannot, however, be expressed adequately by such terms as *less* or *more*. These differences are better illuminated by answering the question: Power for what purpose? Khrushchev's power was expended in efforts to change institutions and policies. Its limits were tested most visibly in his alternating advances and retreats in the face of opposition. Brezhnev never really tested his power in that way. His was used primarily to assure the continuity of Soviet institutions and in the gradual adjustment of policies. Within the context of these aims, his position was strong and stable. Whereas Khrushchev often tried to form a new consensus or to undermine an existing one, Brezhnev was concerned primarily with maintaining consensus.

During Brezhnev's rule, the elite became engaged as never before in real politics. The cult of the top leader, the centralization of the Communist Party and state, and the "planning" that supposedly permeates all aspects of Soviet life could not hide the interplay of different interests and even individuals within the elite. The key actors in the political process are the major bureaucratic structures and their subsections. Alliances are formed on particular issues between and among various bureaucracies and territorial interests. (Khrushchev with his penchant for succinct characterization called one such interest group the metal eaters, a combination of civilian and military managers who sought even greater investments in heavy industry.) In the Brezhnev era, those interest groups developed a high degree of corporate identity, displayed a broad range of opinions on specific issues and were able as never before to resolve those issues through bargaining and compromise.

The conflicts and agreements between various bureaucracies and their subdivisions testify to the broadening on the elite level of the policy-making process. Yet, one bureaucratic hierarchy, the Party apparatus, requires particular attention. Brezhnev restored and even strengthened the central position of the Party, a position that Khrushchev had attempted to undermine in his radical reorganization of 1963–64 in order to achieve independence from any single bureaucratic constituency.

Under Brezhnev, the Party apparatus on all levels, but especially in the central secretariat, became the chief agency in charge of appointments to leadership positions in all bureaucracies. In the early years of Soviet power, the Party was primarily engaged in propaganda and in checking the loyalty of the state bureaucracies. In the Khrushchev period, it largely fulfilled the function of mobilizing other bureaucracies for the attainment of the prescribed state goals. Under Brezhnev, the main function of the apparatus became the coordination and arbitration of the activities of state institutions on the regional, republican, and central levels.

It would be incorrect, however, to conclude that the Party was simply a broker among various institutional interests. First of all, it was not a neutral coordinator. Moreover, on all levels it was in charge of the key element of policy-making and implementation, namely, agenda-setting. The setting of the agenda defined the boundaries within which conflicts over policies were resolved: that is, the limits of the options which could be considered by the policy-makers. From the study of Western decision-making we have become conscious of the importance of non-decision-making, that is, of excluding several options from consideration by governing bodies. In the Soviet Union such exclusion was the prerogative of the Party. In agriculture, for example, the Party excluded from the agenda the option of the reprivatization of land, the course followed in the 1980s by China, or the idea of transforming the agricultural collectives and state farms into virtual capitalistic enterprises, which has been one of the successful policies of Hungary's New Economic Mechanism.

Under Brezhnev the old conservative themes of law and order, national unity, and intolerance towards those who defy these norms remained the ruling principles of society.

A major dimension of Soviet conservatism as it entered the 1980s was the stability of the leadership and political elite. To a degree unequalled in any other period of Soviet history, the composition of the leadership and key hierarchies remained stable and unchanged throughout the Brezhnev era. Brezhnev's leadership gave them security of office. The turnover rate in the membership of the Central Committee of the Party was extraordinarily low, as the figures below demonstrate:*

TABLE 1 SURVIVAL RATIO OF MEMBERS OF THE CENTRAL COMMITTEE AND THE COMMUNIST PARTY OF THE SOVIET UNION AT CONSECUTIVE CONGRESSES †

Khrushchev			*Brezhnev*			
XX	XXII		XXIII	XXIV	XXV	XXVI
62.4	49.6		79.4	76.5	83.4	89.0

† The extraordinary XXI Party Congress that took place in 1959 is omitted from the table. Because of its special character, devoted to the unveiling of Khrushchev's program after he became firmly entrenched in power, no elections to the Central Committee took place.

This stability was partly a spontaneous reaction to the experimentation and turmoil of the Khrushchev period and partly a secular trend representing the further bureaucratization of the political system, with its stress on gradualism and orderliness. Until recently, this stability represented the basic desires of elite groups, and the leadership responded positively. But one major consequence was that the Soviet Union entered the 1980s with the oldest group of central and regional elites in its history. The replacements for those members who died or retired during the Brezhnev era were selected primarily from Brezhnev's generation. For instance, when Prime Minister Alexei Kosygin retired in October 1980 at the age of seventy-six, he was replaced by the seventy-five-year-old Nikolai Tikhonov. So the leadership and elite worked together for an extraordinarily long period of time, and were able to design a set of rules for their relationships that was widely accepted and relatively benign in light of Soviet tradition.

Whether by Brezhnev's choice or because of the oligarchic nature of the Soviet leadership and the compromises that it entailed, the price of the stability of the Brezhnev era was primarily the lack of structural re-

* Except where noted, this and the tables which follow are drawn from the following sources: *Narodnoe Khoziaistvo SSSR* (Moscow); *The Soviet Economy in a Time of Change* (2 vols., Joint Economic Committee, U.S. Congress, U.S. Government Printing Office, Washington, D.C., 1979); *The Soviet Economy in the 1980s: Problems and Prospects,* Parts I and II (Joint Economic Committee, 1983); and *East European Economies: Slow Growth in the 1980s,* Vol. I: *Economic Performance and Policy* (Joint Economic Committee, 1985).

forms. The most striking changes took place in policies. Despite the reforms of the Khrushchev and post-Khrushchev period, despite all the discussion on improving the planning and economic mechanisms, all the tinkering with indices of success, and all the progress made toward modernization, the Soviet economic system remains virtually unchanged in its basic characteristics from the Stalinist model. Supercentralization, the absence of autonomy of economic subdivisions, tight and detailed planning, the stress on quantitative output, and the lack of any self-regulating mechanism that relies on competition or promotion of technological progress, are still the hallmarks of the economic system. Policies have changed; the structure remains.

During the Brezhnev era, the Soviet Union faced a number of difficult problems. Its achievements were impressive but uneven. At the outset, Western analysts defined long lists of trouble spots and potentially destructive problems that would confront the leadership. But on the whole, the leaders performed better than expected. Most importantly, despite the fact that they did not solve or for the most part even diminish any of these major problems, they prevented any of those problems—taken singly or in the aggregate—from becoming the source of a paralyzing and destructive crisis. Crucially also, the popular standard of living continued throughout most of the Brezhnev period to increase significantly.

While there was virtually no institutional change during the Brezhnev era, there was considerable policy innovation. Some policies constituted a major shift from those of the Khrushchev period, while some continued or even accelerated what Khrushchev had done. Some of the policies were failures, some produced marginal results, and some were successful.

The major success story of the Brezhnev era was the military buildup. The impressive growth of military strength was not a result of an extraordinary expansion or spurt of spending. It was rather the consequence of a steady increase in expenditures of about 4 percent per year throughout most of the period. Starting from an already broad base, the compounded increase in expenditures produced a qualitative change in military strength both in absolute terms and in relation to the forces of its adversaries.

The production of arms for all branches of the armed forces expanded enormously. Year after year it exceeded by a large margin that of its main opponent, the United States, whose military expenditures decreased or stagnated through most of this time. As a result, the balance of military strength between the two superpowers moved in a direction favorable to the Soviet Union. Moreover, the Soviets steadily enlarged their military-industrial base, expanding their capacity for future growth, while the existing American potential for military production declined after the Vietnam War.

In military technology, the Soviets dramatically closed the gap between them and the United States. They modernized and upgraded both their forces facing NATO and those on the Chinese border. They reached a greater balance between their land and sea weapons and their land, naval, and air force mix, and, for the first time, attained the capability to project military power—their own and that of their proxies like the Cubans—far from their own borders.

Brezhnev's other central and highly visible policy concerned agriculture, which during most of the period received the largest budgetary expenditure. There was a large infusion of capital in the form of long-range programs to upgrade the soil, to develop the non-black-earth regions which produced low yields and needed major capital investments, and to increase the production of fertilizer and agricultural machinery. There was a major commitment to the production of meat, so that Russians could have an improved diet, and a willingness to import large amounts of feed grain from the West. Khrushchev's grain imports were primarily for flour, Brezhnev's for livestock feed. By 1963 the Soviet Union was still a net exporter of grain, but by 1981 it imported about 40 million tons, equal to about 20 to 25 percent of its average grain production in the late 1970s and 1980s.

Huge subsidies for agricultural produce continued on the official market, which kept the prices down and thereby translated improvements in agricultural production into higher consumption, particularly of products like meat and butter. While Soviet flour consumption per capita dropped from 156 kilograms per year in 1965 to 139 kilograms in 1980, the consumption of milk and milk products rose by about 25 percent, of eggs by more than 60 percent, and meat and poultry by about 35 percent. Soviet meat production during the Brezhnev era increased from 8.3 million tons in 1964 to 14.9 million in 1975, and then, until Brezhnev's death in 1982, stagnated at a level slightly over 15 million tons.

Other policies included the lifting of many restrictions against production on the private plots of farmers and state farm workers; the increase of incentives to collective farmers through the state's assumption of partial responsibility for their welfare in the form of minimum pay, social security benefits and insurance against bad harvests; and an attempt to stem the migration of the young from rural to urban areas.

Brezhnev's program was successful in that at its peak grain production reached a level almost three times larger than that of 1953, and even in bad years only once went below double the output of 1953. However, after an initial upsurge, productivity of Soviet agriculture, that is to say, the percentage of return on the money and labor invested, declined precipitously in the later years of Brezhnev's rule. As Table 2 shows, in the 1970's the growth of agricultural net product was lower than the increase in population, while the inputs into agriculture were rising steadily.

The inherent weakness of Soviet agriculture and its vulnerability to weather conditions became apparent in 1979–81, when the harvest was disastrous and food shortages in the cities were the worst of the Brezhnev era. The basic policy failures of Soviet agriculture were identified in the resolution of the May 1982 Plenum of the Central Committee, which implicitly recognized the incongruity of the vast sums of money spent with the poor results. The Plenum introduced a Food Program to be in place until 1990. In his speech to the plenum, Brezhnev made a statement that showed the leadership's fears of the consequences of a continuous shortage of food. He said that providing a reliable supply of foodstuffs is not only a "top economic priority, but also an urgent sociopolitical task." As Anton F. Malish, an authoritative American expert on Soviet agriculture, remarked: "Touted as a radical solution, the 'Food Program' seems more a slowly evolving process that differs little from themes identified at Brezhnev's first plenum (1965) on agriculture. In highlighting the problems, however, the Soviet leadership would seem to be inviting massive dissatisfaction if the program fails to show results."*

TABLE 2   SOVIET AGRICULTURE: RATES OF GROWTH, 1951–1979

	Average Annual Percentage Rates of Growth		
	1951–60	1961–70	1971–79
Grain	3.4	4.0	−0.3
Potatoes	−0.8	2.0	−0.5
Fruits and Vegetables	6.5	5.3	3.3
Technical Crops	4.6	4.0	1.3
Net crop output	2.6	3.7	0.7
Meat	4.1	3.3	2.7
Milk	5.7	3.0	1.3
Other	9.0	5.5	−0.9
Net livestock output	6.1	3.7	1.0
Net agricultural output	4.3	3.7	0.9

* Anton F. Malish, "The Food Program: A New Policy or More Rhetoric?" in *The Soviet Economy in the 1980s: Problems and Prospects,* Part II. Selected papers submitted to the U.S. Congress, Joint Economic Committee (Washington, D.C.: Government Printing Office, 1983), pp. 49–50.

Industrial policy in the Brezhnev era brought no major surprises. Until the final years the leadership was able to boost investments year after year in the heavy and extracting industries, as well as in the consumer-oriented industries. Plant and production levels rose substantially during Brezhnev's first decade, but then the growth rate started to decline.

Most importantly, however, the industrial system of planning, management, pricing, and incentives retained its basic characteristics and was unable to promote higher productivity of capital and labor. It remained a system geared to extensive growth—requiring ever larger inputs of the factors of production: labor, capital, and land.

Technological innovation and its diffusion within industry remained unsatisfactory. In the 1980s, Japan is overtaking the Soviet Union as the world's second largest producer of combined industrial goods and services. A study by a group of scientists, engineers, and economists from Birmingham and Yale universities concluded that between 1953 and the mid-1970s, the technological gap between the Soviet Union and the West in most branches of civilian industries did not narrow at all.

TABLE 3   SOVIET INDUSTRIAL PRODUCTION:
AVERAGE ANNUAL RATES OF GROWTH (Percent)

	51–55	56–60	61–65	66–70	71–75	76–80
INDUSTRIAL MATERIALS	10.5	8.9	6.8	5.8	5.4	2.6
Ferrous metals	11.1	7.6	7.2	5.1	4.0	1.1
Nonferrous metals	12.8	6.9	7.6	7.4	5.9	2.6
Fuels	9.4	8.9	6.3	5.0	5.0	3.3
Electric power	13.1	11.4	11.5	7.9	7.0	4.5
Chemicals and petrochemicals	11.6	10.5	12.0	8.9	8.6	3.8
Wood, pulp, and paper	7.4	5.8	2.6	2.9	2.6	−0.1
Construction materials	15.7	14.7	5.4	5.7	5.4	1.8
TOTAL MACHINERY	9.6	7.9	7.4	6.9	7.9	5.4
Including:						
Producer durables	11.8	12.4	8.9	7.8	8.6	5.8
Consumer durables	17.7	10.4	9.6	11.3	11.7	6.0
CONSUMER NONDURABLES	10.3	7.4	4.8	6.4	3.4	1.6
Light industry	10.4	6.4	2.6	7.2	2.7	2.6
Processed food	10.2	8.4	6.8	5.9	3.9	0.7
TOTAL INDUSTRY	10.2	8.3	6.6	6.3	5.9	3.4

While industrial technology imported from the West increased significantly, it constituted only about 3 to 4 percent of total Soviet investment, and its impact on general technological progress in the civilian sector remained negligible. Yet the high technology imports may have had a significant impact on the military-industrial sector, and moreover, were important in the realization of key Soviet projects in the late 1960s and 1970s. In contrast with Poland, which imported Western technology in the 1970s on a great scale and in a haphazard manner, the Soviet Union concentrated most of its industrial technology imports on a few projects, such as the Togliatti car complex, the Kama truck factory, the Kama electrical power facility, the Baikal-Amur Railroad, and the gas pipeline from Siberia to Europe.

In the cultural field, Brezhnev's policies, almost from the beginning, adhered rigorously to the old Stalinist approach. They emphasized culture as the major instrument of political education. There was marked intolerance for experimentation in form or substance. The relative openness and creative turmoil of Khrushchev's years gave way to orthodoxy, which found its initial expression in its treatment of the Stalinist past: The anti-Stalin campaign was aborted, and, while it was not replaced, except on occasion, by glorification, criticism of Stalin's criminal deeds was at best perfunctory. The official attitude toward the Stalinist era was laudatory of its basic policies such as collectivization, and silent about its criminal methods and effects.

TABLE 4   USSR TRENDS IN CAPITAL AND MANHOUR PRODUCTIVITY
BY PERIODS, 1966–79 (Annual average percentage changes)

	Capital Productivity			Manhour productivity		
	66–70	71–75	76–79	66–70	71–75	76–79
Industry	−2.2	−2.8	−3.3	3.2	4.1	1.6
Agriculture	−4.3	−8.0	−5.2	3.2	1.5	0.7
Construction	−6.3	−5.5	−6.1	1.1	2.4	0.8
Transportation and communications	−0.1	−1.2	−3.6	4.2	3.6	1.2
Trade	−1.9	−3.3	−4.3	2.0	1.3	0.9
Services	−0.4	−1.7	−1.7	0.4	0.3	...
Manufacturing and mining	−2.0	−3.2	−3.6	3.2	4.0	1.5
ECONOMIC AGGREGATES:						
Material production sectors	−2.3	−4.4	−3.5	4.0	2.7	1.9
Economy	−1.9	−3.8	−2.9	3.1	2.3	1.3

Source: JEC 12/31/82, pp. 172–73.

One major theme of Brezhnev's cultural policy was patriotism, which kept the memory of victory in the Second World War alive in the national consciousness; another was the cult of Lenin, which on such occasions as the fiftieth anniversary of his death, in 1974, was celebrated in a circuslike manner reminiscent of Stalin's seventieth birthday in 1949. In the mid-1970s still another theme was highlighted—the cult of Brezhnev. Following the old examples, this campaign presented Brezhnev as the "great helmsman," the "great military leader," the "great writer of our era," and so on. The main engineer of this campaign was Konstantin Chernenko.

One of the very few liberal gestures in the Brezhnev cultural policy was the permission given to some major artists to emigrate. Yet even this policy was far from liberal in its intent; many of them, notably Alexander Solzhenitsyn, were actually thrown out of the country against their will. Emigration and exile were ways to get rid of troublesome figures and at the same time to underscore in the eyes of foreign public opinion the magnanimity of Brezhnev's rule. Those who were thus got rid of included many of the country's truly creative figures: the cellist Rostropovich, the poet Brodsky, the writers Solzhenitsyn, Sinyavsky, Nekrasov, Aksyonov, and many others.

Towards the end of the Brezhnev period, along with the officially optimistic style of socialist realism, an increasing degree of pessimism began to penetrate Soviet culture. Themes of the "happy tractorist," the all-knowing party functionary, and the fusion of "progressive" sociopolitical consciousness and positive work with personal happiness were displaced in many books, movies, and plays by unhappy endings, doubts in the mind of the "positive hero," insoluble problems, disbelief in "progress," the search for new spiritual guidelines, praise of the "simple" values of the Russian village as contrasted with the corruption of life in the cities, and the search for the Russian past and for personal happiness outside the collective. As one student of Soviet cultural and intellectual life, Maurice Friedberg, concluded:

> The virtual absence of goals such as those that once inspired the Soviet population and helped it endure hardships and sacrifices serves to intensify obsession with the past and to underscore a pervasive sense of vague dissatisfaction with the seemingly aimless present. All of these trends describe an immobile and aging society at once restless and insecure.*

With regard to ideology in its pure form, that is to say, doctrine, what happened in the Brezhnev era may best be evaluated by comparing it to the Khrushchev period. Both the Khrushchev and Brezhnev eras saw a pronounced expansion in the output of ideological literature, much more attention to its mass dissemination, and greater stress on ideological training and Party schooling than in the Stalin era. Both regimes responded to the disappearance of terror by upgrading the role

---

* Maurice Friedberg, "Cultural and Intellectual Life," in Robert F. Byrnes, ed., *After Brezhnev: Sources of Soviet Conduct in the 1980s* (Bloomington: Indiana University Press, 1983), p. 251.

and weight, if not the effectiveness, of ideological and economic social controls.

Yet the doctrinal tendency of these two periods differs. The association of the Khrushchev period with goulash communism and with an attempt to reorganize the Party along functional economic lines sometimes concealed what was in fact the dominant theme of this period: an unsuccessful attempt at ideological revival. The reformist zeal and flux of the Khrushchev period was founded on the belief that ideological truths can impress and inspire the masses. In Khrushchev's last years, the manipulation of ideological symbols was increasingly intended to link the leader directly with the Party and the masses, bypassing the bureaucracy.

The basic theme of the Brezhnev era was ideological retrenchment and partial retreat. The materials used in mass and Party indoctrinations had a dogmatic, uncritical, monotonous tone. Most importantly, there was no serious effort to go beyond the routine slogans and precepts in the attempt to propagate the doctrine to nonbelievers or doubters. Instead the emphasis was placed on resistance to, and defense against, alien ideas.

One sign of this partial retreat was the line drawn between science and doctrine. The issue of the possible incompatibility between the substance of some scientific thought and ideology was simply dropped. With it went the attacks on, reinterpretations of, and even suppression of particular scientific theories. The Party philosophers have ceased to be the ideological watchdogs of scientific research. Their main function became to provide a justification for the accommodation between science and doctrine. The other indication of partial retreat—ambiguous, uncertain, and much less clear—is the debates in professional journals and at conferences concerning a wide range of social, ecological, and economic issues. The participants do not try, and are usually not pushed, to link their factual analysis and recommendations to doctrinal truths. The doctrinal position on policy issues is now ambiguous, nonauthoritative, and ill defined. Discussions, therefore, are conducted neither against doctrinal prescription nor in support of it, but rather parallel to doctrine. Doctrinal entrenchment does take place on one level, where rigidity and dogmatism are very pronounced—in propaganda and culture, general education and Party schooling, and with regard to the central questions of Soviet history. At the same time, direct doctrinal intervention into expert deliberation is limited, and therefore the impulse to issue binding verdicts on unresolved policy questions has been curtailed.

An example of this change may be seen in cancer research. In 1966 a researcher in a medical institute wrote a letter to the Central Committee reporting that in his medical institute there were two different views on the question of hereditary immunity in relation to susceptibility to cancer. The writer asked the Central Committee to issue a verdict on which of these views was correct. In response, *Pravda* replied in an editorial that the question of scientific truth should be determined by scientists themselves in experiments, and that the Central Committee had no qualifications for issuing binding verdicts on scientific issues. In Stalin's time, the attitude to such questions would have been very different. After all, it was Stalin who in the late 1940s proclaimed which of the respective schools of theoretical linguistics were ideologically pure and which were contaminated by un-Marxian influences. Even in Khrushchev's time, the pseudoscientist Trofim Lysenko was supported by the Party leader against the attacks of his opponents. This backing of Lysenko's theories of the crucial role of environment as opposed to heredity was very costly to the Soviet Union; Soviet biology fell behind Western research by at least ten to fifteen years. Only after Khrushchev's ouster was biology left to the biologists.

Nonetheless, a Soviet proclivity for intermixing politics, ideology, and science occasionally resurfaces even today. The question of heredity versus environment has remained a subject of continuous discussion in the biological and psychological community; and in 1984, Konstantin Chernenko's daughter, who is a psychologist, published a blistering attack in *Pravda* on those who stress the importance of heredity. *Pravda,* of course, publishes only articles that are approved by the Party. This was a clear example of ideological interference in scientific discussions.

Thus, communist doctrine could retain a semblance of consistency, and disagreements about its meaning and consequences for practical action could be minimized, by continually increasing its aloofness from social practice, that is, by its escalating ritualization. However, the staying power of the doctrine depends not only on its logical coherence and consistency, but also on the social functions that it performs. The continuation of these functions is crucial, and so the leadership has tried to find ideological formulations that will reinforce them. A typical formulation of the Brezhnev era was that of "mature socialism" and "scientific management of the society," which implied new functions for the Party apparatus that it alone could perform because of its mastery of "scientific socialism." These formulas sought to reinforce the role of the Party bureaucracy by presenting it as the main force behind technological progress and the chief promoter and coordinator of the adaptation of society to new technological realities.

The most important function of doctrinal orthodoxy is to legitimize the Party's and Party apparatus' dominant power position within the elite. It is not that the Party's administrative role is parasitic—its function of coordinating and overseeing the activities of all other bureaucracies is a necessary one in the Soviet system. But it is not the only institution that can perform this function. The basis of legitimacy of the Party and the regime is nationalism, but to nationalism the Party has no unique claim. Only when it is combined with doctrinal orthodoxy does the position of the Party and its apparatus become unique: The Party is the sole repository of the founding revolutionary myth and the bearer of the mantle of Lenin.

The Brezhnev period saw an acceleration in the withering away of the concepts of utopia and utopianism in the thought and practice of the political elite. Under Khrushchev, this utopianism, traditionally the central element of the doctrine, still constituted one part of the vision of the future. Incorporated in the Party program of 1961, the promise of the leader read, "The Party solemnly proclaims: The present generation of Soviet people shall live under communism." The Brezhnev (and post-Brezhnev) leadership disliked and discouraged this kind of fantasy. *Delovitost,* "businesslike behavior," has become the ubiquitous slogan, the leadership quality most praised in written and spoken word. The *delovitost* of the top leaders signifies an overriding concern with the rationalization of an uncritically accepted system, and above all with reinforcing their own power.

The many policy reforms that Brezhnev introduced stressed the preservation of the existing institutions, such as centralized planning. The reforms were designed to make the institutions more effective by better training of their personnel or greater utilization of computers. The impulse to reshape society faded. For the leaders, the social structure has found its permanent shape—at least for the foreseeable future. What the Party now proposed to the population was nothing more than the indefinite continuation of the basic existing social relations and gradual material progress.

The leadership and elite retain a fundamental belief in the idea of progress. They are committed as much as before to the goal of growth, particularly economic growth. Their belief in the inherent goodness and instrumental value of technological progress and science remains deeply rooted. This is one of the reasons that, despite widespread political cynicism and a clear decline in the operational importance of communist doctrine, they retained under Brezhnev a basically optimistic outlook. Progress is still defined by the standards established by the developed Western societies. What declined radically in Brezhnev's last years was the confidence that catching up was possible.

Nationalism has grown more important. Partly in its great-power Soviet version and partly in its cultural, traditional Russian variety, it constitutes the major effective, long-lasting bond within the bureaucracy and between it and the citizenry. The old conservative theme of pre-1917

Russia—national unity and the condemnation of individuals and groups who threaten to impair it—provides the emotional base for an authoritarian political outlook and is in turn reinforced by it. In this sense the Soviet leaders reach into their Russian past to provide a basis for their own rule.

Lastly, within the leadership there is deep-seated fear and mistrust of spontaneity in political and social behavior, a bias in favor of intervention to repress it, and the conviction that strong central government, organization, and order are necessary.

In the West, the Brezhnev era is often regarded as a period of immobilism, traditionalism, and rigidity. Immediately after Khrushchev was ousted in late 1964, the Soviet system started to be portrayed as a government of clerks, or the dominion of gray bureaucrats. Although this initial image stuck throughout the whole period, it was not wholly accurate at the beginning. The elites were intelligent and experienced. But the characterization was valid as it referred to the lack of structural, as distinctive from policy, reforms; and in the last years of Brezhnev's tenure, it became completely true. By the end of the 1970s, the economic situation had worsened drastically. Decline in growth of the industrial and service sector combined with bad harvests and technological stagnation. The need for economic and political steps to counteract the slippage in growth and the unraveling of plans at home and abroad became urgent. The inability in most cases to deal with these problems revealed to Soviet citizens the immobilism and procrastination of the Soviet decision-making apparatus and the rigidity of ideas and personnel. The relative stability under Brezhnev did not, therefore, create conditions that would ensure such stability in the 1980s.

While the balance sheet of Brezhnev's legacy is mixed, it may well be that in historical perspective his era will be primarily remembered as a time of lost opportunities. The leadership succumbed to its conservative tendencies and the pressures of vested interests. It lost the opportunity for major reform of the economy. The first decade of Brezhnev's rule offered the conditions for such reform—a high rate of growth and necessary reserves to support the transition to a less centralized economic system. Yet, the respectable economic performance weakened the rationale of a radical reform. Now the new leaders must choose between reform and decline in a much harsher environment, and they will encounter greater social, political, and economic obstacles to reform.

Externally, the Brezhnev leadership exploited temporary American weakness in the aftermath of Vietnam and Watergate and pursued an ambitious expansionist policy by military means. In the 1970s, when the military strength of the United States and Western Europe remained basically stable, the Soviet Union lost the opportunity to secure durable arms control agreements by sustaining a constantly high rate of military buildup. The predictable American response set back prospects for accommodation and regulated competition, perhaps for a very long time.

Shortly before Brezhnev's death, I was struck by the complexity of official Russia's feeling about the dying leader. They liked and respected him for the achievements of his leadership, but primarily because he was good to them. At the same time they were troubled by his inability to deal with the most pressing issues, especially the economy. They had become impatient with his paralyzing hold over the levers of power. His rule had clearly outlived its usefulness. They hoped for another leader who could restore the dynamism of the system, even while they were apprehensive about what a new leadership would mean for their own positions. All in all, however, the overwhelming impression to an outside observer was that these people considered changes in the regime that they served long overdue and highly desirable.

4

The Harsh Decade

Brezhnev bequeathed to his successors profound economic, social, and political problems that have their source not in a particular policy of the leader or in the lack of intelligent leadership but in the very nature of the system. They represent the cumulative effects of inherent weaknesses in basic Soviet structures. The most immediate problems are economic. They will inevitably bear heavily on society and the political system. Without decisive action by the leadership, they promise to become even more acute over time. While they are not as catastrophic as some Western analysts would have us believe, they are far from being as routine as the Soviet press maintained for a long time. For many decades the political superstructure has shaped and controlled the socioeconomic base in the Soviet Union. Now the time has come for the base to take its revenge on the superstructure.

The policies shaping social and economic development over the past thirty years have produced many unintended consequences with troublesome implications for future development. The problems have been rendered more difficult by the social evolution of the country, which the leadership has been unable to control. Soviet leaders are becoming increasingly conscious of these developments.

Hardly anyone today who studies the Soviet Union doubts that it faces serious troubles and challenges in the late 1980s. The list of serious economic problems is extensive. Some have their sources in and are symptomatic of the maturation of the economy; some are the consequence of specific policies and their inertial continuity; and some are of an external nature, the result of circumstances that the leadership cannot control. Soviet economic problems can be described simply as an unsuccessful quest for modernity. This quest is strongly hampered by the insufficient level and diffusion of technology, by the decline in the growth of production and productivity, by the unresponsiveness of the managers and workers to the needs of modernity.

When the absolute size of the industrial sector was relatively small and the level of its technology relatively low, the rates of growth in proportion to the size of the economy were very high. During this long period, the first Soviet industrial revolution, which coincided with the Stalin era, a number of unique factors contributed to this growth. The improvement of the backward technological base that rested on foreign examples was swift and had a significant effect on labor productivity. The rapid expansion of the industrial labor force provided huge reserves for growth. Cheap raw materials were available and investment capital multiplied at an impressive rate. As had occurred in Western economies, after this initial burst of industrialization, growth rates in the economy began to decline. However, unlike in the West, the Soviet economy did not have built-in regenerative and innovational capacity to prepare itself for the onset of the second and third industrial revolutions—that is, for the advent of the mass-consumption society and the era of high-speed communication.

The maturation of the Soviet economy led to a decline in its growth rate. The projection for the rest of the 1980s, on which there is very little disagreement among Western experts and no convincing challenge from Soviet officials or economists, suggests an estimated range of 2 to 3 percent expansion. It is probable that the slower increases might mitigate the conflicting requirements for slower growing resources. That is to say, there may be a more or less stable floor to the decline in growth rates, and the slower development may eventually produce a lower demand for resources. For instance, lower investment growth will lead to declining demand on, let us say, steel or energy. Yet the absolute level of growth will still remain low.

The Soviet leaders do not possess economic indicators by which to measure these trends or instruments through which to counteract them. The prices, costs, and profits in the economy are artificial. They provide no true measurement of performance and little guidance. Prices, which are determined by the state, do not reflect actual costs of production; these costs do not accurately reflect the scarcity of human and material resources. The fulfillment of the industrial plan, and hence the profit margin of individual enterprises, is measured largely by the quantity of gross output and does not take into account the quality or specific mix of products.

With prices and fiscal investment playing a passive role in the economy, Soviet macro-planning is detached from the realities of economic performance. Gross output is a poor standard of judgment, because it leaves out of account both the quality of products and labor productivity—two crucial indicators for assessing performance overall. The focus on quantity is reinforced by an incentive system that distributes rewards on the basis of size of output. For instance, the year-end bonuses received by the managers of factories, mines, restaurants, or shoe-repair stores depend almost entirely on their meeting their output quotas imposed by the ministries in Moscow. Aside from fostering a deleterious effect on quality, such a system of incentives very much influences the mix of the products turned out. A nail factory, for instance, has an incentive to manufacture large nails in order to fulfill a production quota faster than it could by making small nails. As a result, there is a shortage of small nails. Restaurant waiters have an incentive to sabotage, by slow service, clients who order only food, and push hard for the consumption of vodka. The price of vodka is very high, partly to discourage its consumption. Yet for the restaurant manager and the waiter it is primarily the sale of vodka that makes it possible to fulfill their quotas. Moreover, even this incentive structure has become less and less effective in recent years as the shortage of consumer goods has created strong, albeit hidden, inflationary pressures.

A survey conducted in 1981 by Radio Liberty of 782 Soviet travelers in Western Europe concluded that only 3 of 19 foodstuffs were regularly available at the time in the cities in which the respondents lived: vodka, bread, and sugar. *Defitsitnye materialy* (commodities in short supply) are, of course, not limited to foodstuffs, but include a whole range of consumer goods. But inadequate supply may be only one of the causes of widespread shortages. Indeed, shortages are also caused by increased demand backed by purchasing power that is only partially reflected in the level and structure of official prices. The shortages go hand in hand as well with inflationary pressures. The reselling of goods bought in state stores for higher prices, the major increase in prices in local *kolkhoz* markets, the illegal black market—all point to an increased money supply and savings in search of consumer goods, and hence to strong inflationary pressures. Shortages and inflation together render monetary incentives quite ineffective.

A major problem of the economy is its monstrous overcentralization according to strict, vertical lines of authority that lack coordination among themselves. There is a triple economic control system, consisting of direction from the ministries, the planning bodies, and the Party apparatus. The directions from above are often contradictory, and the incessant stream of inspectors and controllers push the manager in diverse directions favoring different priorities. On the other hand, there is too little centralization, coordination, and supervision of investment policies.

The declining growth of labor productivity is a decisive factor in the economic dilemma. As Table 5 shows, in the second half of the 1970s the downward trend of productivity intensified sharply. In the eleventh five-year plan (1981–85), labor productivity was supposed to go up by 35 percent, but in 1981–83 it went down by 4 percent. (Incidentally, labor productivity in Soviet industry is about 55 percent of the American level, while in agriculture it is about 10 percent.)

TABLE 5   GROWTH OF SOVIET OUTPUT AND PRODUCTIVITY

	1960–65	1965–70	1970–75	1975–80	1980
GROSS NATIONAL PRODUCT	5.0	5.2	3.7	2.7	1.4
Labor Productivity (output per man-hour)	3.4	3.2	2.0	1.3	0.2
Total Factor Productivity (output per combined input of manhours, capital, and land)	0.6	1.1	−0.5	−0.8	−1.9
INDUSTRIAL PRODUCTION	6.6	6.3	5.9	3.6	3.4
Industry Labor Productivity (output per man hour)	3.6	3.1	4.4	2.0	2.4
Industry Total Factor Productivity (output per combined input of manhours and capital)	−0.1	0.5	1.1	−0.6	−0.2

The most important source of labor productivity growth is new technology, both from domestic and foreign sources. This has had only a limited influence on economic performance. In order to take advantage of advanced technology, it is essential that this technology be broadly diffused and assimilated. The Soviets cannot do this. Their failure is partly caused by the faulty system of management and planning, which does not reward technological progress. It is also due to the lack of coordination and cooperation between the applied science and technology organizations (above all the institutes of the Academy of Science and of the economic ministries) and the producing units. The technological gap between the major sectors of American and Soviet industry remained, as previously mentioned, basically unchanged between 1953 and the late 1970s. It is probable that the gap will grow wider because of the backwardness of the Soviet electronics industry.

Past rapid growth was to a large extent based on the availability and relatively low costs of natural resources. The era of cheap and abundant raw materials, however, has come to an end. In order to satisfy the demands of its own economy as well as those of its empire, the nation must develop rapidly the expensive natural resources of Siberia. An almost inaccessible area in West Siberia, for example, is the only region where major output increases have been achieved in the last ten years. While in 1965 West Siberia accounted for about 2 percent of total oil production, in 1980 it produced more than half of Soviet oil. Siberian development will require the redirection of substantial portions of its investment resources from other goals.

A major part of the resource problem has to do with energy. The level of energy production in the 1980s is unfavorable to economic development. While natural gas extraction is rising, the production of coal and oil is stagnating or declining. Even setting aside the worst-case scenarios of CIA analysts, and they do seem unrealistic, the slow growth or stagnation of energy will impose significant constraints on the economy, limiting the full utilization of existing productive capacities, and impinging on the living standards of the public. Moreover, even the effort to keep oil production from declining will require huge expenses because of the sharply increasing costs of drilling and of developing new fields. In addition, an energy squeeze will necessitate switching large funds from investments in labor productivity to ventures in energy conservation. Oil output slipped slightly from 12.32 million barrels a day in 1983 to 12.26 million in 1984. In 1985 its further decline to 12.0 is predicted. (The output plan for 1985 calls for 12.54 million.) The Soviet Union may succeed in stabilizing oil production at the 12-million-barrel level for the rest of the decade, or beyond it into the 1990s, only if it radically increases its investments and adopts emergency measures.

TABLE 6   COMPARATIVE FIXED ASSET RETIREMENT RATES
(Retirement as percentage of stock at the beginning of the year)

	Non-residential plant	Producer durables	Housing
West Germany	3.7	10.2	2.5
France	5.7	12.5	2.5
Italy	4.0	11.1	1.7
Great Britain	2.5	7.3	2.5
Canada	4.2	9.0	2.5
United States	3.3	8.5	1.7
Soviet Union	1.5	4.1	1.0

In the 1950s and 1960s, because of the rebuilding of industries destroyed during the war and rapid growth, the Soviet Union possessed an industrial plant that was to a high degree equipped with new machines. This situation has changed by now. Industry is operating with aged machine stock, which in times of labor scarcity should be steadily replaced with new, more advanced machines. As Table 6 shows, the average retirement rates of capital assets in the 1970s in Western countries were much higher than in the Soviet Union. According to one calculation, Soviet capital stock retirement (capital retired during a year as a percentage of the capital stock at the beginning of the year) for the economy in the 1960s and 1970s averaged about 1.5 percent, while for the industry it was a little higher, but still below 2 percent. For the United States the comparable figures are more than twice that level, 3.7 and 4.2 percent.

To improve labor and capital productivity, new machinery must increase dramatically in the 1980s. Yet the capacity of the machine-building industry to meet the demand is limited, and investment funds for machine stock will be hard to come by. This squeeze is the result of past government policy, which concentrated on easier, more traditional ways of extracting large outputs from industry and postponing technological change. Because the Russians have always enjoyed an abundance of cheap labor, they simply did not modernize existing industry, but rather emphasized the building of new factories that were, however, equipped with the same technology as the old ones. As a result, a high percentage of machinery is obsolete. An example of an industry that grew fast but in which the technological structure of the plant is outmoded is steel, as shown in Table 7.

TABLE 7   STEELMAKING CAPACITY BY TYPE OF FURNACE
(Percent of total)

		USSR		USA	JAPAN
	1975	1980	1985 (est.)	1980	1980
Open-hearth	65	61	58	12	—
Basic Oxygen	25	29	29	61	75
Electric	10	10	13	27	25

Commenting on the situation in the steel industry (and the difficulties in supplying it with new materials) a CIA report concluded: "In effect, by neglecting modernization, the Soviets seem to have painted themselves into a corner. They must modernize the steel industry to break the current logjam in production. At the same time, the Soviets will have to defer any major program to modernize steel-making capacity as long as uncertainties exist in the supply of iron ore, coking coal and scrap metal." Now, with a shortage of labor, the Soviets can no longer afford simply to build new factories in order to secure continuous high growth. Yet the decline in the growth of investment resources, coupled with the broad range of claims on these resources, will make the renewal of the machine plant in older factories extremely difficult. Capital investment, which had risen at an average annual rate of 7 percent in 1971–75, slowed down to 3.4 percent in 1975–79, and for the 1980–85 period was planned at 1.8 percent. Gosplan Chairman Nikolai Baibakov, in his speech to the Supreme Soviet in November 1981, said "For the first time in the practice of national economic planning, the planned growth of national income exceeds the planned growth of capital investment."*

One of the original sins of forced industrialization has now returned to haunt development. Throughout their industrial and agricultural development, the Soviets concentrated their investments of labor and capital on manufacturing and neglected almost entirely the development of the industrial and agricultural infrastructure. In 1981 the Soviets had fewer telephones than France or West Germany. The United States has about nineteen times as many cars, six times more trucks and buses. The Soviet stock of passenger cars in 1980 was estimated at about 7 million units, fewer than are produced in one year in the United States or Japan. The total length of concrete or asphalt roads in the largest country in the world was in 1980 only 239,000 miles—just short of that in Texas alone. In fact, between 1965 and 1980, the total length of all roads in service declined by about 5 percent. As for railroads, there is the comment of two American economists, Holland Hunter and Deborah Kaple: "Just as motor vehicles can clog an urban highway system, sending costs of all kinds soaring, a similar phenomenon seems to be appearing in Soviet railroad freight traffic."† The shortages of railroads, of roads, of adequate truck parks, of storage facilities, of repair shops and spare parts for machinery and cars, and of communication facilities result in dangerous bottlenecks and create major obstacles in the planning and execution of major investment projects. And, while Soviet levels of growth in railway, automotive, and construction machinery were never adequate to meet demand, in each case average annual growth rates for these items actually declined in the 1976–80 period.

Capital aging and slow growth of capital stock contributed to the sharp decrease in the rate of growth of railroad freight traffic in the period after 1975. Railroad freight traffic grew at an annual rate of 5.1 percent in the period 1965–70 and 5.3 percent in 1970–75, then plunged to 1.2 percent in the period 1975–80. While this dramatic slowdown could

---

* Nikolai Baibakov, *Pravda,* November 16, 1981.

† Holland Hunter and Deborah Kaple, "Transport in Trouble," in *Soviet Economy in the 1980s: Problems and Prospects,* Part I. Selected papers submitted to the U.S. Congress Joint Economic Committee (Washington, D.C.: Government Printing Office, 1983), pp. 239–240.

have been caused by the reduction in output, it is more likely that in itself it is an important factor in the falling off of productivity growth in the rest of the economy.

The shortcomings of transportation involve not only the inadequacy of the existing plant but also its ineffective employment. "What may be at the bottom of these problems," Hunter and Kaple observe, "also constitutes the most fundamental difference between East and West: the attitude of enterprises toward transport is indifferent, for it is viewed as a service to be squandered because it costs them so little."*

The most vivid manifestation of this shortcoming is the level of losses of finished products. The Soviet Union, for example, is the second largest producer of fertilizer in the world, but the lack of storage facilities on the county (*raion*) level or on the collective or state farms results, by Soviet estimates, in a one-third loss in fertilizer quality; again, according to Soviet sources, about 20 to 25 percent of the harvest is lost each year because of the lack of storage and transport facilities. But the expenditures necessary to correct the situation are high and, with the pressure on investment funds coming from so many directions, hard to make.

These and other infrastructure problems are more characteristic of a Third World nation than of an advanced industrial power. They disclose a basic truth that is often not grasped by Westerners: One cannot understand the Soviet Union without regarding it as both a developed and an underdeveloped country, one that combines a successful space program with an inability to produce durable shoes or sharp razor blades.

The industrial economy had virtually been built on the bones and by the sweat of the enormous labor force. The large population and population growth, the high percentage of new female labor, and the unceasing flow of peasants into the urban areas, provided an unlimited reserve army of industrial labor. This is no longer the case. For cyclical demographic reasons and because of the low quality of health care, the influx of newcomers into the labor force is declining and will decline even more sharply in the late 1980s. The drop is precipitous. Between 1970 and 1982 the working-age population rose by 26 million, that is, by about 2.2 million people per year. Between 1982 and 1995 the growth will be 6 million, that is by about 400,000 per year—almost five times lower. This problem is magnified by the already high level of employment of women, which leaves almost no reserves to improve the labor picture.

The graph opposite shows the dramatic decline in the growth of the

---

* Holland Hunter and Deborah Kaple, "Transport in Trouble," in *Soviet Economy in the 1980s: Problems and Prospects,* Part I. Selected papers submitted to the U.S. Congress Joint Economic Committee (Washington, D.C.: Government Printing Office, 1983), p. 233.

working-age population. The anomaly becomes especially vivid when one considers that in the technologically advanced United States, the labor force between 1970 and 1982 increased by 32 percent, while in the technologically backward Soviet Union it rose by only 19 percent.

A further complication is that the new entrants into the labor force will be overwhelmingly non-Russian. Over the rest of the 1980s and through the early 1990s, approximately 90 percent of new workers will come from the Central Asian republics and Kazakhstan. This ethnic imbalance represents a dilemma for the authorities. They can try to force a migration of non-Russian, predominantly Central Asian, labor to European Russia, where most of the existing industrial capacity is located, or to Siberia, where the new mineral sources are found. Such a policy, however, seems unlikely. The native populations of Central Asia and Transcaucasia have deep cultural and economic roots in their own republics and a life-style different from the Slavs'. In the absence of terror, more than marginal migration to Russia proper is doubtful even if economic incentives are offered. The alternative is to invest at great cost in the industrial development of Central Asia and Transcaucasia. Given the present fiscal bind, this seems equally unattractive. Moreover, either solution will undoubtedly exacerbate the tensions between the Russians and the non-Slavic minorities.

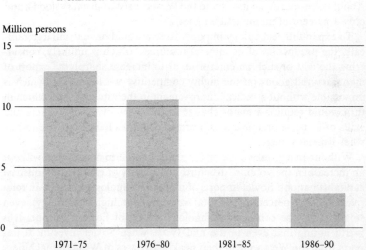

INCREASE IN SIZE OF THE SOVIET WORKING-AGE POPULATION *

Million persons

* Males 16–59 and females 16–54

In the 1970s the Soviets managed to alleviate their technological problems of backwardness to some extent by imports from the industrial democracies. Even when President Reagan imposed a *de facto* embargo on American technology sales to Russia and made the sale of West European and Japanese technology, which included American produced or licensed components, very difficult, Western nations continued a substantial trade with the Soviet Union. But in the late 1980s the flow of Western technology is not so much a question of supply but of ability to pay. The Soviets must pay for their imports with hard currency. Because of the slow growth of energy resources and stagnation in the production of oil, the main foreign-currency earner, the Soviets will probably be unable to increase their hard currency transactions for technology and foodstuffs with the West.

The Soviet Union is one of the few communist countries without a significant international debt (relative to its resources and volume of its foreign trade). Its financial soundness, backed by exportable oil, gas, lumber, gold, etc., is unquestionable. Yet for a giant country with enormous natural resources and an industry that is still modernizing, the volume of its trade as a percentage of the GNP is quite small at about 5 percent.

The structure of its imports and exports resembles that of an underdeveloped country. Russia is the world's largest importer of grain and food and an importer of machinery. Its exports in general, and to the capitalist world in particular, consist primarily of raw mineral resources. About three-fourths of its sales to the West consist of primary goods, and only 3 percent of manufactured goods.

To expand its technology imports, Russia would have to enlarge radically the production of its mineral resources, which is unlikely, considering the cost of such an enterprise, or to increase sharply its export of manufactured goods on the highly competitive world market, which is impossible without a radical improvement in their quality, and which in turn would require a major change in the mentality of its leaders and skills of its trade organizations. Foreign countries have no desire to buy what Russians make.

Without an aggressive search for major long-term credits, and without an increase in the volume, structure, and quality of exports to industrial capitalist nations, Soviet imports of modern technology will remain relatively small (2 percent of the total world trade in high technology), even smaller than the combined technology import of Eastern Europe. It is worth noting that even in the mid-1970s, when Soviet investment imports from the West were at their peak, purchases of Western machinery never rose to more than 5 to 6 percent of domestic investment in equipment.

This is one of the reasons that foreign technology was and is unable to provide a spark for the Soviet modernization effort. The other, and equally important, reasons are the quality of its managerial cadres, the habits of its workers, and the general economic domestic environment, which is not conducive to the diffusion of technological progress. The role of imports of technology and know-how was and is important to the Soviet Union because they are primarily concentrated in the key projects of the five-year plans. But imports of foreign technology have failed as the engine of modernization because the volume has been insufficient, and because the Soviet system cannot diffuse the new technology beyond key projects or duplicate it in themselves.

Finally, agriculture, the chronic weak spot of the economy, may steadily slow the rate of growth of the GNP through its inability to keep pace with population growth. The fluctuation from year to year of agricultural production may have a larger influence than before on the size of the GNP.

Agriculture employed 35.5 million people in 1980. This represents 26 percent of the total work force according to one account, and as much as 31.1 percent according to another—a remarkably high percentage for an industrial state. In the United States, agriculture employs only 3.2 percent of the labor force. In absolute figures the number of Soviets employed in agriculture is twice as large as the total of farm workers in the United States, Canada, Japan, France, West Germany, and Italy combined. Yet the Soviet Union still requires major feed grain imports from the West.

Agricultural performance in 1979–83 was unprecedentedly poor in Soviet and Russian history. The weather caused four bad harvests in a row. But even if the weather factor returns to its usual pattern of one very bad harvest every four years, agricultural productivity will remain embarrassingly low or even decline. The Brezhnev program of investment in irrigation and land improvement in the non-black-earth regions of Russia proved to be a costly fiasco—throwing money at the problem has failed so far. (Agricultural investment accounts for about 27 percent of Soviet total investments in the economy.) And, even if the new leaders wish to continue this policy, they will not have the necessary funds to do so. Therefore, the emphasis in agricultural planning for the 1980s, as indicated by the Food Program announced in 1982, is clearly shifting to increased efficiency of existing agricultural assets, a goal that in agriculture is as difficult to achieve as in industry.

The forecast for the next decade makes it almost inevitable that even with an increasing grain output the Soviets will require high, and maybe even rising, levels of grain importation. Without such imports, which are almost exclusively utilized for livestock feed, the Soviets will be unable even to preserve their herds, the basis of their improved diet, and will face even greater interruptions in the supply of food to the cities.

The economy entered the 1980s mired in a vicious circle that presents planners with severe dilemmas: To increase labor productivity, major sums must be spent on technology investments and on the growth of the consumer-goods sectors, including agriculture, which will provide incentives for the work force, and to speed up the development of the infrastructure in order to relieve the bottlenecks. Yet the rate of growth of investments, and maybe even their absolute size, will be much lower in the 1980s than in the 1970s. In the early 1980s the Soviet government, hard-pressed to maintain the rise of military expenditures while preventing a decline in the standard of living, decided to cut the growth of investment by almost half. This kind of a policy amounts to mortgaging the future, and especially modernization, in order to delay imposition of the necessary civilian and military austerity. Reductions in military expenditures would, from a short-term point of view, alleviate the situation only slightly, however. In any event, such cuts are not likely to be made at a time when a new arms race with the United States seems imminent. The Soviet economy remains a flexible and workable instrument when costs do not matter and the economic effort concentrates on a few selected priority areas. But unlike in the past, what the country needs now is economic development on a broad front with a wide spectrum of priorities. Without such development, even growth of military production may be affected in the 1980s.

How difficult the economic situation in the late 1980s will be is a matter of conjecture. At worst, there will be low growth intermingled with stagnation and decline. But even the more optimistic predictions foresee an economic crunch far more severe than anything encountered in the 1960s and early 1970s.

The problem of the relative backwardness of the economy concerns not only the question of how it produces, but also what it produces and at what cost. In all three respects, the Soviet Union is highly deficient not only by the standards of such capitalist giants as America or Japan, but even of the newly industrializing countries like South Korea or Taiwan. The methods and organization of production seldom go beyond the outdated labor-intensive assembly line.

By the early 1980s the inventories of both machine tools and metal-cutting machinery were about twice as large in the Soviet Union as in the United States. These are striking ratios when one considers that Soviet industrial output is estimated as being less than two-thirds of the American output.

Moreover, about one-third of the machine-tool stock is reportedly under constant repair. In automation and computerization of production flow, the Soviets are at least a generation behind the West. The average managerial skills are still archaic, and center almost exclusively on the production process, with little attention paid to the relationship between production and sound economies. (The bulk of Soviet managers, administrators, economic officials are engineers, not economists.) The work habits of the labor force are slovenly, sloppy, and uncaring. Very few workers take pride in their jobs. Labor is cheap, but one wonders whether it is, in fact, not being overpaid relative to the quality and quantity of the work done. There is a familiar saying among Soviet workers: "They pretend to pay us, and we pretend to work."

Labor productivity is of course uneven in different economic branches, yet one can get a sense of it from the fact that the Soviet Union, with a labor force about 30 percent larger than that of the United States, has a GNP of only half the size. The level and quality of skilled labor is a major factor in productivity. Soviet quantitative achievement in this respect is enormous. They employ twice as many engineers as the United States and graduate close to three times as many every year. The number of scientists and engineers working in research and development is more than 50 percent higher than in the United States. The reality of Soviet production and technology, however, suggests that the quality of education and productivity of these engineers must be much lower. This, indeed, is confirmed by the fact that, unlike mathematicians and physicists, Jewish engineers who emigrated to the United States during the period of détente had difficulty finding work in their profession, because their level of competence was not high. In agriculture the Soviet Union educates great numbers of specialists every year (agronomists, zoologists, mechanics, combine drivers, and the like). Yet only a small percentage of these specialists ends up being employed in agriculture. For example, in 1979, 1.4 million tractor, combine and truck drivers/mechanics were trained for agricultural work, but the number employed on farms increased only by 32,000. The prospect of urban employment is irresistible to many when compared to what Karl Marx called the "idiocy of rural life." Even so, the Soviet Union employs three times as many specialists in agriculture as the United States.

The product mix of civilian manufacturing is heavily weighted in favor of smokestack industries. A mass market for electronic consumer goods is almost nonexistent. But even the products of traditional industries are archaic in design though often difficult to obtain. Exceptions include cotton goods, shoes, radios, big ungainly watches, cameras, and electric shavers, which seem to be abundant beyond demand. The products that are usually classified as electronic are often too old-fashioned for such a designation—the most modern part in radio and television sets is still the transistor, or even the vacuum tube, not the microchip.

Soviet civilian computers are considerably more than a generation behind those in the West, and are produced only in small quantities. Minicomputers and copying machines are almost entirely missing from the market.

The most neglected sector in Russia is that of services. Many of them are strictly in the domain of the unofficial second economy. One is forced to wait forever for home services such as painting and plumbing, and car repairs, if one relies on the normal bureaucratic route. Moreover, the repairs will be of low quality and done with inferior materials. In the non-elite hospitals nurses must still reuse needles for injections. Run-of-the-mill doctors still cannot get basic Western medical textbooks and literature.

Moscow still does not have a telephone book (this is, of course, for reasons of "secrecy"). Despite major help from Sweden, the telephone service is still very bad, and the city is not part of the international network of direct dialing.

Except at Moscow's international airport, the passenger service by Aeroflot, the Soviet airline, is abominable. Airport facilities are dirty and primitive. The plane seats are hard, the stewardesses arrogant, the flight timetables almost never observed.

To buy anything imported or of good quality in the state stores, one has to stand in three long lines: one to select goods at the counter and receive a bill for the product, a second to pay the cashier (who still uses an abacus), and a third at the first counter again to pick up the product. Those who suffer most from this system are women, who usually have full-time jobs and are still expected to carry the full burden of housekeeping and shopping. (A Russian friend told about the first time his wife was permitted to accompany him on a business trip to the West. After their first day in Vienna his wife started to cry, and for the whole week of their visit refused to leave their hotel room. She simply did not want to carry back to Russia the picture of abundance, care, and beauty which would make her life in the drabness, not of a small town, but of the Soviet showcase, Moscow, so much more difficult to bear.)

This neglect of the service sector has philosophical underpinnings. The Marxian dogma, taken straight from its Ricardian roots, is based on the notion of the "labor law of value." This "law," which reflects the mechanistic approach typical of the mid-nineteenth century and the early-industrialization stage of capitalist development, divides work into "productive" and "non-productive" kinds. The first produces tangible items, machines, steel, cloth, and so on. The second is what we call service. It may be useful to society but because it has no specific product as its end goal, is considered largely parasitic. The first type produces value; the second type (that of a barber, banker, a scientist) is financed by the redistribution of the primary value. Thus passenger rail transport is nonproductive while transporting commodities is productive.

The psychological approach to production and economics which this Marxian law inspires in Soviet leaders and economists automatically puts service into a subordinate category. The official measure of economic activity in the Soviet Union is not the generally accepted change in GNP, which includes all goods and services, but the National Income, that is to say, the net product of productive labor. The estimates of the GNP are entirely Western.

The waste of primary materials, quality, and durability are especially problematic. For example, the Soviet Union produces almost 50 percent more steel than America and Japan, yet steel continues to be a bottleneck of growth. Steel is used wastefully in producing both consumer and capital goods. Soviet machinery is sometimes twice as heavy as its Western counterpart. Anyone who has tried to lift a television set in a Moscow hotel has learned this at first hand.

The low quality and durability of goods are evident at a glance. Shoes that can be worn for less than a year, furniture that is warped at the time of sale, new buildings that require repairs from the moment they are complete, are the rule rather than the exception. In addition, the design of the products is often so ghastly that despite the shortages, and buying power that outdistances supply, there are large inventories of unsellable goods in the big cities. Some stores have to declare "fire sales."

The low quality of goods is a hidden depressant of productivity and a real cost. Much greater output is required to meet demand than in the West, making the costs of production enormous despite the fact that wages and salaries are lower than in any industrialized country. Thus many quantitative comparisons of Soviet and Western output are simply meaningless.

If the economic difficulties are not effectively handled by the leadership, they may have important consequences for social stability. In each period of its development the Soviet Union faced challenges to its social stability that it was able successfully to resolve. Under Stalin the main threat came from the peasantry—alien, anti-Soviet, and counterposed to the narrow layer of industrial workers and the Communist Party. Stalin dealt with the threat in a radical and brutal way.

In recent years concerns over social stability were directed towards the behavior of the intelligentsia and youth and their relation to the newborn open dissidence in society. All in all, this challenge was successfully if only temporarily contained. The dissidents have remained isolated in society. Finally, the Soviet Union is probably the only industrial country that has not passed through a youth revolution. While Soviet youth in the major urban centers became much more Westernized and attracted to Western culture than ever before, they remained nonetheless basically career-oriented.

In the 1980s it is the industrial workers who pose the most notable potential threat to social stability. And this because over the next few years the factors that have heretofore assured labor peace will most likely be considerably weakened. The police state, of course, will not only remain but most probably be strengthened. Still, the urban working classes, whose expectations remain relatively low, are accustomed to a steady growth in their standard of living; and how they will react to years of stagnation or decline is difficult to predict. Moreover, any serious industrial reform undertaken by the new leaders will require the imposition of austerity on the workers, with a cut in the subsidies for basic consumer goods and services, and at the same time a demand for more work and higher productivity. Finally, the mobility of workers into the middle and professional classes is decreasing and will continue to decrease. There will be fewer new professional and managerial jobs in a stagnant economy and the children of the large middle class will compete for them. The combination of these factors may erode the patience and political apathy of the Soviet workers.

During the Khrushchev and Brezhnev eras another potential source of social instability—the non-Russian nations in the USSR—was handled on the whole successfully. But the job of preserving social peace will be more difficult in the immediate future because the economic base, and thus the "carrot" part of policy towards the non-Russians, will be less robust. Yet, while in the long run this problem is potentially explosive, and while in the 1980s it may be more difficult than before to maintain ethnic peace and Russian control, there is no evidence that it will become the focus of social instability. The often-quoted figure showing that the Russians are only half of the population is significant only to the extent that the other Slavs—that is, the Ukrainians and Byelorussians—display different attitudes from, and do not identify with, the Russians; that they do so is a highly questionable proposition, and will probably remain so in the 1980s. The Russians, Ukrainians, and Byelorussians together constitute about 76 percent of the Soviet population.

The socioeconomic problems may have a spillover effect on the political arena. The two most immediate and most important political problems will be the familiar questions of social discipline and bureaucratic lethargy and inertia.

During the last years of Brezhnev's leadership, social discipline deteriorated to an extent remarkable even by Soviet standards. Absenteeism at the workplace skyrocketed; the turnover of industrial workers, that is to say, the percentage of workers who leave their jobs to seek new ones, reached by some estimates the unheard-of level of over 20 percent a year; the quality of production, let alone of services, deteriorated to the point where, according to some estimates, it actually lowered the level of GNP by 10 to 15 percent; the unofficial corruption and thievery became so enormous that it in fact amounted to a redistribution of national income.

Soviet citizens' own recognition of their work habits is reflected in the joke about a foreign trade-union delegation visiting a Soviet factory. After looking around its main work hall the leader of the delegation says to his host: "I didn't know that sit-down strikes were permitted in your country."

When discussing social discipline, one has to make special mention of the scourge of Soviet society, the almost uncontrollable alcoholism. In 1976 alcohol poisoning accounted for 39,800 deaths in the USSR, 88 times greater than the comparable figure for the United States. The extent of Russian alcoholism can be comprehended through a bizarre story reported from Czechoslovakia and printed by respected West European publications. Four Soviet soldiers who got lost during maneuvers in Czechoslovakia "traded their tank to a tavern owner for two cases of vodka and were found sleeping it off in a forest two days later. . . . Czech communist authorities later learned that the tavern owner dismantled the tank and sold the pieces to a metal-recycling center. . . . The tavern proprietor was quoted as telling authorities he had acquired the tank for twenty-four bottles of vodka, with about seven pounds of herring and pickles thrown in as 'a gesture of comradeship.' " One cannot, obviously, vouch for the accuracy of this story. But the fact that this tank-and-vodka episode is plausible is sufficient to make the point.

The visible decline of social discipline has become a political issue. It impinges heavily on the ability of the directors of the system to achieve their economic goals. Moreover, these forms of deviant social behavior should be and to some extent are regarded as the expression of mass disaffection, a loss of morale, and a lack of response to incentives of persuasion and political appeal. Without a major strengthening of social discipline, no improvement of economic performance is possible. This disturbs the rulers because it is precisely economic performance that, with the disappearance of terror, provided a source of political legitimacy for the post-Stalin regime.

Yet the regime will require more than coercive measures to improve social discipline. And here we again encounter the kind of vicious circle that plagues attempts at reform. Social discipline would increase if the material incentives were to grow substantially; but without stricter social discipline and the attendant rise of labor productivity, the leadership has no resources to provide for better and higher incentives. The demoralization of the working class is so profound, its disillusionment with the regime's more lavish promises so deep, that some American and Soviet economists and sociologists wonder if the entire present generation of workers is not irretrievably irresponsible.

The stagnation within the governing bureaucracy during the last years of the Brezhnev leadership has no equivalent in Soviet history except perhaps the last years of Stalin's rule. The system can only be energized from the top; therefore, the process of decision-making, already cumbersome under the best of conditions, was made even more intractable by Brezhnev's infirmity. Bureaucratic routine took over in the central and local organizations and any attempts at reform were simply tabled. Important policy decisions waited too long to be adopted. The crash program to prevent an energy crisis, and particularly to increase oil production, was not adopted until 1977 and not announced until 1981. Costly policies that obviously did not bring the expected results were continued.

Bureaucratic stability was higher than at any period in Soviet history. The nation had an aged elite, older than that of any major industrial country in the twentieth century. The logjam at the top created a whole generation of frustrated middle-aged and middle-ranking officials whose career paths were blocked by those in their late sixties and early seventies.

The low level of horizontal mobility resulted in a shortage of the most important type of Party functionary, the generalist, whose skills are critical to the coordination and integration of the diverse bureaucracies. Clientelism—coteries of officials with well-placed protectors—became widespread and bred major-scale corruption. The most famous cases were those of Brezhnev's close friends, Sergei Medunov, First Secretary of Krasnodar province, and Nikolai Shchelokov, Minister of Internal Affairs of the USSR. The corruption of both officials was common knowledge in Moscow, but they remained safe under Brezhnev's protection. Immediately after his death, they were arrested.

With the old bureaucrats monopolizing important offices, very little could change. The bureaucracies have to be shaken up and renewed, and they must provide greater opportunities for the advancement of officials in their fifties. Without such renewal and mobility, and without at least some change in the political-managerial structure, even a strong leader in the Kremlin will find innovative policies being sidetracked, sabotaged, and absorbed by the system.

Another political challenge that the leadership must face is the preservation of an equilibrium among various elites and bureaucracies. In a period of austerity, it will be much more difficult to achieve a peaceful consensus. In past successions, top-level bureaucrats were optimistic about getting more from the new leadership than they had got from the old. Now these senior officials are pessimistic, fearful of actually getting less than in the past.

There is regional conflict as well. Four areas are competing for the allocation of scarce growth resources—European Russia, the Ukraine, Siberia, and Central Asia. European Russia and the Ukraine have a developed industrial infrastructure but lack natural resources and labor. Siberia is rich in resources, but has neither a significant industrial base nor plentiful labor. Central Asia has a significant labor supply but lacks both industry and natural resources.

In the past, the Soviet Union faced a number of domestic challenges that seemed more dangerous to the stability of the system than those it now faces. The enormous problems of development and consumption were recognized as such from the time of Stalin's first *piatiletka* (five-year plan). Socially, the crisis of mass collectivization was surely much more destructive than any threat to stability in the 1980s. In political terms the death of Stalin, the anti-Stalin campaign, and the schemes of Khrushchev were similarly a test of the stability of the regime much more dangerous than the political challenges it now faces.

The present crisis is not one of survival but of effectiveness. Yet the challenges are in many respects quite different from those of the past, and they will have to be dealt with differently, in ways for which the system is unprepared. The economy is a case in point. At many times in the past, it has been in much worse shape than it is in today. There has hardly been a year without crises and major emergencies. The economic system has been characterized by institutionalized crisis and emergency management. Anyone watching a factory operating in December—the last chance to fulfill the annual plan—or witnessing any harvest—which always seems to require the mobilization of every white-collar worker, student, and military unit in the country—knows that this is so. There is even a special word in the Soviet lexicon to describe this movement from one emergency to another—*shturmovshchina*, which means "storming" or "taking by storm." In the past, however, these crises and emergencies could be handled with at least partial success by the old and tried methods of mobilizing massive quantities of labor, natural resources, capital, and land. These were the methods of extensive growth. The political and economic systems were not constructed to deal with the present need for intensive growth.

In the past the emphasis of the economy was on achieving ever-larger output, a goal which the system could achieve. Today the focus is on quality, costs of production, and the conservation of inputs—problems that defy the present economic organization and managerial patterns of behavior.

Moreover, in the past, economic troubles occurred in a fast-expanding economy with cheap resources. To a large extent they were problems of growth, and a 5 to 6 percent yearly growth of the GNP could cover a lot of sins. The economy is now gaining slowly and will slow down even more if corrective qualitative measures to increase the productivity of labor and capital are not introduced into the planning, managerial, and incentive systems. Even a partial improvement of growth and productivity requires much greater adjustment than in the past and significant reforms in the system.

Historically, the political system became accustomed to scarcities, shortages, and stringencies. Dealing with those problems was its normal *modus operandi*, together with a process of highly uneven development concomitant with rapid overall economic growth. Moreover, during this time the system was underpinned by the Stalinist terror. In the post-Stalin period, the relatively high rate of growth, while still uneven, ensured the flow of new resources to all sectors of the economy, including those totally neglected during the Stalin era.

The political system, however, is not accustomed to dealing with prolonged periods of low economic growth. Moreover, priorities have not so much changed as significantly broadened. Military production still comes first; heavy industry, second; and consumer goods, third. In the past, despite the system's immense inefficiencies and bureaucratization, the priorities, the major projects of every five-year plan, were by and large accomplished through a concentration of skilled labor, the best managers, prime resources, and constant control. This is still possible today with a small number of supremely important projects. What has changed, however, is that the priority items have increased dramatically, and the ability to accomplish them requires the balanced growth of the economy as a whole. Without such growth, bottlenecks will multiply and could endanger even the achievement of high-priority projects. The Polish economist Oskar Lange noted that the essence of the Soviet economy can best be described as a war economy during peacetime. Such an economy is radically less effective now even in the old sense of ensuring a timely attainment of priorities.

There is another important way in which the economic situation differs from the past. The leaders cannot regard their problems of growth in isolation from what is taking place in advanced industrial societies. It must seem ominous that Japan is becoming the second largest producer of industrial goods and services in the world. No longer can the leadership formulate the problem as it has in the past—"To catch up with and overtake" the level of production and technology of the advanced capitalist countries. The Western technological explosion is so overwhelming that now Soviet efforts must be focused on merely catching up.

In this area the greatest problem involves the utilization of computers.

In 1974 the Soviet Union had an estimated 12,500 computers in use compared with 207,000 units in the United States. By 1977, the last year for which reliable data is available, this gap had widened substantially—an estimated 20,000 in the Soviet Union compared with 325,000 in the United States. According to some estimates provided by Soviet specialists, in the early 1980s the proportion of Soviet to American computers in use was close to one to twenty-five. This gap in production is paralleled by a gap in technology. In addition, Soviet software is still quite primitive by Western standards.

The exact figures of the number of computers in the Soviet Union, especially of the third generation, are neither reliable nor illuminating. There are several reasons for this:

• The Soviets now produce their most advanced large computers in conjunction with the Council of Mutual Economic Assistance (the Soviet-bloc equivalent of the Common Market). This is called the ES or Riad series. It is indeed a third-generation computer, which has gone through many stages and developments. It is based on the IBM 5/360 and 5/370 models.

• The Soviets do not replace antiquated equipment as we do. Hence, any knowledge of the number of most advanced computers in use does not, in and of itself, indicate how many computers of all generations and styles are still on line.

• A substantial portion of Soviet computer capacity is devoted to classified purposes. Without such figures any gross estimates of the absolute numbers of third-generation computers in use there would be quite meaningless.

In any case, attempts to computerize the economy could turn out to involve "vast and futile expenditure," Academician Anatolii P. Aleksandrov, president of the Academy of Sciences, has been warning. Writing in *Izvestia*, Aleksandrov alleges that the nation is failing to make proper use of "even the comparatively small amount of computer equipment" that it manufactures. The main difficulty, according to Aleksandrov, is the shortage of trained personnel and a lack of awareness of the potential of computers among the population at large; overcoming these deficiencies will be a task comparable with that of eliminating illiteracy after the Revolution.

The computer situation is also indicative of much broader problems in high-technology information and data processing. One can evaluate the present Soviet politicoeconomic system according to its compatibility with various areas of production and technological progress. Such an evaluation would conclude that the system is best suited for the production of military hardware where costs are not a primary concern and the mobilization of resources on a priority basis works quite well. The compatibility of the system with heavy industrial production yields still impressive if declining results. However, the system is poor at producing consumer goods and very bad in its management of agriculture. It is almost as bad at producing and using data-processing technology.

With its paranoiac secrecy, control of data, compartmentalization of responsibilities and knowledge, virtual absence of individualistic innovative spirit and venture capital, the political system is simply not compatible with the communications revolution. The use of computers in the Western manner would encroach on Soviet principles governing the distribution of information and would require a basic change.

Secrecy often leads to ridiculous situations. Some time ago I had a conversation with a high-ranking economist who works on a model of the Soviet economy at an economic institute of the Academy of Sciences. I asked him where he got his primary data, and his matter-of-fact answer was "from the green books." It took me a while to understand what he meant. Every two years the Joint Economic Committee of the U.S. Congress produces, in the form of a two-volume work with green covers, a detailed overview of the Soviet economy written by the top American authorities within and outside the government. The Soviet economist I spoke to found more, and more accurate, information in these volumes than in the meager data supplied him by the Soviet Planning Commission. The leadership has to weigh the gains possible through the efficient use of computers against the danger to the system that a computer revolution would pose. Until now, the leaders have opted for a narrow and limited use of computers, control of their data banks (similar to their strict control of the use of photocopying machines), and limited access to computer technology. Loren Graham has defined the problem in the following way:

What are the characteristics of a culture that make it receptive to the new computers and which cause them to spread rapidly? A great many factors influence this receptivity, and in all of them the United States seems to have the edge over the Soviet Union. They include:
—A tradition that successful technology should be privately owned and controlled if it is advantageous to do so.
—A tradition of free access to information.
—A tradition of creating large amounts of reliable and accurate data about the economy and about society.
—A financial system offering a diversity of business and consumer services.
—Widespread education in business and technological skills, including typing and programming.
—Excellent telephone lines that can be used for remote access to data bases.
—Close relationships between sellers and buyers of technology which include consulting services, maintenance and spare parts when needed.

—A tradition of entrepreneurship and innovation under which a person who develops a successful product—whether hardware or software—can legally make an attempt to sell it.

The Soviet Union has major problems in every one of these areas. . . . Soviet authorities often say that "history is on their side." In the computer revolution, time is on the side of the West. Therefore, if we can gain time by controlling the military technology that can so easily destroy us all, the civilian computer technology that is now penetrating to the lowest level of society—the individual—will give a real advantage to societies that do not try to control information.

Whether the Soviets can maintain their international status atop an already backward economy that falls increasingly behind a computer-dominated world must be a profoundly troubling question for the rulers in Moscow. *

There are indications that the lack of technological development is starting to affect the military sector. Draftees are ill prepared to serve in a technologically modern army; the barrier between the civilian and military economic sectors prevents feedback, thus hindering the development of a sufficient technological base for the military; the relative costs of priority projects and high-quality military buildup are greater than in the post-Stalin period. The Soviets will do everything necessary to keep up with the West in defense production, but without a change in the entire economy, the process will be much more difficult and costly than in the past.

The population upon whom the leadership must now impose austerity is different from in the past. It is better educated and probably, therefore, better able to evaluate its situation. It is very young and therefore possesses no memory of Stalin's terror. Most important, it is a population that, with the exception of the past few years, has become accustomed to a steady increase in the standard of living and therefore has at least slowly growing material expectations. If popular expectations have in fact changed, then labor unrest in the 1980s is a real possibility. Unrest among urban workers, a class that is ideologically central to the regime and is socially concentrated, would cast doubts on the legitimacy of the Soviet Party-state. At the very least, the disillusionment of the work force will have a detrimental effect on any attempts to increase its productivity.

So the struggle for a piece of the allocation pie will probably be greater in the 1980s than it was in Stalin's or Brezhnev's time, though probably less than during Khrushchev's stormy rule. Probably more important than the potential for divisiveness are the indications, which are difficult to formulate—based almost entirely on meetings, discussions, and private conversations with bureaucrats over a long period of time—

---

* Loren Graham, "Science and Computers in Soviet Society," in Erik Hoffmann, ed., *The Soviet Union in the 1980s* (Montpelier, Vt: Capital City Press, 1984), p. 131.

that the spark has gone out of the thinking and the hopes of the elites. There is no lack even now of devotion to the regime and to the system, but under Stalin and Khrushchev, and in the early years under Brezhnev, the depth of their belief in the system and in their future was still quite pronounced. This optimistic attitude was deeply shaken, and has been replaced by more pessimistic expectations. What remained at the time of Brezhnev's death were great-power ambitions, the inertia induced by a rigidly ideological outlook on the world, private careerism and materialism, and spiritual emptiness.

5

Andropov's Interregnum

The ailing Brezhnev could not deal with the social and economic problems that plagued the Soviet Union from the mid-1970s. He continued to monopolize political power but shrank from using it for innovation and change. Both in the Soviet Union and in the West a consensus formed that changes in the system, and even only in policies, would have to wait for a new leader.

In November 1982 Brezhnev died. Yuri Andropov became the general secretary of the Communist Party of the Soviet Union and thus the heir to the legacy of four formidable predecessors in sixty-six years. Lenin, the founder, had led the Party through revolution and the consolidation of power. Stalin, the tyrant, revolutionized the political system and society through unbridled coercion. Khrushchev, the innovator, shook the Stalinist mold, invigorated foreign policy, and ended the country's self-imposed isolation. Brezhnev, the administrator, attempted to institutionalize the bureaucratic policy-making process, and achieved a degree of unprecedented domestic stability. He also oversaw the transformation of the Soviet Union into a truly global power.

The situation after Brezhnev combined some characteristics of past successions with a number of exeptional features, a combination with major political implications for the 1980s. The most important was of course the fact that the leadership of Andropov lasted only fifteen months. It was no more than an interregnum. Moreover, the incumbency of Andropov's successor, Konstantin Chernenko, was even shorter, which simply served to delay the emergence of a strong leader.

From the long-range point of view, the single most important characteristic of the leadership after Brezhnev has been the overlap of the succession process itself with the burning need to resolve the accumulated domestic and international issues. Some of these problems, such as economic growth, are different from those of the post-Stalin and post-Khrushchev successions in that they require nontraditional methods and new organizational arrangements. In this respect they more resemble the issues after Lenin than those after Stalin.

By all accounts, Andropov was a sophisticated person whose knowledge and tastes were acquired through self-education. Although he never visited a noncommunist country, he was very well prepared, thanks to his experience as head of intelligence, to guide foreign policy. His experience in managing the troubled and troublesome Eastern European empire was extensive. His knowledge of internal Soviet politics, including those of non-Russian areas, was also wide-ranging. As head of the KGB, he was well qualified to enforce law, order, and discipline. He did lack direct experience in managing the economy, and therefore had to rely heavily on specialists in this area.

Foreign expectations, and those of the Soviet political elite, were that Andropov could become a strong and relatively innovative leader. This assessment was based on his personality and his history, combined with the fact that ambition, power, and a desire for innovation all meet in a succession, and in doing so prepare the ground for change. A new leader is exposed to ideas and surrounded by people who want action. In addition, and most importantly, initiatives are an important resource in the struggle to consolidate a leader's position. Succession, then, is a period not only of power plays but also of policy initiatives. He who wins and is able to consolidate his authority is most often not only the one who wields power most effectively, but also the one who best meets the elites' and the Party's perceptions of national needs. Members of the Moscow political community believed that Andropov's leadership would be much more gradual, orderly, and realistic than Khrushchev's was, but more innovative than Brezhnev's.

Successions of leadership are milestones in Soviet history—events of great consequence for policies and political structure. There are a number of reasons that a succession is such an important phenomenon in Soviet political development and at the same time so difficult for both participants and outside observers to analyze. No predetermined tenure of office is attached to the post of top leader. The terms of the office, the rights and obligations attached to it, and the power and influence involved are not standardized, nor is the procedure for relinquishing the post. Most important, the degree of uncertainty in the procedures of selecting a leader, and in the process of consolidating his position is much higher than in other societies. This makes a period of succession much more unpredictable.

The consequences for the political system are profound. Probabilities of deep personal and policy conflicts within the leadership structure are increased. Possibilities for resolving the conflicts in more extreme ways by bloodless purges are maximized. Large-scale personnel changes at other levels are likely. The period of succession offers great potential for destroying the bureaucratic inertia associated with departed leaders and for changing their policies. In sum, the succession, aside from its own intrinsic importance, acts as a catalyst for pressures and tendencies already present within the Party and society that previously had only limited opportunity for expression and realization. Equally important, it can lead to a realignment of the existing political coalitions and to the amassing of power and influence by the new leader, who thereby becomes less constrained by his previous institutional commitments in the selection of his preferences and priorities.

The struggle for Brezhnev's mantle began well before his death. It intensified after the passing, in January 1982, of the chief Soviet ideologue, Mikhail Suslov, who had possessed sufficient authority among his colleagues to keep the Politburo together. Because of the debilitating illness of Andrei Kirilenko, the organizational secretary of the Party and heir apparent to Brezhnev, Konstantin Chernenko became a key contender for the top position. Chernenko took over many of Kirilenko's duties (which had in turn been shifted from the ailing Brezhnev), and became the man in charge of the day-to-day running of top Party institutions. A crony of Brezhnev's with an undistinguished career, Chernenko was clearly the incumbent general secretary's personal choice for his successor. The transfer of Andropov from chairmanship of the KGB to the Party Secretariat in May 1982 was a decision of the Politburo majority (only the Politburo could have made the move) and provided evidence of the sharp decline of Brezhnev's power and of conflicts and divisions about policies and personal loyalties. The fact that Andropov could secure a majority vote in the Politburo while Brezhnev was still alive and formally in charge shows that many members were at least undecided about who should succeed the general secretary.

At the time of Andropov's transfer to the Party Secretariat—and his emergence as a contender for the top position—the retirement of Brezhnev would probably have resulted in the elevation of Chernenko, while the death of Brezhnev in office favored Andropov. Chernenko's strength and power base lay in his closeness to Brezhnev. His major problem was his dependence on the transfer of commitment from Brezhnev's loyalists to himself. This was not automatic upon the death of Brezhnev.

Andropov's advantage was his reputation as a strong leader and a generalist, a combination in short supply within the Politburo. The coalition that brought him to the top probably included both some of the oldest members of the Politburo and the youngest members of the Secretariat. Old men like Defense Minister Dimitrii Ustinov who, because of their age, and known physical frailty, no longer aspired to the top position, felt more comfortable with Andropov, who had had a distinguished independent career, than with Chernenko, whose entire career consisted of being Brezhnev's aide. The young secretaries of the Central Committee like Vladimir Dolgikh or Mikhail Gorbachev probably wanted change rather than the continuation of Brezhnev's policies that Chernenko's victory would have augured. In addition, they desired a strong leader from among the younger members of the old generation, who could understand their own aspirations. Andropov fit these criteria.

The scarcity of plausible choices for the post of Party general secretary was caused primarily by three factors, all attesting to the general failure of the system of political leadership. First of all, the nature of the modern Soviet society and economy requires the formation of a leadership stratum which is highly specialized. Most of the leaders on all levels are specialized in a narrowly defined field of activity. (This is also largely true of the Party's provincial first secretaries, whose expertise reflects the economic profile of their provinces, be it extraction of oil or coal, agriculture or military industry.) Yet, at the same time, because of the fusion of polity and economy and the centralization of the Party and state, the leadership structure requires generalists, which the system no longer produces.

Second, Stalin's purges ushered into office a generation that was very young and assumed its leadership positions almost all at once. This generation was able, because of its youth, to stay in office for a very long time. Third, the replacement of this group was continuously delayed by Brezhnev's policy of personnel stability.

Every succession in the Soviet Union goes through four stages. The first is the battle for the top position while the incumbent leader is still in power and directly after his death or ouster. The second is the actual transfer of authority to the new leader, his accumulation of positions, and the acquisition of the nominal prerogatives that go with them. The third is the consolidation of the new leader's power through bureaucratic and political alliances and through defining the boundaries of rights embodied in his new positions. The fourth, which overlaps partly with the third, is the decision of the new leader concerning how he will use his newly acquired power.

Before his death Andropov had clearly passed the second stage of the succession. He accumulated all Brezhnev's titles and offices. He became the general secretary of the Party, the chairman of the Supreme Soviet, the chairman of the Defense Council, and commander-in-chief of the Soviet armed forces. The speed with which he achieved this was not only a sign of his ability to use his power, but of the desire of the leadership and political elite to get over the transitional period quickly and start to cope in earnest with the accumulated problems. The domestic and foreign issues and dangers facing the Andropov leadership argued for the unity of the collective leadership and elites, that is to say, for a repetition of the 1964 pattern of succession from Khrushchev to Brezhnev, which was characterized by compromise and conciliation.

The struggle for power did not end with Andropov's ascendancy. Especially in the period from late summer 1983 until his death in February 1984, there were attempts to circumvent the power potentially inherent in his position as general secretary. At the Politburo meetings of November 4 and 5, 1983, there apparently developed major differences among members over whether to quit the INF (Intermediate-range Nuclear Forces) negotiations with the United States after the deployment of American Pershing II and cruise missiles in Europe. The deadlock was allegedly broken in favor of quitting by a forceful memo from the absent Andropov.

Throughout his tenure, Andropov could not feel safe in his position without replacing some members of the Politburo, Secretariat, and Presidium of the Council of Ministers with men of his own choosing. This was particularly true since he almost certainly intended to be a leader who made major changes that would endanger many vested interests.

The need of a new leader to consolidate his power leads to the consideration of Soviet successions from a broader point of view. Replacement is likely to be followed by major changes in the core leadership group and in the central (that is, Moscow-based) Party-state elites. In all probability, significant replacements also take place among the leadership's advisory groups. At some point the turnover spreads to the republican and provincial leadership. The leaders and elites during the final years of Brezhnev's rule were so old that their replacement was bound to occur quickly. The turnover was predictable on the basis of actuarial calculations, even in the unlikely event that the process of succession did not generate replacement for political reasons. Indeed, during his fifteen months, Andropov still managed to effect major personnel changes, especially when compared with the stagnation during the last years of Brezhnev's leadership.

In one important respect, Andropov's successful bid for power differed from his predecessors'. Stalin, Khrushchev, and Brezhnev all attained the post of Party leader from the same initial power base—the professional Party apparatus. Andropov came from the KGB. For the fifteen years before he attained the top post, Andropov did not work in the Party apparatus, and only from May to November 1982 did he again resume the position of secretary of the Party's Central Committee. But while from the late 1960s to the early 1980s he was not *in* the party apparatus, he was *of* the Party apparatus. Before becoming head of the KGB, he served as a Communist Youth League functionary, as the Party secretary of the Karelo-Finnish Republic, and as a secretary of the Central Committee. He was a professional Party man, not a career KGB official. Still, his position in the Central Committee Secretariat was marginal to the Party machinery's main tasks, which both Khrushchev and Brezhnev had performed before reaching the leadership. Andropov's job was that of the secretary in charge of relations with Eastern Europe, which was not a domestic responsibility.

So he was remarkably free of the obligations both Khrushchev and Brezhnev had owed to the Party apparatus. His base of initial support stemmed directly from his Politburo colleagues and was therefore narrower than his predecessors'. He needed a broader backing in the Party machine and the state bureaucracy if he planned any major innovations. But at the same time, he owed very few debts to particular branches of the political elite—although he was under obligations to individual members of the Politburo and the Secretariat, most notably Defense Minister Ustinov.

Andropov's attainment of the top leadership position marked the final rehabilitation of the security and intelligence services in the post-Stalin period. In the Khrushchev period and at the beginning of the Brezhnev era it would have been unthinkable for a man who spent the longest period of his political career as head of the KGB, and who was chairman of the security and intelligence services longer than any of his predecessors, to aspire to general secretaryship of the Party and to succeed with relatively limited opposition from his colleagues. Apparently, in the harsh climate of the 1980s, when everyone desired a strong leader, Andropov's personality and reputation and his record in the KGB were assets rather than liabilities.

Andropov owed no political debt to the KGB, nor did he have to fear its pressures and possible future aspirations to play a more central and visible political role. While he permitted the final rehabilitation of the agency and its increased weight in the political arena as a junior partner of the Party, it is now clear that he was determined to preclude a political challenge to his new powers from the KGB. He was using his loyalists in the KGB to solidify his power. He appointed Geidar Aliyev, the former KGB chief of Azerbaidzhan, as first deputy prime minister. He replaced the Brezhnev loyalist Nikolai Shchelokov, as the minister of the interior with a loyalist from the KGB, Vitalii Fedorchuk. Most important, Andropov wanted the KGB to be under professional, not political leadership. The newly appointed head, Viktor Chebrikov, was promoted from within the ranks. His chances of becoming a major political figure are small. Andropov's policy, which might have been successful had he reigned longer, was to use the KGB to strengthen his control over the Party and state, while at the same time preventing a KGB challenge to his authority, which could come only if a ranking political leader were to be appointed its director.

It is sometimes asserted that Andropov's success was primarily secured by the alliance of the KGB and the Soviet military. As far as his relationship with Ustinov is concerned, this was clearly true. Yet this personal partnership did not signify in itself an institutional concordat between the KGB and the professional military leadership. Such an association would imply a potentially greater role for the military. Because of the lack of any supporting evidence for a significant military role in Andropov's succession, we must rely on what we know about the role of military leaders in politics and policy formation in general, and particularly during a succession process. This suggests that the idea of Andropov's succession being primarily the result of a KGB/military connection is probably erroneous. If anything, Andropov's accession was accompanied by an attempt to increase civilian control over military and national security policies.

The change in leadership was full of uncertainties. None of Brezhnev's colleagues in the Politburo, the pool of likely candidates, had a clear edge over the others. The lack of preparation for Brezhnev's succession was particularly evident from the ages of Brezhnev's personnel appointments to replace leaders who died or retired. There was a shortage of qualified candidates for the top positions—men who would combine the experience of generalists with the age (or rather youth) and health that would make probable an extended tenure in office.

However, in all past successions the man appointed to the position of general secretary survived the later challenges of other contenders or coalitions to become the undisputed leader. The inherent power of this office is so great that a politician of even average skills finds the odds stacked decisively in his favor. His prerogatives include the chairmanship of the Politburo and the ability to decide the agenda and timing of that body's deliberation; the role of the chief executive of the Party apparatus; the position of the head of state as chairman of the Supreme Soviet; the chairmanship of the Defense Council, which oversees the military-industrial complex; the supervision of the *nomenklatura*, that is, the right of appointments and dismissals of key office-holders throughout the bureaucracies; and symbolic legitimization from the onset of his position as the top leader. The odds were overwhelming that Andropov would be able to consolidate his position beyond any challenge from his colleagues, that he would be able to purge personal opponents and opponents of his policies. Having been head of the secret police and intel-

ligence service for the previous fifteen years, he must have known where
the skeletons of every member of the Central Committee were buried,
and so could have exacted obedience, if not out of loyalty and agreement
with his policy initiatives, then at least out of fear.

Every past succession has represented a major change in either domestic policies or political structures or both. Every succession provided
the platform for new policy initiatives and new configurations of the
major political sectors. After Brezhnev, the Soviet Union was at a potential turning point comparable to that of the late 1920s, when the New
Economic Policy was replaced by the Stalinist revolution from above,
with its clarity of purpose, extremist policies, and coercion and terror; or
to that of 1953–57, from which emerged the hybrid system, combining
Stalinist totalitarianism and traditional authoritarianism, that exists
today.

That the leadership after Brezhnev recognized the need for a change is
clear, if only from the appointment of Andropov. His style and substance were likely a response to the personnel stability and policy incre-
mentalism under Brezhnev. During each past Soviet succession, the new
leader responded at least partly to the yearnings of the political elite,
especially of those groups that were his main constituencies. Obviously,
in the Andropov succession as in the past, the desires and hopes of the
elite group were primarily concerned with the fate of the particular institutions over which they presided. With Andropov's transition to
power, however, there were also hopes that seemed to cut across all
groups and that represented a consensus of expectations. The most visible concern was a desire to get the country moving again, to reverse the
stagnation and decline of recent years. Another common hope was to
strengthen social discipline, to enforce law and order more decisively.
There was a clear expectation that the new leader would be forceful. No
one in the Politburo seemed better qualified to fulfill those wishes than
Andropov. Of course, the law-and-order desires of the elites were
directed toward society at large and not their own bureaucratic fiefdoms.
In this respect the various bureaucracies, and particularly the Party apparatus, would not have been happy when and if Andropov applied the
discipline to them.

Finally, there was a major segment of the elites who saw their most
productive middle years passing by and who felt frustrated by the se-
niority blockage. They hoped for a quick retirement of the old generation and quicker promotion for themselves. Andropov started to respond
to the expectations of these middle-aged "young Turks," thereby building his power base on their gratitude and personal loyalty. The later
Chernenko leadership did not so respond, but was still unable to stop the
accession to increased power by this group.

In early 1983 I wrote that after almost two decades of stability of personnel and leadership in the Soviet Union, a longer period than any other such period in Soviet history, we might well see two successions in one decade, with all their destabilizing effects. In this sense one might say that Andropov came to power ten years and one heart attack too late.* Events overtook this estimate, and with Andropov's death and the selection of a frail Chernenko to the position of general secretary, it became inevitable that the 1980s would see at least three successions.

In the last months of Andropov's rule the Politburo seemed to be determined not to repeat the virtual paralysis of decision-making that characterized Brezhnev's final years. Andropov's colleagues decided that if he became incapacitated to the extent that he could perform his functions only on a part-time basis, they would force his retirement. The situation was complicated by the fact that with the exception of Chernenko and of Moscow secretary Viktor Grishin, the candidates to succeed Andropov were either too old, again risking the repetition of a short-lived leadership, or too young and inexperienced by Soviet standards.

In the late summer or early fall Andropov underwent major surgery, which incapacitated him for two months. He is said to have returned to Moscow late in October. Though he became more active, his condition did not permit him to appear in December at meetings of the Central Committee or the Supreme Soviet. Yet his memoranda—presumed to come from his bedroom—were heeded, his speeches read, his policies implemented, his loyalists promoted, his writings published. His personal qualities continued to be celebrated. In November Ustinov praised Andropov with unusual warmth and emphasis to a meeting of high-ranking military officers. And in December, several of Andropov's protégés were appointed to higher positions.

How can we explain the political survival and even apparent prosperity of an incapacitated and absent leader? Clearly important was his colleagues' belief—during the period from October 1983 to his final relapse the following January—that there was a good chance for his recovery. Yet to answer this question adequately, we would have to know more than we do about Andropov's apparent success in taking over all the key leadership positions, the strength of his support in the Party apparatus and KGB, and the degree of consensus among elites on his domestic policies, especially those concerning the economy. Beyond all this, there was simply no experienced and attractive candidate who could aspire to dislodge Andropov and his supporters while there was hope for him.

Among other factors that help to explain the paradox of Andropov's resilience, one is particularly germane to Soviet-American relations. Ex-

* Seweryn Bialer, "The Andropov Succession," *The New York Review of Books* (February 3, 1983).

ternal danger impels Soviet leaders to preserve unity at all costs. They were genuinely persuaded that President Reagan and his policies presented a grave test of their will to maintain and improve their international position. They wanted the sort of strong leadership that Andropov was able to deliver until August 1983 and that they hoped could be renewed with his recovery.

Despite the hopes of the political elite, most of his comrades in the Politburo, and probably large segments of the population, by early January Andropov had suffered a mortal relapse of his illness. His rule ended on February 9, 1984. The interregnum was far too short to leave a major impact on the Soviet system. Yet a balance sheet of his policies offers important clues to the direction in which domestic efforts will be moving in the years to come.

Andropov did leave his mark on the Soviet Union. He represented a style of leadership, a direction of personnel policies, a sober assessment of the situation, and a desire to improve performance, which act as a model for many, and perhaps most, members of the leadership, elite, and political public. Without any doubt he remains an object of reverence in Gorbachev's Russia and for Gorbachev himself. This in itself makes the analysis of his short rule significant for understanding the Soviet Union in the mid-1980s.

The most noticeable contrasts I observed between Brezhnev's last autumn and Andropov's first were the disappearance of the black marketeers from the back rooms of the Aragvi restaurant in Moscow, and the hesitation of taxi drivers to insist on payment in hard currency. The general mood in Moscow, however, was harder to define. The ordinary Muscovite seemed to be slipping back into his normal state of political apathy after the initial burst of expectations that followed Andropov's accession. The wish that Andropov prove a new *khoziain*, a boss who would get things going again after Brezhnev's last stagnant years, was yielding to the suspicion that nothing seemed to be happening apart from a few changes in detail.

This popular attitude was not shared by many members of the political elite, academic experts, and a segment of the intelligentsia. For them, the slow start indicated not a lack of ideas and political will but rather a gradualist approach and methodical preparation characteristic of Andropov's style of work, one that promised a genuine change from Brezhnev's paralysis. Their sentiments were reflected in a story that circulated among them. When appointed chairman of the KGB in 1967, Andropov reportedly assembled his top personnel from around the country and delivered a speech. "I don't know much about your work," he said. "I'm not a professional. I want you to feel secure in helping me learn what you do and in giving me advice." One year later, very few of his listeners remained at their old jobs; they had been fired, promoted, and transferred. Two years later, Andropov's control of the KGB apparatus and operations was beyond dispute; he reorganized and streamlined this immensely powerful institution and brought modern technology to bear on its activities. Those who recounted the story clearly hoped that Andropov would employ a similar style of leadership as general secretary of the Communist Party.

The average Muscovite and the Western observer could detect little of Andropov's activity and purpose. Most striking were the initiatives that he launched shortly after assuming office in order to demonstrate that Russia was moving again, even if no substantive changes in the system were taking place. The first was greater candor in relations between leadership and population. The press openly reported serious shortages of food and consumer goods and pervasive bureaucratic foot-dragging. It said straightforwardly that economic plans remained unfulfilled and a major share of allocated investments frozen, and that wages and income would not rise without a significant improvement in labor productivity.

The second initiative sought to convince the public that the new leader was hard at work, on top of his job, and capable of resolving the difficulties inherited from Brezhnev. There were unprecedented announcements of weekly Politburo meetings that contained information on the agenda and the results of the deliberations.

The third was a visible and repeated effort to show that the new leadership was strong and united, and ready and able to defend Soviet power and prevent its enemies from taking advantage of the period of transition.

The fourth was probably the most important and impressive. It sought to enforce greater discipline in the workplace and society at large, as well as to reduce blatant official and unofficial corruption. The immediate effects of these efforts were evident even to outsiders: Worker absenteeism declined; bureaucrats displayed a greater sense of responsibility; and illegal private traders no longer staked out tourist hotels in such large numbers. In all probability it was the stress on social discipline among workers and greater responsibility among managers and bureaucrats that accounted for the overfulfillment of the Soviet industrial production plan in the first half of 1983.

Of course these changes were for the most part cosmetic, without lasting effects on the performance of the economy and the conduct of the citizenry. Much more important were the deeper currents of activity, less visible to the average citizen or Western visitor, that suggested preparations for change in personnel, institutions, and ideology.

Personnel shifts began at the upper-middle and top levels of the Party-state machine. In the Politburo, Andrei Kirilenko was retired and

Geidar Aliyev was elected to full membership. In the powerful Secretariat of the Party's Central Committee, Nikolai Ryzhkov, deputy chairman of the State Planning Commission, was named secretary in charge of economic affairs, while Grigorii Romanov was brought to Moscow from his post as Leningrad Party secretary. Mikhail Solomentsev vacated the position of prime minister of the Russian Republic to assume a much less significant post as head of the Party Control Commission. Another Central Committee secretary, Ivan Kapitonov, was fired while the head of the party's propaganda department, Evgenii Tyazhel'nikov, was sent to Romania as ambassador—a demotion. The important organizational department of the Central Committee received a new head, former first Party secretary of Tomsk province, Yegor Ligachev; and the department itself was placed directly under Andropov's supervision.

As for ministerial positions, Foreign Minister Andrei Gromyko became a first deputy prime minister. Vitalii Vorotnikov, whom Brezhnev had exiled to Cuba as ambassador, was named a candidate and then full member of the Politburo en route to appointment as prime minister of the Russian Republic. The minister of trade of the Ukrainian SSR, Grigorii Vashchenko, was promoted to minister of internal trade for the USSR. Andropov's successor as KGB chairman, Vitalii Fedorchuk, replaced Brezhnev's close friend Nikolai Shchelokov as minister of internal affairs, while the KGB was taken over by another Andropov stalwart, Viktor Chebrikov, who was also elected an alternate member of the Politburo. The composition of the Politburo, of the Party secretariat, and of the central Party apparatus was significantly changed. In addition, about one-fifth of the provincial (*obkom*) Party first secretaries—the core functionaries of the Party machine—were new. Within the Council of Ministers, fifteen ministers were retired or fired, and in most cases they were replaced by one of their deputy ministers. On a lower but still important level of the bureaucracy, a few dozen officials were removed (some were even arrested), transferred, or promoted in ways reflecting their competence and loyalty to Andropov. In almost all of those changes, the new leaders belonged to the younger generation. It is difficult to ascertain what these new people represent, and what their previous ties to Andropov might have been. In most cases they were also promoted from among the deputies of the retired officials. Of importance, however, was the very fact that the old guard was replaced and a loyalist group of senior officials created.

The new look attested both to Andropov's surprising authority and to his preparation of major policy changes that required new people in strategic positions. Personnel shifts would have surely continued as Andropov worked to place trusted supporters in government and Party posts and to increase the efficiency of these organizations. Without control over the central and provincial Party organizations, neither the support of the KGB nor the consent of the Politburo and Secretariat would suffice to bring about major administrative and policy reforms.

Andropov's program also included a redefinition of functions in Party and state institutions. Potentially significant was the newly defined jurisdiction of the Party secretary for economic affairs, Ryzhkov. He was empowered to transform the function of the central Party economic apparatus from its former concentration on detailed supervision of the state economic bureaucracies to a primary concern with strategic planning decisions and the formulation of economic reforms. Such a major shift in direction logically requires the abolition or drastic reorganization of existing economic departments of the Central Committee, which replicated the structure of the state economic bureaucracies. The main role of these departments has been supervising the activities of parallel governmental units, such as the economic ministries, which actually run the economy. The change could make the Central Committee apparatus the focal point of future reform activity. De-emphasis of the supervisory function from the Party center would have also necessitated the promotion to state economic bureaucracies of younger, better-trained, and loyal officials from both Party and state organizations, to act from within the government as the general secretary's watchdogs and the implementors of his ideas, a process well under way under Andropov.

These indications of a more substantive role for the central Party apparatus in economic matters was echoed by the direction of appointments in the bureaucracy, which suggested centralization and greater control of it from within. Two new appointees to the position of first deputy prime minister were given newly created jurisdictions. Geidar Aliyev, known for his determined fight against corruption in Azerbaidzhan, was expected to apply this experience to the central government. He was named to control and supervise the state bureaucracy. Andrei Gromyko supervised and coordinated virtually all government activities relating to foreign affairs, excluding, presumably, the intelligence activities which were directed through Chebrikov to Andropov. Gromyko's responsibilities included the making of foreign policy, foreign trade, technological transfers from abroad, participation in international financial arrangements, and Soviet export industries. These two appointments narrowed dramatically the jurisdiction of the ailing Prime Minister Tikhonov. With them, for the first time since Stalin's death, three Politburo members also served in the Presidium of the Council of Ministers. At the time, Andropov's leadership reflected his desire to limit the Party's supervising function with regard to governmental agencies and to impose stricter discipline and supervision of the governmental organs from within.

Andropov's reorganizations could also have affected the Defense Council, the decision-making body in military, military-political, and military-economic matters. Chaired by Andropov, as it had been by Brezhnev, the Council included, in addition to the minister of defense and his principal military commanders, the prime minister and the civilian managers of military industries, the head of the KGB, and the minister of foreign affairs. Without a sizable staff of its own, the tasks of setting the agenda of meetings, preparing briefings, and presenting options fall to the general staff, which thereby exerts considerable influence thanks to its monopoly of military expertise. Andropov was said to have planned to establish an independent staff for the Defense Council, composed in part of civilian specialists on military, economic, and political questions, and in part of military specialists who would be permanently transferred to the council from the ministry of defense and the general staff. This could have offered him greater flexibility in dealing with proposals and requests from the armed forces.

There are no indications that Andropov envisaged sweeping institutional change. To an outside observer it seems that he was determined to improve Soviet labor and management discipline partly by coercive measures and partly by marginal policy and administrative reforms. Nonetheless, one should not dismiss out of hand the positive effects of even such marginal reforms. And one should remember, moreover, that these were only initial steps which in time would have been supplemented by more serious efforts to improve—though not to restructure—the system.

A third current of activity was the preparation of ideological arguments and justifications for organizational-administrative and economic change. Novel ideological formulas were beginning to appear in speeches and articles by Andropov and some of his associates, which in turn were broadcast by the standing army of Soviet propaganda experts. The aim was to prepare the Party and state bureaucracies and the population at large for coming reforms. The two most important of the new formulas concerned "the potential for growth of socialist society" and "contradictions in the development of mature socialist society."

According to the first, the alleged superiority of socialist over capitalist societies was said to constitute only a "potential" that would not be realized unless wisely exploited by the directors of socialist society and vigorously pursued by the workers. The clear implication, at times explicitly stated, was that this potential had not been properly nurtured.

The second formula stated that contradictions occur constantly between the potential for Soviet development and the actual growth and development of the means of production, particularly with regard to new technology. To overcome such contradictions, economic mechanisms and organizations had to be continuously adjusted and reformed in order to take full advantage of the unrealized potential inherent in the socialist organization of labor. Both formulas, firmly planted in the garden of quotations from holy writ, alerted bureaucrats, managers, and the populace to the necessity of reforms that could then be regarded as products of the "law of socialist development."

Andropov's ideological formulations, which were designed to shake the Party from its complacency about the domestic situation, were expressed in the article "Marxism-Leninism and the Contemporary World" in the October 1983 issue of the Party's theoretical journal, *Communist*. According to reports, when Andropov's speechwriters—high-ranking Party ideologists to whom he entrusted the writing of this article—brought him its first draft, he gave them a short lecture about what he expected from them. The gist of his remarks was as follows: You still do not understand the seriousness of the economic and social situations in which we find ourselves now, when the international situation is dangerous and the pressure to engage in a new arms race spiral may be irresistible. In the last decade we adopted the formula that our country had entered the period of mature socialism, a stage next to full communism. But what kind of a mature socialism do we have? How can one reconcile this formulation—which conveys the image of a well-functioning system that possesses the self-generating ability to grow rapidly and generate technological progress and that ensures high social discipline and the proper attitude to work—with the relative backwardness of our economy, the lack of discipline and complacent dogmatism of our managers and our Party? We have to change radically our methods of work both in the government and in the Party. We have to understand the need for large-scale innovation and dramatic improvement of our social discipline. We have to forget the nonsense about mature socialism. We have to obtrude into the consciousness of our Party the urgency and difficulty of our task to make our socialism really mature and modern. Our Party has to be armed ideologically for this task, and you had better make this clear in this article.

Changes in personnel, institutional functions, and ideological formulations all point to an accumulation of greater power by a leader bent on preparing the ground for change. How much power did the new leader actually possess?

Andropov's potential authority before and even during his mortal illness was enormous. He monopolized the key posts of command. With office, however, comes not power but the potential for power. Under Soviet conditions, power for the top leaders means several things: that a majority in the principal decision-making bodies are his supporters or—better still—his appointees; that the leadership in the major bureaucratic hierarchies are willing and able to implement his decisions in accordance with his wishes and not their own preferences; and that the leader can adjust and alter ways of operation within the bureaucracies that are consonant with his individual style of leadership and goals.

In this sense, Andropov's power was still limited, first by the absence of clearly defined priorities and second by the significant structural impediments that he inherited—bureaucrats with long tenures in office, a predisposition to inertial policies, and the influence of his predecessor's style and policy goals. Nevertheless, after only seven months in office—that is, before he became ill—Andropov's actual power far surpassed that of his two predecessors, Khrushchev and Brezhnev, at comparable stages of their periods of ascendancy. This was true because Soviet elites felt a need for a strong chief to deal with the accumulation of problems in Soviet life, and they regarded Andropov as such. It was also true because even though Andropov's power base still rested primarily in the KGB and not in the Party, there were no obvious competitors among the top leadership after Chernenko lost out to him. And it was true because Andropov's style of leadership, with its preferences for gradualism in personnel and policy changes, did not provoke the formation of opposition coalitions within the leadership able successfully to sabotage his policies within the bureaucracies.

In the winter of 1983 in Moscow, I was made aware of two episodes connected with Andropov's pursuit of moderate economic reform and innovative behavior within the bureaucracy. The local Party apparatus, primarily the *raion* (county) secretaries who constitute the overwhelming majority of the Party machine, inundated the Central Party Secretariat in the early fall of 1983 with letters opposing any change in the Party's policies or style of work. Their chief argument was that in the dangerous international situation, it was necessary to rely on the tried and true techniques of the Party and economic mobilization rather than to engage in economic reforms and changes in the style of Party work. The second incident involved a memo sent by Andropov warning the managers that he would not tolerate a "formalistic," make-believe attitude toward economic reforms and bureaucratic responsibility, and that those found unresponsive to his programs should not be surprised if they were replaced. These episodes, and probably many more of the same kind, convey the resistance to change by entrenched local officials. It would have required major efforts to break it. Gorbachev faces this messy task now.

How Andropov would have used his power will never be known. The impulsive Khrushchev tried to restructure the Stalinist system of rule, to revitalize the bureaucracy and the dormant ideology. Often acting against the consensus of elites, he eventually risked his power against the

Party apparatus, the crucial barrier to the abandonment of Stalinism as well as his own base of power. He was brought down by a coalition of leaders from all the major power groups. The cautious and circumspect Brezhnev reversed many of Khrushchev's attempted reforms and pursued the goal of stability in bureaucratic organizations and society as a whole. He created a policy consensus among almost all elite groups and satisfied most of their yearnings for stability in office. At the same time he achieved strategic parity with the United States while overseeing an impressive rise in the standard of living.

Andropov's use of power would likely have differed from that of his predecessors. Unlike Khrushchev, he would have probably designed and executed reforms only after thorough preparation, in order to secure broad support for them within the elite. Unlike Brezhnev, he would doubtless have pushed reforms beyond the limits of elite consensus, to challenge the vested interests of the bureaucracy. If Khrushchev pursued reform mainly through organizational change and Brezhnev largely through budgetary allocation, Andropov would most likely have combined both approaches. His main domestic objectives seemed to be the inculcation of a strong and durable social discipline in white- and blue-collar workplaces, and the introduction of innovations into management of the economy. The Soviet elite now looks back to Andropov as a leader with great but unfulfilled promise.

6

The Chernenko Episode

To understand the tragic and almost farcical character of Konstantin Chernenko's selection in February 1984 as the new, but very weak, Party leader, one must have some idea of the mood that reigned in Moscow during the last half-year of Andropov's life, and throughout Chernenko's incumbency. This mood grew out of a recognition of the domestic power vacuum. It was also reinforced by the international situation. The elite was angry about the country's immobilism and its own helplessness, and about the challenge from the United States. Outside official circles there was a fear of war and further decline, as well as uncertainty about the future. Among the official intelligentsia there was a feeling of frustration with the direction, or lack of direction, that their country was taking, and with the all-embracing neo-Stalinism generated by the Party machine.

Moscow residents were subjected to an assault of primitive and offensive anti-American propaganda that recalled Stalin's attacks in the 1950s. The neo-Stalinist direction of the press and television was followed by the academic institutes that study international relations. Their researchers were busily grinding out what was officially called counter-propaganda, and was in fact an unbridled vilification of America. Predictably, the experts who might once have appeared soft on America were now anxious to appear most zealous in their attacks.

The turn to neo-Stalinism was reflected also in increased pressure on the tiny dissident groups. Andrei Sakharov was denounced as a warmonger. In the fall of 1984 a new trial of dissenters was being prepared in Leningrad. Dissenters were tried with exceptional speed and sentenced harshly. Their treatment in camps and prisons became more cruel. Experienced KGB managers took control of the uniformed police, who, after undergoing a purge, were unleashed against "speculators, hooligans, and shirkers." Increasingly tough measures were applied in factories and offices to enforce work discipline. American diplomats and correspondents were more effectively isolated. In December 1983 the head of the KGB gained alternate membership in the Politburo, a promotion that preserved the organization's place near the top during Andropov's illness and underscored symbolically its new visibility and power against Soviet citizens. Yet this increasingly intolerant neo-Stalinism in domestic affairs coexisted with urgent advocacy of economic reforms.

In these increasingly difficult, tense, and taxing times, even at the beginning of 1984, the political elite still hoped that Andropov's health would improve and that he would be able to resume his duties at least on a part-time basis. Their hopes reflected their recognition of hard times and the unique degree of respect for Andropov, which was magnified by an especially lackluster Politburo.

Andropov's death was the second worst thing that could have happened to the leadership. The worst would have been a continuation of his debilitating illness for a prolonged period while he still remained in office, paralyzing the decision-making process and repeating the nightmare of Brezhnev's last two or three years.

The pomp, ceremony, and selection process of fifteen months earlier was repeated: the lying in state of the dead leader's body in the Kremlin's Hall of Columns; the eulogy by his comrades in the Politburo; the formation of a funeral commission headed by his heir apparent; his burial in the Kremlin wall with leaders from around the world participating; the selection by the Politburo of their new master; the convening of the Central Committee members in Moscow to confirm the selection made by the Politburo; the short, reassuring, but empty speech by the new leader; and finally the appeal for Party unity by the presumed alternative candidate in the Politburo, in this case Mikhail Gorbachev, the fifty-three-year-old secretary of the Central Committee.

When Chernenko was selected to lead the Soviet Union, *The New York Times* published an article about him entitled "Bolshevik of the Old Mold Rises to Kremlin's Peak." In fact, however, the mold from which he came was not revolutionary Bolshevism, but bureaucratic Stalinism. Yet, even in comparison to his comrades of the Stalinist generation, his career path, and the general level of competence and intellectual capacity he displayed, stamped him as a mediocrity. Most of his responsibilities over the years lay in agitation and administration, the least respected aspects of Party functioning. His writings and speeches, even in a field tightly constrained by dogma, were particularly trite and predictable. True, they were probably composed, as was the practice for many Party officials, by his assistants and speech writers; the point is, however, that he obviously felt comfortable with them. Throughout his career, Chernenko never held an important independent managerial position either within or outside the Party. From 1946 on, he was a shadow of Brezhnev, a loyal self-effacing retainer ascending the ladder of success on his patron's coattails. Never was he in charge of administering any important segment of Soviet life. Only in the last years of Brezhnev's leadership, and particularly during Brezhnev's progressive physical decline, did he get a taste of real, if reflected, power, when he became the spokesman and the organizer for his patron. Opinions about his intelligence, creative power, and organizational talents, both in the Soviet Union and abroad, were rather low. It was unlikely that at the age of seventy-three, by far the most advanced age of any new leader in Soviet history, he would suddenly disclose hitherto hidden talents or change his long-held views.

That Chernenko could become general secretary at all, despite his uncertain health, was in itself an expression of the Soviet Union's problems, of the crisis of the system, in this case in its leadership dimension. The appointment of Chernenko after several years of leadership paralysis expressed the Soviet malaise and at the same time contributed immensely to its perpetuation. What was brewing in Russia during this lengthy period was not a cataclysmic explosion, but an undeniable and continuous erosion of respect for the system and for those in charge of it. The overall legitimacy of the system probably did not suffer an irreversible blow. Yet Brezhnev's near-senility in his last years, and the banality and obsolescence of Chernenko went far to undermine the legitimacy of the position of general secretary.

There are those who say that the archaic leadership style of Brezhnev and Chernenko makes Mikhail Gorbachev's job far easier because of the inevitably favorable comparisons. Yet what the aging Brezhnev and Chernenko did, or failed to do, with the general secretaryship may still come to haunt the Communist Party because this most important office has been trivialized.

The top leader may be a tyrant and a murderer, as Stalin was, but he can still be admired and respected if he conveys the aura of power and statesmanship. On the other hand, while even a well-meaning individual who has little stature or has outlived his time may evoke pity, he will also bear the anger of a proud nation that feels it is not properly represented. The Russian proverb, "Lucky is a country that has a hero; happy is a country that does not need heroes," does not apply to the Russian nation itself. The Russians are happier with their heroes.

It is also possible, but unlikely, that the recent experience with leadership may finally produce an institutionalized process of succession, with established tenures for high officeholders, and regular turnover of incumbents according to the simple rule which is so difficult for politicians and bureaucrats to recognize, that all must retire at some point.

Chernenko's selection as Andropov's replacement was the most conservative, predictable, and cautious of all available choices. Yet when faced with the necessity of picking a new leader two years before, in November 1982, the Politburo had selected a strong man. The choice then was between a strong, influential and respected leader, and a weak Party apparatchik who represented the Brezhnev past and particularly its last years of decline. Andropov was picked because he had knowledge and experience, and because it was felt that the Soviet Union needed a leader of stature and strength. In 1984 Chernenko represented no risks and no surprises, and the old core of the Politburo rightly considered him to be malleable.

Almost without exception, the leaders in the Politburo were either too young and inexperienced or, with the exception of Chernenko, too old and specialized, to be general secretary. Andrei Gromyko had spent his entire career in the foreign service, and Dimitrii Ustinov had headed the Soviet military-industrial complex since 1940. Viktor Grishin had never held a national office. Of the younger generation, Grigorii Romanov had worked only in Leningrad, ultimately rising to the head of that city's Party organization. Even Mikhail Gorbachev, the youngest member of the Politburo when he was appointed in 1980, had only been in the south of Russia, in the agricultural province of Stavropol. When he was brought to Moscow to become a secretary of the Central Committee and a Politburo member, he was placed in charge of Soviet agriculture, the only aspect of Party activity he knew well.

From the second half of 1983, the impression was strong that Gorbachev was being groomed to become Andropov's successor, almost certainly with the latter's approval and support. There were unmistakable signs that he was getting a crash course in areas central to the duties of the general secretary. Retaining his responsibility for agriculture, he also began to play a major role in personnel appointments to *nomenklatura* positions, and became active in the field of foreign policy. Yet by February 1984, Gorbachev was hardly prepared for the job of general secretary. That he became the front-runner for the post among the Politburo's younger members was only one indication of the depressing situation wrought in the leadership by Brezhnev's eighteen years of stability. The selection of a new general secretary became a choice between inexperience and old age.

The fact that Gorbachev made an appeal for Party unity at the Central Committee meeting that confirmed the selection of Chernenko

strongly indicates that his candidacy was at least considered in the Politburo. If Andropov had survived for perhaps another year, Gorbachev
would probably have become his successor. One also has the impression
that what worked in Chernenko's favor was the disunity of the "young
Turks" themselves. Gorbachev and Romanov were strong men with
similar ambitions but with different outlooks and personalities. Gorbachev is by Soviet standards "liberal," deliberate, and a workaholic.
Romanov is an extreme hard-liner, impulsive and self-indulgent.
Moreover, all the members of this generation had a strong motivation
for supporting Chernenko's candidacy. Had one of the younger leaders
been elected general secretary, it would likely have foreclosed the possibility that any of the others could have achieved this position. According
to this logic, by supporting Chernenko, each of these men kept alive his
hopes of one day gaining the top post.

In addition, despite prodding from some of the younger appointees of
Andropov in the Politburo, in the Secretariat of the Central Committee,
in the All-Union Government and central and provincial Party apparatus, Gorbachev, according to all available evidence, did not push his
candidacy for the post of general secretary, but instead lined up dutifully
behind Chernenko. He probably rightly considered that he had no realistic chance to achieve the top position, that by pushing for it he would
undermine his standing with the old Politburo core, that because of his
age time was on his side, and that Chernenko's leadership, precisely
because of its weak and temporary character, would provide him the
opportunity to solidify and expand support for his position as the
second-ranking leader of the Party apparatus and the heir apparent. The
selection of Chernenko did not therefore involve a conflict and division
within the top leadership.

The decisive factor in Chernenko's selection, however, was the position of the old guard. Unlike the Chinese Communist Party, the Politburo does not have a formal standing committee, a small group of the
most experienced members who decide the agenda and the resolutions.
Yet, in fact, the Politburo did have a leadership core composed of the
old guard that carried influence and importance beyond its numerical
strength. It seemed to include Ustinov, Gromyko, Tikhonov, the head
of the Party's Central Control Commission, Mikhail Solomentsev, Grishin, and, of course, Chernenko. In the final analysis, it was they who
carried the day. Their decision was not difficult to understand. To pick
Gorbachev in February 1984 would have involved a major risk. Instead,
Chernenko would be a temporary, transitional leader who was more
popular than Gorbachev with the venerable generation of the Party apparatus. His attitude toward his old comrades in the Politburo would be
deferential, his domestic policies would be safe and predictable, and in

foreign and security policies, he would rely on Gromyko and Ustinov. The Politburo opted for caution in a time of danger on the international scene and major unresolved problems at home. The selection of Chernenko was the "last hurrah" of the old generation.

While in office Chernenko labored under major constraints. He was supposed to lead a Politburo that only fifteen months before had rejected him in favor of Andropov. The new members of the Politburo and the score of high officials who joined the central Party apparatus after Brezhnev's death were all Andropov loyalists. They shared their patron's position on the issues. Almost all belonged to the younger generation. Many had replaced Brezhnev loyalists who were close to Chernenko. Moreover, Chernenko did not enjoy the respect of the older generation, all of whom had had more illustrious careers and more independent positions than he. They controlled major blocs of bureaucratic support from the hierarchies they supervised. Nor was Chernenko personally respected by the younger generation. For them he represented the past, and particularly the years of paralysis at the end of Brezhnev's rule. It was in the interest of all the Politburo members to praise Chernenko and support his prestige within the population at large as a front man for the key Soviet institutions of power. However, it was also in their interest, in order to maintain their independence on policy and organizational questions, to keep him on a short leash.

Most important, however, Chernenko's power and his independence were sharply circumscribed by the widely recognized fact that he was a transitional leader who was keeping the seat of the general secretary warm for the real successor to come. The lame-duck nature of Chernenko's leadership meant that officials were not likely to become preoccupied with an effort to please him, or to identify themselves with him. Rather, they spent their time and political resources jockeying for favor with the two or three candidates for future leadership and seeking to establish their loyalty to them.

The fluidity and precarious balance of forces in the leadership, the separation of power centers within it, and the division of responsibilities under Chernenko were unprecedented in postwar history, though in some ways the situation resembled the three-year period following Stalin's death. There were two centers of power within the leadership; all the major figures gravitated toward one or the other.

These two centers also coincided with a new division of labor and responsibilities within the leadership. The first was composed of the two most influential and visible members of the old leadership core, Andrei Gromyko and Dimitrii Ustinov. It was they who had played the role of kingmakers in the selection of Chernenko. They formed a power center not because they competed with Chernenko for overall leadership but because they monopolized to an unprecedented degree the decision-making in two areas of central concern to the leadership—foreign policy and national security.

For the first time the foreign minister was really in charge of the foreign policy of his country. Gromyko, who began his diplomatic career in 1939 at the age of twenty-nine in the American section of the People's Commissariat of Foreign Affairs, and who by 1943 was already ambassador to Washington, became foreign minister in 1957 and in 1973 was promoted by Brezhnev to full membership in the Politburo. He concentrated his activities almost entirely on foreign policy (and to the extent that they were interconnected with foreign policy, on Soviet national security matters), and thus was unquestionably the most experienced leader in that area. Yet even when participating in the highest councils of government under Brezhnev, he served primarily as an instrument of foreign policy in the service of the top leader, very seldom as its conceptualizer and shaper.

After Chernenko's selection, however, Gromyko became the most influential voice in foreign-policymaking. Indeed, he seemed to hold virtual veto power in such matters. Andropov's effort to build a parallel foreign policy apparatus within the Party to circumvent Gromyko's state bureaucracy (and at the same time to kick Gromyko upstairs by furnishing him with the title first deputy prime minister) was nullified. The influence of the international departments of the Party declined or were forced to concentrate more narrowly on international labor and communist movements. The advisory role to the Party leadership of the think-tanks of the Soviet Academy of Sciences—such as the Institute of the Study of the United States and Canada under Central Committee member Georgii Arbatov, or the Institute of World Economy and International Relations, under Alexander Yakovlev—were diminished.

To what extent Gromyko bore responsibility for the extremely hard line of foreign policy in 1984 is difficult to establish. The line was adopted under Andropov, especially after October 1983, when the deployment of American missiles in Western Europe became a foregone conclusion. Moreover, the entire Politburo, other leadership institutions, and their aides and experts probably gravitated to this position even without Gromyko's prodding. However, one has the impression that Gromyko actually enjoyed the anti-Americanism. He may have felt a sense of personal betrayal, which other members of the Politburo probably did not, at what the Soviets saw as the Reagan Administration's attempts to deny them equality with the United States and the status of a respected global power, a status that the Soviets felt had been conceded to them in the 1970s.

Dimitrii Ustinov's function in directing and deciding national security policies was also unique in Soviet history. What was exceptional about it was the fact that he as defense minister, and not the general secretary or the collective Politburo, played the decisive role in formulating national security policies. His status was extraordinary in the degree of authority and respect he enjoyed in the high command of the armed forces. Ustinov, who had no professional military education and never commanded troops, was nevertheless a leading military hero of World War II. From 1940 when he was thirty-two years old, until his appointment to the post of minister of defense in 1976, he was in charge of the military-industrial complex. During the war, as people's commissar for munitions, and afterward as deputy prime minister and secretary of the Central Committee, he directed the development and production of arms and weapons systems. He was the only person still active of the dozen people who, working under Stalin, were primarily responsible for the Soviet victory in World War II. With the exception of the chief of the navy, Admiral Sergei Gorshkov, who commanded a fleet, all members of the present high command were either junior officers during the war or had entered the service afterwards. The former chief of the Soviet General Staff and first deputy defense minister, Marshal Nikolai Ogarkov, for example, finished the war as an infantry battalion commander. The present chief of the General Staff, Marshal Sergei Akhromeyev, entered the war as a tank commander. The resulting prestige of Ustinov, both among his political colleagues and in the military establishment, was enormous. Finally, his position was further strengthened by the fact that in the reigning mood of hostility and threat in Moscow, any demand of the Soviet high command accepted by Ustinov was assured of passing in the Politburo. As one official expressed it: "No member of the Politburo or of the Government will dare in the present situation to deny the military any request which the military and Ustinov deem necessary for the defense of the fatherland."

The power represented by Gromyko and Ustinov was counterposed in the Politburo, although not opposed, by the alliance formed by Chernenko and Gorbachev. The division of responsibilities for all practical purposes left to Chernenko control over domestic policies and the leadership of the most important bureaucracy, the Party apparatus. At almost any time in the past, and with a more forceful man than Chernenko, ultimate control of domestic political-economic matters, and particularly leadership of the Party, would constitute a firm enough base for taking full charge of the Politburo's activities and decision-making agenda. However, the situation in 1984 defied the traditional logic of Soviet politics. An accumulation of power resources by the general secretary did not occur. Chernenko was never more than a caretaker leader. The situation potentially profited Mikhail Gorbachev.

In a sense, Gorbachev's calculation not to challenge Chernenko was probably similar to that of Gromyko and Ustinov, who were convinced of their ability to manipulate or circumvent the new leader. In Gorbachev's case he may have believed he could fill the gaps in Chernenko's weak leadership and make himself an indispensable ally. By doing this, he may have hoped to place himself in an unbeatable position for the next succession.

With the confidence that time was on his side, Gorbachev was patiently and methodically building his own power base and influence over policy. During the last months of Chernenko's rule there were unmistakable indications that Gorbachev was recognized by the old guard and by a dominant segment of the younger leaders as the heir apparent. This was demonstrated by the continuous broadening of his activities and visibility in making ideological pronouncements, in taking part in meetings with foreign leaders, in playing a central role in relations with the Eastern European satellites, in the preparation of the new program of the Party, and by the atmosphere of hope and even adulation that surrounded him in Moscow political circles.

Gorbachev's domestic policy line was a faithful continuation of Andropov's methodical attempt to prepare meaningful, although only partial, economic reforms and to rejuvenate the Party-state apparatus. His loyalty to Chernenko and his determination not to rush events were helpful to his political plans, but at the same time must have been frustrating. Andropov had envisaged the abolition of the economic departments in the central Party apparatus and their transformation from a supervisory role over the state machinery into a center of strategic economic planning. Yet only a few days after Andropov's funeral, Chernenko assembled the staff of the Central Committee and assured them that no changes would take place in the structure and role of the organization and activities. The same pledge was conveyed by Chernenko in his talks with the provincial and republican Party secretaries. As expected, he both catered to and embodied the political elite and Party apparatus at their most conservative, in outlook and style of work. His own attitude towards economic reforms was strictly incremental and traditional, very much in line with the late Brezhnev approach of tinkering with the system rather than changing it.

In 1984, Gorbachev's strategy seemed first, to solidify his position by defending and enlarging the network of younger officials who had risen under Andropov, and, second, to attempt economic reforms on the margins without upsetting the vested interests to which Chernenko was sympathetic. The post from which Gorbachev acted was secretary of the Central Committee. But he was not simply one among the nine secretaries. His position was defined in practice, although it was not expressed in a special title, as that of a second secretary. (It was similar to that occupied under Khrushchev by Frol Kozlov and then by Brezhnev himself. Under Brezhnev, Andrei Kirilenko played a similar role prior to his illness.) As the *de facto* second secretary, Gorbachev supervised the other secretaries, including his primary competitors Grigorii Romanov, who was in charge of supervising military industry, and Vladimir I. Dolgikh, the secretary of the Central Committee in charge of energy. He also prepared the agenda for the meetings of the Secretariat, chaired these meetings in Chernenko's absence, and even, according to some sources, when Chernenko participated. In the Secretariat his two key allies were Ryzhkov, in charge of economic planning, and Ligachev, who supervised personnel and the *nomenklatura,* the right to appoint and dismiss high Party and state officials. In the Politburo his allies included Vitalii Vorotnikov, the prime minister of the Russian Republic, and Geidar Aliyev. (Aliyev, owing to his non-Russian nationality, had no chance whatsoever to become the new Soviet prime minister. On the other hand, Vorotnikov was probably Andropov's future candidate for this position.)

Three Gorbachev policy initiatives were particularly important. The first and newest was an attempt by Gorbachev through Ryzhkov and two high-placed allies in Gosplan to weaken the barrier between the military and civilian sectors of Soviet industry. The two first deputies of Nikolai Baibakov, the chairman of Gosplan, Lev Voronin and Yuri Maslyukov, were responsible respectively for the civilian and military sectors of the economy. Voronin and Maslyukov were apparently allies of Gorbachev and close associates of Ryzhkov from his days in Gosplan. They apparently tried to build bridges between the civilian and military industrial sectors. The details of their plans still remain unknown, but it seems that their main effort was directed at securing technological and managerial feedback from the military to the civilian sector.

The second measure involved broadening and improving conditions for limited economic reform. According to the original plan announced in the late summer of 1983, five industrial and service branches of the USSR or of a union republic were to start operating on January 1, 1984, under a modified system of management that stressed indices such as cost of production, profit, quality of products, and technological progress. The selected five branches did start work according to the new system in 1984, but Gorbachev was able to introduce two new elements into the project: The number of economic institutions participating in the experiment was doubled, and the time span of the experiment after which its evaluation was to take place was extended from the one year planned under Andropov to two. (It is only fair to note, however, that this experiment is in fact nothing more than a repetition of the reform favored by Prime Minister Kosygin in 1965 and abandoned after a few years.)

The third initiative concerned Soviet agriculture and the fate of the so-called contract brigades. A contract brigade is a relatively small basic unit of production, which unifies fifteen to twenty peasants or state farm workers, tractor drivers, mechanics, etc. The group is assigned a particular plot of land for which it is responsible. The brigade signs a contract with the leadership of the collective or state farm specifying how much it will produce on its land. Anything above the agreed quota belongs to the brigade and can be sold in the free market. Having met some success on a trial basis in Georgia, the system was to be introduced gradually in other republics. What seems to have happened under the direct influence of Gorbachev is that the introduction of the brigade as the standard mode of organization was speeded up; the guarantees concerning the planned production and state delivery quotas were extended from five to six years, therefore securing for the brigade members the free-market profits for production above the state-established quotas.

Any analysis of the balance of power in the Politburo, Secretariat, and upper reaches of the elites would not be complete without mentioning the aging prime minister, Nikolai Tikhonov. When Andropov took office Tikhonov offered his resignation, but it was not accepted. One can only speculate that Andropov did not at that time see a satisfactory replacement and intended to keep Tikhonov on the job until such a replacement was ready. After Andropov's death, Tikhonov, it seems, again expressed his willingness and even desire to retire, and again his resignation was rejected by the Politburo.

This rejection can be explained by the role played by Tikhonov in the post-Andropov Politburo. He apparently was an essential, neutral balance wheel between the two basic power centers. With no ambitions of his own, Tikhonov appeared to act as the mediator and the reconciling force within the Politburo. His retirement probably would have changed the existing power balance.

In a sense Tikhonov's position epitomized the situation in the Soviet leadership in 1984 and its probable future evolution. The balance of power within the Soviet leadership was extremely fluid. The retirement or death of any major figure or any new appointment to a major position would change the situation considerably. The Politburo's restraint in deciding on any important personnel change in 1984 is explained precisely by the fear of such a change. In due course such a change did come.

7

Gorbachev in Power

I was in Moscow for two weeks just before Chernenko's death. The mood was one of gloom, frustration, impatience, and embarrassment—gloom about the country's huge problems, frustration with the inactivity of those who were supposed to lead, impatience with old guard leaders, and the fear that once again they would be able to prolong their dominance despite their inability to innovate. It was the embarrassment of a great power that was for all practical purposes leaderless. The embarrassment reached its apex in the macabre attempt to prop up on television what everybody knew was a living corpse, President Chernenko.

Beneath this grim mood, however, there was also hope that soon there would be a new leader, and that he would be Mikhail Gorbachev. People were so eager to believe that Gorbachev would really be new that during Chernenko's year in power a minicult of personality had formed in Moscow around him—a most unusual development with regard to a Soviet leader before his rise to the top position.

After Gorbachev's election this minicult intensified and spread in an unparalleled way. The mood within the Moscow Party establishment, and among Party aides and experts, can simply be described as exhilaration. As one Soviet official expressed it: "I don't remember any time but the early 1960s when discussion [only among Party activists, of course] was so free and so creative." The nightmare of the last several years has disappeared. Just how realistic is this new mood of hope and expectation is another question. In any case, for a Sovietologist who has been forced to follow the nonevents of the past several years, the analysis of Soviet policy is once again a fascinating enterprise—and more particularly, the question of how long it will take before the present "high" of the elite is replaced by preoccupation with the more mundane and refractory aspects of Soviet life.

The election of Gorbachev as general secretary occurred with notable speed—less than four and a half hours after the announcement of Chernenko's death. The funeral proceedings were hasty, and the eulogies for the old leader perfunctory. It was as if the leadership, the Party, and the country wanted to bury with Chernenko their memories of the unhappy year of his stewardship. As we are learning only now, in February 1985, when Chernenko was already dying, the old guard in the persons of Gromyko and Grishin made its last stand against Gorbachev. The alternative candidate they unsuccessfully touted for the general secretaryship (reportedly with support from a young Party secretary, Vladimir Dolgikh) was another "young Turk," the secretary of the Central Committee for military-industrial affairs, Grigorii Romanov. Gromyko and Grishin apparently believed that they would be able to manipulate Romanov, and that, to the contrary, Gorbachev's rise to the top leadership would mean the end of their days in power.

With the selection of Gorbachev, it was predictable that the fragmentation of power at the top would rather quickly come to an end (though the power struggle may continue for some time to come). Gorbachev is not a transitional leader. He will be in place for years. It may not be so important, as is usually stressed in the West, that he belongs to a new, post-Stalin generation of leaders. What is really meaningful is that Russia again will have a continuity of leadership at the top, with a vigorous and probably strong man at its apex. Moreover, the hope of the people in Moscow that Gorbachev would take over where Andropov, rather than Chernenko, left off seems likely to be realized. (It is worth noting that shortly after Gorbachev's succession a highly laudatory documentary film about Andropov was shown in the Soviet Union.) At a time when the need for change and for breaking the deadly inertia is widely recognized in the Soviet Union, the new leader will be pushed toward innovative policies by his own predilections, by the imperatives of maximizing his power, and by the "public opinion" of Soviet elites.

The western media had a field day with Gorbachev's appointment. Their infatuation with him is easily explainable. In comparison with his aged, ailing, and (except for Andropov) unsophisticated predecessors, this normal man acquires the status of a superman, a giant who will stand up to Reagan and will seek to push and pull the Soviet Union fully into the modern era. Nonetheless, it must be said that even in his own right Gorbachev seems suave, witty, and vigorous. There can be little doubt that his succession carries a potential for fundamental change. The leader of one leading industrial democracy told me that "Gorbachev, in all probability, will be regarded by future historians as one of

the major reformers in Russian and Soviet history." In Moscow itself,
.many members of the elite are convinced that Gorbachev not only will
be a strong leader, but will systematically transform the Soviet economic
system.

What is the life story of this man who has become the focus of so
many hopes and expectations?

An ethnic Russian by origin, Gorbachev was born on March 2, 1931,
in the southern province of Stavropol. His parents were peasants who
lived in a village only a few miles away from the place where Andropov
had been born seventeen years earlier. While still at secondary school he
started to work at the local machine tractor station, which supplied the
surrounding collective farms with agricultural machinery and implements and the personnel to operate them. At that time he also became a
member of the Komsomol. After high school he went to study law at
Moscow State University, where he became a Communist Party member
in 1952. After his graduation from the law faculty in 1955, he returned to
Stavropol and served there in various political positions in the Komsomol and the Party without interruption for twenty-three years. In 1978
he was transferred to Moscow and obtained his first national office as
secretary of the Central Committee of the Communist Party in charge of
agriculture. In 1979, while still a Central Committee secretary, he was
selected as an alternate member, and in 1980 as a full member of the
Politburo.

The Western press often presents Gorbachev as a Soviet lawyer. But
he has never spent one single day of his life practicing law. (It should
also be kept in mind that he embarked upon his university legal studies
at a time when Stalin was still in power and the law was not exactly a
prestigious pursuit.) Neither is Gorbachev a professional agricultural
economist. He graduated, while already a political leader, from the local
correspondence institute of agricultural economics. Gorbachev was and
is, first and foremost, a professional Party politician and an organization
man.

While a student at Moscow University, he became the secretary of his
faculty's Komsomol. From 1955 until his promotion to Moscow in 1978,
he occupied sequentially the following political-organizational positions:
first secretary of the Stavropol city committee of the Komsomol; section
head, second secretary, and then first secretary of the Stavropol Provincial Committee of the Komsomol; Party chief of Stavropol provincial
collective and state farm management (1962); section head, secretary,
then second secretary of the Stavropol province Party committee (1963);
first secretary of the provincial Party committee (1970). In 1971 he was
elected a full member of the Party's Central Committee.

An interesting evaluation of Gorbachev was published in the West by the Italian communist newspaper *L'Unità* (April 9, 1985). It was written by a man who, far from having incentives to praise a Soviet leader, has every reason to be critical. Zdenek Mlynar was a secretary of the Communist Party of Czechoslovakia in 1968 and a close associate of Alexander Dubček, the Czech leader whose reformist regime led to the Soviet invasion of that year. Mlynar is at present an émigré in Austria. In the 1950s, he had been a fellow student and friend of Gorbachev at Moscow State University. He also visited Gorbachev in Stavropol in 1967. His opinion of Gorbachev as a man and politician is certainly positive:

I do not believe that he would be a man for whom politics and power might have become ends in themselves. He has never been a cynic; he was by character a reformer who considered politics to be the means and the people's needs to be the objective. What importance that may have in the function that he holds today is a complicated question, and anyway an open question. . . .

Gorbachev the student doubted that men were to be divided solely into partisans of a given line and criminals. He knew that there can exist, moreover, opponents, critics, reformers, who are not criminals for that reason, and that this can concern even socialists and communists. . . .

Gorbachev the student was not only very intelligent and gifted, he was an open man, whose intelligence never carried over into arrogance, who knew how to and wanted to listen to the voice of his interlocutor. Loyal and personally honest, he earned an informal, spontaneous authority. Not that he was not sure of his own business, certainly. He had the self-awareness of a man who knows that all that he has is due to his own efforts, his own talents, his own diligence, and nothing by virtue of protection or social origin. One must believe that such an awareness would have grown, would have been consolidated with the years. All those who have occasion to have Gorbachev as a political partner or opponent will certainly note it. . . .

Gorbachev did not regret the fall of Khrushchev. He did not consider that the event signified a return to the past. He evaluated the deposed leader above all according to the criteria of internal politics. He considered rather harmful his repeated interventions, generally not well thought out and often completely subjective, in the field of economic management (and particularly in agriculture), let alone in the institutional structures of the Soviet system. His principal accusation against Khrushchev was that, in reality, he had preserved the old method of arbitrary interventions from the center into the life of the whole country. Khrushchev's attempts at decentralization themselves took the form of bureaucratic interventions and command authority that passed from the center over the heads and will of "those who are below," without any regard for their opinions. Khrushchev, in conclusion, had put in motion in a unilateral manner a campaign directed from the center and supported by his own subjective solutions, which were handed out as a panacea, as the only possible way of deciding. . . .

From Brezhnev he expected greater autonomy and responsibility for the "lower" leaders, in the republics and in the individual regions. . . .

A certain share of the credit for Gorbachev's successes in Stavropol belongs, moreover, to his wife, Raisa. Their marriage goes back to their university years: Raisa Tutorenko studied in the philosophy faculty and lived in our dormitory. In London, recently, she shocked the journalists because she didn't fit their image of a Soviet bureaucrat's wife. And how could she have? She was the initiator of the elementary sociological research in the *kolkhozy* which certainly contributed to the changes adopted in the Stavropol region.

According to Italian press reports, "On his recent visit to Moscow Italian Prime Minister Bettino Craxi told Gorbachev that he had read a most interesting article about him written by an old friend of his, Zdenek Mlynar from Prague. 'Oh, Zdenek?' Gorbachev replied, hastening to ask whether the article dealt kindly with him. 'Very much so,' Craxi answered, prompting the following amused comment: 'A Prague Spring intellectual issuing a very positive verdict on me could cause some tongues to wag.' "*

Gorbachev's career until his transfer to Moscow was quite different from that of an old-guard Soviet apparatchik. Far from being broad and varied, it was both geographically and functionally quite narrow. His career pattern was, however, typical of the high Party functionaries of his generation in its bureaucratic gradualism and specialization. According to various sources, Gorbachev's performance as first secretary in Stavropol was very credible, some even say outstanding, in terms of fulfilling agricultural plans and innovation in its managerial style. This does not, however, seem enough to explain his transfer to Moscow and promotion in 1978. It is quite possible that personal qualities such as intelligence or notable organizational talents helped elevate him from among the many to join the few. But when all is said and done, he certainly needed, and had, high-ranking patrons in Moscow.

Over the course of Gorbachev's career, the names of three powerful Soviet politicians clearly stand out: Fyodor Kulakov, Mikhail Suslov, and Yuri Andropov. Kulakov was the Party's first secretary of the Stavropol province from June 1960 until 1964. He was Gorbachev's superior, and Gorbachev's crucial promotion to the provincial level of the Party apparatus (as head of the organizational department) occurred under him. In 1964 Kulakov was brought to Moscow and in 1965 he was promoted to the position of Party secretary responsible for agriculture. In 1971 he became a member of the Politburo (and was considered a

---

* Foreign Broadcast Information Service, *Daily Report: Soviet Union,* July 2, 1985, p. 87.

major prospect to succeed Brezhnev). His respect for Gorbachev and interest in his protégé's career were well known in Party circles.

The second patron, Mikhail Suslov, was a member of the Politburo from 1955 and the chief Soviet ideologist in the Brezhnev era. His connections with Stavropol province were close. From 1939 until late 1944 Suslov was the Party boss in Stavropol, supervising during the war the partisan movement in this province. Suslov visited Stavropol regularly and was well acquainted with Gorbachev.

In July 1978 Kulakov suddenly died, and the post of Central Committee secretary for agriculture became vacant. In November of that year Gorbachev was promoted to the post. He certainly had Suslov's support, and would seem also at this point to have entered the circle of Yuri Andropov. The first clear notice of Andropov's connection with Gorbachev came in September 1978. On their way to Baku, the capital of Azerbaidzhan, Brezhnev and Chernenko stopped in Stavropol province and met Andropov, who was accompanied by Gorbachev. (Andropov was in Stavropol to undergo treatment at the Mineralnye Vody spa.) In January 1982, Suslov died. From that time on, Gorbachev was clearly Andropov's ranking protégé. There is not the slightest doubt that when Andropov became general secretary in November 1982, and throughout his short rule, he regarded Gorbachev as his successor.

What Gorbachev had learned before his transfer to Moscow, at the age of forty-eight, about foreign affairs, let alone military matters, must have been acquired by self-education. This is not an easy job for an overworked provincial Party official, especially given the Soviet Union's scarcity of serious source materials from which to learn. (It should be mentioned, however, that during the 1970s, before his transfer to Moscow, he headed Party delegations to Belgium, West Germany, and France.) The process of participating in the work of the Politburo, and the access to data and analysis available to its members, must have been exhilarating and broadening experiences for Gorbachev.

His career was still crucially linked to the chronically unhappy (and politically dangerous for its supervisors) state of Soviet agriculture. Agriculture performed badly during the years when Gorbachev was responsible for it. Yet his stature was not on this account diminished. This again suggests a very powerful patron, or the judgment of the top leaders that he did everything he could under difficult circumstances, or both.

By early 1982 he had earned a reputation among his colleagues in the Party elite for high intelligence, considerable organizational abilities, political acumen, and a talent for survival. He started to be looked upon as one of the young men of the future.

When, in the fall of 1984, Chernenko became unable to work full-time or systematically, and then disappeared altogether from the public and

Party eyes, Gorbachev became in fact if not in title the second secretary of the Central Committee. He routinely chaired meetings of the Secretariat and he organized the work of the other secretaries during Chernenko's absence.

Chernenko's patronage proved decisive. He established important precedents in the early stages of his illness by opening the meetings of the Politburo and then turning over the chair to Gorbachev—against the wishes of old-guard figures like Gromyko, Tikhonov, and Grishin. There is evidence that in the last few months of Chernenko's life, Gorbachev became in fact, if not in title, chairman of the Politburo. There is also reason to believe that Gorbachev chaired the meetings of the military council, the highest Party-military body, which prepares decisions on security matters for the Politburo's approval.

Defense Minister Ustinov may have been a crucial actor in the succession drama, but little is known about his view of Gorbachev. There were rumors in Moscow after Ustinov's death that he had thrown his support to Gorbachev, both because he was an Andropov loyalist and because he became friendly with Gorbachev in the few months before his death. (Ustinov knew he had a fatal cancer.) There are also clues that after Ustinov's death it was not the Party secretary in charge of military industry, Grigorii Romanov, who became responsible in the Politburo for military affairs, but Gorbachev, in his capacity as *de facto* chairman of the military council.

After Gorbachev became general secretary, his first task was to consolidate his power quickly. The long period of leaderlessness, the emergency nature of the domestic and international problems, the wishes of the elite and of the Party activists argued in favor of bold steps. The position of general secretary is of strategic importance. When occupied by someone with Gorbachev's youth and tactical skill and the expectation that he will be in office for many years, we might anticipate a rush of other state and Party officials to proclaim their loyalty and their support.

But imposing titles provide in the long run only the potential for great power; the opportunistic new loyalists who will flock to his standard give Gorbachev only the appearance of dominance. To establish his ascendancy firmly, he must create a solid political base built on personal loyalties.

He has to deal with the old guard and put an end to the fragmentation of power at the top. This will mean easing out or neutralizing the most important old guard representatives. At the same time it will necessitate bringing into positions of high- and middle-level power, capable, new, and relatively young officials who will owe their advancement to him personally and who are attuned to his ideas about change.

From the point of view of this primary task, the timing of Chernenko's death could not have been more propitious for Gorbachev. It gave him multiple opportunities to build the personal political base he needs.

One opportunity came from the shrunken size of the Politburo, which—with Chernenko's death—had fallen to ten members. This gave Gorbachev a legitimate opportunity to add people loyal to him to this most important body. He could also convene a meeting of the Central Committee, which had been delayed a number of times and was overdue. There he could present his initial policy ideas and make the necessary personnel changes at the top.

Further, the Party leadership decided some time ago to produce a new program to replace the totally utopian one adopted under Khrushchev, now embarrassing. Gorbachev automatically inherits responsibility for the development of this plan and can use it to introduce his own ideas about the Soviet Union's future.

Most important, the new Party congress of February 1986 gave Gorbachev the unparalleled chance to proclaim his long-range plans for domestic reforms to the Party and the nation and allowed him to "clean the stables," by making major personnel changes throughout the state and Party bureaucracies.

In his early months, Gorbachev made major strides in grasping his opportunities. On April 23, 1985, he convened a meeting of the Central Committee which endorsed a number of major changes in the Kremlin lineup. KGB Chairman Victor Chebrikov was upgraded from candidate to full membership of the Politburo; Central Committee secretaries Yegor Ligachev and Nikolai Ryzhkov moved directly into full membership of the Politburo, bypassing the nonvoting rung on the ladder; Marshal Sergei Sokolov, the minister of defense, came in as a candidate member of the Politburo; and Viktor Nikonov, the deputy minister of agriculture, was added to the ranks of the Secretariat. None of these new men had any discernible tie with the Brezhnev-Chernenko machine; most of them were directly linked with Andropov. Also of major importance was what did not happen at the meeting: Marshal Sokolov was not elected a full member of the Politburo, leaving this body without a military representative; Vladimir Dolgikh, the relatively young Central Committee secretary in charge of energy policy and a candidate member of the Politburo, was also bypassed in promotions to full Politburo membership.

In July it was decided that Andrei Gromyko, while still retaining his full membership in the Politburo, would relinquish his position as first deputy prime minister and foreign minister and serve instead as chairman of the Supreme Soviet. The Party boss of Georgia, Eduard Shevardnadze, was promoted to full Politburo membership and foreign minister. Grigorii Romanov was removed from all his leadership positions. Boris Yeltsin, the Party leader of Sverdlovsk, and Lev Zaikov, the Party chief of Leningrad, were transferred to Moscow and appointed secretaries of the Central Committee.

With these changes in the top Soviet leadership Gorbachev has most of his men in place in the Central Committee apparatus. Ryzhkov, an Andropov appointee and a close friend of Gorbachev, was the secretary with overall responsibility for economic affairs, particularly for designing the strategies of economic reforms. Ligachev, also an Andropov appointee, is in charge of party organizational affairs and in control of the *nomenklatura*. A Gorbachev appointee, Viktor Nikonov, oversees agriculture. Yeltsin and Zaikov, Gorbachev's appointees, are in charge of investments and of military industry and technology, respectively. One has a strong impression that Gorbachev wants to upgrade the importance of the Party Secretariat, and to make of it the main instrument of his future policies.

The only man with domestic responsibilities left in the Central Committee Secretariat from the pre-Andropov era is Vladimir Dolgikh, who heads energy programs. During Chernenko's illness it was rumored that the old guard had him in mind as the alternative to Gorbachev. Be that as it may, two facts are clear: the bypassing of Dolgikh in appointing new full Politburo members, some of whom were not even candidate members, did not bode well for his future career; Dolgikh's performance in energy programs is not impressive and has been criticized sharply since Gorbachev's assumption of power.

The elimination of Romanov was also significant. He was the only member of the Politburo of the Gorbachev generation who could, and in the past probably did, challenge his power. He was a man of considerable stature, but he was disliked in the Party both when he ruled Leningrad and in Moscow. He was by all accounts an especially brutal man, known for his ostentatious style of living.

The promotion of KGB-chief Chebrikov to full membership in the Politburo confirms not only the obvious fact that he was Andropov's choice and his loyalist, but also strengthens the impression of an alliance between Gorbachev, and the Party apparatus that he represents, and Chebrikov, and his secret police and intelligence service. Since he assumed power, Gorbachev has also changed five heads of departments in the Central Committee: the crucial organizational department, and the departments of propaganda, construction, machine building, and trade.

Gorbachev's next objective was control of the Council of Ministers, and in particular its Presidium. Although his domination here is not as complete as in the central Party apparatus, it is growing at a rapid pace.

Thus far, in the post-Brezhnev period overall, about 20 percent of the ministers and committee chairmen attached to the Council of Ministers have been purged, and in most cases replaced by their younger deputies. By August 1985 Gorbachev had removed two members of the Presidium and nine more ministers, similarly replacing them for the most part with their younger deputies.

The major change, however, occurred in the fall of 1985. The eighty-year-old Tikhonov retired from both his Politburo post and his position as Prime Minister. He was replaced by Gorbachev's closest associate, the Politburo and Secretariat member Nikolai Ryzhkov.

At the same time, Gorbachev's attention turned to the usually very conservative leadership of the State Planning Commission (Gosplan), a locus of power indispensable to the implementation of his reform plans. The two first deputy chairmen of Gosplan, the relatively young Voronin and Maslyukov, are Gorbachev allies. But the chairman, seventy-four-year-old Nikolai Baibakov—who had occupied high positions in state economic administration since 1940, and had been chief of Gosplan for twenty years—was forced to retire. He was replaced by Ryzhkov's close associate, the fifty-six-year-old Nikolai Talyzin, who was simultaneously made First Deputy Prime Minister. (Talyzin was previously Deputy Prime Minister in charge of economic relations with Eastern Europe.)

It is not certain whether Gorbachev views the other First Deputy Prime Minister, Geidar Aliyev, as his loyalist, or as the right man for the post he now holds. He was appointed by Andropov—under whom he had once served in Azerbaidzhan as the local KGB chief—to be his watchdog within the Presidium. During Chernenko's year in office, however, it was rumored that he was fence-sitting and not helping Gorbachev in his rise to power. What can be ascertained is that since Chernenko's death he has kept, or been forced to keep, a rather low profile. His major responsibility now is the supervision of transportation. He is not a technocrat like Ryzhkov and Talyzin, and it is reported in Moscow that the new Prime Minister dislikes him personally. Or perhaps Ryzhkov simply doesn't want a former KGB chief looking over his shoulder.

Changes in the most important Moscow-based institutions of the party and government are, however, not sufficient fully to cement Gorbachev's power or to give his likely reform program a fair chance. From this point of view, the most important segment of the Party apparatus is that composed of the first secretaries of the fourteen republics and 156 provincial organizations. Most are members of the Central Committee, supervise and coordinate the activities of all the Party and state institutions in their administrative regions, and exercise real power outside of Moscow. More than twenty provincial first secretaries had already been changed under Andropov and Chernenko. In 1985 twenty-two more first secretaries were appointed. Gorbachev has to come to the congress with a largely new republican and provincial team. In the reality of Soviet politics, a Party congress does not make personnel changes but rather ratifies and legitimizes the hiring and firing of high- and upper-middle officials already decided on by the Politburo and Central Committee Secretariat.

The changes wrought in the Party's high command are clearly far-reaching. They ensure Gorbachev against major opposition and put him firmly in charge. Half of the current Politburo members are strong Gorbachev loyalists. More important, among the Moscow-based members, who hold the key executive positions in the central Party and government, Gorbachev has a clear majority. His domination of the Central Committee Secretariat is absolute. Aside from Dolgikh, the only two other members who are not explicitly Gorbachev's men are a relic of the Komintern (the prewar Communist International), Boris Ponomarev, and Konstantin Rusakov, who is in charge of the satellite countries. Both will certainly retire soon.

The changes in the top Party institutions and provincial personnel bring us back to the question of the political orientation of the younger elites. Knowledge of the mood, predispositions, and orientation of the young successors among the elites is of great importance in the evaluation of the mood in the establishment at the present and in the future.

During the late seventies and the eighties, Western Sovietologists have been trying to draw a profile of the new generation of leaders on the basis of very limited evidence. Our contacts have been infrequent and accidental, our knowledge of their predispositions scanty, our evaluation of their political views attained through intermediary sources only tentative. Lately, however, the information available about their instincts and their views has increased dramatically. The picture that emerges of the younger leaders in the Party apparatus, those who are acquiring positions on the republican, provincial, and district levels, is only partly reassuring to a Western observer.

These new leaders seem to be less ideological and more interested in efficiency in domestic policies. They believe that the economic system should be improved by reforms that will stress increased managerial rights, greater efficiency, and technological progress, more rational methods of planning, and the use of pricing and cost-effectiveness considerations. But they do not believe in changing the fundamental principles of the system. They seem to think that a thorough overhaul of the system with its existing structures, conducted by new Party and state managers, will exploit enormous reserves of productivity that were left fallow by the old, tired, and complacent leadership. The primary requirement they believe is discipline. They feel that in the long run partial reforms and enforced demands for greater work discipline and greater responsibility of managers of basic production and service units will produce an upsurge in economic growth. In this respect they are in accord with Andropov's economic reform activity and the present program of improvement in economic performance advocated by Gorbachev.

The instincts and preferences of the new generation must also be considered in regard to the international situation. On foreign policy, various examples, incidents, and reports lead to the conclusion that the new generation is nationalistic and hard-line. There are convincing reports that in the fall of 1983, in the wake of the deployment of American missiles in Western Europe, the office of the general secretary received hundreds of letters from local Party leaders that overwhelmingly stressed the same theme: the fatherland is in danger; one should not be too afraid of the Americans; this is not a time for reforms but for an all-out mobilization of resources to counteract the American challenge under the slogans of Soviet and Russian patriotism. Those letters could, of course, have been staged. But even if staged they might well express generally held views. One should remember that these are also the people who gave a standing ovation when Gorbachev mentioned Stalin's name in his speech at the May 1985 celebration marking the fortieth anniversary of the victory in World War II. While all the evidence is not yet in, it may well be that the combination of support for partial economic reforms, harsh domestic discipline, and a nationalistic, ambitious, and hard-line foreign policy represents the future orientation of the Soviet Union if this segment of the younger provincial apparat has its way.

It should also be mentioned that an unsettled international situation makes it immensely difficult to pursue, not only a relaxed internal line with regard to culture and restrictions on everyday life, but also radical socioeconomic reform policies. It redirects the attention of the leadership from domestic to foreign and defense policies; it creates a siege mentality among the population and it breeds additional intolerance towards moderation and innovation; it requires increased mobilization for military expenditures, which absorb economic reserve resources necessary for reforms; it provides, finally, foreign scapegoats for economic failures and thus obviates the urgency of aiming at economic improvements through reforms. In other words, in the Soviet Union, hard international times almost always produce hard domestic lines.

Our preoccupation with the successor generation should not blind us, however, to the more important dimension of Soviet politics—the views, inclinations, and personal character of the leader and his narrow circle of associates. After all, Khrushchev and Brezhnev belonged to the same political generation, yet the difference between them was enormous. The question of the personality of the leader, his style and preferences, is absolutely central to policy. A leader will have a certain style, a certain method of making decisions, and a certain set of preferences. Often he is ambitious to achieve his goals if only for the sake of history. While the process of policy-making does set certain limits on what is possible, it is the leader who decides how to work within those bounds. Therefore, while the general impression is that Gorbachev is strong-willed and a reformer, it is still too early to be certain how far he and his closest associates want to move in changing Soviet structures and policies.

It is not surprising that Gorbachev started his rule in a way similar to that of his mentor, Andropov. He declared an open season against workers who do not come to work, managers who falsify reports, storekeepers who steal, officials who are incompetent or corrupt. In contrast to the ouster of officials under Andropov and Chernenko, very many of those dismissed by Gorbachev are not benignly retired with honor, but fired for publicly announced reasons such as corruption, irresponsibility, incompetence, and so on.

Yet so far Gorbachev's major wrath has been directed against alcoholism. Very strong coercive and punitive measures have been announced against drunkenness, and especially alcohol consumption on the job, while the price of vodka has been drastically increased. The sale of alcoholic beverages in restaurants, bars, and stores has been ordered to start not earlier than 2 p.m. One of the first results of this partial prohibition was the disappearance from the stores of toilet water, the old Russian substitute for vodka. The element of humor in this anti-vodka campaign is being provided by the pharmacies, which have decided to sell alcohol-based medications only after 2 p.m.

This campaign is probably one of the most unpopular in Soviet history. It is especially evident within the establishment, at official parties and banquets. Banquets without substantial quantities of vodka mean that Gorbachev has scored yet another first in post-Lenin Soviet history. It would be miraculous, however, if his campaign had a lasting impact. It may already be too late to change this generation of workers' dislike of work and addiction to intemperate drinking. Such a change would require a combination of many social policies, such as greater incentives to work, a greater availability of consumer goods, better facilities for leisure time, better housing, and better entertainment on television and in the movies, with less political soap opera or endless repetitions of classical plays and ballets.

Obviously the core of Gorbachev's program goes far beyond such *ad hoc* campaigns. From his statements and writings published since becoming general secretary, one can get a glimpse of the direction in which he wants to move. It is, without no doubt whatsoever, a reformist direction, expressed in sharper criticism of what exists and in more explicit and more determined proclamations of the need for change than were heard even under Andropov.

Gorbachev openly believes in the validity of what must be one of the most candid statements made by Andropov or any other Soviet leader: "We have not yet properly studied the society in which we live and work, and have not yet fully discovered the laws governing its development, particularly the economic ones."

It confirms our perception of the extent of Gorbachev's control even before Chernenko's death, that one of his most interesting speeches was delivered three months before he became general secretary, on December 3, 1984, at a conference of selected Party and state officials. Only a portion of this speech was published in *Pravda*. Reported by the Italian newspaper *La Republica* on March 27, 1985, it sounds authentic in light of Gorbachev's speeches and articles published after he became the top leader. In addition, a number of Soviet sources have confirmed its authenticity to me.

In this semisecret speech (100,000 copies distributed to the Party activists) Gorbachev started with the assertion that "There has been a failure to perceive properly the need for changes in some aspects of production relations" and to overcome "the stagnant conservatism of Soviet production relations." In Marxist-Leninist terms, this kind of statement was at least as critical on economic matters as Khrushchev's anti-Stalin speech in 1956 was on political matters.

In identifying the problems that face the country, Gorbachev spoke about a "titanic task," "an exceptionally huge and multifaceted task." What is at stake, he said, is nothing less than the "ability of the Soviet Union to enter the new millennium in a manner worthy of a great and prosperous power." "Without the hard work and complete dedication of each and every one," he warned, "it is not even possible to preserve what has been achieved." These tasks are now extremely urgent because the crisis of the last decade went beyond a mere "coincidence of unfavorable factors" to the aforementioned need to change "production relations."

Social gains "are the principal factors in society's stability." "It would be illusory," Gorbachev continued, "to believe that a person's relationship to his work can be divorced from material interests." One should have greater confidence in the people, for they "have seen a great deal and lived through a great deal." These people do not accept "simplistic answers to their questions" and perceive "acutely the hypocrisy that stems from inability or reluctance to respond to the real contradictions of social development." In answering the question of what should be done, Gorbachev provided a complete list of generalized tasks:

> In the forefront there are the radical problems, such as ways of accelerating technological and scientific research and stepping up production, the improvement of forms of socialist ownership that will guarantee a more complete bond between the direct producer and the social means of production, the activation and optimization of the system of interests in line with the prevalent common interests, the development of the scientific and practical aspects of economic planning as the chief means of implementing Party economic policies and the improvement of the entire system of distribution relations.

Gorbachev used dramatic language to describe the phase in which the country finds itself and the need to take the qualitative leap forward with "revolutionary élan," to impart a "national character" to the process of stepping up the economy, and to instill "into the social awareness," as has not yet been done, the realization that this is a transformation no less radical or substantial and no less obligatory than the initial process of industrializing the country in the 1930s. Even as he consolidates power, Gorbachev will have to operate for a long while within the context of the collective and oligarchic decision-making process established during the Brezhnev era. An activist approach to the ills of Russia will require disciplined will, political and managerial talent, consistency, and a broad vision. Gorbachev still has to demonstrate that he possesses all these qualities in the right proportions.

The words Gorbachev used to describe the socioeconomic faults of the system are very strong. His language and phraseology go beyond even the anti-Stalinist campaign of Khrushchev. In many respects they revert to the intra-party disputes of the 1920s, with their delineation of the stark choices confronting Russia. The discussions in the press among the lesser party leaders and professionals are immensely interesting and forthright in diagnosing Soviet ills, and these discussions, too, are freer and more far-reaching than anything heretofore observed in the entire post-Stalin period.

Yet what strikes an observer forcefully in all the speeches and discussions is a general failure to penetrate deeply into the underlying reasons, the ultimate causes, for the growth of social and economic difficulties to their present proportions. One is also struck, moreover, by the incongruity between the harsh and honest judgments about the sorry state of the Soviet society and economy and the relatively feeble remedial actions now being taken or being proposed.

Although official pronouncements are devoid of any evidence that the leadership contemplates a market-directed reform, many participants in the economic debate have stressed the virtues of the market mechanism with an openness not witnessed in the Soviet press since the 1960s. Yet, as Philip Hanson has concluded, the evidence is lacking "that those who favor market reform are moving into positions where they would have much direct influence on policy."*

None of the advocates of market reform has thus far been appointed as Gorbachev's advisor. Currently, the leader's top advisor on economic matters is one of the most respected and innovative of Soviet economists, Abel Aganbegyan. His official position now is Chairman of the Commission for the Study of Productive Forces under the Presidium of the USSR Academy of Sciences. Aganbegyan published recently two major articles which outline Gorbachev's economic policy for the immediate future. They confirm fully the impression that the leader's present program for economic change is quite limited in scope.

It may well be that the deepest sources of Soviet ills, which lie in the nature of the system itself, are not being disclosed in order to avoid such destabilizing effects as those produced by Khrushchev's revelations about Stalin's regime. It may well be, also, that the disparity between the assessed gravity of the socioeconomic situation and the countervailing policies so far taken or proposed may simply express Gorbachev's caution and gradualism in preparing the party for reforms to come. In this respect they might be indications of his seriousness of purpose and realism in starting slowly the process of change, in accordance with the Russian proverb: *"Tishe yedesh, dalshe budesh"*—"You will go much further if you start slowly."

What is more probable, however, is that Gorbachev and his team do not intend at all in the foreseeable future to engage in systemic changes that Western specialists and many of his own economists consider necessary to reverse the negative trend of Soviet socioeconomic development. We have therefore to look closer at Gorbachev's views about the reason for the present troubles, and especially his attitude toward the existing sociopolitical system. We have to evaluate the options provided by Gorbachev's reformatory programs. We have to examine the reformatory actions that he has already initiated. Finally, we have to identify the obstacles that he faces if his goal is a truly significant reform of the Soviet system.

The right leader in the right place at the right time can make a major difference. Gorbachev's accession could represent the reassertion of Soviet power in the world, the determination to attack the domestic mal-

---

* Radio Liberty Research, RL 291/85 September 4, 1985, p. 1.

aise and to deal more successfully with foreign and military problems. Soviet elites and, probably, large segments of the population longed for just such a reassertion during the many years of interregnum and paralysis. Now they will discover their country's capacity for dealing with the many grave problems it faces. The sooner Gorbachev consolidates his power, the more severe will be the standards by which his policies are judged.

8

The Politics of Reform
in the Soviet Union

For the rest of the 1980s, economic difficulties and the political conditions accompanying the leadership and elite successions will create
strong pressures for change in the Soviet system. The major problem for
the leadership is to find a way to impose new priorities effectively on old
structures and processes.

There are three major types of reform in the Soviet Union: policy
reforms, organizational-administrative reforms, and structural-insti-
tutional reforms. The first involves change in longstanding social or
economic policies, and its major instrument is the redistribution of resources. The second concerns changing and streamlining the decision-
making process, and its major instrument is the reorganization of
existing administrative units. The third involves changes in basic polit-
ico-economic structures, and its major instruments are the fundamental reorientation of priorities and major shifts in the power of existing
institutions.

The differentiation of these three types follows in many important respects the distinction made by political scientists and economists between changes in the system and changes of the system. Policy and
organizational-administrative reforms occur within the system. Structural reforms alter the system itself. The distinction is not always a clear
one, but in general an in-system reform seeks to improve a particular aspect of the system or to correct its shortcomings, without affecting the
basic character of the system. Such relatively marginal reforms do not
produce cumulative change. Any results they achieve gradually fade
away and in time are simply absorbed into existing structures. The process is something like administering drugs to a body that has already de-

veloped a tolerance for them; only a radically increased dosage will produce positive results.

The nature of in-system reform helps to explain why, despite the sheer number of such reforms constantly introduced in the Soviet Union over the last three decades, the economic system remains essentially unchanged. Their accumulation does not produce structural transformations. Like the elections, which occur more often in the Soviet Union than in any other country and yet do not result in democracy, these frequent reforms do not alter the economic command system.

There is one threshold that is crucial to the system and that subsumes the other structural elements. It has two characteristics: The first is reached at the decision to keep or abolish direct planning from above at the level of a factory, a mine, a store, a restaurant; the second is reached with the decision to keep the "ratchet" principle—planning growth and rewards for one year based on the level of production achieved the previous year. Direct planning of the activity of individual factories, mines, and service establishments, prepared by a superior planning organization introduces a strong element of unpredictability for the manager since somebody else plans the work of his enterprise. This kills any initiative based on intimate knowledge of local conditions, and forces the manager to fulfill the quantitative plan at any cost, even if this means sacrificing quality, costs, variety, and profit. The ratchet principle persuades the manager to prevent overfulfillment of current plans, to fight for low output plans, to falsify information to justify low plans, and to keep hidden reserves in the factory for use in the next period—all of which, as the Polish economist Janusz Zielinski noted, "means keeping actual enterprise productivity permanently below what its managers know to be possible."*

In the post-Stalin era, there has not been a single instance of the implementation of structural reform. Even such relatively far-reaching and comprehensive reforms as the one that Prime Minister Kosygin tried unsuccessfully to introduce in the late 1960s, which were known collectively as Libermanism after their author, the economist Yevsei Liberman, could by no stretch of imagination be described as structural. The distribution of economic power in the system has not shifted significantly since Stalin. Until it does change, no structural transformation of the economy will take place.

The term *radical* should be reserved for the third type of reform. However, the use of *liberalizing* and *conservative* to describe Soviet reforms is of little use. In common usage, liberalizing reform would describe a movement away from the existing system toward a greater devolution of

* Janusz Zielinski, "On System Remodelling in Poland: A Pragmatic Approach," *Soviet Studies,* Vol. 30, No. 1 (January 1978), pp. 3–37.

power. Alternatively, conservative reform would shift toward a greater concentration of power. Yet also in common and logical usage, one would employ *conservative* to describe reforms that move in the direction of a devolution of power, but do it in a limited or unconvincing way.

Another term very often used in describing Soviet economic reforms is *partial reform,* which makes sense only when applied to structural reform. The term *partial* refers to the attempt by the leadership to cross one of the thresholds of the economic system while leaving the other features more or less intact. For example, the leaders may try to change drastically the incentives for managers and workers, rewarding high quality products and low production costs. Yet at the same time they are unwilling to abolish direct quantitative planning and unable to make state prices dependent on supply and demand. In such a situation the quality and cost incentives will have almost no visible effects. In the trade-off between quantity and quality of production, the manager will still opt for the former because it is easier to attain and because his performance will still be judged primarily by his fulfillment of the quota. With regard to lower costs of production, the incentives will also not work because the manager has no control over the changing prices of his raw materials and semifinished parts. These are determined and altered by Moscow often without any clear rationale. Therefore, far from moving the system gradually towards structural changes, the partial reforms are absorbed and assimilated by the system.

The basic truth about effective radical reforms is that they cannot be made on the installment plan. An incentive structure will remain ineffective unless the price system reflects real costs and supply and demand pressures. A more realistic price system will have very limited impact on the effectiveness of production if the centralized economic administration remains intact. The bitter truth for those who want partial reforms to minimize the political dangers and the opposition of vested interests is that for the reforms to be effective they have to cut across all parts of the existing system. Thus there is considerable evidence to support Samuel Huntington's proposition that "Reforms are more difficult to perform than revolutions." It also shows the wisdom and courage of the Chinese leaders, who attacked their economic problems comprehensively, staking their future on mutually reinforcing cycles of change which will emanate from all the parts of their economy.

It is conceivable that the new leadership will initiate an economic reform leading toward market socialism, like the Hungarian New Economic Mechanism. But this is extremely unlikely. No Soviet official or economist would suggest that anything resembling the Hungarian model is applicable to the Soviet Union. The sheer size of the country and its economy, the importance of its military-industrial sector, the necessity of increasing trade and credit dependence on noncommunist nations (which has played a crucial role in the Hungarian success), the radical decline of the work ethic among the Russian working class, and the style of managerial behavior ingrained through many decades, all make the option of the Hungarian model an implausible one. Most important, however, Hungary could afford its flexible economic model because the very existence of the Soviet Union and its military might underwrote the experiment politically; that is to say, the Soviet Union acted as the guarantor that the Hungarian economic experiment would not have political consequences undesired by communist officials.

Andropov's efforts and Gorbachev's inclination to the contrary notwithstanding, it is quite likely that the Soviet economy will not break out of its Stalinist mold, at least for the rest of the decade. Large-scale reforms will certainly be tried. However, there will be no bold and rapid steps to do away with the archaic economic institutions. Both Western observers and the Soviet leaders believe that such a policy would carry a high political price domestically and internationally. Yet the question today is no longer whether the Soviet Union will engage in significant reforms or simply muddle through as it did in the last ten years. The question today is whether it will make real improvements or muddle down. Without major reforms, the slide of the Soviet economy will not be arrested, and its effectiveness will decline further.

The vested political and economic interests that oppose change are powerful and will remain so even in a period when the turnover of leadership is high and when the pressures to get the country moving again are strong. Brezhnev and his close associates opposed major reforms, as did Chernenko. Gorbachev and his close associates clearly seem to favor reforms, but even they remain apprehensive of the potential negative political repercussions. This apprehension on the part of the top leaders, however, is minor compared to the fear of the numerous officials at lower levels of authority. Even the short-lived and mild experience of Andropov's campaign for reform reaffirmed this basic truth. Middle- and low-level managers and bureaucrats did in fact sabotage, by inaction and falsified reports, the leaders' efforts and instructions to pay more attention to quality and costs and to increase labor discipline. In November 1983, Andropov, who was then recuperating from his operation, sent an angry telegram to all local managers warning them that he would not tolerate their foot-dragging. The planners and ministerial bureaucracies would foresee the decline of their powers, and managers and technocrats at lower levels have learned to live and work within the system as it now exists. One author has aptly remarked that "After sixty years of experience with the Socialist economy run by government agencies, . . . nearly everyone seems to have found ways to turn its shortcomings to individual advantage."*

Gorbachev seems to understand well the practical opposition that his reforming activities will encounter among middle-level bureaucrats. He seems ready to meet them head on and to purge anyone who stands in the way of his revitalizing Russia. At a meeting with the Leningrad Party organization on May 17, 1985, he made this amply clear: "We must, of course, give all our cadres the chance to understand the requirements of the moment at this stage and adapt themselves accordingly. But anyone who is not prepared to adapt and who, moreover, impedes the resolution of these new tasks, should get out of the way. Get out of the way and not interfere."†

The newspaper *Socialist Industry* is already reporting cases not only of opposition, but also of plain bewilderment among middle-level officials and managers. The Ministry of Instruments, which is heavily engaged in manufacturing computers and other electronics, appears to be the first to have found out about one aspect of Gorbachev's plans. It has had to begin eliminating its intermediate level of management, the industrial associations (*promyshlennye ob'edineniia*). Eight hundred officials must somehow be moved. As Thane Gustafson has calculated, if one multiplies 800 by roughly the current number of production ministries, then the total number of officials whose jobs will disappear in this single mini-purge could be about 50,000.‡

The *Socialist Industry* correspondent comments, "Although no one is objecting openly to the restructuring, I think that many don't yet believe in its inevitability." The majority of the 800 officials displaced were to be transferred to management positions. The ministry assured one and all that no one would be fired, although the article hinted that those who wished to retire would not be discouraged. One-sixth of the 800 were to be reassigned to factories.

One of the central points of the Gorbachev program is a reduction in the number of plan indicators compulsory for the ministry and its production units. The chief planner at the Ministry of Instruments states what they should be for his ministry: First, production sold in accordance with supply contracts; second, profits; third, labor productivity.

But the planner reveals that the rhetoric is racing ahead of the actual

---

* Gertrude Schroeder, "The Soviet Economy on a Treadmill of 'Reforms,' " in *Soviet Economy in a Time of Change,* Vol. I. A compendium of papers submitted to the U.S. Congress Joint Economic Committee (Washington, D.C.: Government Printing Office, 1979), p. 340.

† *Kommunist,* No. 8 (1270), May 1985, p. 32.

‡ Thane Gustafson, *Sovset' News: The Electronic Newsletter of Soviet Studies,* August 7, 1985.

changes: "We're preparing the annual plan for 1986 and the twelfth five-year plan using the old structures and the old indicators. We should be doing it under the new ones, using the smaller number of indicators. But I am not personally convinced that the number of indicators will be cut any time soon. Yet it is simply dangerous to go over to the new structure without them."

The planner describes where the opposition will come from inside his ministry: its enterprises have to follow an instruction book 200 pages long containing 208 plan indicators. Behind each indicator there lurks an official who will fight for it because his job depends on it. "No," comments the reporter, "the officials won't give up without a fight, don't imagine otherwise."

The replacement of old cadres, of incompetents, of shirkers on all administrative management levels is a major undertaking. Yet the process of replacement is proceeding rapidly and will probably, on its own terms, at least, be quite successful. One should be clear, nonetheless—and Gorbachev himself certainly understands—that even a large-scale change of personnel on all levels of administration and management will in itself have only limited impact on the way the economy is managed. The old guard can, of course, be replaced by bureaucrats who will be more energetic and eager to please the leader. Yet they themselves were brought up and trained in the old system of practical management; their experience, their socialization, their instincts, are geared to the old school.

The other and more difficult part of Gorbachev's personnel reform will be to educate the newcomers to be more truthful, more responsible, more flexible, and to display more initiative than their predecessors. One can easily predict, however, that neither persuasion nor coercion alone will achieve the desired results. Successful reeducation will require also a change in the economic environment in which managers operate: the introduction of new primary indicators of performance that will stress quality, cost control, and profit over quantity. This in turn will necessitate a virtual revolution in central planning, involving both the drastic reduction of centrally planned items imposed on the manager, and the reordering of their priority and weight; this revolution will require in its turn a monetary transformation that will reflect both the real costs and the real scarcities of raw materials, of components, and of finished products.

In sum, the basic Soviet management difficulty is not simply the attitudes and behavior of the old managers—their lying and stealing, their general lack of concern with the quality of what they produce. These attitudes and behavior result from the pressure generated by the system they work under; and unless the system is drastically changed, the old managers' replacements—even though they will be on the whole better educated, better motivated, and more ambitious—will inexorably be forced into the mold of their predecessors.

At the higher bureaucratic echelons, moreover, prodding from above will push the new administrator or Party official to adopt the desired style of leadership, but his deeply ingrained instincts will push him constantly in the opposite direction. I am reminded in this connection of a conversation I recently had in China with a Shanghai party leader. "Whenever," he told me, "I have trouble with supervising the economic managers, whenever I am infuriated with their mistakes, my instinct cries out and tells me—centralize, centralize, centralize. I have then to repeat to myself many times what I am learning in practice, and what my guidelines from Beijing tell me, that centralization is not a help but in the long run a hindrance. I know that this is right, but the struggle between my instincts and my mind is often excruciatingly difficult." The Soviet counterparts of the Shanghai party secretary will be inevitably exposed to the same dilemma and inner struggle. In view of how much less reformist their environment is and will be in comparison to that in China, their instincts may well prove stronger than their minds.

The Party bureaucracy, and especially the central Party apparatus in Moscow, is often depicted as the main political-administrative obstacle to economic reforms. This most probably is true of the lower Party echelons. At the county or town levels they would be excluded from the administration if local factories, and collective and state farms acquired a high degree of independence. But, in the Central Committee's Secretariat there were supporters of economic reforms even before Brezhnev died. What is most important is that the top Party bureaucracy is concerned with the performance of the economy as a whole rather than with local problems. Within the system and for the system, they represent the national interest, although of course with a strong ideological coloration.

In the face of widespread and strong opposition at all levels, reform, if it is to be even modestly successful, will require energetic initiative and a constant push from above, especially from the new general secretary. An oligarchic leadership, which by its very nature has to operate through bargaining and compromise, is ill suited for initiating and executing major reforms of structures, procedures, or even policies. Thus, the future of reform depends to a large degree on the inclinations of the top leader, and on his ability to accumulate power and to pursue and realize those inclinations.

Even if Gorbachev becomes convinced of the necessity of radical reform—and this is still a large assumption—it will be some time before he can consolidate his power sufficiently to make serious efforts in this direction. Moreover, given the powerful forces allied against radical reform, it is unlikely that any leader can consolidate his strength while openly promoting fundamental change. And once he achieves a position of unchallenged strength, it is perhaps unlikely that he will reverse his previous positions and wholeheartedly pursue such a program. In short, a set of complex and contradictory political conditions must be fulfilled before the leadership can implement serious reform.

For Gorbachev to be a dedicated reformer, it is not enough that he be liked, admired, and supported by his comrades in the Party's top echelon. In the present situation he can accumulate adulation and support quite easily, since his policies of change are still in a modest beginning phase. If, however, he should later seek more fundamental reform goals, the support of some of his comrades may evaporate. He may then find it necessary to be ruthless and feared by his colleagues and subordinates— a basic truth about reformers both in tsarist Russia and in the Soviet Union. In his nominating speech for Gorbachev, Andrei Gromyko remarked, clearly as a token of respect, that the nominee had an "iron will" behind his amiable exterior. At another point he attested to Gorbachev's alleged "steel grip." Both will be indispensable if he is to bring about serious reform.

The contradictory nature of the political requirements in this situation may explain Gorbachev's present tactics. These consist of a sharp and far-reaching critique of Soviet performance, and the granting of freedom for professional discussion of economic mismanagement, combined with apparent avoidance of either an analysis linking these shortcomings to structural characteristics of the system or practical actions that would move beyond marginal changes.

The critique of Soviet shortcomings combined with major personnel changes prepare the ground psychologically and politically for future reforms. They provide the rationale for such reforms and serve to rapidly consolidate Gorbachev's power base. The actions being taken to improve economic performance and social behavior build support for Gorbachev on the one hand, while on the other, these actions are too marginal in nature to stimulate the formation of an anti-reformist coalition. But all of this is based on a big assumption—that Gorbachev and his close associates are in the final analysis convinced of the need for truly fundamental reform. The limited evidence that will be presented later casts doubts on the validity of this assumption. Rather than being a prelude to more sweeping change, Gorbachev's present tactics quite likely reflect a basic intention to avoid such fundamental reform.

The growing dependence of the leadership and elites on the expertise and advice of professional groups also has important implications for the fate of radical reform. Stephen Cohen is probably right when he stresses that the spirit of reform and liberalism was not dead, but only dormant, under Brezhnev. Moreover, during the recent period of leadership paralysis, and its attendant economic stagnation, the desire for change, even if ill defined and vague as regarded specifics, became stronger and more widespread.

It is a well-known phenomenon in politics that a party out of power becomes radicalized by its isolation from, and lack of responsibility for, national decision-making. Very often, however, when the party returns to power, the weight of its responsibilities moves it inexorably back to the center. Just so, the length of the period of leadership paralysis in the Soviet Union, and the endless and unseemly delay in passing the baton to the new generation of leaders, seemed to have a radicalizing impact on younger officials: they came to adopt radical views concerning the nature of economic changes necessary in the Soviet Union. What we see now, when they are at last in power, may well be the process of their deradicalization and movement to centrist positions. Among the Soviet "intelligentsia," however, the unquestionable radicalization of expectations during the late-1970s–mid-1980s period shows no sign of giving way to a centrist stance now that the young leadership has taken over. It is among the professional groups, especially the economists, that the greatest support for basic reform continues to be found.*

That leading Soviet economists are well aware both of the depth of the troubles that beset the economy and of the social and political roots of these troubles, is attested to by a remarkable document that surfaced in the West in the summer of 1983.† Written by a leading Soviet sociologist and economist, Tatyana Zaslavskaya, a section chief in the Institute of Economics and Organization of Industrial Production of the Soviet Academy of Science in Novosibirsk (a very large research center), this paper was presented at a symposium in Moscow in April 1983. It confirmed most of the essential points being made by Western students of the contemporary Soviet economy, in identifying obstacles to a more effective economic performance. Most revealing, original, and never seen in the Soviet Union in published form, was the author's stress on the catastrophic degeneration of the work ethic among the work force as a key obstacle to reforms that could improve the economic situation.

In light of their significant advisory capacity, professional groups, and especially economists, could have substantial influence if they could unite and address the leadership in a single voice on the need for real

---

* Stephen F. Cohen, "The Friends and Foes of Change: Reformers and Conservatism in the Soviet Union," in Stephen F. Cohen, Alexander Rabinowitch, and Robert Sharlet, eds. *The Soviet Union Since Stalin* (Bloomington: Indiana University Press, 1980), pp. 18–19.

†The Novosibirsk Report, in *Survey*, Vol. 28, No. 1 (120) (Spring 1984), pp. 88–108.

change. In Hungary, the unity of the economics profession was critical to the implementation of reform. But in the Soviet Union these professional groups are fragile, fragmented by various interests, and divided on the kinds of reform needed. This situation neutralizes their potential to influence change and enables the factions in the leadership and the bureaucracy to manipulate them with ease. If the professional groups continue to speak with conflicting voices, both proponents and opponents of radical reform within the leadership will be able to find, or to mobilize, experts for their respective positions.

In addition to this opposition, the economic and technical difficulties of radical change are formidable. Reform would certainly involve a temporary decline in production and in productivity, would significantly increase the need for real incentives, and would entail the enormous task of reeducating the labor force and management. The difficult transition period from old to new would require large reserves of capital and consumer goods. In the 1980s, however, the economy will be stretched to its outer limits, planning will be especially taut, and reserves will be dwindling. The leadership thus faces an acute dilemma: the shortcomings of the system are creating enormous pressures for a radical change, but successful reform requires previous performance to subsidize the transition. The political risks of attempting a radical reform during a period of declining economic growth must seem grave to the leadership, probably graver than the consequences of living with a somewhat improved old system and its shortcomings.

The leaders also recognize that major economic reform would require both a thoroughgoing change of the pricing system and a major readjustment in the workers' position in the industrial marketplace. Prices of consumer goods, particularly of food and basic items, are kept low through immense state subsidies. Subsidies to agriculture increased from about 17 billion rubles in 1970 to more than 37 billion in 1980, accounting for about 50 percent of the national income produced in agriculture. They include not only artificially low urban prices for agricultural products but also for manufactured goods sold to agriculture, such as fertilizers and machinery. For example, in 1978 the average state procurement price for meat and poultry was about 3,088 rubles per ton, and the average state retail price was 1,730 rubles. Yet this costly subsidy policy did not have the expected positive impact on labor productivity in agriculture.

Any thorough and far-reaching reform would have to abandon artificial prices for prices determined by real costs and, at least in part, by the levels of supply and demand—or by a rationing system. Here the leadership cannot help being sensitive to the Polish experience, where price increases of basic commodities repeatedly led to labor unrest—in 1970, in 1976, and finally to the major upheaval in the summer of 1980, when the workers' union Solidarity was formed.

Radical reform would also require a dramatic change in the workers' habits and in the system of rewards: They would have to work better to receive more in return. Moreover, as we have already seen, it appears that not only would the worker not be paid more in the initial stages of a radical reform, he would also be burdened with an austerity program, higher prices designed to bring basic commodity prices in line with their costs and availability. Furthermore, reform would eventually impinge on job security, the most important achievement under communism. A small-scale experiment—in which the optimal size of the work force is determined by the productivity of labor—could be introduced with relative ease, for instance, in a factory in Shchekino, a showplace of industrial efficiency. But its application throughout the Soviet Union would cause large-scale displacement.

Initially, then, a thoroughgoing reform would have a high cost for the workers and might well produce combustible social and political pressures. It is important to remember that the situation most conducive to popular turmoil and revolutionary upheaval is not one associated with a high level of popular deprivation, but rather one that results from the decline (or stagnation) of a working-class standard of living after a period of visible improvement. The austerity of radical reform would bring such conditions, and the leaders are probably aware of this.

Any discussion of reform must also consider the relationship between Moscow and Eastern Europe. Frequently, Eastern Europe is regarded as the funnel that channels Western influence and reformist tendencies to the Soviet Union. That this view has some merit is clear from the attention the Soviets currently devote to East German managerial experience and the market mechanism in Hungary. In most instances, however, the very existence of an Eastern European empire is a thoroughly conservative influence on the domestic situation in the USSR. The Soviets' total commitment to the maintenance of their empire, coupled with the region's potential instability, exerts a powerful pull on internal policy. The more restless Eastern Europe becomes, the more conservative this influence will be.

When contemplating a thorough or even modest reform, the leaders must therefore consider its impact upon a potentially unstable area. They will recognize that change in the Soviet Union can only encourage the forces of liberalism in Eastern Europe. Therefore, only an enormously confident—or desperate—Soviet leadership will initiate internal policies that would be certain to challenge its external holdings. Since the situation in Eastern Europe for the rest of the 1980s will be very difficult economically, explosive socially, and precarious politically, it will have an antireformist influence on the leadership.

The multiethnic and nominally federal character of the Soviet system also exerts a conservative influence on reformist tendencies. Undoubtedly, a decentralizing reform would diffuse economic authority. If the rewards were high enough, the leadership might tolerate such a diffusion among the Russian provinces, but it would be much more reluctant to introduce similar changes among non-Russians. During the Brezhnev period, the leadership was able to achieve relatively peaceful relations between the Russians and non-Russians through a shrewd carrot-and-stick policy. Nevertheless, the balance of these relations remains precarious. A fundamental economic reform could—and probably would— upset the balance. Indeed, the leaders may well believe that radical economic reform would necessarily entail a thorough restructuring of the relationships among the nationalities. This is a price they are probably unwilling to pay.

The workings of the present arrangement are predictable even in smallest details, and it has become rigid with the passing of generations. It was shaped by a political elite, but it in turn has shaped the nature and major characteristics of the political system. In another place I wrote:

> The key characteristic of the Stalinist model of economic growth was its lack of *economic* self-generating, self-regulating, and adjusting features. To run at all, let alone to perform well, it required an enormous political edifice to provide the decision making, and the push, the regulation, supervision, and coordination. *In fact, the Soviet political system was developed largely to run the economy and was shaped by running the economy* in line with the chosen growth strategy.*

When one considers the task of radical reform in the light of a political process, three aspects appear as central: the explanation for the poor results of the existing arrangements; the setting of the agenda prior to the decision-making; the deliberation of options open to the decision-makers.

With regard to the first aspect, what is remarkable about the Soviet Union is the trivialized explanations of the existing system's shortcomings to be heard from the leaders and elites. They now identify the shortcomings of the system in harsh words, and this itself is major progress in comparison to the past. Yet their explanations are trivial, and do not address the structural underpinnings of the problems. They do not ask whether the system is wrong, but simply what unacceptable results the system has produced. Most often the answer concerns the fallibility, incompetence, and neglect of certain people in positions of

---

* Seweryn Bialer, *Stalin's Successors: Leadership, Stability and Change in the Soviet Union* (Cambridge: Cambridge University Press, 1980), p. 19.

responsibility. There is something rather pathetic in Gorbachev's harsh, if justified, criticism of ministers and Party secretaries, coming from a man who for over thirty years was an integral part of the system and bears no less responsibility for the country's poor economic performance. (This phenomenon of blinders in explaining situations or events, incidentally, is even more pronounced in Soviet evaluations of foreign affairs. In a meeting about the invasion of Afghanistan, no one asks "Were we right in going there?" The discussion centers exclusively on the explanation of why the United States reacted to the invasion as it did. I suspect that this kind of approach is typical not only of middle-level party meetings but also at the Central Committee level and above.)

The agenda for decision-making follows logically from the evaluative steps. The most vital function of ideology lies not in *prescribing* behavior but rather in *proscribing* behavior, that is to say, in defining what should not be on the agenda of decision-making. This phenomenon, which is known as "non-decision-making," is of importance in the process of change and directly related to the question of radical reforms.

Since a thorough economic reform would constitute an overhaul of the system, it would require a basic change in work habits, and would have a significant impact on other spheres of Soviet life. One does not embark on such a serious undertaking unless one is convinced that the existing system has exhausted its potential. The old leadership and the elite did not reach this conclusion, and there is no compelling evidence that their successors have done so either.

The old elites apparently believed in the basic viability of the system they directed throughout their lives. They were realistic people who recognized many of the system's operational shortcomings and strove to improve its functioning. Nevertheless, they remained convinced that it was workable and appropriate for the Soviet Union.

Although we know much less about the attitudes of the younger leaders, it is clear that they are less patient with the deficiencies of the system. Possibly there are individuals among them who are fed up with it, but in general they appear to feel that its potential has not been exhausted. Like successors in any other country, they believe that the system is not run well, and that they will be able to do much better than the older generation. Once they are operating the system themselves, they may of course conclude that *it* is the problem after all, but by then they may well be so caught up in its day-to-day operations that they will not be able to draw back and consider broad changes. It is, in sum, difficult to place the question of the system's basic viability on the Soviet political agenda.

From numerous Gorbachev speeches and Soviet writings it is clear that the new leadership by and large knows what is wrong with the economy. Their diagnoses of the socioeconomic ills that hinder development are not much different from the analyses of Western economists over the last decade. At the same time, the conclusion is inescapable that the leadership does not locate the sources of their problems in the very nature of the system they have inherited. Eventually they assign the major share of blame for their predicament to the failure of previous leadership. From the early 1970s on, they argue, the system required urgent adjustment in the forms of planning, in the directions of socioeconomic policies, and in managerial style. But these adjustments were not made; economic management proceeded heedlessly on its old conservative path. There was no serious effort to rouse the economy from the stupor of bureaucratic inertia, and malfunctions that at the start could have been corrected relatively easily were permitted to grow to dangerous proportions.

If one takes this diagnosis at face value, the new leadership's basic belief is that the Soviet system is an intrinsically superior form of sociopolitical and economic organization that was prevented by their predecessors from realizing its true potential. The top leaders grew self-satisfied and conservative in office; the elites were not properly supervised; the middle- and low-level managers learned how to take advantage of the system for personal gain and lost their sense of responsibility to the state; the working people, without pressure or good examples from their superiors, adopted the old Russian attitudes *naplevat; vse ravno; moia khata s krayu, nichevo ne znayu* ("the hell with everything"; "nothing makes any difference"; "I'm an observer, I don't want to get involved").

Thus it is not surprising that changes in personnel and an all-out attempt to restore social discipline should become the priorities of Gorbachev and his team. The purge of the old guard is dictated as well, of course, by Gorbachev's basic need to consolidate his political power through the loyalty and support of his own appointees. In addition, however, these new appointees are central to his plans to restore health and dynamism to the society and economy. Yet Gorbachev and his closest colleagues—Ryzhkov, Ligachev, Vorotnikov, Talyzin—must be aware that personnel changes, while politically important, will not by themselves significantly improve economic performance or alter negligent and uncaring social behavior. Far from being the end, the extensive purge marks only the beginning of Gorbachev's plans for improvement. The more difficult and more important part of his plan requires education in new levels of responsibility and new styles of work. At the same time, a long-range campaign will be waged to improve social discipline by coercion, by material incentives, and by appeals to patriotic duty.

The new leadership's analysis of the causes of Soviet failures obviously dictates the relatively narrow scope of remedial actions. The

Gorbachev attitude to radical reforms can be partly deduced from a speech he made in late summer of 1985 to the secretaries for economic affairs of the Central Committees of East European parties. The three most notable themes were: an attack on reforms directed at creating market socialism; a defense of centralization of economic control; and a negative evaluation of both the Yugoslav model of socialism and the Chinese economic revolution.

Gorbachev warned his East European comrades (he is probably issuing similar warnings to his Soviet comrades) about the false glitter of market-oriented reforms and the dangers of moving towards market socialism. He acknowledged the difficult situation of the East European economies, and that on this account "Many of you see the solution to your problems in resorting to market mechanisms in place of direct planning. Some of you look at the market as a life-saver for your economies. But, comrades," he then admonished, "you should not think about life-savers but about the ship, and the ship is socialism."

Gorbachev attacked the tendency to consider economic centralization as the source of the failure of communist economies to secure continuous growth and technological progress. He argued that with regard to the important objectives of socialist development, centralization not only is necessary but in all probability has to be even strengthened. With regard to investments, he said that the mistake of the past leadership lay not in overcentralization but, to the contrary, in insufficient centralized control that left enormous capital expenditures frozen in unfinished construction. Centralization, he further maintained, is absolutely necessary in socialist pricing policies that make basic consumer supplies accessible to the working class and which constitute an important pillar of social stability. Centralization in the allocation of resources, he suggested, is also indispensable in pursuing the correct policy toward national minorities in a multiethnic state: A distribution of resources based entirely on criteria of profit would give an undue advantage to the most developed ethnic regions and would inevitably result in ethnic disharmony and discord. Finally, centralized administration and control is necessary in foreign trade, particularly in the acquisition and disposition of advanced technology. In a situation where the hard-currency resources of the socialist states are sharply limited, decisions as to what to buy and how to distribute must perforce be highly centralized.

In this same speech Gorbachev commented extensively on what he termed the "negative examples" of Yugoslavia and China (a theme which, especially in the case of China, has often appeared in the Soviet press). The market socialism of Yugoslavia was described by Gorbachev as a failing experiment on at least three counts: first, the immense inflationary pressures in Yugoslavia; second, the country's dependence on foreign trade and the export of labor, and a payment balance subject to the cyclical vicissitudes of the capitalist world market; and, third, ethnic strife within Yugoslavia, which he attributed to the lack of a centralized policy to upgrade backward regions, with the market instead being allowed to decide the ratios of development. As far as the economic revolution in China was concerned, Gorbachev's approach was very revealing about his attitude to Soviet development itself. He sees contemporary China serving as a warning about the dangers of two policy tendencies. The first is exemplified in current Chinese policies which are non-socialist: spontaneity dictates the course of economic development, and creates dangers for the survival of the Chinese socialist economy as well as the political system itself. The second concerns the policies obtaining during the Maoist period, with their neglect of economic factors, and their stress on economic autarky and international self-isolation. The thrust of Gorbachev's evaluation of the Chinese course was very clear: the fanaticism and leftist excesses of the Maoist period led to the excesses and "right wing" orientation now manifest in post-Mao policies. Gorbachev's position with regard to China was simultaneously a warning against both Stalinist inflexibility and anti-socialist deviation.

While Western analysts employ the term *reform* for the new leader's program of improving economic performance, this is not a word used by the Soviets themselves. The phrase they most often employ is "improving the economic mechanism." At present this reflects exactly the way they are thinking. They want to improve the mechanism but not to change it. A comment made by Eduard Shevardnadze during Andropov's rule when Shevardnadze was still the Party boss of Georgia provides explicit confirmation of this. "The improvement in our economic mechanism," said Shevardnadze, "will take place on the basis of the already existing mechanism."

It is only in the third dimension of decision-making, that of selection among options placed on the agenda, that one can plausibly, and in the case of Gorbachev certainly, expect a broad innovative approach. The options could cover a broad range of changes, and which options are accepted as the Party's general line can make a major difference. But the outright abandonment of the system will not be among those options. For there is no evidence whatsoever that the new leadership has a critical attitude toward the classical, that is Stalinist, economic system and the post-Stalinist political system. As a matter of fact, Gorbachev and his lieutenants are quite optimistic that the economy can be made to work well and that the political system is basically sound. Their guarded optimism is of course predicated on their belief that all the system really needs is better leadership and more effective policies.

It is also important to ascertain how leaders and elites see the prospects for the economy beyond the 1980s. Though there are indications that they recognize that the rest of the present decade will be difficult, we do not know whether they see this as a temporary situation that can be corrected in due course by a combination of their own actions and a change in the "objective circumstances." Two factors could be decisive in bringing them to an optimistic assessment: the demographic trend and Siberia. In the 1980s, the trend that has recently been bringing so few new people into the labor force will probably be reversed, providing an important reserve for the functioning of the economy. The natural richness of Siberia, probably the largest unexplored reserve of mineral resources in the world, must be a powerful influence on the leadership's evaluation of their country's future prospects. With the exploitation of Siberian wealth only just beginning, the Politiburo may believe that it will be able to tackle the task of its development on a large scale—a belief and possibility it may prove quite unwise to dismiss. Such relative optimism could only reduce the magnitude of the economic transformations that it would be willing to introduce in the 1980s.

Another serious obstacle to liberalizing change is the pattern that reform has taken under the conditions of post-Stalinist politics. Far-reaching reforms must be carried out across the board without hesitation and not in piecemeal fashion. However, until the effects of such reform are tested and recognized as effective, the determination and persistence necessary for such bold action will most likely be lacking. Past experience tells us that the response to this contradiction tends to be largely self-defeating. From the range of possible reforms, the leaders usually select a compromise that will cause the least disturbance and require the least cost and effort. Moreover, they usually introduce it as an experiment on a limited scale, virtually ensuring that the results will be far from conclusive and often disappointing. This outcome in turn fuels the arguments of the reform's opponents, who successfully block its further implementation. The leadership soon reverts to the traditional way of doing business, tinkering halfheartedly with the system and thereby allowing it to absorb and nullify the well-intentioned reform. This pattern explains the inherent stability of the traditional economic system and shows why the recurrent attempts at reform prove so ineffectual.

An example of this pattern is provided by the educational reform introduced by a Central Committee edict in 1983. Of all its clauses the improvement of vocational training was probably the most important. It is unlikely, however, that this reform will significantly change the educational system. This judgment is based on the fact that twenty-five years before (in 1958), an educational reform was introduced with almost identical goals and procedures. If the 1958 reform had been effective there would have been no need to reinvigorate it in the 1983 decree. One of the things that is so striking about the Soviets is the way they continually rediscover the same troubles and then resort to the same solutions, resolutions, prescriptions, and decrees. In a graduate seminar, I once selected a dozen *Pravda* editorials from various years of the post-Stalin era and erased the specific dates, names, quotes, etc. They resembled each other so closely that it was almost impossible to identify the years of their appearance.

A variation of this pattern, which might be called the hothouse phenomenon, constitutes yet another obstacle to radical change. In such a case, the leadership initiates reform on a carefully restricted scale amid conditions specially designed to encourage success. Ensuing attempts to expand the reform to different geographic areas or to other economic units find that these hothouse conditions simply cannot be duplicated, and the positive consequences of the initial experiment do not follow.

So, the odds are against successful, far-reaching reforms that will move significantly in the direction of market socialism. In their reluctance to embark on a program of radical reform, the leadership is not dissimilar to political elites in other countries who opt for continuity rather than changes that might lead to the dilution of their power. The crisis that the leaders face today is one of effectiveness, not of survival. Only when they are convinced that the system's continued existence is threatened will they be apt to relinquish the benefits of continuing inaction and pay the political price of radical reform. In the end, perhaps only a dramatic revolution from above by an unchallengeable leader like Stalin can effect radical change in the Soviet Union. But a leader of this kind probably cannot emerge in the foreseeable future, and in any case changes thus arbitrarily imposed would be quite unlike those we are discussing here, which involve a devolution of political power.

It is ironic that the strongest push for reform would certainly come from the top leader and from some of his highly placed associates, while the source of major opposition would be the middle rank of managers and officials, the very people who in the long run would be the main beneficiaries of such reforms. At the same time, a program of reform might produce unpredictable ripple effects in the political arena, a possibility that probably frightens the same politicians who would like to implement the reforms. So radical reform is a policy option from which the leaders can hope to gain limited benefits, but one from which they may lose a great deal.

There is a tacit assumption among U.S. analysts that nothing short of radical reform would improve Soviet economic performance. The validity of this assumption in terms of a comparison of Soviet and Western labor productivity, levels of technology, and efficiency is unquestionable. What is doubtful, however, is that this assumption is correct when actual Soviet performance is compared with its current potential. The economic system and the political-economic relations existing in the Soviet Union contain so much slack, are ridden by so much irrationality, and therefore contain so much unused potential that could be mobilized by a strong political leadership, that even without a radical change, economic performance could be improved.

It is noteworthy that in the two leadership successions after 1953 and 1964, the new leaders, Khrushchev and Brezhnev, were initially able to improve economic performance without resorting to structural changes. This was accomplished through a combination of organizational and policy reforms that partially eliminated the irrationalities built into the economic system and the bureaucratic inertia tolerated by the old leader and his idiosyncrasies (as in Khrushchev's pet project of corn production). In the present succession, the determination of the new leader to combat the inherited irrationalities and to use the existing reserves of growth will be even stronger than in the case of his predecessors. The urgency of such policies and reforms is stronger today than at any time in the post-Stalin era.

Support for reform may come from unexpected places. The declining growth rates and uneven and narrow technological progress are far from being sacred cows for the Soviet military high command. The slowed growth creates strong pressures on military spending from the supply side, and especially on the expansion of the military industrial plant. The technological level of the economy as a whole may become inadequate to support the burden of a global power and the required technological progress in the military sphere itself. In April 1984, in an interview in the Soviet press, Chief of Staff Marshal Nikolai Ogarkov spoke about the need for further modernization of the armed forces. His worries, so it seemed, were not about the ability to sustain a strategic military buildup in response to American moves. They concerned rather the non-nuclear forces whose effectiveness is jeopardized by the explosion of military technological innovations in the West, such as guided missiles, antitank weapons, mines, and greatly improved communications. And it is the conventional forces that are more dependent on the overall technological base of the economy at large than the strategic forces.

Reforms that do not change the military priorities of the economy but improve overall economic performance are both politically and economically advantageous to the armed forces. They may ease the pressure of competition with other interest groups and could improve the supply of goods to the military sector. By preventing the stagnation of the standard of living, such reforms may also contribute to higher morale in the population, something in which the military is deeply interested. This would not be the first time that the high command exhibited less than wholly conservative policy preferences. When the U.S.-Soviet détente developed in the early 1970s, the Soviet military was far from opposed, if for no other reason than the hope for a flow of Western technology.

A combination of administrative and policy reforms could prove temporarily efficacious in areas plagued by sluggish economic performance. Reform is most necessary in the countryside in the wake of an unprecedented series of bad harvests, which have reversed the consistent rise in the standard of living that has characterized the post-Stalin era. Agriculture must be given a high priority because of the critical role it plays in the economy and society. Food is the largest and most important item in the average citizen's budget. In the mid-1970s, food, beverages, and tobacco accounted for close to 50 percent of total income consumption. The figure for the United States at that time was about 20 percent. For the government, the availability of food is a guarantor of social stability and the foundation on which rests the effectiveness of incentives for higher industrial productivity.

Given the critical investment squeeze, the present leadership can no longer follow Brezhnev's example by throwing huge sums into agriculture without satisfactory results. It seems almost certain that the new form of agricultural organization, the "contract brigade," will be extended throughout the Russian republic, the largest.

In 1981, the rules affecting the private plots of farmers and workers were significantly relaxed. The new leadership has already moved further in this direction. Private plots are held by some 13 million collective farm families, over 10 million state farm workers, and more than 10 million workers and employees in other sectors of the economy. The size of the private plot of land went up to 0.5 hectares (1.2 acres). Private agricultural activity is highly labor intensive. The production and ownership of livestock on the private plots as a percentage of total agriculture rose sharply after Khrushchev's ouster in 1964. (He opposed support of private plots as ideologically impure and as an obstacle to getting farmers to pay greater attention to collective work.) From early 1973, production has stagnated and its share in total agricultural production has steadily declined. Yet private plots remain a very impressive supplier of food to the Soviet consumer.

Current discussions on the private agricultural sector mention the abolition of limits on the number of livestock owned by individual farmers; permission for grazing private cattle on collective land; and provision of credits, fertilizers and implements from the collective farm to individual farmers. In addition, industrial enterprises are being encouraged to provide food for their own workers by investing where possible in farms and truck gardens.

The increased attention to these plots and the proposed relaxation of the existing constraints on their production will be, however, measures of relatively limited consequence. In collective farms located near large cities, where the produce can be sold for prices higher than in the subsidized state shops, the new incentives for the peasants' private-plot production would be effective. On the more isolated *kolkhozy,* however, given the lack of roads, trucks, and storage facilities, the peasant would still have little incentive to produce more than he needs himself and can sell to his collective farm. A case in point is the effort in the early 1980s to distribute calves to individual peasants free of charge, in the expectation that they would raise them at their own expense and, in time, provide more meat to the cities, thus profiting both the state and the peasants. This effort produced very limited results. While many peasants living close to large cities took advantage of the opportunity, peasants on the outlying farms mostly ignored it. An equally important barrier to increased production in the private agricultural sector is the narrow feed base and the almost total lack of small machinery usable on small plots.

Yuri Andropov actively tried to improve coordination among all the central and provincial agricultural institutions. There were also signs that the immense expenditures on the less fertile nonblack earth regions of Russia were drastically cut. This may free some investment resources that could be applied more productively in other areas of the agricultural economy. Since investment in soil improvement sometimes requires a whole generation to show results, it is possible that in the late 1980s, Brezhnev's investment will start to improve the dismal state of agriculture. Yet, however important these measures may be, the new leadership's agricultural policy will prove successful only if they find the means to overcome the countless bottlenecks resulting from the appalling underdevelopment of agriculture's infrastructure—roads, transport, storage facilities, repair shops, and the like. Substantial improvement of the infrastructure is absolutely essential for sound agriculture; it will be extremely expensive.

The pursuit of the reforms mentioned here may bring improvements in agricultural production for a few years. They can only be deemed modest, however, when contrasted with China, which has actually returned agriculture to private hands, or with Hungary, which has transformed collective farms into quasicapitalist enterprises.

It is abnormal for an industrial country like Russia to have almost 26 percent of its labor force still working in agriculture. (The figures for America, France, and West Germany are 3, 8, and 6 percent, respectively.) It is even more unusual that this large agricultural population cannot provide an abundance of food. Considering the amount of culti-vated land in the Soviet Union and the United States, the number of machines employed in Soviet agriculture is clearly insufficient, yet nev-ertheless quite large. In 1981, the Soviet Union had 2,598,000 tractors as compared with 4,655,000 in the United States, 741,000 combines as against 674,000 in the United States, and 1,653,000 trucks as compared with over 4,000,000 in the United States. Yet the qualitative factors of sturdiness, maintenance, repair facilities, and availability of spare parts provide one reason for the major difference in the productivity of Soviet and American agricultural labor. By some Soviet estimates about one-third of the agricultural machinery is inactive or under repair at any given time. At the present level of agricultural technology, rather than providing labor resources for the cities, agriculture is judged by the au-thorities to be suffering from a shortage of labor. The reason is that in 1980 scarcely 20 percent of the collective farm labor force was made up of able-bodied men—that is those between fifteen and fifty years of age. The typical *kolkhoz* workers are older women. As many as 40 percent of the collective farms may be producing food sufficient only for their own members. If these collective farms were abolished, the cities, in all prob-ability, would be unaffected.

In industry, as much as the present leadership may recognize the de-sirability of reforms, no authoritative statement has yet heralded them. The discussion in the press focuses on less ambitious ways to improve the quantity and quality of manufacturing, to raise labor productivity, and to promote new technology. Proposals discussed during the first three or four years of Brezhnev's rule have reappeared. The reluctance to tout industrial reforms with the same energy as the proposed agricul-tural reforms surely derives from the greater degree to which they must impinge on vested interests of the bureaucracies, the intermediate levels of the Party apparatus, and even the industrial workers, who would have to work harder with little immediate reward.

It is likely that the leadership will continue to tinker with the eco-nomic system, intensifying its "organizational" and "mobilizational" re-forms. Other options will also probably be attempted. They may occur at the margins of the official economy, and be directed at relieving the pressures on the consumer sector. As suggested by Joseph Berliner, this would entail

a NEP-type reform [the New Economic Policy of the 1920s, based on the coex-istence of the private and public sectors] which retains the centrally planned economy largely intact but allows for a flourishing small-scale private sector. Since it entails no retreat from central planning but, rather, the development of a new secondary economy that offers some promise of spurring new imitation and innovation, it may be entertained seriously by the proposed successional leadership.*

It is ridiculous, and can be explained only by ideological blinders and the old guard's inertia, that over two-thirds of a century after the Bolshevik Revolution Soviet leaders still fear the existence of private restaurants or repair shops even on a scale where their turnover would constitute only a limited share of the volume of trade or service sectors.

There can be no doubt that Gorbachev will initiate many policy and organizational reforms. These reforms will have centralizing as well as decentralizing features. Investments in all spheres will certainly be more centralized and controlled from Moscow. The practice of diffuse investment decisions directed and supervised from many centers has had unwanted consequences. The critical and costly period between the allocation of investment funds for a project and the time when the project starts to produce is much too long by world standards and almost always longer than planned.

A Moscow economist described the situation as follows:

Construction time for large industrial projects is five to ten or more years and three to four years for medium-sized projects. This is much longer than the construction time in the United States and other developed countries, where large enterprises in ferrous metallurgy are built in less than twenty-four months while enterprises in the majority of other branches are built within a year. The project planning time (frequently two to three years or more) and the time required to reach the technical and economic potential of newly activated production capacities are excessively long at the present time. As a result, when a new or rebuilt enterprise begins operating at full capacity it is already technically obsolete. This is not surprising when we consider the modern tempo of scientific and technical progress.†

Between 1970 and 1980, the volume of unfinished construction has more than doubled. In 1980 it was equivalent to about 6 percent of the value of the total capital stock in the economy, and amounted to almost 80 percent of fixed capital investment. Moreover, the volume of unfinished construction is largest in machine building and ferrous metals, which are basic for Soviet modernization. In part, this is the result of lax control from Moscow, its permissiveness in terms of time and cost overruns. In the past, it derived from the chronic shortages in the Soviet

---

* Joseph Berliner, "Planning and Management," in Abram Bergson and Herbert S. Levine, eds., *The Soviet Economy: Toward the Year 2000* (London: George Allen and Unwin, 1983). See pp. 375–80.

† Robert Leggett, "Soviet Investment Policy in the 11th Five Year Plan," in *Soviet Economy in the 1980s: Problems and Prospects,* Part I. Selected papers submitted to the U.S. Congress Joint Economic Committee (Washington, D.C.: Government Printing Office, 1983), p. 133.

economy: The director of a project is often forced to postpone his time-table because the delivery of critical items is delayed. Yet in large part it is the inheritance of an entire philosophy of growth and investment.

From the time of the initial industrialization under Stalin, Soviet leaders have been enthralled by the expansion of the industrial plant. Growth for them has meant primarily the addition of new factories, mines, power stations, and so on. The modernization of the existing plant was less enticing, and thought to represent a nongrowth mentality. As a matter of fact, in their ideological writings on the superiority of their system over capitalism, they claim to have overcome what Marx called moral amortization, the alleged socialist ability to use aged enterprises and old machines, which would go bankrupt or be abandoned under capitalist conditions. Moral amortization worked, though with diminished effect, when the Soviet Union seemed to enjoy an unlimited supply of cheap labor. But the period of extensive growth had ended late in Brezhnev's regime. The key sources of Soviet growth are no longer in building additional factories but in modernizing technology. The industrial plant has been heavily weighted in favor of old machinery. It is relatively less modern now, as compared to America or Western Europe, than it was when Stalin died. It is therefore perfectly logical that one of Gorbachev's early edicts was to cut investment funds for new enterprises and to redirect the money to the modernization of existing facilities. The major question, however, is whether the Soviet machine-building industry will be able to supply the old plants with modern technology.

It is also certain that Gorbachev will impose stricter controls concerning plan fulfillment, particularly with regard to product quality, and will institute greater inducements for plant managers to innovate. The beginnings of such reforms were already initiated in mid-1983.

Under these plans five branches of Soviet industry, construction, and services started to work under revised managerial and incentive structures. If the reform was deemed successful, it was to be broadened to include new branches of the economy. (An official involved in supervising this reform told me that the key indicator of success would be growth in those branches of 5 to 6 percent in 1984. If the results of this experiment are much less satisfactory, the leadership will try another limited reform using different branches of the economy.) In the Chernenko period, Gorbachev was able to persuade the general secretary to double the number of branches involved in the reform and to extend the period from one to two years before a decision was taken concerning their success or failure. It is very likely that these experiments will be superseded by more far-reaching steps.

As decisions are made on budgetary allocations, one critical choice faces the new leadership—the level and distribution of funds for military growth. While the new leadership inherits decisions made earlier on major weapons systems, it can decelerate their development, curtail expenditures on production of existing systems, and even cut current military expenditures, if external conditions permit and internal conditions require. The basic dilemma is not simply guns versus butter, as it is so often presented in the West. It is the choice between direct expenditure on arms and upkeep of military forces versus general investments, especially military-industrial plant, to support future military growth. As long as industrial output was growing by 4 to 5 percent every year, direct military expenditures could increase annually by about 4 percent while at the same time the level of investment in the military-industrial plant remained very high. The drop to an annual growth rate of about 2 to 3 percent, which is expected to persist throughout the decade, poses a crucial question for Soviet leaders. Should direct military expenditures continue to rise at the 1970s level, at the price of depressing the growth rate of military-industrial development or vice versa? To maintain both at the 1970s level is not possible and in the long run may affect social stability through the impact on civilian industry and agriculture.

Even before Brezhnev died, this dilemma was aired publicly by military and civilian leaders. The former advocate the steady increase of direct military expenditures over military-industrial investments; the latter support cuts in direct military growth to permit larger military-industrial investment. With the expected decline in overall economic performance, this conflict will become sharper and reconciliation of the two preferences more difficult. It would appear that Andropov leaned toward preservation of investment growth, even if direct military expenditures had to be curtailed. Gorbachev's choice will obviously depend on the level of Western military spending and his evaluation of the East-West military balance. In any case there will be no return to high growth rates in both areas even in the 1990s in the absence of a major improvement in labor productivity. Such improvement will be less likely and more costly if the Kremlin continues to consume reserve growth resources for military purposes.

In broad outline, at least, it is possible to list the key tasks now confronting Gorbachev. Their order of priority stems not only from the significance of the problems that must be solved, but also from a realistic evaluation of what he can do in the initial stages of his leadership.

• Rejuvenation or change of the personnel who administer the economy at the top, the middle, and, eventually, the lower levels of the Party-state structure, putting in place officials of proven talent and energy, and sympathetic to the new style of management and reforms, combined with a major effort at their reeducation.

• A drastic improvement of discipline among workers and managers, through harsh punishments, better supervision, and appeals to patriotic duty.

• Better utilization of the Soviet strong point—applying the highly centralized system to mobilize and direct massive resources to priority goals.

• A mini-NEP, which would permit, within regulated boundaries, small private enterprises in the service sector, thus improving social welfare and perhaps providing competitive standards for state or cooperative enterprises.

• Strengthened control over the quality of products, perhaps by using the method employed in military industry, where final quality control is taken away from the managers and their ministerial supervisors and given to the "consumers"—senior officers from the Ministry of Defense on temporary duty in the factories.

• An assault on some of the barriers between the military and civilian economic sectors by teaching civilian managers methods of organization and supervision employed in military production, giving some especially important civilian projects to managers in the military sector, and transferring a sizable group of managerial and technical personnel from military to civilian activity.

• The abolition or drastic reduction of credits and hidden subsidies to the Eastern European empire and Cuba (most of the subsidies take the form of low prices for Soviet oil and raw material exports and, more obliquely, the low quality of imports from Eastern Europe); the securing of Eastern European investments for the extraction of raw materials, some of which will be exported to Eastern Europe; a greater division of labor between the Soviet Union and Eastern Europe in specific branches of industry, which would provide savings through longer production runs.

• A reduction in the resources allotted to global aspirations (military and economic), the adoption of a more restrained approach in foreign policy whereby not every target of opportunity would be pursued, and thus a concentration of foreign policy resources on major objectives, where Soviet vital interests or prestige is really at stake.

• A decrease in the size of the bureaucracy at the central, republican, and provincial levels, primarily by abolishing or cutting the number of intermediary organizations between the ministries and state committees on the one hand, and the producing units on the other.

• A rapid and continuous modernization of technology, which could be achieved by switching funds from new construction to the modernization of existing plants, by concentrating investment on the electronics and machine-building industries, by bringing the research institutes of the economic ministries and the Academy of Sciences closer to the enterprises, by encouraging the managers to accept and fully utilize new technology through the stabilization of their production plans for several years after the introduction of a new technology, and the provision of rewards for the overfulfillment of plans not only quantitatively but also with regard to quality, costs, and profits, and by establishing low prices for high-technology producer goods (through subsidies) and a high rate of amortization, while increasing the relatively low (6 percent) interest rate on capital (which encourages waste).

• The increased importation of advanced technology through normal channels of trade with Western Europe and Japan and through intensified industrial spying and smuggling. (It is my impression, however, that Gorbachev's aim is to establish a self-generating technological progress which need not rely primarily on imports. As a Japanese economist once remarked about products already on the market, "What exists is already obsolescent or obsolete.") A dramatically greater use of imported capital and consumer goods could provide standards of competition for industrial enterprises. ("Socialist competition" has proven in the Soviet civilian sector a futile exercise in encouraging efficiency.)

• The expansion of exports to the West beyond the present range of raw materials and gold predominantly, to include manufactured products, allowing direct contacts and ties between the largest Soviet exporting and importing units and foreign firms, thus omitting the intermediary role of numerous foreign trade organizations that constitute a bureaucratic obstacle to effective trade. The improvement of export capabilities in manufacturing could be achieved by creating special zones or special umbrella units that would bring together enterprises working for export and supply them on a priority basis.

• Improvement of the export industry's design bureaus and the provision of strict control over design and product quality, based on Western standards.

• The creation of a unified and centralized energy network that would better exploit existing capacities; a partial shift from the extremely costly plans to acquire new oil for domestic consumption and export from new Siberian fields to a determined and far-reaching plan of oil conservation, which has proven very successful in the industrial democracies (such a program would require industrial investments but, most importantly, it would be based on a revised incentive system for managers and workers); improvement of the export industry's design bureaus and the provision of strict control over design and product quality, based on Western standards.

• A gradual but consistent reduction of the enormous subsidies for basic consumer goods (with the probable exception of bread, lard, and potatoes) to bring their prices up at least to their real costs of production, thus freeing funds for expansion and easing inflationary pressures.

• The development and implementation of a program of improvement in agricultural productivity by abolishing extremely costly and diffused investments aimed at cultivating new lands and concentrating on the productivity of those farms that already provide the bulk of supplies to the urban areas; the introduction of contract brigades on a massive scale, while making them smaller and stabilizing their delivery quotas for several years so as to stimulate their interest in higher production; and the encouragement of production on private plots, especially of meat, by changing the existing limits on their size, providing credit, supplying fertilizers and small machinery, and eliminating any remaining progressive taxation.

• The creation of an all-union market for produce, instead of the presently predominant regional markets, where chronic shortages in some areas go hand in hand with abundance and surplus in other areas (this will require road improvements, and the expansion of truck and railroad transports, storage space, and refrigeration).

• An attempt to change the geographic imbalance of existing labor resources both by providing greater incentives for south-north migration and by intensifying the industrialization process in the south.

• The institution of changes in the curriculum of secondary schools to prepare students for work with computers, an increased flow of elementary school graduates into vocational high schools to learn skills required by the economy, and increased spending per student in the higher education establishments.

These measures can be organized in four categories according to their relative priority: wholesale change in managerial and administrative personnel, and their reeducation; an increase in labor discipline; the diminution in central planning of the number of indicators, and greater stress on quality and cost; and utilization of the Soviet Union's strong point, the centralized mobilization of resources for essential goals.

It is almost certain that the new general secretary will take steps in all of these categories. The question is how successful he will be.

It would be very wrong to imagine an orderly plan of reforms toward the fulfillment of these goals. The situation in Russia rather resembles French society during the revolutionary years 1848–51. It is a picture, to quote Karl Marx, "of the most motley mixture of crying contradictions . . . a more confused mixture of high-flown phrases and actual uncertainty and clumsiness, of more enthusiastic striving for innovation and more deeply rooted domination of the old routine, of a more apparent harmony of the whole society and more profound estrangement of its elements."*

From the political perspective the question of the viability of major economic reforms is to a large extent one of alliances. Nowhere has a serious reform succeeded without coalition-building by its adherents. Since somebody has to lose in a reform, the clout that political alliances provide is necessary. To put it another way, the energy required to push through a major economic reform must be much greater than the energy expended by bureaucratic opposition and the forces of inertia.

Many argue that the need to build alliances in the cause of reforms is confined to democracies, with their free play of political forces and interest groups. The Soviet Union is judged to be not only an authoritarian system but also a dictatorial state effectively controlled by the top leader. Yet alliance building is also a necessity there, both in the cause of serious reforms and in the interest of maximizing the powers of the general secretary, especially in the first few years of his rule.

Truly personal dictatorship ended with the death of Stalin. It was possible only through the ruthless application of terror, directed not only against the population, but also against other leaders and the elite. The oligarchical Brezhnev leadership was formed from the heads of major institutional interests and significant bureaucracies, such as the Party machine, the secret police, the military, the economic administration, the general administration, the foreign policy apparatus, and the leadership of the key republics and regions.

It is true that the general secretary has great power at his disposal from the beginning. He eventually can accumulate enormous power. Yet the extent to which the potential for power is transformed into reality depends on his personal qualities, and on his talent for alliance-building. After all, such a strong leader as Khrushchev was removed from his position after eleven years in office. Gorbachev can ignore the voices of diverse, often competing interests only at his own peril.

Nonetheless, the situation today seems quite different from that of either Khrushchev or Brezhnev at the beginning of his rule. Khrushchev relied primarily on a single power base—the Party apparatus (and to some extent also on general appeals to the population). His ouster occurred at a time when he was trying to become independent of even this base. Brezhnev, learning from his predecessor's fate, was a conciliator who sought the widest bureaucratic support for each step he took. Since Brezhnev's programs were conservative, and entailed an unprecedented

---

* Karl Marx, "The Eighteenth Brumaire of Louis Bonaparte," edited by C. R. Dutt (New York: International Publishers, no date), pp. 19–20.

stability of the leading personnel, such support was not difficult to achieve.

It would be wrong, however, to pose the question of reform and of those who oppose it as a straightforward dichotomy between reformers and conservatives. Stephen Cohen quotes a Czech official who remarked during the Prague Spring of 1968: "The boundary between progressive and conservative runs through each of us."* There are many examples in history of conservatives who become uncomfortable or uneasy reformers. This happens when they come to the conclusion that reforms are necessary to preserve the valued aspects of a system. (Franklin Roosevelt created the American welfare state not to destroy capitalism but to strengthen it.) The conservative reformers will not be consistent allies of genuine reformers on every issue or at all times. Sometimes their alliance may have a defensive character, an attempt to remain on the inside and to keep the genuine reformers from moving too far.

Gorbachev will probably be an innovative leader whose instincts will be close to Khrushchev's reforming zeal, although exercised in a much more gradual and systematic way. He will be a leader who will enjoy at the early stages of his career a honeymoon with his bureaucratic constituencies. He has been accumulating power at a faster rate than could have been expected; the turnover of the personnel at the central and local level, controlled by the general secretary, will probably be more rapid and massive now than at any time in the post-Stalin era. His alliance-building is, and for some time will remain, of a personal nature and largely concentrated in the Politburo, the Secretariat, and the Presidium of the Council of Ministers.

Gorbachev's effectiveness and freedom of action at the present stage, and his initial reforming plans, depend more on the personal loyalties of his fellow oligarchs than on the allegiance of major bureaucratic constituencies. Those whom he and Andropov brought to power should be regarded as the general secretary's loyalists rather than representatives of institutional interests. The time may come when this will no longer be true, but in the near future the alliances about which Gorbachev has to worry are those with his fellow Politbureaucrats. Their personal commitment to him and a general desire for change could remain stronger than their commitment to represent bureaucratic interests for a while. Gorbachev's leadership will for some time remain an emergency leadership, with the rules of the Soviet political game stacked in his favor. His most difficult task will not be to push reforms through the Politburo, the

* Stephen F. Cohen, "The Friends and Foes of Change: Reformism in the Soviet Union," in Stephen F. Cohen, Alexander Rabinowitch and Robert Sharlet, eds. *The Soviet Union Since Stalin* (Bloomington: Indiana University Press, 1980), p. 26.

Central Committee Secretariat, or Presidium of the Council of Ministers, but to assure their implementation by the bureaucracies.

Many Soviet economists, managers, and Party officials know what is
wrong with their economic system as well as any Western analyst. What
they do not know is how to solve the problems while remaining within
the boundaries of the system. A comprehensive model for reform does
not yet exist in the Soviet Union. In Maurice Friedberg's words: "The
Soviet government wrestles with a dilemma which Nicholas I and other
Russian tsars encountered: It wants a fire that will not burn."*

Considering the state of the Soviet economy, many in the West may
have formed a highly negative image of Soviet managers. To a large extent this image is unjustified. As many articles by American management specialists, and especially by David Granick, testify, the managers
are, on the whole, well educated and prepared technologically to administer the organizations and units of production they supervise. They are
quite rational. The problem is that the economic environment within
which they act is nonrational.

An experienced American executive, transferred to the Soviet Union
and appointed manager in the area of his expertise, would act in exactly
the same manner as his Soviet colleagues after a short period of time. He
would concentrate on the quantitative flow of production; he would consider new technology a hindrance rather than a help; he would have
small interest in the preferences of his consumers; he would squander
capital resources; he would learn to doctor, in collusion with his main ac-
countant (*glavbukh*), his reports to the ministry; he would hoard raw materials and semi-products so as to be as little dependent on his suppliers
as possible, actions that would increase costly overhead costs and the
size of his inventory; he would create an illegal slush fund and semi-
legally employ an associate as the *tolkach,* the man who bribes other
managers to get the necessary materials on time. In all this he would be
showing his good sense and capacity for rational thinking. It would be
irrational of him to behave as he would in an American factory.

The Soviet political-economic system separates what is rational for
the individual manager from what is beneficial to the economy as a
whole. Many decades of working in the system warp the average manager's conception of what is right and wrong economically, turning him
into a staunch supporter of the system as it exists, the system in which he
has learned how to deal with his responsibilities, and how to secure legal
and illegal rewards. Yet it is he who will be pushed by the leadership to
reform the system. What comes to mind is a one-liner from the Polish

* Maurice Friedberg, "Cultural and Intellectual Life," in Robert F. Byrnes, ed., *After
Brezhnev: Sources of Soviet Conduct in the 1980s* (Bloomington: Indiana University Press,
1983), p. 251.

humorist Jan Lec: "There is something wrong with the logic of asking the same man who destroyed a machine to be in charge of its repair."

From what has already been said, it should be clear what we do know and what we do not know about the new Soviet leadership. We know that the leaders are deeply concerned about the state of the society and economy; that they blame their predecessors for letting the negative developments go so far; that they are determined to take strong countermeasures; that as of now their reformatory actions are focused on improving social discipline, sweeping changes in personnel on all levels, inducements for a better quality of work and production, and small steps to improve the economic mechanism. What we do not know is the extent to which they will be ready to make radical reforms. We have no picture of their long-range plans, and it is quite possible that they are so thoroughly preoccupied with stopgap measures as to preclude consideration of larger-scale reforms.

The less we know about Gorbachev's future plans, the more important it becomes to try and place the nature of his leadership in the historical perspective of post-Stalin Russia. This period has seen three basic types of leadership, widely divergent in both style and substance. Khrushchev's approach was populist and ideological: He believed in people, appealed to them, and attempted to bring about an ideological revitalization. Brezhnev's leadership was corporatist and conservative: He adhered to rule by consensus and stressed institutional representation of the major bureaucratic hierarchies in the leadership bodies; perpetuating the rule of the old guard, he was fundamentally committed to the preservation of the system in its traditional mold.

The nature of Gorbachev's leadership seems to be managerial-reformist. It is managerial in the sense that it seeks to reinforce strict, vertical lines of authority rather than engage in compromise and bargaining; it is reformist in the sense that both in its attitude to personnel and in its socioeconomic policies it recognizes the need for innovation. Gorbachev and his closest associates (primarily Ryzhkov and Ligachev) do not make a fetish of the reconciliation of institutional interests, as Brezhnev did. They seem determined to strengthen discipline and to encourage innovation in the face of, and overriding, entrenched interests in the Party apparatus, in economic management, in foreign policy, and in the armed forces. It is not consensus they seek, the lowest common denominator of all institutional interests, but the advancement of their reformist line while adhering, again, to strict vertical lines of authority and control. Their style appears to be not that of a wheeling-and-dealing corporate board of directors but rather of strong chief executives actively supervising, controlling, and laying down the lines of action for their subordinates.

The reformist aspect of their leadership is most clearly manifest in their decision to pursue far-reaching personnel replacements that in effect constitute a generational changeover in the elite; their determination to reexamine thoroughly the policies and organizational framework they have inherited, and to institute a broad range of policy changes and administrative reorganizations; and their effort to improve central planning and to concentrate on the crucial issues of technological progress and material incentives, in the interests of faster growth in labor productivity.

The men of the new Soviet leadership are often called "technocrats." This is as good a description as any. It is particularly apt for Prime Minister Gorbachev's alter ego in the economic field, who fits the mold as regards education, profession, and career pattern.

A Russian, born in 1929, Ryzhkov graduated in 1959 from the Ural/Kirov Polytechnical Institute. In 1956, while still a student, he entered the Party. Before and during his studies he was also employed at one of the largest Soviet heavy-machine-building enterprises, in Sverdlovsk. After graduation he became a shift foreman, advancing successively to section chief, shop chief, chief welder, deputy director, and then chief engineer of the gigantic factory. In the early 1970s he rose to the post of factory director and, within a year, became director general of the "Uralmash" Production Association, which, in addition to his old factory, incorporated many other machine-building and metallurgical establishments in the Urals. In 1975 he was transferred to Moscow as First Deputy Minister of Heavy and Transportation Machine-Building. In February 1979 he was promoted to a position of high political and national importance: First Deputy Chairman of the State Planning Commission (Gosplan). But the truly decisive upturn in Ryzhkov's career occurred in November 1982, when Andropov made him secretary of the Central Committee and simultaneously chief of the Central Committee Economic Department. His close association with Gorbachev dates from this time, if not earlier, and after Gorbachev assumed power he elevated Ryzhkov to full Politburo membership. Ryzhkov became economic chief in the Party's central apparatus, Gorbachev's righthand man in economic problems with Ligachev and Vorotnikov.

In October 1985 Ryzhkov assumed his present position, only one step removed from Gorbachev himself: the Prime Ministership of the Council of Ministers. He became the chief administrator and the man in charge of supervising the implementation of plans for Soviet economic development.

What stands out in Ryzhkov's biography, typically for a "technocrat," is his solid education as a metallurgical engineer. Of much greater importance, however, is his knowledge of the industrial and planning systems from the level of a rank-and-file worker to that of a minister and central planner. He knows the production line. He is aware of the obstacles faced by managers, as well as of their tricks and maneuvers to satisfy the ministry in Moscow and the local Party authorities. He is very well informed about the method of supervision of a major ministry. He is well versed in the intricacies of top-level planning. And finally, he understands, and has assimilated, the unwritten rules of political survival and influence. Thus he combines technological expertise, managerial acumen, administrative experience, and political skills.

Yet, to be meaningful, the term "technocrat" must refer to something more than education and career. It must encompass a particular approach to problem-solving, and, even beyond that, a particular view of society and social order. He is an individual confident of his ability to lead, possessing few doubts about what is the "correct" course of action to overcome present difficulties.

The technocrat is primarily a manager and only secondarily a politician—successful political maneuvering is for him merely a prerequisite for the realization of his managerial goals. His formula for a better and stronger Russia can be reduced to four items: discipline, technology, leadership, and stratification.

For the technocrat, the fundamental failing of the old leaders lay in their inability to preserve a high level of social discipline in the society at large, and among workers in particular. The old leaders were too soft and tolerant, too heedless of the decay of the social fabric. The technocrat opposes, to be sure, the methods of ensuring discipline that were used in Stalin's time; he regards Stalinism as a probably inevitable yet unsavory extreme of "primary accumulation of capital" and industrialization that can have no place in a modern society. Yet he is equally opposed to what he sees as permissiveness in work and social life, as well as in culture and human rights. He puts great faith, on the one hand, in coercive methods and, on the other, in material inducements in the pursuit of labor discipline. He has authored the latest Soviet slogan: "It is insufficient to be at work, it is necessary to work." He feels that authority should be just but not liberal. Good work should be promptly rewarded, while bad behavior should be swiftly punished. He has no sympathy for dissenters, whose varied points of view he does not understand at all. He is preoccupied with instrumental rather than normative questions. He is pragmatic and empirical—what works is good, what does not should be replaced.

He is not against centralization per se; he believes in an authoritarian and authoritative structure with a clear delineation of rights and duties. At the same time, he is opposed to excessively detailed supervision of managerial personnel on the production line, and to overly detailed plans from the bureaucracies that would unduly curtail the freedom and initiative of managers. While he still subscribes to the Soviet definition of initiative as "the search for the best way to fulfill an order," he wants to allow the manager as much leeway as possible to find ways to fulfill that order in accordance with specific local conditions and the manager's knowledge of his own business.

The technocrat opposes the egalitarianism promoted (at least to some degree) by the old leaders. In fact he regards the present degree of social stratification as insufficient, the distance between classes and strata as too small, and as counterproductive to the general social interest in promoting intensive and high-quality production. The material gap between the various strata of Soviet society is in his view too narrow—it should be increased upwards, with the greatest benefits accruing to the upper rungs. Responsibility, qualifications, and skills should be better rewarded, in accordance with the country's need for hardworking, energetic, well-trained leaders on every level and in every sphere of activity. Foremen, engineers, managers, and administrators must have a monetary stake in striving for success. Within every vocational and professional group sinecures should be abolished, sloppiness should be punished, material incentives should be provided for those who display ability, good will, and vigor. The technocrat subscribes to traditional conservative values of duty and hard work. He shows no tolerance to indifference and accepts no excuses for failure.

In a society where the technological ethos still rides high, and progress is synonymous with technological advance, the technocrat feels especially stymied by the Soviet Union's relative backwardness. His envisaged solution is to involve academic scientists and engineers much more closely and actively in industry. He proposes to reward them by status and material incentives, not for their accomplishments in their institutes, but for their success in bringing technology to bear on the methods of production and the products themselves.

The technocrat believes in the urgency and efficacy of training both engineers and skilled labor in the use of new technology. He is searching for methods, as yet unfound, of forcing technological progress through the competition of more backward economic units with advanced enterprises. He wants to reorient centralized planning away from a primary preoccupation with quantitative indices of production and more, instead, toward qualitative indices. He is determined to create conditions where managers will be eager to accept new technology because of special rewards along with the inducement of having production plans stabilized for a number of years after the new technology is introduced. In sum, the technocrat's preoccupation with advanced technology comes through loud and clear. What is still unclear is how technological progress can be sufficiently speeded up within the institutional framework of the existing system.

At the republic and provincial levels, the new leadership is not so conspicuously dominated by individuals with a technocratic background. Gorbachev himself, and his righthand man for party organization and personnel, Yegor Ligachev, have educational and career backgrounds different from those of their technocrat colleagues. Thus the leadership may be characterized overall as an alliance of the new generation of Party apparatchiks with the technocrats. One has an impression, however, that top-level apparatchiks have either consciously adopted the technocratic way of thinking and evaluation or are at least very sympathetic to it. They see it as the proper approach to dealing with the economic morass created by the old generation of ideologues and conservative administrators. What is truly amazing is that the technocrats are only now being given the chance to lead, more than thirty years after Stalin's death, and with the Stalinist economic model still in place. The difference with the situation in China is striking.

How is it that China can successfully embark on a program of radical reforms, so soon after Mao's death, while the Soviet Union has yet to attempt a radical economic reform? A comprehensive answer to this question would be very long and complex. Let me concentrate briefly on just one major aspect that is pertinent to our discussion: the aspect of tradition.

The danger of oversimplification is always present in the making of major generalizations. Yet from the societal and economic point of view, Mao's revolution, from the "Great Leap Forward" through the "Great Proletarian Cultural Revolution," went against the grain of dominant Chinese traditions and national characteristics. (Mao's revolution, on the other hand, with its goals of national independence and unification, did fit Chinese traditions and expresses the people's aspirations.) The important traditional elements of the Chinese character are entrepreneurship, pragmatism, a strong work ethic, cultural adaptability, an ability to assimilate alien experience, and a self-confidence so deeply ingrained that acceptance of foreign experience is not considered humiliating. All these characteristics have been reawakened after Mao's death, and they promote conditions favorable to radical reforms. Russian tradition is quite different. The legacy of Stalin or Brezhnev does no violence to Russian tradition. Indeed, it fits the mold quite well.

Two traditional Russian characteristics are noteworthy for their imprint on the Soviet mind-set. First, there is the relationship between status, class, and political power in Russian history: traditionally, political power has been more of a source of high status or class than vice versa. Second, there is the lack of status and class autonomy vis-à-vis the state. Accordingly, even the highest status has always required service to the state and is reaffirmed by that service. The Soviet theory and practice of politics, wherein relations to the Party-state serve as the wellspring of class and social status, falls well within the Russian tradition. This is a tradition that exaggerates the political factor and neglects the value of individual initiative and entrepreneurship.

There is also the military factor in Russian history—sometimes dictated by defensive reasons, sometimes by offensive, but always present as the centerpiece of Russian policies and development. The reforms in Russia's internal order and economic development were to a greater degree than in any European country generated by the military needs of the state. Soviet historical development has reinforced the importance of the military. The organization of the polity, with its centralized vertical lines of authority, economic planning, and development resembling a war economy even in peacetime, the foreign policies—all carry the military stamp. In the absence of a threat to Soviet independence, the military factor provides a rationale against fundamental reforms. (It appears that the clash of military priorities within the economic system is not yet sufficiently strong to argue for fundamental reforms.)

What is most notable about the Russian religious tradition is the fusion of the church with the state, and the resultant lack of autonomy of the church. This traditional pattern of relations between religion and the state is continued in the Soviet Union in two ways. The first is the subordination of Russian Orthodoxy to state domination, and, by and large, the loyalty of the Orthodox church to the state. Secondly, the secular Soviet ideology, which attempts to provide a functional equivalent for religion, is created by the state and is adjusted according to the state's needs. Here again is a factor that reinforces the custom of central controls as opposed to individualism and the diffusion of power.

Russia's enormous economic potential has never been realized to any significant degree. Throughout its history, the country has lagged behind the West, periodically experiencing spurts of rapid development based on direct Western participation and on indirect borrowing from the West. However, at no time has there been self-generating, self-sustaining, long-range economic and technological progress.

All past attempts to modernize Russia, all spurts of actual change were primarily inspired and forced by the rulers. In this respect the Soviet pattern of revolution from above follows Russian tradition. Even today, pressures for change from below are either minimal or find no form of effective public expression. Prevailing periods of mass apathy were regularly interrupted by outbursts of mass violence, times of *smuta* (disorder). Among the elites, the professional class, and the masses there exists a deep fear of uncontrollable violence that may be lurking behind the façade of impressive societal organization and stability. The response of the elites is the condemnation of spontaneity in social and political behavior. Lenin and Stalin made great efforts after the revolution to conquer and control the very spontaneity, the *stikhia*, of larger social groups that had made the Bolshevik victory possible. The highest possible value is placed on order. The authoritarianism of Party rule is in part shared by the masses, who also yearn for order and strong rule and strong rulers. That there must be order in Russia is instinctively accepted by all Russians.

In sum, Russian tradition fosters an aversion to risk-taking, to the spontaneity necessary for economic ventures, to devolution of economic power, to a pragmatic approach in which results would count for more than official presumptions, to any confidence on the part of the leaders in their society and on the part of the society in the leaders' legitimate right to rule—to all those factors that shape the essence of the Chinese modernization drive. The postrevolutionary tradition only reinforces the stigmas of the past.

In any comparison of the different roads to reform in contemporary China and Russia, there is one aspect that is of absolutely fundamental importance. It concerns the difference in the quality of human material with which the leaderships of the two countries have to deal when contemplating reforms. Soviet power in its development destroyed the Russian smallholder peasantry, with its ambition for land and profit. Soviet power never trusted the peasant—it declared war on the peasantry, it exposed them to large-scale violence, it brutalized their lives, it destroyed their dignity and their sense of belonging to the larger society. The Soviet peasantry today is not even a class in the proper meaning of the term. It is an agglomeration of isolated groups with their spirit broken and their hopes abandoned.

In his account of his Siberian exile, the dissident Andrei Amalrik provides a vivid picture of the apathy and indifference on what is probably a typical *kolkhoz*. "There is the mentality of the *kolkhoznik,*" Amalrik sums up; "he has ceased to be a peasant but has not become a laborer, and hence cares nothing about what happens to the result of his work."*

In China, by contrast, the peasant was the central figure in Mao's revolution. During the Cultural Revolution, in particular, he was the model of the workingman which was to be emulated. While the collectivization and communization of the Chinese countryside was certainly coercive, it was by and large nonviolent. The basic characteristics, aspirations, and

* Andrei Amalrik, *Involuntary Journey to Siberia.* Translated by Manya Harari and Max Hayward. (New York: Harcourt, Brace, Jovanovich, 1970), p. 162.

dignity of the Chinese peasantry were preserved throughout the turmoil of the last decade of Mao's rule. The peasant needed his own land, reasonable taxes, and freedom to produce and to enjoy the fruits of his labor. The Chinese Communist Party has encouraged the peasant to revert to his private aspirations for a better life and to his traditional habits of hard work. In Russia, however, such agricultural reform would not succeed—it is unsuitable to Soviet conditions.

The question of the quality of industrial human resources in China as compared to the Soviet Union is less clear. Yet even here the long-range destructiveness of Soviet practices on both blue- and white-collar workers has been much greater than has been the case in China. The relatively shorter exposure in China to the Stalinist tradition of industrial organization and work patterns argues for a greater sensitivity to material incentives and much less diminution of a sense of responsibility and interest in work than is the case in the Soviet Union, where the work ethic of the industrial and white-collar working classes may be beyond repair in the present generation.

When the Bolsheviks took control, they declared war on two symbolic figures of the past that represented the Russian tradition. The first, Oblomov, was the symbol of laziness, of disinterest in any productive work, of economic and political apathy. The second, Manilov, was the epitome of the dreamer, of impracticality, lacking both realism and entrepreneurship. Ironically, for Stalin and other Bolshevik leaders, the American experience was the counter-symbol to Oblomov and Manilov. In 1926 Stalin wrote:

American business ability constitutes . . . an antitoxin against "revolutionary" Manilov-like behavior and fanciful yarn spinning. American business ability is that unconquerable force, which does not know and does not recognize barriers, which washes away by its businesslike stubbornness each and every obstacle, which cannot fail to bring to a conclusion any task once begun, even when it concerns small things, and without which any serious constructive work is unthinkable. The union of Russian revolutionary drive with American business ability—this is the essence of Leninism in Party and state work.*

Sixty years after Stalin wrote those words Russia has lost its revolutionary drive at home, but has not yet acquired American business ability. Gorbachev faces not only the legacies created by his predecessors but the entire weight of Russian tradition.

Mikhail Gorbachev inherited the top position of leadership at a time when in fact, though not in its own perception, the country is more secure from external threat than at any time in history. His predecessors

* I. V. Stalin, *Sochineniia* 6 (Moscow: Gospolitizdat, 1952), pp. 187–188.

bequeathed him a legacy of awesome military strength. Yet the domestic situation has entered a phase of decline, and there is little reason to believe that this trend will be significantly reversed in the remainder of the century.

The deepening slump in the system is best seen in comparison to the advanced industrial democracies. As mentioned, the difference between the technological and productive level of the Soviet Union and the West has not changed significantly since Stalin died over thirty years ago.

The size of the Soviet GNP relative to that of the United States has sharply increased in comparison to the 1950s, but in the last decade it has stagnated:

TABLE 8

	1955	1965	1975	1980
Soviet GNP as percentage of U.S. GNP	31	39	50	49

Besides the relative size of the Soviet economy, another ratio should also be considered. The absolute gap between the Soviet and American GNP's has increased significantly. It was smallest in 1958. By a rough estimate, it is twice as large in the mid-eighties.

By the standards of economic vitality and technological progress and productivity stressed by the Bolsheviks in their self-proclaimed competition between socialism and capitalism, the results are conclusive. Two-thirds of a century after the Bolshevik Revolution, even the slogan that for so long characterized the aspirations and activities of the Bolsheviks after they attained power—to catch up and overtake the advanced capitalist societies—has all but disappeared from government propaganda. The question is no longer how to catch up and surpass, but rather how to keep up with the industrial democracies and not fall further behind.

Technological backwardness and economic inefficiency poses, of course, a major problem for Soviet ideologues and propagandists. One method for dealing with it is simply to lie. More often they rely on omission, on silence about the real state of affairs, in the mass media and sometimes even in professional publications. After 1981, for example, when Japan continued its growth at a faster pace than Russia, the statistical data on Japan was drastically reduced in Soviet publications. The size of the official Soviet Statistical Yearbook (*Narodnoye Khnoziaistvo*), published annually, started to shrink in the mid-1970s. The latest yearbook, for 1983, is one-third smaller than it was in 1959. This is, of course, done primarily to reduce access to data that reflect badly on the state of Soviet society and to conceal the details of unfavorable economic trends.

Another, more sophisticated device employed to explain away comparative economic inefficiencies is to switch the frame of reference from precise economic indicators to an amorphous analysis of the quality of life allegedly associated with the socialist socioeconomic system. When I visited a very large state farm, where the management was quite impressive and the standard of living relatively high, I was struck by its incredibly large work force and inventory of machinery—probably six to seven times larger than in a comparative American farm. When I conveyed my impressions to a sophisticated Soviet expert, he tried to explain the reasons for the overemployment by the restraints imposed on the economy by the nature of the socialist system, which cares more about the quality of life of its people. "You see," he said, "in your system more than half of these people would be unemployed. Since there is no large-scale industry in the part of the Soviet Union where the farm is located, these unemployed would have to migrate to other areas where they could be absorbed by new industries. We in a socialist system, however, can neither permit unemployment nor force the local people to go, for example, to Siberia, where there is great demand for labor."

A still higher level of ideological sophistication (and sophistry) in explaining away the embarrassing problem is reserved for the core of the Party itself, through the use of Marxian semantics. A high Party ideologue used a convoluted argument: "Stalin was wrong when he proclaimed (in the 1920s) that in counterdistinction to other socioeconomic formations, elements of socialism cannot be developed in the economic mainstream of capitalist societies. As a matter of fact, the multinational corporations, for instance, are an example of socialist methods of cooperation utilized for capitalist purposes." In other words, socialist methods of organization are behind the success of capitalism—which begs the question of why they cannot be employed in the service of socialism. Of course, when all else fails, arguments are used about the effects of the Second World War, which, while certainly destructive, did after all end forty years ago and had an effect on Japan and Germany as well. Or there are truthful references to the burden of Soviet military expenditures, which are of course necessary for the defense of peace. Despite all these arguments, and behind them, there lurks in the minds of most of the ideologues and experts the recognition that something is terribly wrong—that neither the capitalist nor the socialist system behaves in a way that was and is expected by the Soviet holy writ. Gorbachev is likely to be very impatient with this ideological explaining away of the reasons for Soviet backwardness. His speeches, the tone of the press, and the critical attitude of many elite members testify to a hardening stance toward the obvious shortcomings of the existing system.

The decline of the system can, however, be considered not only in relative, but also in absolute, terms: that is, in comparison to Soviet performance, and the aspirations of the populace, both material and spiritual, in the recent past. The most visible indicator of overall economic performance is the prolonged decline in the rates of growth. These are now at the lowest level in Soviet history, and it seems unlikely that this trend will be reversed or even stabilized in the next decade. Agriculture, after its initial recovery from the role of internal colony under Stalin, is unable, and by all estimates will remain unable, to overcome the chronic weakness that plagues it. Despite the vast expenditures wasted on the agricultural sector, potatoes and bread grains are the only commodities that are produced in sufficient quantities each year. After a long period of improvement, the growth of the popular standard of living began to decline in the second half of the 1970s and there is little reason to believe that it will improve in the 1980s. The vast economic and cultural gap between the center and the periphery in Russia—between the metropolitan areas and cities, the cities and towns, the towns and rural units—still continues as a testimony to Russian backwardness.

The ideological, political, and economic optimism of the Khrushchev era and the early years of Brezhnev's rule gave way to the irrelevance of ideology to society, the political apathy of all parts of the population, and political fears and forebodings within the elite. The optimism of the past was also displaced by an economic realism on the part of the leadership that offers as yet little more than the promise of austerity, and on the part of the workers focuses the desire for a higher standard of living on the illegal activities of the second economy.

The aspirations of the elites and professionals associated with the last paralyzing years of Brezhnev's leadership and his two successors have revived with Gorbachev. There has never been a period when a popular and elite lack of respect and lack of hope associated with a top leader of the Party were as obvious and widespread as they were with Chernenko in power. When they were then asked about the situation, officials, professionals, and simple people in most cases did not address the subject but expressed their sense of loss concerning Andropov. In the immediate aftermath of the Gorbachev succession, there developed a rare mood of exhilaration in Russia, at least among the elite and the professionals. Their expectations about how much Gorbachev can do to leave behind the traditional cyclical Russian *smutnoye vremia* (times of trouble) probably exceed what his leadership, vision, and effectiveness can realistically provide.

The stultified cultural wasteland of official Russia is embodied in the endless and stereotyped repetitions of the nineteenth-century heritage on the one hand, and hack activities produced on "social demand" on the other hand. Yet even here the official optimism of "socialist realism" and the predominance of the "positive hero" are increasingly giving way to visible elements of pessimism, wherein the obligatory "happy ending" is often quite ambiguous. The old ideological hope of creating a new, Soviet culture is overshadowed by the spontaneous mass movement to preserve, reclaim, and rediscover traditional Russian (or non-Russian) ethnic culture, moods, and values. The "Association for the Preservation of the Monuments of Russian Culture" is said to have more than 5 million members, and is certainly the only large, truly voluntary organization in Russia. Finally, one can discern the stagnation of the social structure in the declining mobility and the overwhelming corruption and moral rot visible behind the Victorian façade of both official and unofficial Russia. This rot only serves to underscore the moral strength, courage, and purity of those small groups of dissenting individuals and their sympathizers who through their embrace of religious or simply moral norms seek spiritual survival in a sea of iniquity.

The caution and moderation in expectations, one might say even pessimism, of the new leadership can be seen in the new Party program that they have prepared for the Twenty-seventh Party Congress in February 1986. This is a basic document designed to replace the program adopted under Khrushchev some twenty-five years ago. That program reflected the apogee of the leadership's and elite's optimism in the post-Stalin era. "The present generation of Soviet citizens will live under full communism," "the Soviet Union will reach the per capita production of the United States by the year 1980," "the most important countries of the Third World will select a socialist way of development," "the world communist movement will remain monolithic and the world socialist system will expand enormously," etc.—these were only some of the predictions of the 1961 Party program. When compared to the realities of the 1980s, this program is a major source of embarrassment for the leadership. (The fate of Khrushchev's program is best told through a Soviet joke: "Communism is like the horizon, the closer you move to it the further it moves away.")

The new program, first presented by Gorbachev at the October 1985 plenary meeting of the Central Committee, is quite different from Khrushchev's utopian vision. It is a relatively short document, restrained in its claims of achievement and expectations about the future. It avoids by and large making any predictions about the time span necessary to attain its goals. It stresses sharply the necessity of overcoming serious obstacles in domestic development. It acknowledges the continuing strength and vitality of the "world capitalist system." It describes the international situation as being "complex and difficult," with as many dangers facing the Soviet Union and "the progressive forces" in spreading their influence as there will be opportunities for such expansion.

The program's most striking features are its prescriptions for moving the Soviet Union to higher stages of socioeconomic development. Again, as with the speeches of Gorbachev and his close associates, the program defines accurately the shortcomings of the system but does not really identify their systemic sources. It proclaims the need for realistic, pragmatic measures to improve Soviet performance radically, but fails to identify the specific elements in the system's *modus operandi* that will have to be replaced by new arrangements if the new program's fate is to be different from that of Khrushchev's.

In describing the Soviet Union during the post-Brezhnev transition, scholars have frequently used the term *systemic crisis*. This term simply means that the system does not work effectively in achieving the goals of the leadership. One may also define a systemic crisis in two additional ways: declining stability and a declining ability to adjust to changing circumstances, and the inability of a political system to utilize its potential. All three definitions apply to the Soviet system in the 1980s.

Yet while *systemic crisis* certainly describes a serious situation, it does not by itself define how serious the situation is. There is a distinction between a crisis of survival and one of effectiveness. It is clear that the systemic crisis in which the Soviet Union finds itself today, and that in all probability will not be resolved in the 1980s, is one of effectiveness.

The economy is not going bankrupt, and it is capable of delivering the necessary minimum of sustenance to the population. It can support the upkeep of its military machine. The crisis does not mean rebellious behavior on the part of the working class. It does not mean that large professional groups will join the movement of open dissent. It does not mean we will witness a visible decline of Soviet ambition to expand its power and influence in the international arena. It does not imply an inability to provide the minimum resources necessary for the support of the nation's international status. Finally and most importantly, it does not presage a fundamental disunity among the leadership and the functional elites, nor their loss of will to preserve the existing system.

What a crisis of effectiveness does mean is that the stability of the social order is declining and will continue to decline. The political instruments of power will have to be applied with greater weight, which means increasing coerciveness. Belief in Soviet ideology has plummeted, its teachings being irrelevant to the problems faced by the country, while the optimism of the elite about the country's future has given way to ill-concealed pessimism, frustration, and growing doubts. The slow growth or stagnation of the economy will continue. The relative social, political, and economic costs of Soviet determination to compete for power and influence in the international arena will increase immensely.

Obviously there comes a point at which a crisis of effectiveness becomes a crisis of survival. One should stress, however, that the present situation may last for a very long time before signs appear that the survival of the system is endangered. Such a transformation could best be predicted by designating thresholds of the effectiveness crisis that, when reached, indicate a menace to the survival of the system. In the social arena, such a threshold is reached when such social behavior as absenteeism, corruption, or alcoholism becomes politicized and produces unrest. In the economic arena, such a threshold is reached either when the technology and economic effort cannot sustain competitive growth in military strength or when, without recourse to full-blown Stalinism, the growth of the economy is entirely utilized for investment or military expenditures over a prolonged period of time. Politically, such a threshold is reached when pronounced and enduring fissures appear within the leadership and among the elites concerning the basic structural or procedural characteristics of the system, rather than mere tactical issues. None of those thresholds is in sight and none is likely to appear in the present decade.

Yet it is also clear that the cycle of revitalization in Russian history inaugurated by the Soviet seizure of power has exhausted its domestic potential. The Soviet Union has not yet completed the first industrial revolution of creating basic industries and an adequate infrastructure. It has made only a sputtering start of the second industrial revolution, that of mass consumption. It fights, as yet unsuccessfully, to participate in the third industrial revolution, that of electronics, information, and mass communications. Democratic countries as well as authoritarian regimes in both the West and the East generate and participate in new technology. Of all developed countries it is only the Soviet Union and its vassal states that are left behind, thus representing the past and not the future of mankind as their revolutions proclaimed.

The hammer and sickle has been the emblem of the Party and state from their inception. On the Party banner it symbolized its defense of workers' and peasants' interests. On the Soviet flag it symbolized the representation of the working class of the state. On the banners of the communist states and parties that adopted the emblem from the Soviets, it symbolized the worldwide community of Soviet and communist interests. In all these respects the claim of the hammer and sickle was doubtful.

Yet sometimes in history symbols of political movements and states acquire new meanings and become true in a sense not anticipated by its inventors. This is what happened to the hammer and sickle. Today, in one specific sense, it is an appropriate emblem of communism, and particularly of the Soviet Union. The emblem depicts hand tools which belong to the past and represent a bygone era. The programs and movements under the hammer and sickle are simply irrelevant to the vital problems of today and tomorrow. Most importantly, they are the proper symbols of the Soviet Union's economic and technological backwardness and the attachments of its leaders to ideas and policies which belong, together with the hammer and sickle, to the past.

Western specialists usually can find large areas of agreement with Soviet officials and experts about the crisis in Soviet society, but they differ on its root causes. The Soviet points to the lack of strong and imaginative leadership. He remains convinced that the socialist system has immense untapped potential for improvement. The Western specialist considers the paralysis of Soviet leadership in the last decade as one factor contributing to the aggravation of its domestic woes. The underlying root cause, however, he assigns to the very nature of the system.

In Mikhail Gorbachev, the Soviet Union now has a strong, intelligent, energetic leader, who, by his own preferences and in response to the widespread desire for change, will most certainly be an innovator. He is the best of what the Soviets have. The next few years will show whether the Western or Soviet interpretation of the domestic crisis will prove sounder. Gorbachev's leadership and reform program may constitute the last Soviet chance to make the hammer and sickle represent more than the social, political, and economic past.

In an ironic historical twist, the internal decline of the Soviet Union coincides with the height of its military power. Generations of sacrifice forced on the population have produced military might that has become the instrument of the basic rationale for the regime from the time of the revolution—to create a new civilization that would defiantly face the surrounding world and try to change it by any means available. While most of the utopian dreams of the original Bolshevik Revolution have been discarded or become a hollow ritual, the universalistic claims have largely expanded with the growth of military capabilities. This then is the Soviet paradox of today and of the foreseeable future, which both its leaders and the West have to face squarely in the 1980s: internal decline coupled with awesome military power directed toward external goals. The effect of this paradox on military policy and foreign behavior, on the Eastern European empire, on the threat of nuclear confrontation, on turmoil in the Third World, and on relations with China, Europe, and the United States is the subject of the rest of this book.

II

COMMUNIST ENCIRCLEMENT

A t Stalin's death in 1953, his successors inherited the concept of capitalist encirclement, the wellspring of Soviet military and foreign policy. To the degree that fear of capitalist encirclement has receded with the growth of Soviet power in subsequent decades, another set of problems has arisen which may be termed communist encirclement.

This second kind of encirclement may be envisaged as five concentric arcs at varying spatial and political distances from vital Soviet interests, each of which generates problems of differing intensity and danger. The first encompasses the internal empire, the belt of non-Russian nations dominating the periphery of the USSR. The second includes the external empire, Eastern European nations that owe their existence and survival as communist states to Soviet force, threatened and actual. In the third is the People's Republic of China, the colossus on the southeastern border. The fourth contains the outer empire, Cuba and Vietnam, which have no common borders with the Soviet Union and whose revolutions, like that of China and unlike the "revolutions" of Eastern Europe, sprang from indigenous sources, and also the seven or eight Marxist-Leninist regimes in and around Africa, like South Yemen and Ethiopia. The fifth arc, farthest from the center, includes the remains of a once-cohesive international communist movement dominated from Moscow, the many communist parties in democratic states that now exhibit autonomous tendencies that are troubling to the Soviet leaders.

In this part of the book I will concentrate primarily on the Soviet Union's empire in Eastern Europe, and its relations with the People's Republic of China.

9

The Dream of Revolution
and the Reality of Conquest

Karl Marx expected socialist revolutions to take place in highly developed capitalist countries. Only these countries possess the level of economic development necessary for the construction of socialism, and a large, cohesive working class capable of seizing political power. The combination of these two elements, according to Marx, makes a socialist revolution a realistic possibility. It is also clear that both Marx and Friedrich Engels envisioned the proletarian, socialist revolution as being international in character. They believed the revolution would quickly spread victoriously throughout the highly developed capitalist world (or as Marx would sometimes characterize it, the "civilized world") which encompassed Western Europe and North America. The socialist revolution had to be international because otherwise it would confront a united front of capitalist countries that would smother it.

In the Russian revolutionary movement, the true Marxist position was represented to the end by the Mensheviks, the moderate and democratic faction of the Russian Social Democratic Party. The Bolshevik wing of the Party under Lenin, and particularly the minuscule Trotskyite faction, proclaimed the possibility of a socialist revolution in agrarian countries like Russia with only semideveloped industrial and rural capitalism. Lenin, and especially Trotsky, envisaged the possibility of Russia, under certain circumstances, becoming the vanguard of the international socialist revolution and the first country in which the revolution would be victorious. The principal condition for such a revolution in semideveloped Russia, in their judgment, was the inability of both the tsarist authoritarian regime and the newly developed capitalist class to solve the problem of agrarian reform. By taking advantage of this, the

175

socialists could ride to power on a combination of worker unrest and peasant hunger for land.

The tsarist regime was overthrown with unexpected ease. A broad array of forces combined to bring about the February 1917 Revolution: popular anger leading to widespread bread riots in the capital; the disaffection of the local garrison troops which precluded their use against the rioters; the pressure of the moderate, constitutionalist, and populist parties in the Duma (parliament) for a change of the authoritarian regime; and a palace rebellion by the representatives of the upper classes, which looked with horror at the inept leadership of the tsar, the failing Russian effort in World War I, and the rapid decline of the tsar's authority among all classes of the population. Of all these factors the crushing defeat of the Russian forces in war was clearly the primary source and catalyst of the February Revolution. The tsar abdicated, and after intensive bargaining among the moderate parties, a provisional government was established to rule Russia until a constituent assembly could be called and a new, democratic constitution established. The overthrow was not at all in keeping with Lenin's vision of the Bolshevik Party leading the masses and creating a revolutionary government. The Bolsheviks played no role in the February Revolution—Lenin was in exile in Switzerland. Yet he recognized the opportunity for seizing power. None of his colleagues saw this until Lenin declared it in April 1917 on his return to Petrograd (as St. Petersburg had been renamed during the war out of anger at all things German).

The regime that evolved after the February Revolution had three major characteristics that were crucial to ensuing developments. It was a democratic government, which gave full freedom to every political group. In Lenin's own words, "it was the most democratic regime on the face of the earth." It was committed to social and agrarian reforms and constitutional government. But, because of its unshakable alliance with the French and British in the war against Germany and Austria-Hungary, it was determined to continue Russia's war effort and was therefore unable to proceed with these reforms. And it was a regime that almost from its inception, and increasingly over time, faced competing centers of power: the soviets (councils) of workers in cities, and the workers and peasants in the military units.

During the period from February to October 1917 this regime was unable to take harsh measures against the enemies of democracy. Moreover, it gradually lost popular support because of its inability to win or end the war or to engage in practical social reforms. The political situation then can best be described as a system of dual power—including both the provisional government and the system of soviets. In turn the balance shifted gradually to the soviets, which were increasingly dominated by the Bolsheviks. The delay of social reforms and further defeats at the front created a power vacuum, which was filled in October 1917 by the Bolshevik-controlled soviets in Petrograd. During the Civil War from 1918–1921 the political power of the Bolsheviks spread throughout Russia.

The Bolshevik victory in Russia was the result of a unique and unlikely confluence of circumstances and events:

• the vacuum of power left by the fall of the tsarist regime, which the provisional government did not succeed in filling;

• the organization of the industrial working class in the capital and a few other key urban centers into councils (soviets) over which the Bolsheviks gradually gained control;

• the Bolshevik decision to carry out a coup d'état in Petrograd and establish its own government;

• the desertion from the army of peasant soldiers who "voted with their feet," not for the Bolsheviks but against the war and the provisional government;

• a wave of spontaneous peasant rebellions throughout Russia in which the farmers divided the landed estates among themselves;

• the diversity of the opponents of the Bolsheviks both in 1917 and during the ensuing Civil War, which made them unable to unite in the face of growing Bolshevik power;

• the continuation of World War I, which precluded any major anti-Bolshevik actions by the European powers, and the unwillingness of these powers to provide any meaningful level of support to Russian opponents of Bolshevism in the immediate postwar period.

After seizing power in October, the Bolsheviks managed, slowly and with great bloodshed, to extend their monopoly of political control throughout Russia. No one in the Communist Party, and especially the leaders, imagined that revolutionary Russia would remain a socialist island in a sea of capitalist enemies. The tacit assumption of Lenin and Trotsky, and the belief of their followers, was that their revolution would provide a spark that would ignite the proletarian consciousness in Western Europe, particularly in Germany, and thus set off a series of revolutions in the capitalist countries. In 1920, Lenin made his last attempt to force the issue, when the newly created independent Poland under Marshal Joseph Pilsudski invaded Russia. The incursion was halted by the Red Army and thrown back to the Russo-Polish border. Despite the warnings of some of his associates, particularly Karl Radek, a top Party journalist and propagandist, Lenin decided to carry the Bolshevik counteroffensive into Poland. By doing so he hoped to create a revolutionary regime there and thus build a bridge between the Russian Revolution and the revolutionary movement in Germany. As predicted by Radek, who was of Polish origin and knew the country well, the attempt failed, Pilsudski was able to mobilize Polish patriotism against the specter of a Russian-imposed communist regime. That this was Lenin's goal was clear from the fact that during the Soviet military offensive a provisional Polish communist government was established to follow the expected victory of the Red Army. This government was led by two prominent Polish communists active in Russia, Julian Marchlewskii and Felix Dzerzhinskii, the head of the newly created Soviet secret police. The Red Army was too weak; the Russian offensive faltered, and it was thrown back to Russia's borders.

The idea that the Bolsheviks would have to build their own brand of socialism without the participation of other socialist governments established in capitalist societies did not enter the leaders' minds during the Revolution and early phases of the Civil War. As Lenin said many times, the proletariat and its vanguard, the Bolshevik Party, were placed by unique historical circumstances in a situation in which they were able to assume power. But to make this power safe and secure and to build socialism in Russia, proletarian revolutions in developed capitalist countries were indispensable. "We will start," Lenin often stated, and they (the developed capitalist countries) "will follow and finish the job." After the war with Poland, it became clear that the Russian revolutionaries were on their own. They were left with the question of the morality, not to mention the efficacy, of the use of Bolshevik power to spread communist power abroad.

The Soviet pattern of spreading its gospel, its form of rule and its power beyond Russia proper, was first tested in Lenin's time and then practiced in a much more ruthless fashion by Stalin. The old Russian empire embraced a large number of non-Russian nations. At the time when Bolshevik rule was enveloping Russia proper, many of these peripheries were beyond Russian control, and in some areas like Georgia independent, anti-Bolshevik governments were established. These areas, which had belonged to imperial Russia since the eighteenth or nineteenth century, were reconquered by the Russian Bolsheviks. In the Ukraine, in Byelorussia, in Central Asia and Transcaucasia the Red army waged war to preserve the former tsarist holdings under communist rule. The man in charge of the non-Russian areas and nationality policies in the new Soviet regime was Joseph Stalin, the people's commissar for nationalities. And while Lenin at times criticized Stalin's harsh policies in the non-Russian regions, he basically accepted both the goal of restoring Russian rule there and the idea that revolution could be carried into other countries by Russian bayonets. To Lenin, and to the Bolsheviks in general, the cause of socialist revolution was morally and politically superior to the principle of national self-determination that Lenin had in fact espoused before the Revolution.

Lenin did not see himself as a hypocrite. His views on the question of self-determination were developed publicly in his dispute with the prominent German and Polish communist revolutionary, Rosa Luxemburg, before the First World War. He believed that the victories of the socialist revolution, wherever they occurred, represented the supreme moral value. All other goals, such as agricultural reform, trade union activity, and movements for national independence had to be subordinated to the goal of communist revolution, even if it was undertaken by a small minority of the population. In order to gain victory, the revolutionary parties had to "unify the diverse streams of dissatisfaction and opposition" to the authoritarian or democratic government that the revolutionaries sought to overthrow. Therefore, the revolutionary parties were to proclaim their support for national self-determination in order to mobilize support for revolution and to activate the strata desiring national independence under the old regime. The actions of these groups would weaken the antirevolutionary government and thus strengthen the revolutionaries. Finally, after the victory of the revolution, revolutionary goals took supremacy over the principle of self-determination.

In the early 1920s, during the last years of Lenin's rule and the interregnum that ended with Stalin's acquisition of power, two questions preoccupied the Bolshevik Party and its leadership: what policies to pursue in Russia in the face of the failure of revolutions in the West; and what part of resources and effort to devote to domestic tasks? Lenin's answer to both questions was the establishment of the New Economic Policy. In domestic policies NEP stressed a long period of coexistence between the urban, Bolshevik rulers and the peasant masses. In the international arena, it pursued a dual policy of coming to terms with the powerful capitalist enemies and helping revolutionaries abroad. Lenin's position, and that of most of his comrades after his death, was to hope for the development of authentic communist revolutionary movements in the East and West. With Soviet help as a secondary element, it was envisioned, these movements would at some future point be victorious and end the revolutionary isolation of the Soviet Union.

The post-Stalin leaders have asserted that their theory of coexistence between capitalist and communist countries stems directly from Lenin and is therefore not a pragmatic maneuver but an integral part of communist ideology. Yet in Lenin's views on the relations of Soviet power with capitalist countries, the term *coexistence* was used in conjunction with NEP. It signified the temporary necessity of developing relations with some capitalist countries while the revolutionary movement and the

Soviet Union were weak. It described a transitional situation, a breather (*peredyshka*), in Russia before the inevitable military clashes between capitalism and communism were renewed. In the fifty-five volumes of the fifth edition of Lenin's collected works, the term "peaceful coexistence," according to its cumulative subject index, is mentioned only fifteen times.

From the time of Lenin's death and to an increasing degree with the growth of his own power in the Party's leadership, Stalin's answer to the questions was unequivocal. Under the slogan of "socialism in one country" the main efforts of the Party were to be devoted to the development and strengthening of Soviet power, increasing the control of the Party over the population, and economic modernization primarily oriented toward enlarging the military power of the state. In the 1930s, after Stalin had defeated his opposition and established personal domination over the Party and state, the conflict between the domestic and foreign interests of the state and the international commitment to the world revolutionary process was resolved in a straightforward and simple way. The interests of the state were declared to be the principal concern of revolutionaries everywhere. It became the duty of communist revolutionaries worldwide to accept without question Soviet goals and to support without hesitation Soviet foreign policies. As expressed in Stalin's own words, an internationalist communist revolutionary was whoever supported the Soviet Union above all else. As far as support for the world revolutionary movement was concerned, it had to become subordinate to the national interests of the Soviet Union and its foreign policy.

There was, of course, no socialist revolution in the West. The victory of the revolution in Russia appeared more and more to be a historical accident, impossible to repeat in the modernized democracies of Western Europe and North America. It was becoming clear that modernity—in Marxist terms, "the advanced development of capitalist relations"—far from being a precondition of socialist revolution, constituted a decisive obstacle to its victory.

Despite the obvious differences between the revolutionary conditions in Western Europe and tsarist Russia, Stalin's rise to power brought to the Comintern (the Communist International, to which all communist parties had to belong, and whose resolutions were binding for all parties) the process of "Bolshevization." This process successfully pursued two goals: to gain unquestioning obedience from the foreign communist parties, and to adjust the organization, strategy, and tactics of those parties to the Bolshevik example. Of course the actual Bolshevik experience in 1917 and its prescriptions for future revolutions had little relevance for revolutions in other countries. It is in fact arguable that every successful communist revolution in the twentieth century was victorious only when it abandoned the actual or mythical Bolshevik experience. In the late 1920s and 1930s it was already clear to Stalin that despite the presence of sizable communist parties in some developed capitalist countries, the Soviet Union in its own policy planning could not count on their victory. The Soviets instead became primarily interested in using those parties as tools of their foreign policy, with the aim of disrupting the policies of Western governments directed against the Soviet Union.

In this respect Stalin was a realist, especially since he saw a much greater revolutionary potential in the East, particularly in China, than in the West. Despite this realism, however, there still existed in the minds of Stalin and Soviet communist militants a residual belief in the possibility of revolution in Western Europe. Particularly in the period of the Great Depression, this lingering hope helped perpetuate some illusions about the sympathies, commitments, and strength of the Western European working classes and their communist representatives. The leadership thus exaggerated the internal difficulties that a Western government would face in pursuing anti-Soviet policies and particularly in organizing a crusade against the Soviet Union. These illusions were shared to some extent by Stalin himself and were a major factor in his initial misjudgment of the meaning of the Nazi takeover in Germany. Stalin did not believe that the Nazis would be able to destroy the German communists, whose party was the largest and strongest outside the Soviet Union itself. He saw Hitler's coming to power as an act of desperation by the "German bourgeoisie" in its effort to stem the communist tide. He expected that Hitler's rule would be short and would only hasten the victory of the German communists. He underestimated Hitler's hold over German society: The Nazi experience and the Second World War put an end once and for all to the illusions and dreams about authentic socialist revolutions in capitalist countries and about potential working class support for the communist goal.

The Nazis have shown that the Marxist, and even Leninist, idea that workers in capitalist societies would inevitably develop a socialist consciousness (if a revolutionary party exists there) is basically wrong. The hold of the Nazis over the German working class demonstrated that nationalism, or even racism, can have a greater impact on workers than communist ideology. Moreover, aside from recognizing the strength of nationalist movements, the Soviets came to Antonio Gramsci's conclusions, although in a much less sophisticated way, that workers in developed capitalist countries are under the sway of bourgeois culture which is very difficult to break. They drew a logical conclusion from this lesson—trust the strength of your arms more than Western workers.

Before the Second World War there were instances of subordinating

the cause of international revolution to state interests, and of substitut-
ing expansion by force of arms for an authentic revolutionary process.
An example of the first was Soviet behavior in the Spanish Civil War.
The Soviet goal was primarily to protract the war, and thereby redirect
German attention to the West. Stalin also hoped that Western democracies would support the Loyalists and would therefore come into conflict
with the Italian Fascists and Nazi Germany, whose expeditionary forces
were helping General Francisco Franco. Military help for the Republicans was short-lived. By the end of the first year of the Civil War, Stalin
estimated that without massive Soviet assistance, the Spanish republic
was doomed to failure, and he decided to cut his losses. Spain was one of
the first and far from the last cases of the Soviets' placing higher priority
on their control over the revolution rather than on the success of the
revolutionary process itself. The Soviet secret police and their Spanish
collaborators instituted bloody purges of the other elements in the Republican armed forces, the Anarchists and Trotskyites, and this contributed to their defeat by Franco.

The Stalinist pattern of conquest and expansion by force of arms
rather than reliance on an authentic revolution was already evident at
the founding of the Soviet Union by the annexation of the former tsarist
colonies in Transcaucasia and Central Asia. The next round of such
"revolutionary" annexations was carried out partly in competition with
and partly with the acquiescence of the Soviet Union's newfound friend,
Nazi Germany. In the fall of 1939, the Soviets participated with the
Nazis in the partition of Poland, annexing its eastern territories. Foreign
Minister Vyacheslav Molotov gloated that Poland, "the bastard of Ver-
sailles," had ceased to exist. When in 1939 Stalin sent a congratulatory
telegram to Hitler in which he spoke of Nazi-Soviet friendship as "ce-
mented in blood," it was the blood of Poland to which he was referring.

In an aggressive war against Finland in 1939–40, the Soviets took over
large pieces of their neighbor's territory. These were incorporated into
the new Soviet Karelo-Finnish Republic. At the beginning of the war,
Stalin formed a Finnish government in exile headed by the leading
Finnish communist in Moscow, Otto Kuusinen. Apparently he hoped
that the war would be a brief affair, that all of Finland would be occupied, and that a "Finnish" government could follow in the footsteps of
the victorious Soviet troops. It was the heroic efforts of the Finns that
prolonged the war, and, along with the displeasure of their Nazi friends,
the revulsion in the West, and the possibility of Western help for Finland, led to more limited Soviet demands at its end.

In 1940, Soviet forces simply occupied the independent Baltic states of
Lithuania, Latvia, and Estonia and the northeast province of Romania
(Moldavia) and annexed them. In these cases, it is difficult to speak even

of the Soviet "export of revolution." There was no revolutionary situation or noticeable revolutionary movement to provide even a fig leaf for Soviet actions. In Estonia, for example, the Communist party had claimed only a few hundred members.

Otto Kuusinen, who had lived in exile in Russia and was one of the vice chairmen of the Communist International, became the gauleiter of the Karelo-Finnish Republic; none other than Nikita Khrushchev took charge of the eastern Polish territories that were incorporated into the Ukraine; P. K. Ponomarenko, the first party secretary of Byelorussia, administered the northeastern Polish territories incorporated into Byelorussia; and P. G. Borodin, a high Party official, became the leader of the new Moldavian Republic. But the real rulers of the annexed territories were the emissaries of the secret police. The NKVD forced "socialist" measures on these countries and arrested, exiled to Siberia, sent to labor camps, or simply killed the intellectual and political leaders. By 1941, the Soviet Union had almost entirely restored the borders of the old tsarist empire by acquisitions that had nothing to do with authentic revolutionary feeling.

One of the army leaders who enjoyed Stalin's trust was Marshal B. M. Shaposhnikov. During the First World War, Shaposhnikov had been a member of the tsarist general staff with the rank of colonel. In 1918 he joined the new Red Army and advanced quickly after Stalin's purge of 1936–38. Shaposhnikov cast his fate with the Bolsheviks because he believed they were the only power in Russia that could reassemble the broken pieces of the tsarist empire and create a strong Russian military force. In 1940, when almost all former tsarist imperial lands had been reoccupied, the old marshal is said to have remarked that what he had hoped for when he joined the Red Army had been attained.

The first phase of the Russian expansionist drive occurred during the Civil War and, in the case of the Central Asian nations of the Soviet Union, lasted even into the 1930s. The second phase was accomplished during the Nazi-Soviet Pact between 1939 and 1941. In 1944–45, the third phase of the expansionist drive began. As the Red Army moved westward, liberating the countries of East and Central Europe from the Nazis and their allies, the Soviets imposed communist regimes by force of arms and through secret police activity. By 1949 Poland, Czechoslovakia, Hungary, Romania, Bulgaria, and East Germany had been transformed into one-party communist systems and satellites of Moscow. These countries were not formally incorporated into the Soviet Union proper, but rather retained the symbolic accoutrements of national independence. Yet until Stalin's death in 1953, for all practical purposes they were treated as Soviet republics. In most of these countries at the end of World War II there were revolutionary situations that, if left to run their course free of outside interference, would probably not only have toppled the existing governments, but also have transformed their regimes in democratic directions. Yet with the exception of Yugoslavia, none of them, left to its own devices, would have experienced revolutionary upheavals leading to the creation of communist regimes. Communism was imposed on each by the direct application of Soviet military and police force or by the threat of such force.

This, then, was Lenin's and particularly Stalin's contribution to the international features of Marxism. The old Bolshevik dream of authentic socialist revolutions was displaced by the commitment to direct military conquest as the only realistic way to spread communism. The goal of decisive control, rather than true socialist revolution, became the highest priority.

In Greece in the immediate postwar years, there developed a strong communist movement with its own military arm that challenged the restoration of the prewar regime. The communist forces were directly supported with arms and training by the Soviet Union and Yugoslavia. By 1948, however, Stalin had reached the conclusion that support of the Greek revolutionary adventure was too risky in the face of British and American backing of the legitimate government, so he cut off the flow of arms and aid to the Greek communists. This move, despite continuing Yugoslav help, dovetailed with British help for the anticommunist coalition and the American implementation of the Truman Doctrine to defeat the Greek communists.

In China, civil war led to the victory of Chinese communist armies, the escape of the nationalist government to Taiwan, and the creation of the People's Republic in October 1949. The Soviet Union did help the Chinese communists by declaring war on Japan in August 1945, by occupying Manchuria, and by transferring captured Japanese weapons to the Chinese communist armies. This aid was, however, of marginal importance in the communist victory. The Chinese Revolution was an authentic one that fused communist goals with nationalism, and particularly the pursuit of national independence from all outside powers, including the Soviet Union. Stalin was surprised at the communist victory. He preferred a China of weakness and turmoil to a strong, unified country, communist or noncommunist. As both the Soviets and Chinese have reported, Stalin advised Mao in 1945 to make peace with Chiang Kai-shek and agree to a coalition government. Mao rejected Stalin's advice and began the civil war that brought him control of China in three years.

The communist revolution achieved by Tito and his partisan armies in Yugoslavia was also an authentic one, both communist and nationalist. The Soviet struggle with the Germans in the Balkans created the necessary preconditions for Tito's victory, but ultimately the credit must go to

Tito and his communist party. The party and its armies were able to attain both the allegiance of the multinational population and control over their opponents without large-scale Soviet participation or help.

What was already clear in Stalin's time, what the break with Yugoslavia in 1948 demonstrated, was that the Soviet Union could not gain lasting control over any country in which the revolutionary forces came to power as a result of their own strength. Moreover, as the Yugoslav example has shown, the highest priority in Soviet thinking about revolutions abroad in Stalin's time was not the survival and stabilization of revolutionary power but rather Soviet control over a new revolutionary government. In fact, one of the most notable aspects of the Soviet experience with authentic revolutions has been their inability to make a satellite of any state in which such a phenomenon has taken place. The reason for this pattern is that in order to gain power, an authentic communist revolution has to be both communist and nationalist. But nationalism precludes subservience to any foreign power, including the Soviet Union. Moreover, most often the leaders of such revolutions do not need Soviet support to stay in power.

In all authentic communist revolutions the national element—nationalism and national interests—has played a decisive role. The defeats and humiliations of Russia in the First World War were more responsible for the rise of Bolshevism than the appeal of its social program to the masses. Without their struggle against occupying Japanese forces the Chinese communists could not have gained power. Tito's partisan war against Nazi and Italian invaders was decisive because of his ability to mobilize popular support. It is ironic that communist regimes were able to come to power riding the wave of nationalism, a force that Marx and Engels totally ignored in their forecast of the future. And it bodes ill for Soviet hopes for the spread of communist regimes that would also be close Soviet allies. The nationalism of these regimes, the necessary condition of their revolutionary success, will limit their relations.

The pattern of giving priority to Soviet control over foreign revolutions was already apparent in Spain in 1936–37. The pattern was repeated by Stalin in Tito's Yugoslavia and was continued toward the Chinese revolution. By 1956 signs were multiplying that the Chinese communists were increasingly dissatisfied with some Soviet policies toward China. They were disturbed at the status of Eastern Europe. They were seemingly surprised and later shocked by the Soviet decision to permit or even press the North Koreans to start the Korean War, which resulted in the clash of Chinese and American forces at a time when the internal development and stabilization of their own country were of utmost importance to the Chinese. They were outraged by Soviet attempts to dictate Chinese internal policies and by their generally patronizing attitude toward China, which they treated as a junior partner in the world communist enterprise. They became convinced that the Soviet Union wanted to keep them militarily weak and dependent, a conviction reinforced by the refusal to give them the technology necessary to produce nuclear weapons. In addition, the Chinese, while still full of revolutionary international fervor, were disgusted by Khrushchev's determination to arrive at a *modus vivendi* with the United States.

By the early 1960s, the Chinese communists had departed in their internal policies from the Soviets, and in their foreign policy pursued a course that outflanked the Soviets on the left in the communist and revolutionary international community. The Chinese simply and straightforwardly advocated a very radical policy for revolutionary and communist movements in Europe and in the Third World. The Soviets, to the contrary, made the degree of their support for indigenous revolutionary movements dependent upon their own state interests and foreign policy. In Indonesia, for instance, where they had good relations with the Sukarno government, they advised communist cooperation. In Egypt, where they played for high stakes in supporting General Gamal Abdel Nasser, they abandoned entirely the local Communist Party. By the late 1960s, there were Soviet-Chinese military clashes on their common border. At the same time, a vicious struggle was being waged for supremacy in the international communist movement, one that split it into pro-Soviet and pro-Chinese factions.

The only shots fired in anger by Soviet armed forces in the postwar era have been directed against other communist countries: Hungary in 1956, Czechoslovakia in 1968, and the People's Republic of China in the late 1960s. Even the invasion of Afghanistan in 1979 was directed initially against the communist regime of Hafizullah Amin (who had overthrown his communist colleague Nur Mohammed Taraki in September of that year) in order to replace him with Babrak Karmal, whom Moscow considered more subservient to Russia and potentially more effective in fighting native opposition to communist rule.

Soviet use of direct military force and their most vituperative vilification have been reserved not for capitalist adversaries, but for heretical communist leaders and countries: Tito, Imre Nagy in Hungary, Alexander Dubček in Czechoslovakia, and Mao Zedong. Heretics have been more despised by the leadership throughout Soviet history than "fascist," "capitalist," and "imperialist" enemies. In 1939 the Soviet Union was willing and able to reach a pact with Nazi Germany while at the same time Stalin ordered the murder in Mexico of Leon Trotsky, whose followers constituted a small and powerless sect of diehard Bolsheviks outside the Soviet Union. Khrushchev and Brezhnev were able to engage in serious talks with American leaders from Eisenhower to Carter, but were unable to prevent a break with revolutionary China or negotiate productively with Chinese leaders.

The reason for this paradox is familiar. Nonbelievers are enemies who are sometimes despised, sometimes admired, and always feared. But at no time, except in a war, do they endanger the legitimacy of Party rule in the Soviet Union or Soviet standing in the international revolutionary or communist movement. It is the heretical communist countries, movements, and leaders whose views and anti-Soviet activities are potentially threatening to the legitimacy of Soviet rule at home and its claim to infallibility among revolutionaries abroad. This continues to be the attitude of the leadership towards independent communist leaders and countries. The political reconciliation with Tito after Stalin's death—which does not impinge on Yugoslavia's independence—was and remains a damage-limiting procedure based on the growing realism and sophistication of the post-Stalin era. Present attempts to normalize relations with China represent a similar effort.

Both Cuba and Vietnam had authentic revolutions that were both communist and nationalistic in their goals. Their relations with the Soviet Union are good. But neither country can be labeled a Soviet satellite in the same sense as the Eastern European nations. In both cases there are special circumstances that explain their closeness to the Soviet Union and their policies that by and large follow Soviet ones.

Three factors explain Vietnam's dependence on the Soviet Union. The first is its disastrous internal economic situation. The second is its isolation in the international arena, which has both political and economic consequences. The third is its centuries-old enmity and conflict with the Chinese giant on its northern border, which represents a threat to its homeland and to its expansionist ambitions on the Indochinese peninsula.

For the immediate future, these factors are likely to cement the alliance between Vietnam and the Soviet Union. Still, it is foolish to believe that a country that fought so hard for its national independence, first from the Chinese and more recently from the French and the Americans, will be satisfied with the role of satellite. Already Vietnam's relationship with the Soviet Union is not precisely that of a subordinate and a superior. It is one of accommodation, mutual compromise, and some coordination of foreign policy issues of great importance to the Soviets. However, Vietnamese policies on Cambodia are not dictated by Moscow. Nor are they entirely pleasing to the Soviets because of the damage that the support of such Vietnamese policies causes Soviet relations with Third World countries, especially in Asia, and with China. The Vietnamese, on their side, are not satisfied with the extent and quality of Soviet economic aid; they are uneasy about the Soviet desire to make Cam Ranh Bay into a permanent naval and air base, and they want to establish relations with the United States and the capitalist states of Europe and Asia, in order to lessen their dependence on the Soviet Union.

The case of Cuba is relatively simpler and more straightforward. In the face of the U.S. and Latin American embargo on meaningful economic and political relations with Cuba, Soviet political and economic support is crucial in creating at least a tolerable, if far from satisfactory, economic situation in the country. (According to some estimates, about one-third of the Cuban GNP is supplied by the Soviet Union and its satellites.) Given especially the attitude of the present U.S. administration, Cuba's political isolation limits its choices to two stark options. The first is dependence on the Soviet Union, which requires Cuban support of Soviet domestic and foreign positions. The second is capitulation to the American determination to effect a significant change in the Cuban government, which would be tantamount to political suicide for Fidel Castro. Such a choice would also be predicated on a basic shift in Cuban attitudes and policies towards revolutionary movements in the Western Hemisphere and in Africa, which would require a fundamental, although possible, change in the beliefs of Havana.

There is an additional complication about Cuba. Under Batista it was a semicolony of the United States. From the outset, Castro led both a social and a national revolution, which initially placed greater stress on national independence than on sociopolitical change. Even after the revolution clearly became communist, Castro continued to use a nationalist stance to attract support from the Cuban population. Anti-Americanism and the state of tension between the United States and Cuba is an important element in the popular support for political stability of the Castro regime. Cuba's America is Vietnam's China. Still the Cuban leadership and political elite doubtless perceive their country as distinct from the Eastern European satellites. They are not treated by the Soviets simply as a satellite, and they would prefer to be less dependent on Soviet economic and military aid and to have greater room to maneuver.

During the Khrushchev era, the dream of international revolution was reawakened. The disintegration of colonial empires, the nationalist and social strivings of the former colonies produced the hope that these countries would select a revolutionary road of development that might make of them Soviet allies or even dependencies. The Khrushchevian image of a victorious march of a revolutionary postcolonial world was reinforced by the phenomenon of "African Socialism," the Marxist-Leninist ideas and vocabulary embraced initially by many leaders and ruling movements of the newly independent countries—Nkrumah in Ghana, for example, and Sekou Touré in Guinea.

The initial attraction of the Marxist-Leninist credo and the enthusiasm for the Soviet model of development is perhaps difficult to understand today. Twenty and thirty years ago, however, in most of the newly independent countries authoritarian regimes came to power whose leaders saw in Marxism-Leninism a justification for their monopoly of political power. The ideology of Marxism-Leninism, as no other creed, combined the two characteristics which were entertained at that time by the elites of the newly independent countries: anti-Westernism and pro-modernization. This ideology reflected the feelings of the local elites, who wanted to erase their degrading colonial experience and turn their backs on capitalism represented by their old rulers, but who were also attracted to the fruits of economic civilization represented by their former overlords. Marxism-Leninism both glorified the economic progress and condemned the capitalism of the colonial systems. Further, the Soviet Union epitomized successful noncapitalist economic development and could serve as a counterweight to these countries' former mentors and a source of political, economic, and military support.

In the Khrushchev period the leadership invented the concept of the "noncapitalist road of development," which was to account for the peculiarities of the newly independent states. From the Soviet point of view, this road was not yet socialist. The expectation was that its trend of development would be towards socialism with an inevitable alliance with the Soviet Union.

After Khrushchev's ouster in 1964 attitudes remained the same but were tinged with growing disenchantment. Present views on revolutionary and pro-Soviet development in the Third World, and particularly Africa, are much more realistic. Perhaps the leaders remember the verdict on the Third World revolutionary movements in the 1920s of one of the most prominent agents of the Communist International, Mikhail Borodin: "They come to us," he said, "and cry 'Revolution, Revolution.' What they really want is arms."

After Stalin's death Soviet leaders rediscovered a new and strange world outside their borders, from which they were isolated and of which they were ignorant. Their initial attitude toward "socialist progress" in underdeveloped countries was certainly overly optimistic and perhaps also somewhat romantic. Toward the end of the Brezhnev period their optimism gave way to greater realism. The leaders no longer believe that economic and military help with no strings attached will gain them a dominant voice in the domestic and foreign affairs of these countries. Except in rare cases like Ethiopia, they are far from believing the revolutionary claims of their friends in the Third World. They are, therefore, having second thoughts on the effectiveness of their aid, which they can ill afford, considering their domestic situation.

As in the past the hope for authentic revolutions gave way to the Soviet commitment to control. There is no reason to believe that the Kremlin leaders in the 1980s will abandon this approach. In the light of the past experience with revolutions the approach seems, from their point of view, altogether realistic.

10

The Decline of an Empire

In the history of Soviet expansion there is no greater or more important achievement than the establishment of the Eastern European empire. Along with its internal empire—the non-Russian republics of the Soviet Union—Eastern Europe is today the only surviving empire in the world. Much of Soviet domestic, foreign, military, and economic policies can be explained by the goal of preserving hegemony there. In turn, Eastern European policies stem from their countries' ties to the Soviet Union and their expectations. The existence of this domain—along with partial control of countries such as Cuba and Vietnam—was and is perceived by the leadership as the basis for the future expansion of Soviet rule and of communism, and as confirmation of the historical trend towards the "inevitable" victory of socialism over capitalism. Leaders from Stalin to Gorbachev, despite some differences in specific policies toward the region, have been steadfast in their total determination to preserve this empire.

Eastern Europe serves a number of important purposes. It is a security belt of allied buffer states on the Soviet Union's western borders, which both defends the homeland and provides a beachhead for actions against the West. Eastern European armed forces are important additions to those of the Soviet Union. These constitute more than one-third of the mobilized armed forces on Eastern European–Western borders. The Eastern European economies together supplement the military and civilian sectors of the Soviet economy. The countries serve also as sources of technical expertise and as conduits through which advanced Western technology finds its way eastward.

Nations like East Germany, Czechoslovakia, and Poland assist the

Soviet Union in pursuing its foreign policy objectives in the Third World. They bolster the Soviet presence among potential allies or clients. They also play an essential role in Soviet foreign policy toward Western Europe, both as hostages that moderate Western European policies toward the Soviet Union and as intermediaries that make Soviet foreign policies more palatable to Western Europe.

The function of Eastern Europe in moderating Western policy toward the Soviet Union is most clearly expressed by the example of East Germany. The 20 million Germans under communist rule are a major preoccupation among West Germans. The predicament of these 20 million is deliberately used by the Soviet Union to keep the level of Soviet-German economic relations relatively high, as well as to moderate American Soviet policy. Moreover, the Eastern European governments are instrumental in explaining Soviet policy to Western Europe and in warning them of the deleterious effects on Eastern Europe if they should follow American policies too closely.

Yet neither security interests—Eastern Europe as a buffer zone and as a military and economic counterbalance to NATO—nor the usefulness of Eastern Europe for advancing Soviet global ambitions suffices to explain the depth of Soviet determination to maintain a hold over the empire regardless of the cost. Considerations of security and utility alone do not require the present high level of Soviet control over social and political developments in Eastern European countries.

The explanation lies beyond pragmatism. Soviet rule provides one of the ideological foundations of Great Russian and Communist Party control within the Soviet Union itself. It also contributes decisively to the credibility of Soviet foreign policy.

Victory in World War II was the central legitimizing experience of Soviet rule at home and is associated with, even focused on, control over Eastern Europe. As the major spoil of war the empire serves to legitimize the Kremlin's rule in Russia. In particular, it helped to form a bond of common interest between the government and its Great Russian and other Slavic populations. It is important to remember that the creation of the empire made permanent the unification of the Ukraine and Byelorussia with the eastern parts of Poland annexed in 1939. It also led to the division of Germany, the historic threat to the Eastern Slavs.

The domination of this empire is expected and supported by the Russian population, both Party and non-Party members alike. When in 1981 the Polish situation was developing in a way that threatened Soviet rule there, a member of the Russian academic establishment, who is a liberal in Soviet terms, told me: "You will probably hate me for what I have to say to you, but I will say it nevertheless: If tomorrow Soviet forces enter Poland I will applaud them, and I can assure you that this is a very widespread feeling in my milieu." Echoes of this attitude prevail among diverse parts of Russian society. To some members of the public, the Eastern European empire represents the fulfillment of the dream of the unification of the Slavs under Russian domination. To others, it signifies the first step in the expansion of Russian power and influence abroad. To many it provides the desired confirmation and reinforcement of the valued belief that Russia belongs to Europe and is a dominant part of the continent's structure of power. For all, it contributes to a feeling of security and pride.

The continuing domination of Eastern Europe also confirms the basic ideological proposition that the establishment of communist rule is irreversible. Soviet rule in Russia and communist domination in Eastern Europe represent in the Party's view the victory of a historical process and the inexorable trend of the future. If this trend can be reversed in Eastern Europe then the question will inevitably arise why it cannot be reversed in the homeland itself. Furthermore, loss of control over individual Eastern European countries, not to mention the disintegration of the external empire, would certainly strengthen tendencies toward greater autonomy or even separatism among the Soviet nations. The danger of the loss of either empire could even lead to a military coup.

Even after Stalin's death the Soviets have insisted on the monopoly of power by communist parties in Eastern Europe. They have not permitted autonomous organizations of a political character to exist for long, let alone to challenge the parties' monopolies. The media are under strict party control, and are monitored with special care for any breaches in censorship and criticism of the Soviet Union. The security organs and armed forces are strictly supervised through a dual system of native party supervision and direct control by the Soviet military and secret police commands.

In the post-Stalin decades, Soviet controls have been relaxed in some areas, particularly in economic affairs. The Soviets have reluctantly tolerated if not encouraged economic experimentation, leaving initiatives in this field to the wishes and policies of particular leaders like János Kádár in Hungary. They have not been overly aggressive in harnessing satellite economies to the service of Soviet goals; economic integration of Eastern European countries with the Soviet economy is not far advanced. They have also tolerated relaxation of restraints on private, if not political freedoms, again allowing such decisions to be made by local leaders. So the countries differ in important ways. In Czechoslovakia, for instance, since the Soviet invasion of 1968, the conservative leadership has pursued a policy that follows the principle "who is not with us is against us." In Kádár's Hungary, by contrast, the principle is quite different—"who is not against us is with us." In the latter case, as well as in

Poland even under military rule, the freedom to express privately one's feelings and views about communism is quite extensive, just as long as it does not lead to political, antistate actions. And until the Polish events of this decade direct daily supervision of satellite party activities was less stringent than under Stalin.

In foreign policy, the satellites enjoy little freedom to maneuver. The relative independence of Romanian foreign policy is an exception, and derives from its strategic marginality to the Soviet Union, the compensating orthodoxy of the Romanian regime, and the determination of President Nicolae Ceauşescu.

Soviet control varies from one Eastern European country to another and is determined by three things. Most central is the strength of the actual or potential opposition to Soviet *diktat* within each country. The more active it is, the more cautious the Soviets are. Hungary is treated differently from Czechoslovakia largely because of its proven willingness to fight Soviet tanks. Poland's historical pugnacity surely influenced Soviet hesitation in terminating the growing power of Solidarity, as well as the eventual choice of an internal solution over outright invasion. And it will certainly affect Soviet toleration of any relatively liberal Polish communism that might emerge in the future. Another variable is the unity of satellite leaders and their individual strength and authority in the face of Soviet pressure. In 1956 Wladyslaw Gomulka was personally courageous and had the support of the Polish Politburo behind him. As a result, the Soviets retreated from their intention of installing another Polish communist in his place. Finally, there is the strategic importance of a given satellite to the Soviet Union, both militarily and politically. Here East Germany is clearly the most important country in the area, and therefore Soviet control over its internal and external affairs is stricter than elsewhere.

The Eastern European communist regimes were established through the force of Soviet arms and intimidation. The leadership hoped that the origins of these "revolutions" and their lack of a nationalist base would cease to matter over time and that the regimes would attain legitimacy in the eyes of their populations.

In the 1950s and 1960s hopes for the popular legitimization of the regimes were based on the belief in the malleability of the younger generations in these countries and their attraction to communist ideals. These hopes were not fulfilled. In the 1970s, the legitimization of these regimes was expected to be achieved on the strength of their economic and cultural performance. This type of legitimacy is much more fragile than that based on traditional values, national identity, or political authority. Yet it appeared to both the Soviets and the native political leaders that such legitimacy, and therefore a measure of stability, was being attained in Eastern Europe. Indeed, in Hungary and East Germany this goal may have been at least partially achieved through credible economic performance and improved living standards in the course of the 1970s. But with the stagnant Czech regime today, the chaotic, despotic, and spiritually empty Romanian government, and the facsimile of communist government that exists in Poland, the general situation from the Soviet standpoint can only be described as bleak. Further decay during the 1980s is likely, which promises a worsening situation. It is now clear that the regimes in Eastern Europe exist only because the populations of those countries—and even segments of their elites—have no other choice in the face of Soviet pressure.

Western policy towards Eastern Europe and its expectations of evolution and change in the countries of the region went through successive stages, each of which ended either unsuccessfully or inconclusively, with expectations unfulfilled. During the Cold War of the late 1940s and early 1950s, the hope existed that a Western military, economic, and political confrontation with the Soviet Union, combined with rebellion in Eastern European countries, would lead to a rollback of Soviet dominance in the region. Eastern Europe was a central issue of the Cold War. Although the military superiority of the West was at that time unquestionable, it soon became clear that Eastern Europe could only be torn away from the Soviet embrace by force.

After Stalin's death in 1953 both the Eastern European political publics and Western governments hoped that a more moderate Soviet Union and pressures from the Eastern European parties and masses would loosen the Soviet grip. The brutal suppression of the Hungarian Revolution in 1956 showed that the Soviets would not tolerate Eastern European efforts to achieve independence through violent means. The invasion of Czechoslovakia in 1968 demonstrated that the Soviets would not tolerate Eastern European efforts to gain even limited national autonomy through peaceful and gradual measures.

Ostpolitik, initiated by West Germany, had as its goal rapprochement with Eastern European countries through the instruments of trade, credit, and the exchange of expertise, people, and ideas. This was expected to lead to a slow evolution of those countries in a more liberal direction. After the invasion of Czechoslovakia the tacit assumption of *Ostpolitik* was that the road to change in Eastern Europe went through Moscow, and that improvements in the region's position required parallel improvements in the West's relations with the Soviet Union.

Finally, in the early 1970s came détente. The hope here, as in *Ostpolitik,* was that through recognition of the legitimacy of Soviet stakes, especially those involving security in Eastern Europe, the Soviet Union would become less uneasy about changes there. Additionally, through a network of relations combining incentives and deterrents it was hoped that the Soviet Union would be willing to tolerate Eastern European sociopolitical evolution and partial economic integration with Western Europe. However, the lack of both incentives and deterrents on the American side, coupled with Soviet expansion beyond the European continent and the events in Poland, ended American hopes for détente, and with them the hopes of Western governments that détente would lead to peaceful changes in Eastern Europe. The international cycle returned to its point of departure: As in the original Cold War, Eastern Europe once again became a focal point of United States-Soviet relations and confrontations.

Eastern Europe remains the primary example of Soviet expansion abroad. The Soviet commitment to its control over its holdings there is unshaken. Yet after four decades of domination, the external empire has peaked; its own decline has commenced.

The historical experience of empires, generalized especially in the seminal work of Professor S. N. Eisenstadt, reveals a number of factors that presage the decline of the system: the internal economic slump of the metropolitan power, the moral weakening of its ruling class, divisions within the ruling class on major imperial issues, the loss of will of the ruling class to pursue its imperial ambition, the growing price of supporting the empire, the military cost of ensuring colonial tranquillity, and finally the inability of the imperial elite to rule, and the growing reluctance of the colony to be ruled. These factors combine to promote the decline and disintegration of empires. Many of these factors are absent in the Soviet empire today; especially the loss of will of the leadership to rule and its overall perception that this rule is unjustified. Nevertheless, while one cannot suggest the growing likelihood of the disintegration of the Soviet empire, one can certainly identify its downslide.

The signs of imperial failing may be found in the economic, military, political, and ideological areas. Most Western and many Soviet economists concur that the Eastern European countries have become an economic burden for the Soviet Union (see Table 9). (Of course, in a broader sense, by dictating the design of the economic systems in Eastern Europe and precluding patterns of their development similar to the rest of the continent, the Soviet Union has exploited the region. There can be little doubt that if the Eastern European countries had not been forced to shape their economies according to the Soviet model and growth strategies, their economic health, modernization, and standard of living as partners in a free Europe would have been more favorable than they are today.) Not only could the Soviets receive higher prices in world markets for raw materials they now sell to satellites that are dependent on them for economic development, they could also earn the hard currency they need to purchase essential advanced technology. Until recently the Soviet Union routinely accepted from Eastern Europe, in exchange for its raw materials, inferior goods unsuitable for sale in world markets, all the more so during periods of recession. The economist Jan Vanous estimates that in the 1972–81 period the debt incurred to and nonrepayable aid from the Soviet Union amounted to $100.8 billion. Furthermore, it appears that the satellite countries do not bear their proportional share of military expenditures as members of the Warsaw Pact.

TABLE 9   DEFICITS IN EASTERN EUROPE'S TRADE WITH THE USSR 1973–82
(billions of current U. S. dollars)

Year	Reported	Trade Subsidies	Total
1973	−0.6[a]	1.6	1.0
1974	0.1	6.3	6.4
1975	0.5	5.3	5.8
1976	0.7	5.6	6.3
1977	1.2	5.9	7.1
1978	0.1	5.8	5.9
1979[b]	0.9	10.4	11.3
1980[b]	1.6	17.5	19.1
1981[b]	2.7	18.6	21.3
1982[c]	3.3	15.1	18.4

[a] Surplus   [b] Preliminary estimate   [c] Forecast

Not only is the potential contribution of Eastern European countries to Soviet military capabilities very limited—the exception being the clear value of Eastern European or Cuban units deployed in Third World countries to enhance Soviet influence and prestige—in the case of a war in Europe, it is probably a negative factor. The Soviets could rely only on select Eastern European elite units, especially in the air force and army, to supplement its own forces. If the war were protracted, moreover, the uncertain motivation and morale of a draft army and of Eastern European civilian populations could well necessitate the deployment of far more Soviet troops to keep order than Eastern Europe would be providing for the front line.

Politically, the external empire has become an embarrassment and a handicap to Soviet pursuit of foreign political objectives. It seriously inhibits renewal of the détente process with the United States. America cannot accept détente with a power that crushes an Eastern European country every decade or so. It cements the defensive military and political alliance of Western Europeans, who are sensitive to this blatant expression of Soviet imperialism. It stands as a most significant obstacle to a cohesive international communist movement under Soviet direction, and is a decisive reason for the spread of Eurocommunism. There is little difference between the Western European right and left in condemning repressive measures in Eastern Europe that are directed not only against dissidents and intellectuals but against workers and free trade unions. Indeed, the détente with Western Europe that has survived the end of détente with the United States may well collapse on the day Soviet troops again invade an Eastern European country. The invasion of Czechoslovakia in 1968 brought the Sino-Soviet conflict to the point of military clashes along the Southeast Asian border and stimulated the Chinese rapprochement with the United States.

From the ideological point of view, Eastern European countries represent not a showcase for Soviet ideology and the model of socialism but a glaring example of their failure. For decades Soviet leaders and ideologues have explained away the political repression, intellectual intolerance, economic backwardness, and social inequality in their own country by reference to the difficult circumstances of Russia's revolution, tsarist underdevelopment and capitalist encirclement. Yet these basic features of Soviet power have not essentially altered, despite the added security of westward expansion. And now they similarly characterize countries that, prior to the Soviet takeover, enjoyed more democratic governments in some cases and higher levels of industrialization in others.

The crisis in the empire is no less apparent when one looks solely at the internal situation in the particular countries. Its deepest source is common to all of them—their lack of legitimacy.

The legitimacy of regimes spawned by revolution may derive from popular backing expressed in traditional or legal forms, from elite support reflecting the cohesion and interlocking strength of key power centers, and from performance. Legitimacy grounded in popular support did not obtain in the great majority of Eastern European countries because Soviet controls and interventionism denied native governments their traditional source, nationalism, and their legal source, free elections. Legitimacy grounded in elite support did obtain under ordinary circumstances, but the cohesiveness of the power structure and the reliability of support from other power centers (the security and armed forces, the communications networks, the official trade unions, etc.) weakened in times of crisis. This form of legitimacy ultimately depends less on internal structures than on external coercion: It is only through economic performance that East Germany and Hungary have gained a limited and grudging acceptance among the population. Yet legitimacy grounded in performance is the most fragile and least dependable form of all, because no government is insured against hard times, and economic performance may decline precipitously. The satellite governments rest finally on Soviet power and determination to sustain them, and on popular fears of the danger from the East. Especially disquieting for Soviet leaders is the now proven fact that the younger generation in Eastern European countries is just as dissatisfied with communist rule as their parents.

The dilemma of communist elites in Eastern Europe is insoluble. On the one hand, they will gain popular support only by advocating the cause of national independence, with the accompanying risks of Soviet military intervention. On the other hand, they will retain power only through unqualified Soviet support and, if need be, military intervention. Communism has been victorious primarily because the regimes that were forged in communist revolutions identified themselves with national interests, nationalism, and independence. It is the crucial flaw of the Soviet-controlled Eastern European regimes that they cannot do so.

Other circumstances also work to thwart acceptance of these regimes as legitimate. In contrast with the Soviet Union, Eastern Europe has failed to produce professional classes that identify more than superficially with the governments. While persons with higher education in the Soviet Union are not generally opposed to the Kremlin, Eastern European countries boast a genuine intelligentsia that is potentially or actually hostile to communist leadership. Eastern Europe also remains immune to Soviet cultural influence. The contempt for Soviet culture, the perfunctory and ritualistic acceptance of dogmatic Marxism-Leninism even in the national parties, the deep attachment to religion and church, the affinity for Western values and traditions—all combine to make the communist leadership an alien and shallow strain markedly different in stability and effectiveness from its counterpart in the Soviet Union. A cardinal truth is that Eastern Europe is an integral part of Western civilization and culture, as Russia never was, is not today, and probably will not be in the future. The border between East and West is not the political boundary on the Elbe River in Germany, but the cultural dividing line on the Bug River that divides Russia from Poland. Anybody who has traveled between Eastern Europe and Russia knows the shock of passing from one type of society to another. From architecture to national character, social behavior, interpersonal relations, and communal and religious beliefs, Poland, Czechoslovakia, Hungary, East Germany, Romania, despite forty years of communist rule and Soviet domination, remain closer to Western Europe than to Russia. Eastern Europe is a part of Europe; Russia is not. Soviet domination is a rule of non-Europeans over Europeans. Of course, geographically, and to some extent culturally, Russia is both a European and Asian country. This geographic circumstance, however, instead of being a source of strength, led instead to its alienation from both Europe and Asia. In political terms Russia shows to Asia its white imperialist face, and to Europe its features of Oriental despotism.

Finally, and what is unusual among modern empires, the Soviet dominator surpasses the dominated in only one attribute, absolute military power. It lags behind in standard of living, economic development, educational levels, and cultural richness. The single index of Soviet superiority has so far sufficed to forestall the disintegration of the empire. Historically, empires do not disintegrate when the imperial power is at the peak of its military strength. But if apocalypse does not threaten the Eastern European empire in the next decade, serious instability surely does.

In the decade ahead legitimacy grounded in performance may founder on the shoals of economic distress. Just because the basis of the legitimacy of Eastern European regimes rests with economic performance, the decline of growth over recent years and the prospects of further disintegration in the mid- and late 1980s will require a degree of improvement in productivity of labor and technological progress that will be almost impossible to achieve.

Because of their small size, dependency on foreign raw materials, limited labor resources and generally higher level of industrialization, the importance of labor and capital productivity growth is even greater for the Eastern European countries than in the Soviet Union. Yet as Table 10 demonstrates, the situation in Eastern Europe is as bad as, and in some cases even worse than, in Russia.

While the direct and indirect military contribution of Eastern Europe to the Warsaw Pact falls far below that of the Soviet Union, it has tended to rise at approximately the same rate as in the Soviet Union. For the Eastern European economies, which are so much smaller and more developed than that of the Soviet Union, the growth of military expenditures is even more burdensome than in the Soviet Union, not least because of slower overall growth.

Moreover, their own economic difficulties force the Soviets to reduce or eliminate subsidies to the satellites, such as the sale of energy and other raw materials below world prices, and buying inferior Eastern European goods that would not find other markets. Moreover, forced Eastern European investments in Soviet development may soon exceed Soviet credits to Eastern Europe.

In June 1984 a frequently delayed meeting of Comecon, the Council of Mutual Economic Assistance of the communist countries, took place.

According to reliable reports the Soviet Union announced at this conference that its prices for deliveries of raw materials and energy to Eastern
Europe would be equal to the world market prices. The Soviets also
pressed their allies to improve the quality of manufactured goods. It is
unlikely, however, that Soviet pressure for a greater division of labor
among Comecon members and for a decisive increase of investment by
Comecon members in the Soviet economy will be successful. Moreover,
while Comecon countries are willing to participate in cooperative projects with the Soviet Union, such as the design and production of the
third generation computer RIAD, they are resisting the specialization of
individual Eastern European countries in the manufacture of specific
products. Such specialization, while providing the economic benefits of
long production runs, would also lead to an increased dependence on
Soviet and other Eastern European markets.

TABLE 10   PRODUCTIVITY GROWTH IN EASTERN EUROPE
(Annual Average Changes in Percentage)

	1971–75	1976–80	1981–82
BULGARIA			
Labor Productivity	7.7	6.1	3.7
Capital Productivity	−1.0	−3.6	−2.9
Overall Productivity	3.3	1.2	0.4
CZECHOSLOVAKIA			
Labor Productivity	4.8	3.1	−0.1
Capital Productivity	−0.1	−2.4	−5.9
Overall Productivity	2.3	0.3	−3.0
EAST GERMANY			
Labor Productivity	5.3	3.6	3.1
Capital Productivity	−0.3	−1.5	−1.6
Overall Productivity	2.5	1.0	0.8
POLAND			
Labor Productivity	8.3	1.3	−7.2
Capital Productivity	1.7	−6.6	−11.1
Overall Productivity	5.0	−2.6	−9.2
ROMANIA			
Labor Productivity	11.1	7.0	2.3
Capital Productivity	−0.4	−2.7	−6.1
Overall Productivity	5.4	2.1	−1.9
HUNGARY			
Labor Productivity	6.2	4.1	2.5
Capital Productivity	−0.4	−3.2	−2.5
Overall Productivity	2.9	0.4	0.0

The increase of Soviet prices for primary products and energy resources, particularly oil, have already had deleterious effects on Eastern European economies. They have, in fact, changed the terms of trade between the Soviet Union and its empire. The relative value of Eastern European currencies in comparison with rubles has visibly declined. "For one million tons of Soviet oil we paid the equivalent of 800 Ikarus buses in 1972"—remarked a Hungarian economist—"last year that same amount of oil cost us 4,000 buses."

Even more pressed than the Soviet Union to earn hard currency for technological imports, Eastern Europeans will find it increasingly difficult to compete with Western goods in Third World markets and to enter Western markets. Home markets in the industrial West are expanding very slowly and may be safeguarded by protectionist barriers erected against imports from non–Common Market countries. At the same time the competition for Third World markets will sharpen as they acquire a more important role for Western industries. The technological, commercial, and financial edge of Western countries over Eastern Europe will grow and can only be counteracted by costly price cutting. An inevitable curtailment of technological imports will in all likelihood be accompanied by continued purchases of grain and foodstuffs from the West, thus exacerbating an already unfavorable balance of trade.

As shown in Table 11, Eastern European countries must service foreign debts that are sizable—in Poland, catastrophic. At a time when their ability to earn foreign exchange is eroding, they must press all the harder to produce goods fit for export, which will in turn further constrict the manufacture of goods for domestic consumption. Yet, while their need to service their debts, pay off part of the principal, and acquire new hard currency continues to rise, export for hard currency has in fact declined or is stagnated. In 1983 it was only 86 percent of its 1980 volume ($31.4 billion). Moreover, after the experience of the early 1980s, which posed the frightening specter of massive default on debts, they can scarcely expect generosity from the international banking community.

Poland's insolvency sorely disturbs regional economic development. Not only has the country failed to deliver goods and credit repayments to its eastern neighbors, the others must commit substantial resources to alleviate its difficulties.

The general causes of the economic predicament of Eastern Europe are similar to those of the Soviet Union and stem from the glaring shortcomings of the centrally planned economies when intensive rather than extensive methods of growth are required. But the situation of Eastern Europe is additionally influenced by factors that are specific to the region (as well as the particular troubles of the individual countries within Eastern Europe).

The most important difference in Soviet and Eastern European conditions is the far greater influence of external factors on the latter—dependence on the Soviet Union for primary products and markets and sensitivity to the changing or cyclical conditions of Western Europe and the world market. Consequently East European leaders are forced in their planning and economic policies to deal with factors that are entirely beyond their control. Soviet policy in oil and raw material prices for its empire made Eastern Europe relive the oil shock of 1973. The depression in Western Europe in the early 1980s played havoc with trade plans. The international financial debt situation circumvented Eastern Europe's ability to secure additional credit from the West.

TABLE 11   EASTERN EUROPEAN HARD CURRENCY DEBT TO THE WEST
(Index, 1970 = 100)

	1970	1975	1980	1984
Bulgaria	100	300	357	357
Czechoslovakia	100	200	566	683
East Germany	100	342	800	878
Hungary	100	383	966	1,366
Poland	100	700	2,000	2,454
Romania	100	193	581	525
TOTAL (in billion current US $)	6.0	21.2	54.2	62.5

All Eastern European countries have undertaken and will have to sustain well into the decade various austerity programs that affect the working class and undermine efforts to raise labor productivity. These measures are politically sensitive because they are applied to populations whose expectations have been rising and because they are generally applied in a way that all but exempts the political elite and the managerial classes from the burdens of austerity by raising the prices of basic consumer goods.

Austerity programs can often be tolerated by the population if they are combined with reforms. But Eastern European leaders will find it difficult to alleviate their economic difficulties by accelerating the implementation of existing reforms or initiating new ones. East Germany's managerial reform as well as the market-oriented reform in Hungary have probably both reached the point of greatest effectiveness. To achieve better results, Hungarian leaders would have to violate the sacred political rule of every communist government: job security for the working class. They would have to accept some unemployment and the likelihood of bankruptcy of unprofitable firms. Other satellite countries would find it economically difficult and politically dangerous even to attempt the Hungarian model for just the same reasons as the Soviet Union—the devolution of political power that such reforms entail, with the additional problems imposed by an unfavorable international market and credit situation.

The common economic dilemmas of the 1980s will in all probability have a greater destabilizing impact in Eastern Europe than in the Soviet Union. The expectations of the Eastern European populations far exceed those of the Soviet working class, and the gap between what is and what they believe ought to be will certainly intensify their dissatisfaction. Moreover, should austerity programs place disproportionately heavy burdens on Eastern European working classes, as seems probable, the disparity in living standards among diverse groups will reinforce the workers' sense of injustice, which happened to be the most important impulse in the Polish eruption of 1980. Paradoxically, it may well be that this source of discontent will have the more dramatic consequences in relatively prosperous Hungary, where the difference between personal income and standard of living is more visible if not much greater than in neighboring Eastern states.

The dissatisfaction of the Eastern European working classes will also feed on the consequences of reduced educational expenditures in a time of budgetary constraints. Education has been the most important avenue of mobility and a major guarantor of relative stability.

The Gorbachev leadership clearly appreciates the potential for serious instability, the main lines of its policy toward Eastern Europe have only recently begun to take shape. In basic respects, they go back to the last year of Brezhnev's leadership. They are based on the lessons of Poland, considered within the larger context of domestic economic difficulties and the state of relations with the West.

Soviet leaders are now persuaded that they committed a number of mistakes in Poland. Impressed in the early and mid-1970s by the country's drive to build a "second industrial Poland," fueled largely by Western credits, the Soviets failed to press for changes in goals and means when the bloody unrest in industrial centers, Premier Edward Gierek's manifest difficulties, and the well-founded criticism by some Polish and most Western economists, exposed the chaos of overambitious and poorly executed plans. The Soviets did not push for such necessary (from their point of view) changes as consolidation and concentration of the diffuse Polish investment program, limitation on borrowing from the West, and improved economic management. A Soviet economist has described the USSR's attitude toward the Gierek regime: Until the mid-1970s the Soviets were both supportive of and fascinated by the Polish experiment of trying to move ahead rapidly through revolving installments of credit from the West. They were even envious of Gierek's initial successes and were discussing the application of some elements of the Polish program to the Soviet Union itself. Gierek was able to convince Brezhnev that the unrest of 1976 was of a local nature and insignificant. When in 1978–79 the scale of the industrial and agricultural failure became alarmingly clear, the Soviets did not act because they had no ideas about how to repair the situation and were not ready to bail the Poles out, and because the firm hold of Gierek on the Polish leadership made drastic political intervention very difficult. The fact that these were also the years of Brezhnev's part-time secretaryship may also have played a role in Soviet inaction when the evolving catastrophe could still have been contained.

Surprised by the scope and strength of labor unrest in the summer of 1980, the Soviets failed to intervene decisively in internal Polish party matters or in relations between the party and Solidarity. The Polish case illustrates, in fact, just how much independence the local leaderships had in domestic and especially economic questions, and how slack Soviet monitoring of internal developments was.

Soviet economic difficulties in the 1980s, exacerbated by the state of the international money and commodity markets, seriously impair the capacity to provide substantial subsidies to Eastern Europe as well as Cuba and Vietnam. Given the lower rates of growth, this burden increases proportionally. Indeed, one recent study argues that from 1971 through 1980, a time when their investments were rising at an average rate of 4.85 percent, the Soviets may have been spending as much as 3.5 percent of their GNP in subsidies to their Eastern European and Third World allies and clients. At the same time they are becoming increasingly impatient with the modest level of Eastern European participation in Soviet economic development.

The vulnerability of Eastern Europe to social unrest significantly complicates Soviet relations with the West and presents irreconcilable contradictions to policy makers. On the one hand, the Soviets have come to fear Eastern European economic dependence on the West, which their press calls the "imperialist trap"; on the other, they fully realize that Western support of Eastern European economic development might ease the pressure on Soviet resources. Similarly, social peace and a degree of cultural liberalism in Eastern Europe cements Soviet détente with Western Europe and is crucial if any hope is to remain for the restoration of détente with the United States; but improved relations with the West, and especially with the United States, encourage the generally anti-Soviet liberal forces in Eastern Europe and impede Soviet efforts to contain them.

Gorbachev has not changed the policy direction of his predecessors but rather strengthened its basic elements. His approach to Eastern Europe can be characterized as an all-out hard-line policy. It includes a much stronger insistence on political orthodoxy, particularly in Poland and Hungary; crackdowns on dissent; encouragement of a siege mentality and of crude anti-Western propaganda; greater pressure against economic experimentation; and rapid reaction to social and political unrest or to signs of attempted greater independence of satellite leaderships. Soviet subsidies of oil and other raw materials to Eastern Europe and Cuba have been sharply reduced, and a warning has been issued that they may be eliminated. The Soviets have also started to insist, with growing intensity, that Eastern European goods exported to the Soviet Union should be sold at prices competitive with the world market and, most importantly, that the quality and durability of the goods should be equal to those sold to the West. In addition, the Soviets are pursuing more energetically the goal of greater integration through Comecon of the Eastern European and Soviet economies in the division of labor, the coordination of investments, technological exchange, collective projects, and especially significant, Eastern European contributions to the development of Soviet resources in Siberia.

According to Eastern European sources these hard-line themes were dominant during the March 1985 visit of then Politburo member Grigorii Romanov to Hungary, Gorbachev's meeting with the Polish junta chief Wojciech Jaruzelski in Warsaw in April 1985, and at the Comecon meeting in June 1984, and the meeting of the leaders of the Warsaw Pact countries in Warsaw, April 26, 1985. During the years of paralysis of the Soviet leadership the leaders of the Eastern European countries, particularly East Germany and Hungary, acquired greater independence and freedom. The main thrust of Gorbachev's Eastern European policy is to strengthen the Soviet hold on its empire and to control the satellite party leaders more tightly.

The political direction of Soviet policy is clear—orthodoxy over liberalism. The line with regard to Soviet–Eastern European economic relations is established beyond any doubt—greater contribution of the empire to Soviet needs. Gorbachev's attitude toward domestic Eastern European economic policies is more complex and less clear. He is, after all, encouraging marginal economic reforms in the Soviet Union itself. Since Andropov's rule, the Soviet press has featured lengthy discussions of Eastern European innovations in planning, management, and incentives; the articles have often expressed the need to adopt creatively some of these Eastern European measures, especially the ones instituted in Hungary and East Germany. Where Eastern Europe itself is concerned, however, the evidence is more ambiguous. Soviet leaders are not pressing to introduce economic reforms where they do not already exist—in

Czechoslovakia, for example. (Czechoslovakia, incidentally, seems to be the only Eastern European country whose internal policies do not use even the existing margin of freedom from Soviet pressures.) Nor are they proposing a return to orthodoxy in countries where reforms are well advanced. At the root of this inconsistency lies the primacy of political over economic considerations. The Soviets apparently accept established reforms and their economic consequences while fearing the political fallout from new or bolder economic initiatives. Thus the major influence on Soviet attitudes comes from Poland not Hungary. In other words, the leaders are more concerned about worker unrest and departures from political orthodoxy than they are interested in encouraging the spread of productive reforms. They fear that, while the market reforms in Hungary were beneficial both to popular standards of living and the stability of the regime, the process of introducing such reforms in other countries would be politically destabilizing.

It is safe to say that Soviet policy in Eastern Europe during the next decade will stress political stability over economic development—which, as I suggested earlier, is very different from Gorbachev's domestic policy, which will probably stress reforms. That stability, however, ultimately depends on improved economic performance, which certainly hinges on potentially destabilizing economic reform. This dilemma mirrors the contradiction between the two main Soviet goals in Eastern Europe—to preserve domination and to ensure domestic stability.

The ominous Soviet line was reflected in an April 1984 article in the journal of Party history signed by "O. V. Borisov"—a pseudonym for O. B. Rakhmanin, first deputy head of the Central Committee's department of relations with communist and workers' parties. This highly orthodox article sharply attacked the Hungarian positions of continuous reform and greater independence from Moscow. It declared that at the present stage the main policy of imperialism is to export counterrevolution and intervene directly into the affairs of socialist states. It condemned "rightist opportunists" (in Eastern Europe) for nationalist tendencies, and their effort to keep their countries outside the "class struggle," that is, to stay out of the Soviet-American confrontation.*

This hard line was picked up and reinforced by Gorbachev after he assumed power. A very important document concerning Eastern Europe and Soviet-Eastern European relations in the first year of Gorbachev's rule was published in *Pravda* in June 1985.† Signed with the pseudonym "Vladimirov," it was the product of the Central Committee Secretariat and clearly embodied Gorbachev's own views. The article amounted to

---

* O. V. Borisov, "Soyuz novovo tipa," *Voprosy Istorii KPSS,* No. 4, April 1984, pp. 34–49.

† *Pravda,* June 21, 1985.

an unbridled attack on any Eastern European "deviations." It expressed the deep concern of the leadership with the potential effectiveness of Western efforts to support Eastern European strivings for greater independence. It reflected worries about and disapproval of Eastern European leaders who are frustrated in their efforts to remain outside of East-West confrontations and to secure new Western credits and trade essential for their economic performance, and thus also for social and political stability. "The pressure of imperialism," wrote Vladimirov, "on world socialism is now of an unprecedented nature. The imperialist circles are placing their bets on breaking the unity of socialist countries."

Defining the danger, Vladimirov's exhortations and prescriptions for Eastern Europe were explicitly and unambiguously conservative. They were also an open attack on the positions of Kádár and Erich Honecker, the leaders of Hungary and East Germany. These two leaders have championed the specific needs of "smaller socialist countries." They have openly expressed the proposition that the national interest of their countries does not always coincide with Soviet interests, and that Soviet leadership should agree to a *modus vivendi* that would recognize the specific needs of its imperial holdings, in particular closer political and economic ties with Western Europe.

In light of "imperialist" pressures, Vladimirov declared, the criteria of Soviet–Eastern European alliance and cooperation must be stricter than in the past. Attempts to pursue a more independent line in recognition of diverse national interests cannot be tolerated at all, and in fact amount to treason. Eastern European experiments with economic liberalization and support of a more efficient private sector are unacceptable. Any partial agreements, let alone reconciliation, with domestic nonsocialist forces reflect capitulation to "imperialist pressures" and must be resisted at any cost. The ideas of "national roads to socialism," as opposed to the Soviet model, are imperialist inventions that cannot and will not be tolerated. The main danger in Eastern Europe is not economic stagnation but the forces of anti-Soviet nationalism, a separate search for effective country-specific policies, and closer economic and political relations with the West. The forces that pursue such policies camouflage their antisocialism by proclaiming their policy and reform plans as the result of their analysis of the "collective national experience." Revisionism, nationalism, and clericalism will not be permitted. The interests of the Soviet Union and its Eastern European empire are by definition identical. Soviet experience in economics, politics, and ideology are sufficient models for Eastern European parties. The examples that the leaders of the satellite parties should emulate are the non-Russian heroes of Stalin's time—the Czech Gottwald, the Frenchman Thorez, the Bulgarian Dimitrov (all the Soviet dictator's puppets).

Although the invasion of Afghanistan destroyed U.S.-Soviet détente, Western Europe would not dismantle its arrangements with the Soviet Union and its empire. Its aim became damage limitation. Since the installation of the American intermediate-range missiles (INF) in Europe in the fall of 1983, the Soviet line towards Western Europe has hardened. Toward West Germany the Soviets commenced a campaign of vilification and pressure.

In Eastern Europe, particularly in Hungary and East Germany, the leaders similarly tried to exclude themselves from the new cold war. East Germany especially wanted to preserve an "intra-German" détente. Articles were published in the Hungarian and East German press stressing that small socialist states could have good relations with the small capitalist states of NATO despite the U.S.-Soviet confrontation, and their role in preserving détente is growing. There was a call for each Eastern European country to be free within the recognized limits (nationalized industry, finances, foreign trade, etc.) to develop economic models and policies that fit its circumstances and needs. The most provocative theme was raised in 1984 by the Hungarian Party secretary for international affairs, Matyas Szuros, who stated that domestic needs should have priority over international factors in the foreign policy of small socialist states.

The boldness of the Hungarian and East German leaders could be explained not only by their difficult economic situation but also by the power vacuum then existing in Moscow. The Soviet response was, as described above, not long in coming. Yet East Berlin and Budapest are certain to persist. Indeed, as Professor Charles Gati suggests, with the possible addition of Warsaw, they may form a minicoalition to press the Soviet Union on such issues as better terms of trade (even if the skewed 1970 prices cannot be reestablished), toning down the Soviet propaganda war against West Germany, and closer political and economic relations with Western Europe and Japan. What they want now and will continue to want in the future is more elbow room from the Kremlin. They seek a slow process of moving closer to the West and of instituting socioeconomic changes that will move them away from the Soviet model. But with Gorbachev's growing power their position will not improve and may even become more difficult. In strictly economic terms, their dependence on Soviet supplies and on the Soviet market may increase rather than decline.

The central Soviet dilemma with regard to its Eastern European empire is reflected in the difficulties facing the leadership of the satellite countries themselves. This is particularly true in East Germany and Hungary. The focus is not so much the question of innovation, as in the Soviet Union, but that of economic, and consequently political, relations with the West, and especially West Germany. In the fall of 1984 major differences between the East German and Hungarian leaderships and the Soviet leadership became public. These differences had been brewing for a year and expressed perfectly the squeeze in which the East German and Hungarian communist leaders find themselves today.

East Germany and Hungary are tied to a technologically backward Soviet Union that in addition is canceling its raw material subsidies for Eastern Europe. They, and leaders of other satellite countries, are well aware that their relationship with the Soviet Union cannot stimulate the sort of breakthrough that the newly industrializing nations in Asia have achieved. Neither Honecker, nor Kádár, nor other Eastern European leaders want to belong to what could accurately be called "The Greater Eastern European Co-Stagnation Sphere." To preserve chances for their growth and social stability, these countries are looking for better relations and economic help from the West and particularly from West Germany. As Honecker has formulated it, his country is looking for a "community of responsibility" with West Germany. Moreover, while Moscow is interested in détente with Western Europe for itself, it has started to describe Western subversion as the major danger to the "community of communist countries" and is seeking to prevent closer East-West European relations. In September 1984, Honecker was compelled to announce the "postponement" of his trip to West Germany, scheduled for that month.

No survey of the Eastern European empire would be complete without exploring its significance for the domestic and foreign policies of the imperial power itself. Eastern Europe is regarded as a bridge between Western countries and the Soviet Union, and this image is certainly valid for the transfer of technology from West to East and economic experimentation. But the far greater significance of the empire is its very existence and instability. Its effect on Soviet domestic policy is to inhibit political and economic liberalization at home. Soviet leaders fear the consequences across borders—in either direction—of any departure from orthodoxy.

The effect of Eastern Europe on Soviet foreign policy is even more complex. To begin with, the commitment to secure the region is far more important to Soviet leaders than either achieving a durable rapprochement with the West or expanding their power in the Third World. Most critical, given the fact that priorities in Soviet policy are directly correlated with geographic proximity to Moscow, difficulties in Eastern Europe tend to reinforce retrenchment in Soviet foreign policy. This retrenchment, one of the major causes of which is the overextension of Soviet foreign policy resources, was particularly influenced by troubles in Poland.

The situation in Eastern Europe bears heavily on the policy of détente with Western Europe and the United States. Considering the importance of the European détente to Soviet interests, Western Europe has the leverage to moderate Soviet policies in Eastern Europe. Less discussed and more important is the leverage that dominion over Eastern Europe affords the Soviets vis-à-vis Western Europe. Twenty-two million East Germans serve as a powerful restraint on West German policy toward the Soviet Union and on West German willingness to support American policy. Moreover, the rebirth of strong German nationalism, this time on the left of West German politics, has raised again the question of reunification, not as a long-range historical prospect but, in the minds of many Germans, as a question to be resolved in this century. Such hopes give the Soviets the opportunity to manipulate German politics. As the missiles issue has shown, the bipartisan German approach to foreign and military policy has collapsed. The leftward trend of the German Social Democratic Party with regard to the Atlantic Alliance has been encouraged by the Soviet Union. As for the United States, Soviet leaders must decide whether the advantages of a renewed détente, hitherto the central and seemingly irreplaceable focus of their foreign policy, outweigh the disadvantages: inevitable pressures from the United States for liberalization and greater independence in Eastern Europe.

It remains to be seen whether Western Europe will exercise its virtually unused leverage—economic aid to the Soviet Union and moderating influence on American policy—to affect Soviet imperial policy. The situation in Eastern Europe during the 1980s will restrain vigorous Soviet policies toward the outside world, but it is wrong to anticipate that the Kremlin will abandon global objectives to concentrate solely on imperial or domestic problems.

The potentially serious troubles in the Soviet Union are not separated from the troublesome questions in the Eastern European empire; they reinforce each other. This is especially true of economic problems but is also relevant to the leadership situation in Eastern Europe and the Soviet Union. The strong leadership that Gorbachev is beginning to provide will restore and reinforce Soviet control over its empire. Yet it is not immune to conflicts. Divisions within the leadership of Eastern European countries, which will probably evolve in the harsh climate of economic austerity, may overlap with uncertainties and dissensions within the Soviet leadership. The communist leaders of Eastern Europe are very experienced in playing the game of Soviet power politics to their own advantage. In this sense Eastern European questions will probably become an issue in Soviet leadership politics.

Like the Soviet Union in the early 1980s, some of the Eastern European regimes will in the near future face transitions in their own top leadership. The one most fraught with potentially disruptive consequences is that in Hungary. The rule of János Kádár, an imaginative leader with unquestioned authority at home, who is greatly respected in the Soviet Union, will probably come to an end in the next decade, exactly at the time when his creation, the New Economic Mechanism, is running out of steam. In Romania the prospect of the end of Ceauşescu's rule holds out major dangers for the stability of the regime. The economic situation is catastrophic, and the wide dissatisfaction with a leader who is both extremely oppressive and capricious is barely containable. Even Ceauşescu's colleagues are growing increasingly frustrated with his personal dictatorship and the central political role played by his wife. The precarious rule of General Jaruzelski in Poland carries with it all the marks of impermanence. And while it may be true that nothing endures like the provisional, Soviet uneasiness with a professional military leader heading an Eastern European Communist Party and regime is quite genuine.

More than ever, the situation in their Eastern European empire is a point of critical vulnerability for the Soviet Union. For forty years it has had the good luck to confront a crisis in only one Eastern European country at a time. This luck may hold in the 1980s, but even if successive explosions fail to rock the region during the remainder of this decade, serious tensions will surely persist, both within client states and between them and the imperial center. And in this respect Poland will remain for years to come a more prominent focus of Soviet attention and fear more than any other country in this region.

11

The Polish Debacle

Among all the dilemmas the Soviet Union faces in Eastern Europe, the Polish question has pride of place. The events that began in the summer of 1980 were unprecedented in the history of the Eastern European empire. They deeply shocked the Soviet leadership and elite. At the same time, however, the Polish situation is an example—albeit an extreme one—of the problems besetting virtually the entire Soviet bloc. It illustrates both the powerful impulse for independence and justice in the satellite nations, and the depth of the Soviet commitment to preserve its external empire whatever the cost.

The struggle of Polish workers for their rights constitutes a critical turning point in the history of the Soviet empire. The situation, still unpredictable despite the reestablishment of communist rule in a militarized form in December 1981, is of greater significance for the future of the world communist movement, the empire, and the Soviet Union itself than the Hungarian Revolution of 1956, the Polish revolt of the same year, the Czechoslovak reforms of 1968, and even the Stalin-Tito rupture of 1947–48. Its international implications are no less grave. Poland is the key country in the Soviet bloc in terms of strategic location, military and economic potential, and size of population. With its 312,700 kilometers, it constitutes about one-third of the entire territory of the Soviet bloc. Its population of close to 36 million is about 60 percent larger than that of the next largest Eastern European country. The size of its GNP, over $200 billion, is about one-third greater than the next biggest economy in the bloc. Its standing army of about 300,000 is close to one-third of the combined forces of the Warsaw Pact countries (excluding the Soviet Union). Strategically, Poland provides the main route to Russia and the central communications and transportation line with the communist forces facing NATO. Instability there—and even the continuing impasse between the communist government and the population—immensely weakens the empire.

Even before the recent events, Poland was far from being a typical Eastern European communist state. It is the only one in which individual small landholders constitute the great majority of the peasantry. The Catholic Church represents a virtual alternate government, with a moral authority unmatched by any postwar civil regime. (As a Vatican joke has it, the most Catholic countries in the world are Poland, Ireland, and the Vatican, in that order.) Culturally, Poland belongs to the West; its cities have a life-style that is Western in character, from their manners and the coffee shops where the intelligentsia meet to their independence of spirit.

It is a homogeneous country of intense national consciousness and pride, with a long tradition of struggle for independence, and of survival under the most adverse conditions of foreign oppression. Even with Soviet troops present, the communist takeover of 1944–45 was resisted in what was for a time a virtual civil war. Since then, forty years of communist rule have failed to eradicate the distinct national identity shared by all segments of society. In recent years, numerous dissident organizations have been able to communicate their views to a broad range of publics; hundreds of thousands of students took part in the so-called Flying Universities, where professors taught courses in private apartments on subjects they could not present in official settings. And in the last quarter-century, industrial workers have confronted security forces in the streets on three occasions, 1956, 1970, and 1976, to demonstrate their opposition to the regime. Of course since the summer of 1980 there has seldom been a month when security troops have not clashed with workers.

What has happened in Poland since the labor unrest in August 1980 is well known. The crisis began with local strikes against price increases. A workers' movement quickly rose and spread across the nation, and a series of broadly based sit-in actions in factories and mines forced the government, under the threat of a general strike, to promise the workers the right—unprecedented in a communist regime—to organize an independent trade union. Other demands, political in nature, were raised, and hard-pressed Polish leaders promised to overhaul the regime, the policy-making process, and the policies themselves. The workers' struggle brought about the resignation of Polish Party leader Edward Gierek and the almost complete replacement of the upper echelons of the Party and the government.

By the late 1970s it had become evident, not only to the working class but to the population as a whole, that the country faced nothing less than the collapse of its planning and management system and the total bankruptcy of its economy. (The only other time when an Eastern European satellite country dealt with a similar, although much milder, situation was in Czechoslovakia in 1967, and it led to the nonviolent Czech revolution under Dubček in 1968.)

Recent trends in Polish economic development provide indisputable evidence for this conclusion. In 1980, for the second consecutive year, the national income showed an absolute decline, a dubious honor not achieved by any other Soviet bloc country. There were immense shortages in the supply of necessities, which, because of their short-range political implications, received the widest attention in the Western press. But of even greater importance were enormous disruptions in the industrial, construction, and agrarian sectors (lack of raw materials, spare parts for machinery, frozen investments, uncoordinated planning, starvation of the farm sector for industrial goods)—problems with long-range implications for an economy already burdened by massive hard currency indebtedness.

In August and September 1980 alone, according to official estimates, industrial production dropped 17 percent below that of the same period in 1979. Total production losses for the July–September period were estimated to be in the neighborhood of $2.3 billion. For the coal-mining industry, one of the mainstays of the economy, the shortfall may have been as large as 10 percent of the total output. In the first three quarters of 1980, only 37 percent of the plan for the construction industry was fulfilled. The grain harvest declined from 21.3 million tons in 1978 to 17.3 million in 1979. Although it mounted, according to optimistic estimates, to just over 19 million tons in 1980, this total was officially declared to be 8 million below current needs, thus requiring expensive large-scale imports. Meat production, which was 3.3 million tons in 1979, dropped to 2.4 million in 1980 and did not exceed 2.2 million in 1981. The potato harvest in 1980 was the worst in twenty years, down almost 40 percent from that of 1979.

The troubles in the economy can be traced to a critical decision made by Gierek in the early 1970s that promised to improve the Polish economic situation radically. He could have chosen to restructure the economy carefully and to reform its unwieldy and cumbersome planning, management, and incentive system, a course with long-term benefits. Instead, he opted for a quick fix. His strategy combined significant imports of Western technology, financed on credit, with heavy investment in the growth of industry. The theory was that Western technology would permit Poland to switch from extensive to intensive growth; and foreign debts incurred in the process could be repaid by consequent rapid increases in exports from a revitalized industry.

Initially, the policy yielded positive results. In the years 1971–75, the net industrial product grew at the rate of almost 11 percent per year; that is to say, about 30 percent faster than in the preceding decade. Real industrial wages, which from 1961 to 1970 went up 1.8 percent per year, rose in the 1971–75 period by 7.2 percent annually.

But from the mid-1970s Gierek's program foundered. Unforeseen world economic conditions, combined with weaknesses in the preparation and execution of Gierek's policy, slowed economic development and undermined Poland's ability to meet its credit obligations. The energy crisis radically increased the cost of oil required for development. The recession in the West impeded the sale of Polish goods in hard currency markets, thus destroying Gierek's hope that expanded exports would repay foreign debts. The government's investment policy proved ill conceived. At some stages as much as 40 percent of the national income was devoted to investment, about 75 percent of this going to heavy and export industries. Agriculture was denied significant investments. The smallholder peasant was left without credits or suitable agricultural machines and was exposed to a progressive tax system (in kind and money) that did not provide sufficient incentives for production growth. Increasing domestic demand for consumer products was left unsatisfied, thus creating immense inflationary pressures and making Poland dependent on expensive imports. Most important, the government did not undertake any of the major reforms in the system of planning and management that might have prepared the economy to cope with the demands arising from increased dependence on intensive growth, the application of new technology, and the growth of productivity. Indeed, Gierek and his party looked upon the program of expansion on the installment plan as a substitute for a structural reform.

Enormous disproportions and bottlenecks resulted from the rapid economic growth sustained by credits and imports. The utilization of foreign technology was inefficient and its diffusion slow; the proportion of unfinished investment projects rose rapidly. The influx of Western technology failed to generate long-term improvements in productivity. Imports of technology and credits could not serve as a substitute for reforms. The mismanagement of the economy became visible to everyone; waste assumed incredible proportions.

Stories making the rounds in Warsaw at that time, and later confirmed, spoke of imported machinery sufficient to equip entire factories lying unprotected in fields around the capital. The plan for the construction of the factories was two years behind that for importing the equipment. Contributing to the waste was the extraordinary scale of corruption in managerial and political circles. The explosion of contracts with foreign firms created new millionaires overnight through payoffs and kickbacks. In contrast to Gomulka's time and to the habits of *nouveaux riches* in the Soviet Union, this new wealth was flaunted and hated. Its visibility and its immunity to governmental control contributed greatly to the sense of injustice among workers that brought on the explosion of 1980.

During the first years of Gierek's program, the economic expectations of the working class soared. Those expectations were satisfied in part—initially. By 1979 and 1980, however, the situation had become unstable. With diminishing returns from an increasingly stagnant economy, consumers experienced both inflation and severe shortages of basic commodities. At the same time the government neither informed the people about the full extent of the economic problems nor adequately prepared them for the necessary austerity measures. The belief spread throughout all sectors of society, including the Party itself, that the economic system had outlived its usefulness, that it had nothing more to offer—in short, that it was bankrupt.

The economic crisis paralleled one of political authority as the Party became totally divorced from the realities of everyday life and stagnated at its core. United under Gierek's command, the leadership allowed no fresh voices to pose questions concerning the relationship between the Party and the working class or the state and the economy—or if such voices emerged, they were quickly silenced. After thirty-five years of communist rule, the Polish population, including the working class, ceased to believe in the Party's authority, its competence, and its right to rule. Nothing so clearly demonstrated the gulf between the legal and the civil society as the overwhelming response to the visit of Pope John Paul II to his native country in the summer of 1979.

The effects of virtual economic bankruptcy and of the crisis of political authority were compounded by the heightened visibility of official corruption and privilege. Workers harbored a growing sense of the injustice perpetrated by a state that incessantly asserted that it represented them and stressed continuously in its propaganda the importance of workers in society. When shortages of foodstuffs developed, there was no system of rationing to spread the burden evenly. A hated symbol of elite privilege was the so-called "yellow curtain" store, which concealed from public view the scarce goods available for sale to members of the Party and state bureaucracy. Another source of irritation was the shops that traded only with foreign currency.

Worker disaffection found still other sources of nourishment. Plans for investment in public housing were not fulfilled. The latter situation became critical, especially for young working couples who wished to marry and had to wait many years for an apartment. Because the higher education system—the main channel for upward social mobility—was not expanding nearly rapidly enough to meet the demand, entry into the middle class became more and more difficult for children of working people. All in all, there developed within the working class a deep sense of grievance against the system that ruled in its name, a grievance that was no longer mollified by reassurances and promises from the Party leadership.

By 1980 the character of the working class itself had changed dramatically from what it had been in the earlier decades of communist rule. The peasants who had flocked to the factories in the 1950s and 1960s had improved their economic and cultural lot by the very act of becoming urbanized. The working class of the 1980s, no longer dominated by peasant recruits, is urban in origin and has a different attitude and a different set of expectations. Moreover, it is not burdened by the memory of Stalinist terror. The workers are better able to compare their own conditions with those of workers in the West or in more developed Eastern European countries. They listen to foreign radio broadcasts, they talk with millions of visiting tourists, and hundreds of thousands of them travel abroad. It was this new working class—whose existence the authorities failed to consider—which demanded social justice.

The first battles against Party authorities made headway, and this success continued into 1981, when General Jaruzelski became first secretary. Despite the fact that by now the military-security regime in Poland has effectively destroyed Solidarity, some of the gains forced by the movement represent significant, enduring concessions by the regime. This consideration raises the question as to why the workers were so successful initially.

To begin with, a workers' challenge to the communist regime was much more difficult to counter than the earlier actions by dissident intellectuals, to which communist regimes had grown accustomed. A massive movement of workers in a so-called workers' state is a much more formidable threat than a small faction of the intelligentsia, which can be managed by intimidation, repression, bribery, and forced emigration.

Furthermore, Polish workers had learned valuable lessons from their earlier experiences, when street demonstrations turned quickly into violence and defeat. In 1980, they adopted a new tactic that was much more effective: Sit-in strikes and occupation of factories put the onus of initiating violence in any effort to eject the workers on the government. They exhibited self-discipline, a high degree of organization, and an unprecedented ability to act in concert.

Also, for the first time, the workers and the dissident intellectuals effectively joined forces. Their union was symbolized by the commissions of experts attached to the newly formed free trade union. While their role should not be exaggerated—the main force behind the Polish events of 1980–81 was a spontaneous working-class movement—the intelligentsia jumped on the bandwagon, and more important, provided the communications network through which news of the workers' actions in Gdansk reached the rest of the country. The ability of workers along the coast to communicate their actions and demands to other parts of Poland forced the government to make concessions, as it faced not simply a localized strike but the threat of a general one.

It was tactically shrewd for the workers to concentrate on one issue—the demand for independent trade unions, which were perceived as the sole guarantee that the government would honor any future demands. The workers were distracted neither by immediate economic demands nor by broad political proposals that would be explosive in their implications.

The existence of an independent church lent enormous support to the workers' activities. Nonetheless, during the strikes, and especially at the beginning, the church hierarchy, and Cardinal Wyszynski in particular, played an ambiguous role. The church clearly supported the workers, but just as clearly it feared that their demands might go too far. It therefore sought to exert a moderating influence.

In the critical days of late summer and fall 1980, the Polish Communist Party found itself in disarray. Gierek was ousted in September 1980, and the new leader, Stanislaw Kania, did not have the time, the support, or the talent to establish firm command. The Party activists and regional bureaucrats became disoriented. The new unions were able to exploit the resulting power vacuum in the political system.

The Polish armed forces remained neutral. It is reliably reported that as the crisis ripened, the commander of the armed forces, General Jaruzelski, informed the Party leaders at a meeting of the Central Committee that the army could not be relied upon to intervene and eject the workers forcibly from the occupied factories. This statement was a turning point, for it left the Party little choice but to negotiate seriously and to consent to major concessions. Threatened with a general strike and a complete breakdown of order, the new regime accepted the workers' basic demands. This decision resulted not only from alarm over the workers' reaction to a rejection of their demands, but also from the apprehension that continued chaos in Poland and a general strike would increase the danger of Soviet intervention. At that point the Polish leaders feared this outcome more than the workers did.

What the Polish workers had won initially was the unprecedented acceptance by a communist regime of independent trade unions and of the right to strike when other means of bargaining are exhausted. In a very short period of time, a workers' organization had been created parallel to the officially sponsored unions. Even in its formative stage it included the majority of Polish workers. The new union would have ended the organizational monopoly of the Communist Party. It would have also given the workers an effective veto power over government economic policies.

The situation within the leadership of the Communist Party must be distinguished from that in Hungary in 1956 and Czechoslovakia in 1968. Hungary under Imre Nagy and Czechoslovakia under Alexander Dubček were led by renegade communist parties which had adopted unorthodox and reformist positions that questioned their political systems and the alliance with the Soviet Union. The Polish leadership under Kania, and later under Jaruzelski, could not remotely be characterized as renegade. Although far from homogeneous, the leaders were basically politically conservative communists who acknowledged the need for reforms, particularly in the economy and in relations between Party and workers. Some leaders were more conservative and some more reformist; none questioned the need to preserve the Party's monopoly, to enforce a policy of censorship, however revised, or, most importantly, to maintain a close alliance with the Soviet Union.

This new leadership at first could not consolidate its power over a Party that remained disoriented and disorganized. Factional struggle persisted between hard line and more moderate elements. But after consolidation was achieved, under Jaruzelski ultimately, the Party's tactics became clear. It aimed to wear down the workers, to subvert their achievements, and to provoke continual skirmishes over specific issues. It attempted to divide the workers, to isolate them from the dissident intellectuals, and to co-opt their leaders. In negotiations with Solidarity, it sought to establish firm, non-negotiable positions on political demands, such as the principle of censorship and the role of the security apparatus. (While the communist leadership never agreed to abolish censorship, the publications of Solidarity materials and the pressures from journalists created considerable press freedom until martial law was declared in December 1981.) At the same time, however, it agreed to compromise on economic issues and structural reform. In other words, it aimed to preserve the essential characteristics of the system while being flexible on certain elements.

These tactics were clearly insufficient, or not successful enough, to satisfy the Soviet and Polish communist leadership. It was not true, as was sometimes believed in the West, that Solidarity became more and more militant, escalating its demands beyond those that were agreed upon by the workers' representatives and the government in August–December 1980 and the early months of 1981. Of course there was always a militant current in Solidarity that advocated more confrontational methods of struggle. Yet relations with Solidarity deteriorated, particularly after Jaruzelski took over the top Party position, because the government either retreated step by step from its initial agreements with the workers' union or was determined not to implement or ratify in Parliament most of the political-economic reforms it had conceded as far back as September 1980. Under such circumstances it was not the workers' militancy and escalating demands that created the tensions prior to the December 1981 internal solution, but rather the intransigence of the Jaruzelski government, its steadfast insistence on a monopoly of power and the perpetuation of political dictatorship. As a matter of fact, the leaders of Solidarity, and particularly Lech Walesa, performed a near-miracle in containing the militants within the union and sticking to the workers' initial demands.

Perhaps the most important reason for the Polish impasse had little to do with worker militancy or government intransigence. It was rather the fatal link of politics and economics. Genuine success of the Polish experiment in the 1970s and in 1980–81 depended on radical improvement in the economic situation. That, in turn, required major reforms. Without a transformation in the economic sector, the real demands of the workers could not be met, and the situation could only deteriorate. Here we come to the truly vicious circle of the Polish situation.

Poland requires far-reaching economic reforms to create a viable economy, to sustain steady increases in the standard of living, and to persuade Western creditors of the country's solvency. It needs a drastic change in agricultural policy, which would entail a redirection of large investments into the agrarian sector, a canceling of restrictions on the growth of private farms, an extension of credits to farmers, and a restructuring of farm prices. It also must achieve reforms in the service sector. Something like the Soviet New Economic Policy of 1921 needs to be introduced, encouraging craftsmen, artisans, and small private entrepreneurs, and the prohibitive level of taxation on their activity should be abolished. But of greatest importance and difficulty, Poland requires a basic reform of the industrial system of planning, management, and incentives that would resemble, or even go beyond, the Hungarian model. Without such changes, which would drastically cut the waste in the Polish economy and increase its productivity, a long-range economic recovery is a fantasy. Soviet experts evaluate the economic situation and future of Poland in more pessimistic terms than does the Jaruzelski government. As one high official expressed it to me, it is premature to speak about basic economic reforms in Poland when the Polish regime has yet to develop a coherent economic strategy with clearly defined priorities.

Difficult and costly reforms would require a transitional period of several years of austerity and self-denial for the consumer. Having lost their trust in government, the workers have no incentive to make sacrifices. Only if more goods can be produced to satisfy their needs will the government be able to gain their trust; yet such production increases themselves presuppose basic reforms.

Aside from promises, the government had only two recourses in 1981. It could meet the demands of workers for a role in running the factories and mines, and ultimately for a partnership in determining economic policies. The wisest Polish leaders must have understood that these demands had to be met halfway. But would such a government policy be acceptable to Poland's communist neighbors, and particularly the Soviet Union?

The answer, as we now know, was a resounding no. And here was the second recourse of the government, either imposed by the Soviets or fully shared by their Polish orthodox comrades: to destroy Solidarity by force. In such a situation, it was not difficult even for formerly "liberal" Polish communists to justify this course as a patriotic endeavor, saving Poland from the greater evil of a Soviet invasion. (Incidentally, while one may understand the Polish communist "liberals," it is impossible to think without revulsion about some Western European politicians, especially from the German Social Democratic Party, who gave a sigh of relief at the success of the solution in Poland and the avoidance of Soviet invasion. Both the dual power situation in Poland and the possibility of a Soviet move clearly disturbed some of the SPD's plans for continuation of détente with the Soviet Union. From this point of view the internal solution was a godsend. It was treated by many Western European politicians as an internal problem that required verbal condemnation but no sanctions and at the same time left relations with the USSR undisturbed.)

In December 1980, five months into the Polish revolution, I wrote.

We do not know whether the Soviets have decided to intervene in Poland. There are a number of options open to them short of full-scale invasion. There is the option they have already selected—to mass [Soviet and Warsaw Pact] troops along Polish borders as a means of intimidating the workers and strengthening the backbone of the Polish leadership in resisting the workers' demands. The effectiveness and workability of this option will decline with time, however. A second option involves the measured escalation of pressure by conducting military maneuvers on Polish soil. This action will push the Polish leaders to intensify their intimidation of the workers' movement. A third option would be the most advantageous to the Soviet Union but highly doubtful in its effectiveness: Soviet troops would watch at the Polish border while the Polish Army and security forces themselves attempted to settle the situation.*

Subsequently it was discovered that in both 1980 and 1981 there had been strong and continuous pressure on the Soviet Politburo and on Brezhnev personally to launch an invasion. Zbigniew Brzezinski's claim that an American warning about disastrous short- and long-range consequences of an invasion influenced the leadership to delay such a decision seems correct, considering that in the Soviet analysis, the behavior of the Polish army and the response of Western Europe to an invasion were unpredictable.

In March 1981 the Soviet leadership was apparently again contemplating an invasion. According to Soviet sources, Brezhnev, ailing but still in control of the Politburo, provided the decisive voice against the invasion. At that point, after the removal of the powerless Kania from the top Party position in Poland and the appointment of a military leader to the post, the Soviets opted for "internal invasion"—something unprecedented in their relations with East European states—as the solution to the Polish problem. By August 1981, a firm accord had been reached between the two governments, and preparations for martial law, stiff internal security measures, and the militarization of the Polish Party proceeded. On December 13, 1981, the security forces and the military, under General Jaruzelski's leadership and Soviet supervision, declared martial law and banned Solidarity.

Given the circumstances existing in Poland at the end of 1981, and their potential impact on the East European empire and within the Soviet Union itself, the Soviet leaders must have considered seriously using military force. Yet it must have been plain to them that the direct and indirect costs of invasion would be truly awesome, incomparably greater than those paid in Hungary in 1956 and in Czechoslovakia in 1968.

An invasion would have led in all probability to a virtual state of war with the workers and the nation. While it is highly unlikely that the Polish armed forces would have stood united against the invaders, it is probable that major units would have resisted. All in all, the exercise might have become a bloody and protracted affair. Such a military operation in the heart of Europe could have had unpredictable consequences, especially because the behavior of other Warsaw Pact countries and armies could not have been forecast with certainty.

Moreover, a military occupation would have resulted in a staggering economic burden. Not only would the Soviets have needed to maintain

* Seweryn Bialer, "Poland and the Soviet Imperium," *Foreign Affairs,* Vol. 59, No. 3, 1981, p. 539.

an occupying army, they would have had to deliver extensive support to a nation of 36 million people—feed them, sustain their economy, and service their debt of $22 billion. The Soviets could ill afford the strain.

An invasion and the possibility of a massacre of workers would almost certainly have shattered the last ties between the Soviet Communist Party and Western Europe. It would also have destroyed one of the foundations, perhaps the cornerstone, of Soviet foreign policy since Afghanistan—the political, cultural, and especially economic détente with Western Europe. A bloody invasion of Poland would have shocked Europeans of all political persuasions and would have gone far to heal the ailing Western alliance.

An invasion at a time when the American administration was beginning to define its global policies would have intensified the anti-Soviet mood that helped President Reagan into office. It would have facilitated the passage of military programs and stepped up the momentum toward closer American-Chinese relations, which was underway during the last year of the Carter Administration and which appeared to face a less certain future during Reagan's early months. Again, Reagan's anti-Soviet trend ran its full course without an invasion of Poland. But his success in pushing through his military and political policies directed against the Soviet Union was not at all assured in 1981 and may well have influenced Soviet behavior with regard to Poland.

Finally, an invasion would surely have affected the military balance in Europe. It is quite possible that close to a million Soviet troops would have been used for the invasion, and that as many as 300,000 would have remained as an occupation force. This might have required some thinning of the twenty-two divisions in East Germany that form the Warsaw Pact spearhead against NATO. But the overwhelming likelihood is that the Soviets would have called up reserves to make up the difference. Such moves, and the very state of mind revealed in a decision to invade Poland, would hardly have been reassuring to NATO members. It would certainly have led NATO to reaffirm and carry through its increased defense program, and possibly even to raise the number and readiness of the troops stationed in West Germany.

It is clear that such calculations of the consequences and implications of an invasion made the decision the most difficult foreign policy question faced by the leadership in the post-Stalin era. This is why the threshold of tolerance for developments in Poland was relatively high. An invasion would occur only in extreme circumstances and only after it was obvious that the situation could not be salvaged by any other means.

Of the available options, the internal solution was the least expected in the West and the most uncertain in its effectiveness. At the same time, it was the option least damaging to Soviet and Polish communist interests. This was the reason it was selected. It had additional advantages: First, if the internal security-military measures had proven insufficient to establish the *status quo ante* in Poland, the Soviets would have lost nothing and could still have invaded as a last resort; second, if the measures had not succeeded, it would have meant that Poland was in open rebellion, or at least in a state of total chaos and disintegration, which would have provided a perfect excuse, and one more acceptable to the Europeans, for a direct military intervention.

As it was, the internal solution succeeded beyond the Soviet and Polish communists' most optimistic expectations. The belief in the unlikelihood of a successful internal solution had been held not only by Western experts but also by the Solidarity leadership itself. In the fall of 1981 Solidarity representatives tried to convince me that a Soviet invasion was improbable and an internal solution unworkable. The fact that they did not want to admit, even to themselves, that their struggle and accomplishments could be cut short by force, external or internal, was psychologically understandable. What was the sense of fighting and sacrifice if one's position was indefensible against the use of superior force? (In 1968 Dubček and his supporters in Czechoslovakia also did not believe that their experiment would be terminated by a Soviet invasion.)

What Western analysts and the Polish revolutionaries underestimated, to one degree or another, were the following elements of the situation in the winter of 1981:

• The blind loyalty, cohesiveness, reliability, and size (about 100,000 in the uniformed, militarized units alone) of the Polish security forces and their officer corps, and the extent of their control by the KGB;

• The discipline of the military elite units, the commitment of their officers to orthodox communism, and the ability of General Jaruzelski to use them as a backup force, present but not active in the crackdown on Solidarity;

• The professionalism of Polish and Soviet intelligence and the quality of their information about Solidarity and its organization, which made it possible to capture almost the entire leadership of Solidarity a few hours before the declaration of martial law;

• The effects of martial law in an industrial and urbanized country, where communication and transportation networks can be suspended in such a way as to deny a rebellious organization means of coordinating its activities, in effect paralyzing it completely;

• The nature of Solidarity itself, as an extralegal but nonviolent organization that was not well prepared for underground activity, relying on its power to mobilize the masses for acts of civil disobedience only, and not equipped with a security apparatus of its own;

• The fear of an all-out civil war in Poland that was shared by the population, Solidarity, and especially the church;

• The debilitating effects of sustained threats of invasion and occupation on the population, and particularly on the church—threats that finally made the sight of one's "own" security and military forces somehow easier to swallow;

• The effect of the threat of invasion on the army and Party leadership, and even on the communist "liberals," all of whom could now paint their actions in nationalistic colors and rationalize them as patriotic duty to save Poland from the worst evil.

The worst outcome from the Soviet point of view, was avoided. Yet the prolonged crisis disclosed fatal weaknesses in the major link of the alliance system. The events in Poland sensitized both Soviet and Eastern European communists to the explosive potential concealed in the external empire.

The prolonged and still unsolved Polish crisis seemed to drive home to the leaders and their advisers the profound dangers in the empire. The Polish case at once demonstrates the dire disruptive potential of the complex problems common to all Eastern Europe. At the same time, it exhibits elements unique in Eastern European experience. For political leaders as well as analysts, the key question is whether it foretells the fate of the empire.

The role of the Polish working class, parts of which initiated, sustained, participated in, and provided the leaders for the organized defense of its rights, was unique. So was the rapid merger of the workers' movement with a majority of the intelligentsia and later with part of the peasantry, in effect the expression of a unified Polish nation against communism. So was the dual power—Solidarity and the Party—which endured for about a year and a half. Security and elite military forces neither disintegrated nor betrayed the government as they did in Russia's revolutionary year of 1917. If in both historic situations the minority emerged victorious over the majority, Poland's fate in 1981, unlike Russia's in 1917, was decided by overwhelming external force.

The depth and coherence of the proposed alternative to orthodox communism in Poland were also unique. The extent of the disintegration within the Party and state apparatus was unparalleled, a situation that was reversed only with forced installation of a military government. And even after the imposition of martial law and the crushing of Solidarity, the persistence of nonviolent active resistance by the nation to military rule and Soviet communism are without historical precedent. Finally, also without precedent was the elimination, for all intents and purposes, of Poland's military contribution to the Warsaw Pact, an alarming turn that obliged the Soviets to redesign contingency plans for a war in Europe. The main function of the Polish armed forces now is to preserve order in Poland. The probability of the inflammation of the Polish problem again in the late 1980s makes Soviet lines of communication and supply to the troops facing NATO in Germany highly unreliable. There are indications that the Soviets are developing alternate routes of communication and supply in the southern tier and in the north.

The installation of a military government was for Polish communists and their Soviet mentors an act of desperation and not a long-term solution. It avoided the more costly and unpredictable alternative of armed intervention. But from the Soviet perspective, nothing is solved. The Pope's visit in June 1983 exposed the vast gulf between a hybrid government without loyal subjects and a disaffected population without influence. Solidarity was defeated as an organization and a representative of dual power, but the Catholic Church not only survived the experience but emerged stronger in authority and, on the level of the parish priests, more radical in aspirations. At the same time the communist establishment has been fractured dangerously along two axes—the Party versus the military, the moderates versus the hard-liners. A polarization took place within the Party elite, which for all practical purposes eliminated the liberal wing as a well-established faction. The entire bureaucracy shifted to the right, so that today it is Jaruzelski along with a few former liberals such as Mieczyslaw Rakowski and Gornicki as advisers, who represent the forces of moderation within the regime.

From its very inception, military rule, with the attendant infiltration of the weakened Party apparatus at all levels, has appeared as the unattractive but only available alternative to chaos. Tsarist and Soviet tradition upholds firmly the principle and practice of civilian and Party ascendancy over the military. Today Soviet leaders fear both the precedent of prolonging a military regime in Poland and abolishing it in favor of civilian Party rule. To avert a popular explosion, to prevent a reemergence of Solidarity, to ensure a minimum of political stability—these are the immediate objectives. Only a military government appears capable of achieving them.

Neither Polish citizens, Polish communists, nor Soviet leaders can find comfort in prospects for the future. A violent outbreak remains possible, with its inevitable armed response from the East. Even should this not occur, the restoration of an orthodox communist regime, whether in civilian or military garb, could provoke civil war. Also impossible is the restoration by workers and their allies of a competing organization modeled after Solidarity, for it would provoke Soviet invasion.

The main factor working in favor of the continuing stalemate is simply the exhaustion of the population. But the spirit of the Polish worker and intelligentsia has not been broken. A new element has also entered

Polish life—a growing mysticism, one could even say fundamentalism, of the religious beliefs of the population. Not unknown in the Polish past, this constitutes a response to the existing frustration and hopelessness. It may also, as in the past, presage desperate measures. The youth, whose consciousness was formed during the heady year and a half of Solidarity, will be entering the Polish work force in the years ahead. The attitude of this generation was well expressed to me by one of its members: "This round is over, but a next round will start. Our elders have tried everything and they have shown us that peaceful means do not work. When we make our move, 'legalism' will not detract us. We will know what to use the lamppost for."

The Polish consumer's lot has improved, but the economy is in a state of chronic crisis which precludes significant growth and modernization. Major reforms require financial reserves, which are unavailable, and a modicum of trust between the nation and the regime, which has not been established. Moreover, the hard line toward Eastern Europe pursued by Gorbachev is not conducive to liberalism and reforms.

In the economically critical period of the early 1980s, the Soviet Union—and to a much smaller extent other countries of the bloc—provided large-scale help in the form of both consumer and industrial goods. This aid had a clearly political goal—to support the Polish regime in its struggle against Solidarity and to provide the minimum necessary to prevent the frustrations of everyday life from exploding.

Elizabeth Ann Goldstein, senior analyst of the Federal Reserve Bank of New York, concludes that the burden of the 1980–81 assistance to Poland

is heavily skewed toward the East, shouldered mostly by the Soviet Union. The estimates show that in 1980, the Soviet Union provided approximately three-fourths of Poland's foreign assistance. This share increased to roughly 90% in 1981.

The help provided by the rest of Eastern Europe was quite limited at best. In 1980 they provided between 1–2% of the total assistance, and by 1981, this share had fallen to an estimated .3%. The CMEA banks however increased their 1981 contribution to almost 6% from less than 2% in 1980.

The West also provided a relatively small share of Poland's foreign assistance for this period. In 1980, the West's share was roughly 21%, falling sharply in 1981 to about 4%. Western governments provided about 12% of Poland's assistance in 1980, rising to slightly over 22% in 1981. In addition, the estimates show that 1980 commercial bank loans accounted for approximately 9% of Poland's assistance while in 1981 this share dropped sharply to negative 18%, indicating Poland's payments of approximately $1.1 billion to Western commercial banks.

The main conclusion drawn from these results is that, although the Soviet Union has granted only a relatively small amount of formal loans to Poland (mostly hard-currency and ruble-trade credits), when account is taken of the "hidden" transfer of resources to Poland through implicit trade subsidization, it is apparent that the Soviet Union has been the major source of Poland's external economic assistance during 1980–81.*

Foreign assistance to Poland in 1980 and 1981 was very substantial. In 1980 it was equal to approximately 6.8 percent of Polish GNP, and in 1981 it rose to almost 8 percent. Since 1983, however, aid from the Soviet Union and Eastern Europe has drastically declined. Russia is clearly not ready to shoulder the burden of Polish industrial recovery, which is only now approaching the level of 1979 and is still far from the peak level of 1978. It is even less willing to take any responsibility for Poland's hard-currency debt, as many misguided bankers in the West had hoped. Poland is thus in a very difficult situation with regard to its international financial standing. Since Polish exports are too small to cover the servicing and repayment of the debt, Poland's situation is even worse than Brazil's, notwithstanding the latter's much larger debt burden.

Given their own economic troubles, the Soviets could ill afford to continue throwing money into the bottomless pit of the Polish economy. They became convinced that the active rebellious spirit of the Poles had diminished, and their preoccupation with day-to-day economic survival had become central. They were also reassured that the tight grip of the military regime was sufficient to prevent mass trouble and to provide the necessary element of stability.

Emotional and psychological factors also played a role in the decision to leave the Poles on their own economically. The Soviets have always disliked and distrusted Poland. They are infuriated by the Poles' historically unbending anti-Soviet feeling and their contempt for anything Russian, and are angry at what they consider Polish ingratitude. The new Soviet attitude may simply be summed up in the psychologically satisfying phrase, "Let the bastards suffer." Many in the Soviet Union are convinced that the Jaruzelski regime was engaged in a policy of unceasing blackmail toward Moscow. Painting pictures of unrelieved doom, the general warned the Russians constantly of what might happen if Soviet help were not forthcoming. The Soviet leaders called Jaruzelski's bluff. With large-scale aid from Western sources uncertain, despite the lifting of the American embargo, the Polish economic disorder, stagnation, and the lack of realistic reform plans will continue for a considerable time to come.

The sole feasible short-term solution to the crisis would involve a compromise mediated by the church that would gradually reorganize

* Elizabeth Ann Goldstein, "Soviet Economic Assistance to Poland, 1980–1981," in *Soviet Economy in the 1980s: Problems and Prospects,* Part II. Selected papers submitted to the U.S. Congress Joint Economic Committee (Washington, D.C.: Government Printing Office, 1983), p. 568.

the regime and reestablish its overall political monopoly, while at the same time permitting sanctioned free trade unions in the factories, mines and construction sites, thereby realizing some of Solidarity's demands. The restored government would recognize the church's place in Poland's spiritual and, to some extent, secular life. It would issue binding guarantees on human rights, on travel abroad, on relaxed censorship. It would redirect its economic planning toward modest satisfaction of the consumer. A number of years would be required to stabilize the economic and political situation and to commence planning for major change in the economic system. It seems safe to predict that the level of political, social, and economic stability in Poland will remain low throughout the 1980s, and that any changes in policies and structures will have to be introduced very gradually and with only partial effect.

Zbigniew M. Fallenbuchl, one of the foremost experts on the Polish economy, reached the following conclusion from his review of the Polish situation:

Increases in production will undoubtedly tend to induce increases in imports, while it appears that it may not be possible to expand exports. In this situation it will not be easy to achieve external equilibrium and, therefore, also internal equilibrium. There is a serious danger that the stabilisation of the economy will take place at a very low level of per capita income and consumption and will be followed by a prolonged period of stagnation. *A very explosive social and political situation would, therefore, continue to exist.* To avoid this unsatisfactory scenario, the leaders would have to change their policy and look for a "political solution." They would have to win the support of the workers and, indeed, of the entire population and make it possible for the Western governments to remove sanctions. This could lead to more favourable multilateral debt renegotiations and the re-establishment and expansion of links with the world economy. [Emphasis added.]*

But given the unfavorable climate in Moscow on questions of political orthodoxy and Soviet demands for greater contributions to its own development, only the first part of Fallenbuchl's analysis is relevant. The chances of significant steps in the reconciliation of the nation with its government are uncertain.

Yet whatever policies Jaruzelski and Gorbachev may adopt, the lessons of 1980–81 will not be lost on the nation and its working class. "And the lessons are," in the words of Alex Pravda, "that the new [Polish] working class is a repository of revolutionary potential; that it is capable of organizing itself, formulating demands and acting upon them; that it is at once the creature and adversary of the communist system;

---

* Zbigniew Fallenbuchl, *Soviet Studies,* Vol. XXXVI, No. 4 (October 1984), p. 562.

above all, that it is no longer a pillar of continuity but a force for change."*

Moreover, however unique the workers' revolution, the present impasse, with an unprecedented military regime in power, has disturbing implications for Eastern Europe and the Soviet Union itself. The danger of the "Polonization" of the external empire and even of the metropolitan country itself can never be far from the minds of all communist leaders. It is the final irony that the famous words with which Marx and Engels opened their *Communist Manifesto* are applicable today only to the communist states: A specter has indeed arisen to haunt Europe, the specter of a workers' revolution.

* Alex Pravda, "The Workers," in Abraham Brumberg, ed., *Poland: Genesis of a Revolution* (New York: Random House, 1983), p. 91.

12

The Sino-Soviet Conflict

In one of his last speeches to the Communist International, Lenin made a prophecy. He declared that the ultimate fate of humanity and its inevitably communist future would be decided by the hundreds of millions of Chinese and Indians: If they embraced communism in alliance with the Soviet party, communism would become invincible. In October 1949, it looked as if Lenin's prophecy was at least partly coming true. Communists under the leadership of Mao Zedong established their control over the Chinese mainland. As Stalin was creating and consolidating an empire on the Soviet Union's western borders, on its southeastern border a powerful communist state came into being. An alliance was formed, ostensibly to advance the goals of communism, between the world's largest state and its most populous country.

Yet in the three decades since Stalin's death, Soviet leaders have encountered the greatest risks and highest costs of communist encirclement in their relations with China. Along thousands of miles of their southeastern borders, they have deployed men and weapons against their former communist ally. Military planners have felt obliged to make expensive preparations for war on two fronts—the Western and the Chinese. While the Soviet-American contest is, and for the foreseeable future will remain, the central focus of international relations, the Sino-Soviet conflict will continue to influence all aspects of those relations. It will itself be influenced by the changing international environment, but it has an impetus and an internal logic of its own.

By the mid-1950s it was becoming clear that Stalin's Eastern European empire would resist Soviet rule. In the late 1950s and early 1960s it also became obvious that Soviet influence over Communist China was in question, and the alliance was in trouble. After prolonged disputes couched in the esoteric language of Marxist-Leninist dogma, the conflict burst into the open at the Soviet Twenty-second Party Congress in 1961.

The conflict centered on the question of Soviet and Chinese roles in the communist world and the international communist movement. The Soviet Union saw itself as the undisputed leader of world communism. China regarded itself as an equal partner with the Soviet Union and not its vassal. From the late 1960s to the mid-1970s China's main objective was to protect itself from possible Soviet military actions. The Soviets wanted China isolated. In the mid- and late 1970s the Chinese concentrated on obstructing Soviet expansion abroad and trying to exclude the Soviet presence in Asia. The Soviets focused on preventing a Chinese political and military alliance with the United States and Japan.

The bloody border clashes between the two states near Zhenbao Island in 1969 set the tone for Sino-Soviet relations in the 1970s. The clashes were in all probability provoked by the Chinese. They turned political and ideological tensions into a military conflict. Chinese behavior became an important Soviet security concern, and Moscow began to view the conflict from a long-range strategic perspective.

By this time neither side perceived the other as truly socialist any longer. The Soviet Union ceased to regard the relationship as one between socialist states and between communist parties. This redefinition signaled a radical lessening of hopes about any eventual resolution of the conflict. The Twenty-fifth Congress in 1976 declared that henceforth Sino-Soviet relations would be based on the principles of peaceful coexistence, a term the Soviets reserve for their relations with countries that have different sociopolitical systems and that are thought to be hostile or potentially so. For Beijing, this redefinition also precluded any Soviet claim, on the basis of the Brezhnev Doctrine, to intervene legitimately in internal Chinese affairs.

The Chinese military attack on the Soviets' principal Asian ally, Vietnam, in February 1979, although far from successful, humiliated the Russians, who for all practical purposes looked on as their ally was being invaded. China's abrogation of the thirty-year Friendship Treaty with the Soviet Union, which had been signed in 1950, brought the troubled decade to a symbolic close. Soviet hopes that Mao's death would open a way for a reconciliation with China were dashed. During Mao's lifetime some Soviet leaders and analysts had still believed that the antagonism was intimately linked to his personal biases, his political maneuvering, and his domination of the Chinese scene. By the end of the decade, however, the truth was inescapable: The conflict was a clash of national purposes and interests, not one of personalities or ideologies. The Soviets began to realize they would have to live with it for the foreseeable future.

The primary objective of Soviet policy toward China in the 1970s was to minimize tensions along the border through both intimidation and positive inducements, with the goal of avoiding the necessity of redirecting resources there. At best, this policy counted on a shift in the hostile Chinese attitude as a result of a number of fraternal gestures on the part of the Soviets; at worst, it aimed at the military, political, diplomatic, economic, and ideological isolation and neutralization of China.

When the Chinese failed to respond to the conciliatory efforts, modest though they were, Soviet policy became heavily weighted toward coercion and intimidation. As William G. Hyland has written:

Where Khrushchev had relished polemicizing with the Chinese and set some store by his ability to persuade other Communists of his own cause, the Brezhnev regime downgraded the purely polemical aspects of the contest with Beijing. Whereas Khrushchev brought primarily political and psychological pressures on China, without any real threat of military action, the Brezhnev regime began building up its military forces, with the implicit threat of intervention. Where Khrushchev wanted to win over the majority of the Communist movement and reestablish Soviet preeminence, the Brezhnev regime came to see the contest more in conventional power terms. In short, in the years that followed Khrushchev's removal, the Soviet leadership began to pursue policies designed to contain and counter Chinese influence. The conflict was transformed from an ideological contest to a power struggle between two potential enemy states.*

New peaceful initiatives were consistently pursued by the Soviets. There were intermittent border negotiations during which the Soviets made many limited concessions. After one round of negotiations would break off, the Soviets would try to begin a new series as quickly as possible, changing slightly the details of their position on issues in the dispute. The last negotiations commenced on October 17, 1979, and ended inconclusively in the spring of 1980. Deng Xiaoping may well have instructed the delegation to stonewall the Soviet proposals because of his central interest in developing his American connection.

The Soviets offered to conclude a nonaggression treaty with the Chinese, which would preclude the use of force to solve the issues under dispute. They tried to expand trade with China and promised the resumption of deliveries of industrial equipment on beneficial terms. Directly after Mao's death the press temporarily halted its polemics against Chinese internal and foreign policies. This was to signal a readi-

*William G. Hyland, "The Sino-Soviet Conflict: A Search for New Security Strategies," in Richard H. Solomon, ed., *Asian Security in the 1980s* (Cambridge, Mass.: Oelgeschlager, Gunn and Hain, Publishers, Inc. 1982), pp. 39–40.

ness to talk business with the new leadership. The Soviets also proposed broader cultural, technological, and scientific exchanges with China, and more exchanges of journalists. Finally, they issued an invitation for a summit meeting in the hope that it would provide the impetus for the resolution of the conflict that lower-level talks did not.

As Kenneth Lieberthal put it: "The substance of the offers was consistent with the continuing Soviet effort to communicate the USSR's willingness to engage in a far-reaching rapprochement with the leadership in Peking, should leaders who were willing to tread this path come to the fore in the Forbidden City."*

There was as well a military side to policy toward China in the 1970s. A Soviet-Mongolian defense treaty was concluded, which led to the stationing of Soviet troops in Mongolia, the strengthening of Mongolian defenses, and the consequent increasing threat to China's security on its northern border. There was a dramatic military buildup along the Soviet side of the border, where fifty-two divisions with major air and armored elements were. (In the mid-1960s, only twenty divisions had been stationed there.) These were brought up to the level of modernity of troops deployed against the NATO alliance in Europe. Both the command system and the second-line troops in the Far Eastern, Siberian, and Central Asian military districts were upgraded. The Pacific fleet was bolstered; for the first time it included nuclear submarines. There were as well increases in the naval presence in the Indian Ocean, on China's southern flank; the Soviets retargeted significant strategic rocket forces against China, and introduced new intermediate-range ballistic missiles (the SS-20) aimed at Chinese targets. Finally the Soviets continued to try to secure naval and air bases in Vietnam. When they finally were obtained, they markedly upgraded the military deployment against China. Strategic bombers, known as Badgers, are stationed in Da Nang and the Pacific fleet uses Cam Ranh Bay regularly.

The Soviets took diplomatic steps to put pressure on China: the conclusion of an alliance with Vietnam, and economic and military attempts to strengthen it; repeated endeavors to isolate China diplomatically and to expel it from the international communist movement; and a continuing, though unsuccessful, effort to create an Asian Collective Security System, to which all the continent's countries were to be invited, but which in fact would be directed against China.

The Soviets also tried to counteract Chinese activities in Third World countries, sometimes even going so far as to condition help for a particular underdeveloped nation on its taking the Soviet side in the conflict.

*Kenneth G. Lieberthal, "Sino-Soviet Conflict in the 1970s: Its Evolution and Implications for the Strategic Triangle," R-2342-NA (Santa Monica, Calif.: RAND Corporation, July 1978), p. 18.

They engaged in vociferous polemics against the Chinese in international forums, especially the UN, and attempted to mobilize Third World members on their side.

The leadership exerted pressure on Japan and West European countries to limit their economic help and to abstain from military deliveries to China, making it clear that they would consider such assistance to be unfriendly and would respond accordingly by stiffening their position in arms negotiations. During the early 1970s, détente with the United States was partly motivated by an attempt to head off a Sino-American alliance. When détente crashed, major pressure was brought to bear on the United States, partly through its allies, to keep relations between America and China from developing into a full-fledged military alliance. The Soviets indicated that the arming of China would preclude any effort to tone down the growing Soviet-American confrontation.

Underlying the carrot-and-stick policy were the convictions that Chinese leaders were divided on the question of Soviet policy and that both peaceful initiatives and threats would provide ammunition for those among them who wanted improved Sino-Soviet relations. At the beginning of the 1980s, however, it was clear that this policy towards China had failed, as had the effort to isolate China through détente with the West.

Links between the United States and China grew closer during the 1970s, achieving a momentum partly independent of the triangular Soviet-American-Chinese relationship. The first steps were taken by the United States toward extending military aid to the Chinese. Although a formal Sino-American military alliance is unlikely, that disturbing possibility has been introduced into Soviet thinking and calculations. Furthermore, despite Soviet efforts to prevent it, a Japanese-Chinese treaty was concluded in 1978 that includes an "antihegemony" clause clearly directed against the Soviet Union. Whereas the appeal of Chinese communism to ultraleft revolutionary groups has declined visibly (partly because of Sino-American reconciliation), its appeal to established communist parties who want to find a counterweight to Soviet domination of the international movement has grown. China has also heightened its economic ties with developed capitalist countries and can now count on significant help in its program of internal modernization. The current plan of internal development, known as the Four Modernizations, even if only partly successful, will make China a more formidable adversary. After a long period of debilitating upheavals, China has finally moved toward internal stability.

Soviet policy failed because the carrot offered too little and the stick had the opposite effect than the one intended. Chinese national pride and contempt for Russians, bred by a deep awareness of past injustices and humiliations, doomed the policy of threat and intimidation. It is also possible that the Soviet leadership vastly overestimated Mao's personal role in the perpetuation of the conflict and the degree to which the Chinese leaders were divided on their policy toward Moscow.

In the final analysis, however, the reason for the failure of policy toward China lies in the contradictory nature of overall Soviet foreign policy. There is a deep and insoluble contradiction between the Soviet desire to avoid confrontation with major antagonists and normalize relations with them while simultaneously engaging in a program of expansionism in which military power plays a dominant role. It is a Soviet illusion that stable relations with China (or America) are compatible with the uninhibited exploitation of stability in the Third World. But such behavior confirms the worst fears of others about the aggressive character of the Soviet system and cancels out friendly gestures and peaceful initiatives.

The conflict between the Soviet Union and China has lost much of its virulence. Yet, the prospects for a détente remain dim, and the strategic realities of the disagreement are basically unchanged. Why is the dispute so intractable?

The discord has deep historical roots, and longevity fuels it. The Soviets have developed a hatred and fear of a powerful, united China. Moscow views the Chinese as irrational and unpredictable. And while often feeling inferior to Westerners, the Soviets are contemptuous of the Chinese. Furthermore, over the years various parts of the bureaucracy have developed vested interests in the conflict. Among Kremlin ideologues the Chinese apostasy is seen both as a danger to Soviet influence in the international leftist and revolutionary movements (now as a rightist-revisionist danger) and as the most powerful device to mobilize domestic public opinion in support of the state. The military uses the Chinese danger, and lately the developing military relations between China and the West, as a lever to extract economic resources for itself.

China's potential status is a further complication. Few countries in the world have a great past and a great future. China is foremost among them, and it is its future that the Soviets fear more than its present. They do not overestimate China's strength. They see quite clearly its enormous weaknesses, but conclude that now is the time to keep the Chinese down, to teach them lessons, to isolate them as much as is feasible, to delay as long as possible their emergence as a superpower. At the same time, they would like to improve their relations with China if the costs of doing so remain low.

The Soviets apparently believe that real concessions in the border dispute will only encourage greater demands from China as it grows stronger. Moreover, they are afraid that border concessions—even if they only entail symbolic recognition of the justice of some Chinese claims—would inspire other nations, like Japan and Romania, to press similar claims. They worry that it might lead to a surge of irredentism in Eastern Europe.

The question of the enormous Sino-Soviet border and of the conflicting claims surrounding it has a complicated history. During the nineteenth century the decrepit Chinese empire suffered a variety of encroachments upon its sovereignty by the great powers of the world. Most of these were in the nature of economic concessions and rights of extra-territoriality.

It was at this time that the Chinese signed what they now call "unequal treaties," ceding substantial frontier regions to the Russian empire. Most of these areas were inhabited by non-Chinese ethnic groups, but they had long been ruled by China and were recognized as part of the Chinese state both at home and abroad. China has been demanding that these treaties be reviewed, asserting that the border will never be legitimate until renegotiated on a basis of equality. The Soviets, of course, consider the border to be legitimate as it stands, and have refused to renegotiate the treaties.

Soviet suspicions of China create a disagreement about timing that blocks efforts to improve relations. The Chinese want the Soviets to initiate a large-scale troop withdrawal from the border. This they would regard as a real sign of sincerity, after which the relationship would improve. The Soviets, on the other hand, see the withdrawal of some troops from the border as the final step in the process of improving relations. They fear that the demand for substantial removals is a trap designed to leave large parts of sparsely inhabited Soviet territory at China's mercy.

The general Soviet attitude toward China is logically faulty. If the Soviets believe that China is now weak and may at some point attain a superpower status, the time to make peace is now rather than later. But this logic does not take into consideration two points: The Soviets consider themselves militarily strong today—much stronger than China—and therefore feel that they do not have to make major concessions; and they think that possible developments inside China, for example the failure of the Four Modernizations and particularly the disillusionment with the "American card," might in fact make China more susceptible to Soviet pressures in the future. Other possible internal developments in China that the Soviets do not exclude are an intensification of factional struggle, a weakening of the central government, and an ultimate fragmentation in the wake of internal social and political turmoil. But even more important is the question of what the Soviets can gain by making concessions now and what costs would be incurred by the improvement of relations with China. In Soviet eyes, what is to be gained by such improvement is quite limited. The Russians have no illusions that the alliance can be restored. The strategic threat that China poses will not disappear with modestly improved relations. The burden that it imposes on military planning will not lessen appreciably. Most important, improvement will not make the Chinese tolerant of expansionist Soviet policies in the Third World.

One dimension of the conflict did make it much more dangerous to the Soviets than the antagonisms with their capitalist enemies and competitors. The United States and its allies have generally not questioned the legitimacy of the Soviet state. They have long since ceased to pose a threat to the internal system, and are reconciled to a policy of containing it within its imperial boundaries. The Chinese, on the other hand, have accused the Soviet leaders of sins that are anathema to communists. These have included, at various times, "hegemonism," the practice of imperialism under the guise of socialist slogans; the virtual annexation of the states of Eastern Europe, the abandonment of revolutionary movements, and attempts to reach compromise agreements with imperialist states; and the resurrection of a class society in the Soviet Union. Such a powerful challenge to Soviet legitimacy has to be treated seriously because it has come from a country that underwent an authentic and victorious revolution, and whose leader, regarded as one of the central figures of the Marxist-Leninist tradition, possessed an authority as a theorist unequaled by anyone in the Soviet Union since Stalin.

The ideological dimension of the rivalry, which played such an important part in the initial stages of its development, has been reduced sharply. The conflict has become primarily a clash of national interests and ambitions. Disputes do sometimes stem from one set of circumstances and then are perpetuated by different ones. The present struggle is grounded above all in the sharp competition between one state that has attained the status of global power and now wants to taste, unhindered, the fruits of its achievement, and another that seeks to maximize its power status in the face of Soviet opposition. Yet the original ideological dimensions should not be neglected. For the Soviets this aspect still plays an important role.

In the Soviet Union, and to an even greater degree in China, the conflict can be expressed verbally only through ideological language, which alone provides each country with justification for its conduct toward the other. And such ideological formulations, in turn, have a very real influence in shaping actual events. The Soviets have tried to come to grips with the changes in Chinese internal polices and have advanced sometimes convoluted arguments to the effect that despite Mao's death and the anti-Mao campaigns, Maoism retains power in China. The Chinese in turn have attempted to tie expansionist Soviet behavior to the domestic character of the Soviet system. The Chinese ideologues are no longer satisfied with the formula that the Soviet Union has become a "regular" capitalist-imperialist state, yet they are at a loss to find a suitable replacement. The Chinese have also been engaged in a reevaluation of the Stalinist heritage, which bears a close resemblance to their traumatic Cultural Revolution, an experience they now reject totally.

Anyone who has traveled in the Soviet Union and has talked about China with Soviet citizens is struck by both the primitiveness and the intensity of their views. Such conversations leave the inescapable impression that in the Russian popular mind, China looms as a danger of overwhelming proportions. The citizen will give some lip service to the danger from the "Western imperialists," will express his dissatisfaction at a particular policy of the American government, and, even during the Reagan Administration, will voice regret that Americans do not understand the Russians. But when it comes to the Chinese, his deepest feelings are unconcealed fear, distrust, aversion, even hatred. This was expressed to me in a recent conversation with an ordinary Russian who first attacked President Reagan's policies towards the Soviet Union and then said: "I don't understand you Americans. The Chinese are barbarians, they don't know better than to wish a war with us. But you Americans are civilized, we admire you, why do you want war with us?"

The popular Russian mind is greatly fearful of the "yellow peril," the conjuring up the dire threat of one billion Chinese ready without the slightest provocation to move beyond their borders in search of living space. There is a clear association between China and Genghis Khan and the Russian suffering under the Tatar-Mongol yoke. The average Russian also believes that the Chinese are repaying with ingratitude the enormous help they received in difficult times, and fears that the Chinese are trying to push the United States into direct confrontation with the Soviet Union.

A historian of contemporary Russia, Sidney Monas, in his postscript to the essay by the Soviet dissident Andrei Amalrik, *Will the Soviet Union Survive Until 1984?* depicts Russian feelings toward China in these words:

China, whether metaphorically perceived as the "yellow menace" or the "red dragon," is in itself an image of menacing power for the Russian reader. Russian racial feeling about "Orientals"—though often repressed, sometimes successfully, and publicly of course unacknowledged—is strong and widespread. It applies to Chinese, to Japanese, to Uzbeks and other Turkic peoples, and it is sometimes passionately reciprocated. No doubt such feelings go back to the days of the Mongol conquest, the Muscovite princely wars for independence, the imperial expansion of Russia and the subjugation and attempted integration of Asiatic populations. Russia's defeat at the hands of the Japanese in 1904 may have played a certain role here. The writer Andrei Bely, for example, had a pathological fear of "Orientals" and used to hide when he saw a slant-eyed face approach on the street. In his great novel *St. Petersburg,* set on the eve of the Revolution of 1905, the "Orient"—whether represented by Japanese, or merely Japanese fashions among the upper classes, or the Mongol ancestry of the central characters—stands for the forces of destruction....*

On the basis of conversations with members of the intelligentsia, I believe that their image of the Chinese does not differ substantially from that of the average Russian. The Soviet Union, after all, has become a country without distinct elite and mass cultures. Although the world of privilege may separate "we" and "they" in Soviet society, origin and culture unite them.

We also have direct testimony of the Soviet leadership's attitude toward the Chinese from the Khrushchev memoirs.

You might say that China is both close to us and far from us. It's close in that it's our next-door neighbor and shares a long border with our country. At the same time, China is far away in that the Chinese have little in common with our people.... It's always difficult to know what the Chinese are really thinking.... It's impossible to pin these Chinese down. There is, however, one thing I know for sure about Mao. He's a nationalist, and at least when I knew him, he was bursting with an impatient desire to rule the world. His plan was to rule first China, then Asia, then ... what? There are seven hundred million people in China, and in other countries like Malaysia, about half the population is Chinese.... His [Mao's] chauvinism and arrogance sent a shiver up my spine.†

It may well be that one of the secondary reasons for Khrushchev's ouster was his inability to control the conflict with China. His successors made an initial effort to repair the damage they thought Khrushchev had wrought. They failed and then they went far beyond Khrushchev's policies in trying to deal with the Chinese from a position of strength. Those ruling the Soviet Union until recently came from the same background as Khrushchev did. There is nothing to suggest that their basic views of China differed from his.

The Soviet view of post-Mao Chinese domestic affairs is often incon-

* Andrei Amalrik, *Will the Soviet Union Survive Until 1984?* (New York: Harper and Row, 1970), pp. 84–85.

† *Khrushchev Remembers,* ed. Strobe Talbott (Boston: Little, Brown, 1970), quotations from pp. 473 and 474; see also pp. 475–478; *Khrushchev Remembers: The Last Testament,* ed. Strobe Talbott (Boston: Little, Brown, 1974), quotation from p. 235; see also pp. 283, 288–289.

sistent, hesitant, and ambiguous. The Soviets, however, developed in the early 1980s a clear and consistent perception of the foreign policy of post-Mao China: It has joined the imperialists. In Soviet terminology, Chinese modernization involves the creation, with the help of the United States, Japan, West Germany, and other capitalist states, of a stronger, more stable military, economic, and scientific-technological basis for accomplishing Great Han expansionist plans.

According to the Soviets, counterrevolutionary change has occurred in the international activities of the Chinese leadership. The title of a 1979 editorial in the main theoretical journal of the Communist Party, *Kommunist,* neatly summarized the Soviet position: "Beijing: Yesterday—reserve of imperialism, today—its ally." The Chinese problem is portrayed as not only encompassing Sino-Soviet relations but also directly threatening the peace and security of other nations.

The Soviets depict the Chinese as in open and direct confrontation with an increasing number of socialist countries, and attempting to intervene in their internal affairs. This intervention sometimes even takes the form of military action—as against Vietnam. They also see the Chinese problem made manifest in China's relations with world capitalism: in an open convergence of Beijing's foreign policy with the anticommunist stratety of imperialism; in coordinated actions with the most reactionary historical forces; in open opposition to the world socialist system; in various cooperative ventures with the imperialists; and in the buildup of military/economic potential.

Where developing countries are concerned, the Soviets portray the Chinese as giving increasing economic, political, and military support to reactionary regimes, developing good relations with such regimes, and helping forces of internal reaction.

The goals and methods of Beijing's policy in the early 1980s are considered by the Soviets to differ very little from the policies of imperialist states. If previously it was possible to speak of the desire of the Chinese leaders to exploit the contradictions between the two world systems for their own profit, the Soviets believe the situation is now quite different. Viewed in class terms, China's coordination of its activities with those of the imperialists signifies that it has been transformed into a link of the capitalist system. The extent to which Soviet leaders believe this is difficult to say, but it is clearly their line.

The current Soviet view of the Chinese internal changes is as follows: Without changing their basic stategic goals, the Chinese are engaged in broad tactical maneuvers in search of more effective ways to realize their hegemonic plans. Policy shifts have been instituted to preserve and strengthen the leaders' power over the country and the Party, to search for more effective ways to transform China into a militaristic superpower, and to reduce the growing social tension that aggravates the political instability of the "militaristic-bureaucratic" regime.

The Soviets believe that changes in the methods of economic management were forced on the Chinese leadership by the bankruptcy of their previous efforts, but do not alter the antisocialist essence of China's economic activity. The absolutely central goal of the modernization program is to accelerate the increase of military-economic power. Soviet figures suggest that in 1979 China occupied third place in the world in total military expenditures. They claim that while investment in the national economy declined in absolute figures in that year, direct military spending rose 20 percent. Thus the Soviets reason that the modernization program is in fact a program of forced militarization. These assertions, it should be noted, are purely propagandistic. In the early 1980s there were no major increases in the Chinese military budget.

Despite its new economic policy, the Chinese leadership, in Soviet eyes, has no new "scientifically valid" program of development. Moreover, some of the changes instituted by the Chinese—in both the domestic and international spheres—are proof of a growing danger to China's socialist accomplishments. As Moscow views it, China is at a new, dangerous stage, where socialist forms of development are being diluted by the encouragement of private enterprise, by the reprivatization of agriculture, by the introduction of elements of market socialism, and especially by the risky decision to enter into large-scale joint ventures with capitalist firms in basic industries. Beijing's creation of mixed companies is said to follow a general political line of allying with imperialism. Previously one could speak about the deformation of the socialist bases of Chinese society as a result of the exploitation of China's economic resources for antisocialist goals. But the Soviets now talk about the danger of the move toward a private economy in China, about the overall weakening of both the state and the collectivist economic sectors, and about attempts to introduce into China forms of economic activity foreign to socialism.

In its present form, the modernization program impels the Chinese leadership to seek support primarily among skilled workers, rich peasants, the intelligentsia, and remnants of the national bourgeoisie. The urban and rural poor cannot serve its goals. Moreover, modernization will not result in the improvement of the masses' material situation because, the Soviets charge, it is aimed primarily at the buildup of Chinese military power.

It is not entirely clear how the Soviets judge the prospects for the Four Modernizations. Impressed by the commitment to this program, the Soviets are deeply afraid that the Chinese will eventually succeed and that within half a century they will become a powerful adversary. Indeed, there exists a genuine belief among virtually all Soviets that the Chinese are committed to a long-term and aggressive anti-Soviet policy.

In the Soviet view, the official Chinese line—seen as anti-Maoist only in word, while in deed following slavishly in Mao's footsteps—masks the authentic, broad, and spontaneous anti-Maoist movement developing in China. This movement is being fought fiercely by the regime with extreme methods of coercion and intimidation. The Soviet leaders are placing their hopes on its destabilizing potential, which may even force the regime to change their basic policies. Yet those hopes are not very high, because, as the Soviets often repeat, one should not exaggerate the forces of the anti-Maoist movement in China; the fact of its existence does not signify that it can undermine the dictatorship in the near future. Nonetheless, it would also be wrong, the Soviets assert, to underestimate the importance of the movement, especially under China's present unstable conditions.

According to the Soviets, the purge of the Gang of Four has not served to heal the divisions within the Chinese leadership and factionalism still splits China's Party from top to bottom. In both their published material and in private conversations, Soviet observers see factionalism as being of the greatest value for their country in the weakening of China. They do not contend that any of the factions now fighting one another represent diverse opinions on the basic direction of Chinese policies, particularly foreign policy and especially relations with the Soviet Union. Their judgment is that the struggle is primarily a fight for personal power and only secondarily involves tactical differences over internal policies.

Soviet observers do not ignore the ideological revisions of Maoism that have taken place in China. Yet in their opinion the recent "modification" does not change Maoism's basic nature. Moreover, they stress that the revisions reinforce those elements of Maoist ideology that are most hateful: militant great-power nationalism, hegemonism in foreign policy, anti-Sovietism, and reliance on war and coercion as the main means of solving China's international and domestic problems.

In short, the general Soviet interpretation of China is that the situation has gone from bad to worse. It is grudgingly recognized that Chinese internal policy has moved away from the extremes of Maoist "permanent revolution," from the Great Leap Forward and the Cultural Revolution, and that the behavior of the leadership has become more rational and calculating. But from the Soviet point of view this is a change for the worse, because the opponent has become more formidable. Early hopes following Mao's death that the newfound rationality of the Chinese leadership would lead to the tempering of their hostility toward Russia have not been fulfilled. Abandoning its isolation and anti-Western xenophobia and assuming a more active role in the international arena, China has entered into a virtual alliance with developed Western countries—particularly the United States—and is both being used by the United States against the Soviet Union and itself using the Americans in its conflict with Russia.

If logic were a guide to policies, despite the virulence of both Soviet and Chinese attitudes and attacks on each other, one would have predicted an effort on both sides to improve their relations. The failure of détente with the United States, economic difficulties, the overextension of foreign policy, and the uncertainties of post-Brezhnev successions all argue for better relations with China, or at least deescalation of the conflict.

And indeed, since 1982 the virulence of the conflict has lessened. Both countries have moved quietly, cautiously, and slowly toward an improvement in relations. Before long, if nothing like the shock of another Afghanistan intervenes, they will probably achieve a degree of rapprochement that would have appeared highly unlikely just a few years ago.

Signs of accord proliferate. They recall the initial steps taken toward Sino-American reconciliation early in the 1970s. There are conversations among diplomats and exchanges of journalists, scholars, and athletes. There are adjustments in the ideological formulation of respective interests. There is a scaling down of the propaganda war. There are reevaluations of policies and restatements of the preconditions for serious negotiations. Some limited bargaining has commenced, although not without occasional setbacks. The May 1984 visit of the Soviet first deputy prime minister, Ivan Arkhipov, to Beijing was canceled by the Soviets one day before it was scheduled to take place. (When I asked Soviet Far Eastern experts whether the cancellation was connected with the growing tension on the Sino-Vietnamese border or with the visit of President Reagan to China, their answers invariably stressed the latter.) While striking results have yet to be realized, the mood on both sides heralds clear improvements in bilateral relations.

The move toward better relations, however tentative, owes its primary stimulus to shifts in Chinese attitudes and policies. The Chinese have publicly revised their ideological formulations. The United States has lately become a "hegemonic" superpower. The Soviets are criticized with less vituperation than before. Most important, the Chinese have gradually moderated their position on three preconditions essential for serious negotiations and improved relations: Vietnamese withdrawal from Kampuchea (Cambodia), Soviet retreat from Afghanistan, and reduction of forces on the Chinese border together with total withdrawal from Mongolia.

The Chinese now say that serious negotiations can commence if the Soviet Union shows willingness to begin partial fulfillment of any of the preconditions. (Incidentally, conversations with Chinese and Soviet officials suggest that the Chinese place greater stress on and expect greater success with regard to Kampuchea, while the Soviets are more sanguine about movement with regard to Mongolia.)

Why has China shifted its policy in the last three years? The answers lie in its evaluation of its domestic situation, the balance within the Sino-Soviet-American triangle, and the changing international environment. Reagan's first-term policy toward China clearly damaged Sino-American relations and accelerated the process of Sino-Soviet rapprochement. Chinese leaders were embarrassed and affronted by America's handling of the Taiwan issue, and especially by continued deliveries there of advanced military equipment. They deplore the symbolic rather than actual effect of Reagan's actions, while realizing that the United States has not fundamentally altered its China policy. Chinese sensitivity to the Taiwan issue has not diminished. Beijing's fears are now centered on the approaching succession in Taiwan. They take seriously the possibility that, after Chiang Kai-shek's son, Chiang Ching-kuo, relinquishes power, his successors may declare the independence of Taiwan. Such a policy of "two Chinas" will destroy the "one China" basis of Sino-American agreement. The political elite is pressing America to prevent such a development, and will consider America partly responsible if it takes place.

In addition, the Chinese do not want to be associated with American policies such as those toward South Africa or Central America that elicit dismay from a power that applauds Third World aspirations and seeks to lead their struggle.

Ironically, America's consistent hard line toward the Soviet Union—a posture urged by China in the past—now works to distance the Chinese from the United States. Reassured by Reagan's anti-Soviet stance, China can be less vigilant against Soviet "hegemonism." As one official expressed it to me: "We no longer have to strengthen the backbone of an American president and convince the American political elite about the Soviet danger." Poor Soviet-American relations tend to draw the Chinese toward the Soviet Union, while good Soviet-American relations bring them closer to the United States. In the first case, China is sure of friendly links with America even if it improves its situation with Russia. America in this situation simply needs China more. In the second case, China is eager not to be left out in the cold and relies on the United States more actively. While we speak about America's "China card" we should recognize that China has two cards—America against Russia, and Russia against America.

The softening of China's preconditions for normalization with the Soviet Union stems less from specific American policies, however, than from the need for stable relations with a less threatening neighbor in order to pursue internal modernization. The Chinese perceive less danger from a Soviet Union beset by domestic and especially economic difficulties. They expect retrenchment to persist in Soviet foreign policy. These considerations strengthen the position of those Chinese who criticize close alignment with the United States and counsel more independence in China's position within the strategic triangle. In the last two years it has become clear that while Sino-American relations kept improving, China wanted to play a more pivotal role in that triangle (or rather quadrangle, since Japan should be included). Moreover, as much as its leaders would not want to see a new Soviet-American détente, they are uninterested or even opposed to an escalation of the new cold war and dangerous U.S.-Soviet confrontations. What suits them best is a managed conflict that stays clear of either détente or confrontation. (In May 1985, discussions with top Chinese military leaders made clear to me the depth of Chinese opposition to President Reagan's Strategic Defense Initiative ["Star Wars"]. They concur in the Soviet fear that it will provide the United States with a first-strike capability, will upset the existing balance, which they regard as one of strategic parity, and will touch off a new cycle of the arms race, in offensive strategic weapons. The second, and unspoken, reason for their anti-SDI posture is obvious—it will make obsolete China's own meager strategic nuclear forces.)

The ambitious program of post-Mao reforms demands a concentration on domestic affairs and a need to minimize the danger from the Soviet Union. Of the "Four Modernizations"—industry, agriculture, science and technology, and military defense—the Chinese place military modernization last; and the relatively low priority of military needs is not challenged directly or vociferously by the generals. Yet, in 1985, Chinese attitudes toward relations with Moscow and the United States were rather skeptical. At the beginning of the 1980s, it was the politicians who pushed for closer relations with America in preference to any steps improving relations with the Soviet Union. Today it is primarily the military leaders who do so. The reason is plain. Despite their unhappiness with the American position on Taiwan (for the military this issue is probably more emotional than for any other group), the only chance for accelerated military modernization rests with closer relations with the United States. Indeed, it is in this field that the Chinese have given closest attention to the prospects for Sino-American cooperation.

The process of de-Maoization, the opening of contacts with the West, problems in the industrial sector (especially the high level of unemployed youth), and the continued success with experimental economic policies (reminiscent of the 1920s in Russia) have presented the Chinese with the trade-off between political control and economic effectiveness so well known from the history of other revolutionary regimes. At present, they have opted for economic effectiveness, while the Russians are held in check by their fear of losing control over the economy.

Abandonment of old slogans, devolution of economic power, reevaluation of the past, uncertain plans for the future—all heighten the anxiety among China's leaders and bureaucracies that they will lose control over the population and particularly over the youth and intelligentsia. They therefore seek a new ideological compass by which to indoctrinate the population and strengthen authoritarian control. In this regard the West constitutes a greater danger to the regime than does the Soviet Union, as the leadership implicitly acknowledged by terminating the short-lived "democracy" campaign of the late seventies.

If in the autumn of 1982 Soviet specialists were stressing the slowness of the reconciliation process and the unlikelihood that it would alter the basic shape of the Soviet-Chinese-American triangle, in the following spring they were arguing that the process would be quicker and broader than anticipated. Some even spoke of improved relations at the Party as well as state level. Chinese analysts, on the other hand, have consistently warned Westerners about underestimating the difficulties of the process and overestimating its likely extent. If the Chinese wished not to endanger their American connection, the Soviets wanted to bring home the dangers of Reagan's policy toward the Soviet Union by flaunting the likely consolation prize of speedy and successful negotiations with the People's Republic. But in fact the movement toward normalization has been taking place neither as fast as the Soviets would have us believe nor as slowly as the Chinese maintain.

Among the political elite and the expert community in Moscow, Gorbachev's ascension to power created great expectations of change in both domestic and foreign policies. Their exhilaration with a young, energetic, and pragmatic leader after almost a decade of inertia and frustration leads to exaggerated estimates of what is possible in the conflict with China. Unquestionably Gorbachev, like every new Soviet leader before him, will try to speed up the process of Sino-Soviet normalization. Vilification of China has disappeared from the Soviet press. In the general secretary's speeches on international relations an olive branch to China is always extended. Visits by high-ranking officials and experts to China have multiplied. Chinese Deputy Prime Minister Yao Yilin visited Russia in July 1985, the highest official to do so in twenty years. And yet, a radical change in Soviet-Chinese relations is not feasible.

Just as Western policy-makers and analysts were once likely to exaggerate the durability of Sino-Soviet tensions, now they are prone to exaggerate the process of reconciliation and its susceptibility to Western and especially American influence. Rapprochement will certainly end the reciprocal vilification in the press; will stimulate scientific, educational, cultural, and athletic exchange; will increase the communication of unclassified materials and facilitate the visits of journalists and economic experts; will reduce the isolation of accredited diplomats; will reinstate Chinese relations with pro-Moscow communist parties; and, more important, will expand trade, perhaps even substantially. Quite possibly, the border dispute will move toward a compromise. (The Soviets have, after all, vacated all islands in the Ussuri River with the exception of one opposite Khabarovsk.) Eventually, there could be mutual troop reductions along the border and even, perhaps, a nonaggression treaty.

But there will be no political or military alliance, nor even détente. Nor will friendly relations between the two communist parties be restored. Tensions will lessen, but Chinese suspiciousness of Soviet hostility to their ambitions will not disappear. The Chinese will continue to negotiate with Japan on issues of defense and trade. Finally, despite normalization, China will perpetuate tensions by opposing Soviet expansion in the Third World.

Improvement of relations, however far and fast it occurs, will also not alter certain cardinal facts of the Sino-Soviet-American triangle. The Soviet Union and China will remain potential enemies, each seeking its own security partly through the other's weakness. The Soviets will continue to be a danger to China, while the Chinese will always fear little and gain much from a United States that remains hostile to the Soviet Union. The Soviet Union will try to prevent or delay China's attainment of genuine great power status.

The improvement of relations will not obviate the perceived need to keep one-third of Soviet armed forces and one-quarter of their rocket forces poised on the Chinese border. Nor will it relieve the military of the necessity to plan for "two and a half wars" (against America, China, and a regional conflict) and economic planners of the need to finance these preparations.

Given Chinese fears, requirements, and interests, the strategic triangle will remain skewed in favor of the United States. Sino-American relations will remain much closer than either Sino-Soviet or Soviet-American relations.

As a Chinese Party official expressed it in May 1985: "For the foreseeable future there will be no strict balance, no equality in attitude and treatment of other nations and especially the two superpowers. We will continue to tilt toward the United States and this will remain our long-range policy." The United States remains the pivotal country and will derive greater advantages than either of the other two powers. What China is now doing is simply trying to improve its position without at the same time strengthening the Soviet position vis-à-vis the United States.

Soviet policy toward China today differs only marginally from that of Gorbachev's predecessors. There is a greater urgency, rooted in the disintegration of the Soviet-American détente, the threatening U.S. military buildup, and the potentially greater Japanese political and military presence. If Soviet fears of encirclement subsided somewhat during the early 1970s, they surfaced again by the end of the decade. The Soviets began to exaggerate the growth of both the Western and Eastern menace. Andropov's and Chernenko's efforts to accelerate the rapprochement with China were as much an attempt to break out of this encirclement as was their policy of trying to divide the United States from its Western European allies. As for China, the pursuit of this new direction in foreign policy represents merely another, if significant, expression of how its leaders regard their national interests. That is to say, the process of reconciliation has its own dynamic, largely independent of the conduct of the United States.

The question of the "China card," a trump to be played in the global game with Russia, is often discussed in the United States. The value of the card is, however, very problematic. America should simply be satisfied that there exists an independent China that, by its very existence, its geographical location, its historical attitude toward Russia, its military power, and its trying experience of dealing with the Soviet leadership, provides an important obstacle to the expansionist plan of its main adversary. America should, of course, help this China, but should be aware that it can influence its attitudes and actions only in a limited way.

As a prominent Soviet Sinologist said some years ago:

It may be that American analysts, when delving into Chinese policy changes, may be making the same mistake we made in the 1940s when the Chinese revolution triumphed. We expected that China for many years would become a strategic ally of the Soviet Union in matters of foreign policy. We paid rather dearly for these hopes. They cost us a lot. Now, on another level, the United States has done more or less the same thing. I remember how after Nixon's trip to China, especially in the mid-1970s, the American press and American official circles took quite a favorable view of the high level of animosity against the Soviet Union in China. Everyone was saying these anti-Soviet feelings must be fostered and fanned. Peking must be helped, strengthened, this anti-Soviet animus must continue to be fostered in order to change the strategic balance on the planet. I think it was also a mistake for the United States to believe that China could become a long-term ally of the United States. I think a more realistic view on either side must convince us of one very important element: that on this globe a great power has appeared, with its own interests, with its own strategic considerations, which do not jibe with the national interests of either the United States or the USSR. At present we have a sort of bi-polar idea that two great powers more or less guide the destiny of the world. This is true if you think of the balance of forces, but we should not forget that soon the Chinese leaders will burst upon the world arena as a third superpower. We may disagree as to whether that is possible soon or not. Whether China will achieve such power or not is another question. We may see it in our own way but the fact that China wishes it is something else. This is the motive force of Chinese policy. This is why it has distanced itself from the United States and come closer to us.

This message has to be seen first of all as an expression of hope that the United States will have no more luck with China than the Soviet Union has had. It was also a warning that in the long run, a modernized China will be a danger not only to the Soviet Union. Yet one element of what he was saying rang true: Do not believe that you can manipulate China, for China has its own views on how to manipulate both of us.

The Soviet fear of China, and the view of Chinese importance in the global correlation of forces, has not diminished with the slow improvement of relations. A pragmatic China represents an even greater threat to Soviet ambitions and security than the China of Mao, whose ideological fanaticism, while connected with extreme anti-Sovietism, fragmented and weakened China and allowed the gap between Soviet and Chinese military power to widen. Now, China has moderated its anti-Soviet tone and made border clashes less likely than in the past. Yet the long-range modernization program holds the promise of a much stronger China. It therefore presents a greater future danger.

The Soviets are only starting to recognize the scope, the dimensions, and the possible worldwide consequences of the post-Maoist social and economic revolution. In this they are not very different from the West, which even today is preoccupied with immediate events and present strategic realities, but not with the long-range and global impact of China's potentially successful modernization. It is beginning to enter the Soviet consciousness that Deng Xiaoping has been approaching the problem of modernization in a way that the Soviet Union has not yet dared to adopt. Instead of piecemeal reforms that are devoured by the bureaucracy, China has audaciously attacked all phases and dimensions of the Stalinist-type economy at once.

Their bold and innovative program seems to have reached a point of no return; that is to say even when Deng Xiaoping leaves the scene these reforms will be carried on by his successors. No doubt, there are forces who consider the present course too extreme. Certainly modernization will proceed through the politically necessary method called "two steps forward and one step back." The danger of bureaucratic inertia and of

252 THE SOVIET PARADOX

corruption on a large scale is ever present. Yet the overwhelming impression is of a nation that has found its vocation in economic innovation and profitable work.

China's radical reforms started in agriculture, which has been virtually privatized. The first meaningful effects of this drastic step are by now visible. As Table 12 illustrates, agricultural output rose dramatically in five years.

TABLE 12   GROWTH OF AGRICULTURAL OUTPUT (1978 = 100)

1978	1979	1980	1981	1982	1983
100	121	139	157	178	264

The industrial growth has also been spectacular, but the main struggle for efficiency and modernization has only just started. One may conclude, as does an authoritative Japanese publication, that:

It is still too early to speculate on the directions in which China's bold new economic policies may develop in the future. On the other hand, it is already clear that they have made a substantial contribution to infusing life into the economy, raising the national standard of living and increasing stability throughout society as a whole. It also seems fair to say that China's leaders, looking back over the last three decades of history, have concluded that extreme fluctuations in government policy are all but certain to retard economic development.

When we follow the process of China's gigantic modernization plan, there is a tendency to think in terms of the one-billion-plus Chinese, of whom 85 percent are peasants, becoming modern in the next thirty to forty years. Such a view is unrealistic and can hardly be used as a standard of success. China is trying to fashion a number of diverse economic units and geographic areas which will be modern in differing degrees. Its supreme goal is to create islands of high technology on the level of the most advanced world standards around such existing industrial centers as Shanghai and Canton. These centers will coexist for a long time with more traditional industrial centers and with a sea of peasants who will remain backward. Assuming that they succeed, however, the high technology enclave will incorporate, let us say, only 10 percent of China's population, but that constitutes about 120–130 million. What this means in practice is that the equivalent of another Japan will burst upon the global economy and world market. This, and not China's strategic position today or tomorrow, should be the primary preoccupation of Soviets and Americans alike.

Ideology has come to play a lesser role in China and in Sino-Soviet relations. When Mao ruled, one of the major threats to Soviet plans in the international arena came from Chinese revolutionary radicalism, which split the international communist movement and outflanked the Russians from the left. Obviously this danger has passed. But it is quite possible that China's present course also creates a troublesome ideological problem for the Soviet Union, this time from the pragmatic right.

Some time ago I had the opportunity to discuss the new course with a high-level Chinese Party official. How could he explain the calamity of Mao's rule (the Chinese formula by that time was, "We wasted thirty years"), and how could he ideologically justify the new course? "You see," he said,

the tragedy of our Party was that it never knew and learned Marxism as it was thought by its founders. We got our Marxism from the Russians, in their own already corrupted version. Marx has determined that real socialism can be built only on the basis of the highest level of modernity attainable under capitalism. There are no shortcuts and alternatives to this precondition of successful socialism. What we are doing now is starting to create this precondition. To achieve this goal we need forty years of capitalism in China. We believe, however, that this goal will be achieved with the Communist Party in power.

(The Chinese are, indeed, engaged in an effort to translate and disseminate original Marxist literature.)

The political and ideological threat from China may materialize if its gigantic experiment is even halfway successful and at the same time the Soviet effort at revitalization under the new leader makes only slow progress or no progress at all. This would serve as a powerful argument for reformers in Eastern Europe, and perhaps even in the Soviet Union. Within the international communist movement, even among hard-line parties, and in the leftist parties in the Third World, the Soviet economic model has largely lost its credibility. China, this time from the right flank, may compete with Russia for their emulation and allegiance.

China's international isolation belongs to the past. Solid, friendly relations with the United States and Japan provide a foundation for the trade, credit, and transfer of technology necessary for modernization. Fear of China on the part of Asian neighbors has diminished. China's opposition to Vietnamese expansion in the Indochinese peninsula finds supporting echoes, and the odds favor China rather than Vietnam's distant protector, Russia.

Chinese military strength is increasing, and the foundations are being prepared for the modernization of the armed forces. Japanese technological help is of importance here. In this respect, however, the decisive factor is provided by Sino-American military relations, which in the last few years have grown gradually but steadily. Deliveries of defensive weapons, trade in applicable technology, strategic consultations between high-ranking Chinese and American military personnel, are the main forms of American military assistance. The present trend is very far from a military alliance, which neither side wants at the present. Yet if the Soviet-American arms race continues, and arms reduction talks fail, closer Sino-American military cooperation is probable. The potential for these relations provides an additional and fundamental reason why their links with the United States are pivotal for the Soviets.

The Soviet experience with other communist countries shows the bankruptcy of their key ideological precepts even more than the unhappy situation in the Soviet Union itself. The idea that the international spread of communism will bring peace among nations in place of the conflicts and wars engendered by global capitalism has suffered a mortal blow. The workers' unrest in East Germany in 1953, the invasions of Hungary, Czechoslovakia, and Afghanistan, the conflict with Yugoslavia in the 1940s and 1950s, the border skirmishes and warlike tensions with China, the unending political and economic conflicts with their satellites, the need to keep large contingents of Soviet troops in almost every Eastern European country, have demonstrated that the spread of Marxism-Leninism is far from a prescription for peace. Eastern Europe, instead of being a zone of domestic tranquillity and international peace, is a powder keg. The four-thousand-mile Sino-Soviet border, the longest in the world, has the world's largest peacetime concentration of troops.

The idea that Stalin's tyranny and authoritarian harshness were made necessary by Soviet backwardness and the conspiracy of world capitalism has been refuted by the nature of the regimes in Eastern Europe, Cuba, Vietnam, and Ethiopia. All of them exist under Soviet protection. Yet all of them have been forced to reject democracy and have been beaten down by their Soviet protectors whenever they showed any inclination in a democratic direction. The Soviets and their allies have demonstrated incontrovertibly that the association of Marxism-Leninism with democracy is unfounded.

The idea that the Eastern European regimes represent the interest of their working classes was destroyed by the Polish Solidarity movement. The Soviet Union has achieved in Eastern Europe what would have seemed an impossible task before World War II—an end to sociopolitical fragmentation and a far-reaching unification of working classes and the intelligentsia in opposition to communism and in defense of nationalism in almost every country.

Communist encirclement constitutes a threat to the Soviet Union, and it is likely to increase with time. It may become the nemesis of Soviet international aspirations and of the Soviet system itself. Unless and until the psychology of the leadership changes radically in this respect, the empire confronts insoluble political and economic problems. The peoples, and even many of the elites, of Eastern Europe have proven throughout their forty-year existence that the initial Russian hope of legitimizing these illegitimate regimes was futile. Generational changes rather than working for the Soviets have intensified the difficulties of their imperial rule. Time is not on the side of the Soviet Union. This is also true in the case of China. Improved Sino-Soviet relations, which are likely, do not change the basic situation of suspicious neighbors with conflicting interests and aspirations. Moreover, it is probable that the Sino-Soviet correlation of forces in the coming decade will move in a direction favoring the Chinese. The twenty-first century may not be Chinese, but it will certainly not be Russian.

A few years ago, during the Polish crisis, Fritz Ermath wrote a paper with the provocative title "The Crisis of Soviet Empire: So What?" Even in short- and middle-range terms, the "so what" is unjustified. The Soviet Union's external and internal crises feed on each other and compound each other. Empires are expensive. The Soviet version is expensive despite the efforts of Stalin and his successors to make it pay. Eastern Europe has to be garrisoned. Cuba and Vietnam have to be armed and fed. African expeditions are not cheap. And this does not even include the force permanently stationed on the Chinese border. What the Soviets spend abroad they cannot spend at home. And the more poorly the domestic economy performs, the greater the strain that keeping the empire, securing the southeastern border, and engaging in foreign adventures place on domestic expenditures. The crisis of the empire and the conflict with a modernizing China therefore make the alleviation of the domestic crisis much more difficult.

The costs of the empire and the conflict with China make reforms at home all the more necessary and all the more difficult. Improvements at home require innovations that depart from Stalinist orthodoxy. Control of the empire requires political orthodoxy and economic traditionalism. The existence of the empire limits options at home for fear of their impact on Eastern Europe. At the same time, the Chinese modernization program creates an additional rationale for drastic reforms at home. The Soviet Union is trying to diminish the cost of its empire by reducing its aid to Eastern Europe and demanding the investment of more resources from there into Soviet development. But in doing so, they only increase the dangers of East European instability.

How erosion of the Soviet Union's domestic and imperial power will influence its international ambitions and expansionist efforts is uncertain. What is certain is that the way the West manages the relative decline of Soviet power will depend largely on Soviet foreign policy and on U.S.-Soviet relations.

III

SOVIET FOREIGN POLICY AND RELATIONS WITH AMERICA IN THE 1980s

> ... nuclear arms control, though the most sharply contested is *not* the most important issue in Soviet-American relations. Many would challenge this assertion. Yet while weapons themselves do not cause wars, political collisions between the great powers may. Any conceivable treaty delimiting the number and characteristics of missiles, warheads, etc., in the hands of the United States and of the U.S.S.R. would still leave each superpower with enough to devastate the other.
>
> Adam Ulam,
> *Foreign Affairs,* Fall 1985

We now turn to Soviet global aspirations which can contrast with the domestic decline, but have not as yet been abandoned. How does decline affect Soviet international aspirations and resources? To what extent do international goals contribute to decline?

The Soviets believe that the world is an arena of struggle, conflict, and competition between capitalism and communism. The struggle is to be conducted in various ways: politically, as the effort to undermine, to weaken capitalist alliances and strengthen and expand their own and to remove capitalist influence in the countries of the Third World; ideologically, as the competition for the minds and hearts of peoples who, while not communist themselves, may serve the goals of Soviet foreign policy; economically, as the competition between capitalist and communist nations for the largest share of global production and the leading role in technological progress and labor productivity; militarily, for superiority in the balance of strategic forces and successful intervention in civil wars and regional conflicts.

The three decades that followed Stalin's death saw the transformation of the Soviet Union into a global power. For Stalin, the outside world was a place against which defenses to keep out contaminating influences had to be built. For his successors, the world increasingly represented not only dangers but opportunities for the expansion of Soviet influence and power. This shift toward a more activist foreign policy reflected not only the greater Soviet capabilities but also an attitude different from Stalin's isolationism and dogmatism. While for Stalin the Third World countries were primarily an "indirect reserve" of the imperialist nations, for his successors they loomed as opportunities and potential "reserves" for the Soviet bloc.

Within this general framework, Soviet-American relations became the main axis of international competition after 1945. It is the conflict between the two superpowers that carries with it the danger of nuclear confrontation, extends beyond one particular region, and involves parties with the resources to wage a struggle on a global scale.

Each side has tried to downgrade the conflict's importance and to concentrate more on other aspects of international relations. In the beginning of the Carter Administration the intended policy of "benign neglect" foundered on the nuclear arms race and Soviet expansion in Africa and Asia. Midway through the first Reagan Administration, the Soviet attitude was expressed as "we can wait out Reagan," but this gave way to a preoccupation with American policies even greater than in the 1970s. As for the Reagan Administration itself, at no other time since the late forties and early fifties have all the foreign policy activities of an American government been so firmly subordinated to the Soviet-American rivalry.

To understand Soviet foreign policy it is not enough to follow the country's international activities. It is important to look at its motivating forces, its capacities, and its formation. Therefore, we will analyze ideology, policy resources, and politics, with a special focus on the military factor and the military sector; the cycle of Soviet foreign policy and relations with America that appeared with détente and closed with the present slide into a new cold war; typical American assumptions and perceptions concerning the Soviet Union, which constitute an important aspect of the superpowers' relationship; and the lessons to be derived from the stormy relationship and the prospects for managing their conflict in the foreseeable future.

13

The Roots of Foreign Policy

Any country's foreign policy is to a large extent determined by international conditions. But it is also based on geographic location, history, traditional social structure, culture, religion, economics, politics, the experience of relations with other nations, and the way in which the unique configuration of these factors affects the outlook of the people, elites and leadership. Soviet and Russian national characteristics and traditions are reflected in the mind-set of its people and leaders and in contemporary foreign policy.

Geographically, the Soviet Union is the largest country in the world. Because of its enormous size and ethnic diversity, it has always had the problem of maintaining control of its periphery, and the imminent danger of disintegration should there be a lapse in the power of the center.

Russia and the Soviet Union have been invaded from the East and particularly from the West, and have also expanded in both directions. While in the earlier periods of Russian history the invasions and defeats came primarily from the East, subsequently the greatest threats originated in the West; and while the object of Russian expansion was once located in the East and Southeast, in the later and Soviet periods the emphasis shifted to the West. Only from the mid-1950s have Soviet ambitions moved beyond the areas of the Eurasian land mass bordering the Soviet Union. Russia's exposure to frequent invasions and wars, its relative weakness, its subjugation for many centuries to the Tatars, created in the peoples and especially in its elites and rulers an obsessive security-mindedness. This has been magnified in the Soviet period by the experience of foreign invasions and hostility, self-imposed estrangement

259

from the world, and by what was until recently relative military weakness. In 1932 Stalin justified the need for rapid, forced industrialization, by enumerating one by one the instances of past defeats repeating after each "we will never be beaten again." The leadership, like Russian rulers before them, is influenced in domestic and foreign policies by the trauma of past weakness and defeat.

At a Soviet-American conference in Moscow, I discussed the American view that Soviet secrecy and security-mindedness is abnormal, almost paranoic. During a recess one of the top leaders of the Soviet scientific establishment reproached me: "You know our history. How can you say that we are overly security-minded? If we were less security-minded, this conference would have been taking place in a fundamentalist Muslim state or in fascist Germany."

As a great power in Europe and Asia, Russia and the Soviet Union have suffered from a cultural-political schizophrenia. Russia is plagued by a deep sense of inferiority towards the West. On the other hand, the nation is sensitive to its exceptional status. It feels it is endowed with a unique mission. It is this vision of Russia as the third Rome, and of the Soviet Union as the base of a new civilization, that inspired the mission of carrying the message of spiritual renewal to the West and of modernization to non-Europeans.

In the West there are extreme and contradictory views about the effect of beliefs and tradition on Soviet policy. Stanley Hoffmann suggests that there are three principal Western approaches and interpretations on this subject, which can be presented as ideal types.* I would call the first interpretation the fundamentalist school, the second the insecurity interpretation, and the third the opportunistic approach.

The fundamentalist school sees the Soviet Union as relentlessly and inherently expansionist with nothing less than world domination as its goal. The leadership is seen as ready to risk a general war if only the damage to the Soviet Union can be limited. The insecurity interpretation views Soviet behavior as primarily defensive and conservative. The military buildup is a traditional Russian way of dealing with insecurity. Forays, both close to its borders and far away, are designed as preventive moves thwarting the calculations of hostile countries. The opportunistic approach asserts a lack of a Soviet master plan for world domination and considers its drive for supremacy as nothing more than a hope. The desire for preeminence does not determine middle- or short-range goals. Long-term Soviet policy, however, is not only defensive, but has strong offensive elements and expansionist ambitions. Its

* Stanley Hoffmann, from an unpublished paper presented at a conference titled "Psychology of U.S.-Soviet Relations," Spring 1985.

basic objective is to change the "correlation of forces" and translate them into tangible achievements of international power and influence. Its fundamental approach is disruptive and against the status quo. The three schools differ obviously on a number of subordinate issues, such as the nature of the leadership, the effects of domestic difficulties on Soviet international behavior, the elements of risk taking and deliberateness in constructing foreign policy.

There is merit in all three interpretations when specific events or Soviet moves are to be explained, but the third school appears to be the most plausible. The fundamentalist school sees too much continuity in Soviet policies and doctrinal views from the period of revolutionary Leninism to the present. It denies the importance of specific circumstances in shaping policy. Doctrinally dogmatic itself, it excludes the possibility or plausibility of changes in approaches both to the international system and to particular conflicts within it.

The insecurity interpretation concentrates too much on the moving force of Soviet insecurities. That they are real and still remain strong is not in question. Three characteristics of this position, however, confuse more than they explain.

1) This school sees no distinction between qualitatively different types of insecurities: that of the homeland, that stemming from the imperial position, and that of status as a global power equal to the United States.

2) The "insecurity" school often mixes the causes and consequences of specific Soviet policies and actions. Actions such as the continuing, large-scale deployment of SS-20 missiles in Europe could very well derive from a perceived need to improve the Soviet Union's defensive position. As a result, however, this deployment could be and has been used to intimidate West European governments and has triggered a new cycle in the arms race in Europe. Moreover, an act which derives from Soviet insecurity may have offensive consequences and produce an unending cycle of offensive actions. If the invasion of Afghanistan was a defensive move to preserve the communist regime there, an invasion of Pakistan or Iran, the key sources of weapons and refuge for Afghan partisans, could stem from Soviet insecurity about Afghanistan and would also be launched with defensive goals in mind.

3) Those who explain away Soviet expansion by one or another form of insecurity are applying a double standard to Soviet behavior and to the behavior of other great powers in history. In fact they do not acknowledge for the Soviet Union even the traditional attributes, the expansionist aspirations, which almost every great power has displayed in the past; especially if the great power, as for instance Germany, was a latecomer to the international power game and to the colonial feast.

Determining the roots of any power's foreign policy is, of course, very complicated—indeed it is almost as much an art as a science. In the Soviet case it is made additionally difficult by a penchant for extreme secrecy, the lack of documents, memoirs, or access to top policy-makers.

Yet the evaluation of the role and substance of the beliefs of Soviet foreign-policy-makers is of great importance. As John Strachey has remarked: "It is is a military maxim that in framing a country's defense policy, the capabilities alone, never the intentions, of other nations must be taken into account. But this is one of those maxims which however dutifully they are preached in the staff colleges, can never be adhered to in the cabinet rooms."* And it is the concern with Soviet intentions over long periods of time that leads to the discussion of its beliefs as the motive force of its conduct. The only, and far from ideal, way to form opinions and pass judgments is through an examination of Soviet writings, the study of past Soviet practice in specific instances, and discussions with officials and experts that are often and unintentionally very revealing.

The beliefs of the policy-makers provide a self-evident answer in view of their incessant proclamations of Marxist-Leninist doctrine as the guiding light of the party over which they rule. Yet to accept their claim at face value and simply consider Marxist-Leninist doctrine the basis for their foreign policy would be mistaken. Doctrine does play a role for policy-makers, but it is not the only influence on their thinking and is certainly not a precise guide to political action.

Marxist-Leninist doctrine, like others developed in the nineteenth and early twentieth centuries, provides a *Weltanschauung,* a world view, on a high level of generality far removed from a rapidly changing reality. It expresses its "laws" of continuity and change in a highly theoretical, abstract way, and, partly because of its complex methodology, provides uncertain guidelines for understanding the changing world, let alone for determining the actions necessary to achieve its goals. The doctrine cannot explain Soviet international behavior. The level of its generality can seldom be translated directly into policies and can be so broadly interpreted as to leave enormous latitude to the policy-maker. As Alexander Dallin has put it:

In substance, the belief system now sanctions the view that anything is possible; any one thing may or may not occur; revolutions may or may not take place; force may or may not be needed; Communists may or may not be in control of "bourgeois" or "mass democratic" movements; non-western countries may or may not opt for a non-capitalist path, which in turn may or may not lead to socialist revolution. Soviet doctrine (which thus cannot be falsified) becomes use-

* John Strachey, "Communist Intentions," *Partisan Review,* Spring 1962, p. 215.

less as an analytical or predictive tool. It is rather a distorted reflection of a political system trying to come to terms with the present without betraying its past.*

Finally, Soviet foreign policy-makers truly do not know much about Marxist-Leninist doctrine. In all probability, Party ideologue Mikhail Suslov, who died in 1982, was the last Politburo member to have read even the first volume of Karl Marx's *Capital* or some of the more complex works of Lenin, and the elderly Boris Ponomarev would be the only current member of the Secretariat who could claim familiarity with the literature. The policy-makers are practical politicians like Khrushchev or Andropov rather than theoreticians and propagandists like Piotr Pospelov, Ponomarev, or Suslov. The primary role of the theoretician and propagandist is to provide a doctrinal justification for the policies adopted by the "practical" policy-makers.

Yet Marxism-Leninism is not entirely irrelevant. It has three significant consequences for Soviet foreign policy. It stimulates a long-range and systematic approach to international problems. The speeches of Soviet leaders at Party congresses are very different from an American president's State of the Union messages. In their programmatic speeches and in their way of thinking, the leaders analyze and draw conclusions about "the correlation of forces," which goes far beyond military strength to include global political, economic and social trends and their consequences for Soviet foreign policies. They refer to much broader trends and take a longer perspective than is usual for most Western statesmen. As early as 1924, in a series of lectures to a workers' university, Stalin systematically commented on purposes and concepts of strategy and tactics. Such themes as the definition of changing strategic goals, the main enemy, direct and indirect reserves of one's own and enemy forces, and the relationship of tactics to strategic goals provided a stable framework for the analysis of international relations.

This approach does not by any means prevent foolish hopes or unwarranted fears, nor does it preclude frequent shortsightedness. The misreading of the gradual change in America's moods in the 1970s, the initial failure to understand Ronald Reagan either as a candidate or as president, the out-of-hand rejection of America's innovative March 1977 arms control proposal—and the failure to anticipate the worldwide consequences of the Afghanistan invasion are examples of Soviet myopia.

Secondly, one has to distinguish between the influence of doctrine on specific policies and its impact on the overall way of thinking of the So-

* Alexander Dallin, "Retreat from Optimism: On Marxian Models of Revolution," in Seweryn Bialer, ed., *Radicalism in the Contemporary Age,* Vol. III: *Strategies and Impact of Contemporary Radicalism* (Boulder, Colo.: Westview Press, 1977), p. 146.

viet leaders. While their knowledge of doctrine is shallow, and they are unlikely to make references to doctrinal propositions when making policy, the Soviet version of Marxism-Leninism does provide a generalized, though often primitive, framework for the leaders' thinking. The general projections, predilections, and biases of the doctrine, and simplified versions of its basic concepts (such as class warfare), are adopted automatically, and probably unconsciously. Thus, when Khrushchev declared "We will bury you!" during his visit to the United States in 1959, he did not mean it in the way it was interpreted in the American press—that the Soviet Union under his leadership would destroy America. He meant that the American system was anachronistic, and that history, the Soviets' greatest ally, would vindicate communism and "bury" capitalism. This view was so natural to him that he must have been surprised by the effect of his simple ideological statement.

Most important, doctrine has to be distinguished from ideology. Doctrine is a set of highly general and internally consistent theoretical propositions. Ideology can best be understood as a part of culture, a slowly changing combination of doctrinal inputs and the historical experience and predispositions that run parallel to doctrine. This ideology, these beliefs, are operational for Soviet foreign policy-making.

Some Western analysts declare that ideology is dead in the Soviet Union, as the nineteenth-century positivists declared that religion was dead, and that the mainspring of its foreign policy is Soviet national interest. Yet this approach begs the question of the roots of the nation's foreign policy. Aside from some geopolitical realities and shibboleths about security, there is no such thing as "pure," or, as the Soviets would say, "objective," national interest. In authoritarian societies it is defined according to the will and the predispositions and aspirations of the leadership and elites. The study of Soviet ideology provides a key to understanding the changing Soviet definition of its national interest.

The Soviet mind-set reduces all the intricacies of Marxist-Leninist doctrine to a number of simple, and usually untestable, general propositions. From historical experience it adopts a set of fears and predispositions concerning relations with other nations. From the cultural heritage it follows a way of looking at Russia in a historical perspective that defines its role in relation to other nations.

The doctrine declares that the interests of socialist and capitalist countries are antagonistic to each other and in the final analysis irreconcilable. The cooperation of capitalist and socialist nations, when their immediate interests overlap, does not in the long run halt the inexorable course of international class warfare. Historical development favors communism as the future of all mankind.

All socioeconomic systems can be defined in terms of the rule of particular classes. While the political superstructure in any country enjoys a level of relative autonomy from the economic base, it is the latter which designates the class that rules and spells out the nature of the political order and the direction of its policies, including foreign policies. The foreign policies of any country are a reflection of domestic politics and of the interests of the ruling class.

Socialist foreign policy is justified by its ideological ends. Any tactics are acceptable as long as they promote socialism. The spread of socialism requires revolutionary upheavals. The expansion of the socialist system necessitates support from nonsocialist forces whose immediate interests are anticapitalist or only partly socialist.

Soviet historical experience creates, in the mind-set of foreign policy-makers, the following "practical wisdom":

Communist victory in industrial capitalist democracies is unlikely in the near future. Communist movements in developed capitalist societies are undependable allies and of limited help in the execution of Soviet foreign policy. Socialist gains more probably will occur in less-developed countries, as the Bolshevik Revolution has shown and the experience of the last half-century has confirmed.

Soviet security may be identified with the achievement of a communist world. Only such a victory will provide final security for the state. For all practical purposes, communist internationalism is tantamount to the unquestioning support by all other communist forces of Soviet foreign policy. The most valuable assets on the international scene are not the proletarian movements in developed capitalist societies, but the contradictions and splits among these countries, and the socialist or Soviet-oriented revolutionary movements in the less-developed nations.

While Marx pronounced revolutions the midwives of historical progress, the Soviet experience has shown that military power is the midwife of revolutions and revolutionary regimes. The only guarantee of the pro-Soviet orientation of Third World revolutions is the control of the military and security forces of the revolutionary country by the Soviets or their proxies. The major enemies of "correct" revolutionary movements in Third World countries are the spontaneity of mass participation and the liberal democratic institutions that may develop.

Beyond considerations of doctrine, the Russian cultural heritage gives mixed signals about the Soviet Union's place in the world community. The question of Russian nationalism and the relationship to the outside world produces a multiplicity of answers.

First, Soviet nationalism is shaped by past experiences that can best be characterized as defensive in nature. It grew out of the traumatic experience of repeated invasion and constant weakness, of being defeated and sometimes nearly destroyed. The next disaster or crisis always looms just over the horizon. It stresses the separateness of Russia from other nations in a world that is always assumed to be at least potentially hostile.

It is also an as yet undiminished imperial nationalism—in all probability the last one left on the globe. It is committed to the empire that Stalin built in Eastern Europe, which his successors are still ready to defend at all costs. This expands the preoccupation with security to include not only the Soviet Union proper but all of Eastern Europe as well.

Furthermore, and most important for the future of international relations, Soviet nationalism is to an increasing degree that of a great power attaining global stature, that is still young, growing, ambitious, and assertive, and that yet entertains hopes and illusions about what the application of power in the international arena can accomplish. It is the nationalism of the older generation of leaders who worked so hard, waited so long, and hoped so fervently to achieve a dominant international position; who barely saw the complications and limitations of their newly acquired status; and who did not want to face the difficulties of translating their power into tangible international recognition and rewards. It is also the nationalism of the younger generation of leaders who share the ambitions of their elders but not the lingering insecurities and memories of historic weakness, and who lack the maturing experience of past sacrifices.

It is, finally, a nationalism that is still fused with a perception of universal mission. This attitude was present in Russia long before the Revolution. It took root in Soviet soil and has combined with the communist world outlook.

One source of strength of the Bolshevik outlook is the way it combines two major and distinctive currents of thought among the nineteenth-century Russian intelligentsia: those of the Slavophiles and the Westernizers. With the Slavophiles the Bolsheviks shared, and still share, a view of Russian exceptionality and world mission. With the Westernizers the Bolsheviks shared, and obviously still share, the belief in technological progress and the necessity of modernizing. For the Bolsheviks, Western-style modernization had, however, to be decontaminated of democratic political institutions. The various components of this nationalism propel foreign policy-makers into an activist and interventionist direction.

The distinctions among the various elements of the belief system are in reality not separate or contradictory. Under certain conditions, these elements—for example Marxist-Leninist doctrine and great power nationalism—are inseparable. They are fused in the perceptions and feelings of the elite. Of course, particular groups and individuals will differ in their devotion to particular principles or pronouncements and in the intensity of their nationalistic feelings and commitments. These differences are, however, not as clear-cut as they are sometimes made out to be. It is an oversimplification, to take an extreme example, to counter-pose a group of ideologues whose devotion to doctrine is paramount, to a military group composed of pure and simple nationalists. The differences among foreign policy-makers are differences of degree.

It is not really possible, for example, to separate doctrinal elements from divergences of national interest in the Sino-Soviet dispute. Doctrinal differences and commitments—each side's belief that it represents the truth—reinforce nationalism and mutual dislike and fear. To take another example, the defensive dimension of Soviet nationalism provides a basis for the extraordinary preoccupation with security; but so does the ideology, with its view of the world as divided into hostile, irreconcilable camps and its image of the Soviet state as the bastion of progress, that has to be preserved at any cost for the sake of communism.

When the implications of doctrine and nationalism conflict, there is an ambiguity that does not exist when they reinforce each other. When such ambiguities are present, the ways in which the leadership and political elite assign priorities to particular goals, rewards, or expectations take on special importance. One may infer such order of priorities from the long-term tendencies of Soviet foreign policy.

There are absolute priorities, the constant features of Soviet international behavior. They have not changed perceptibly over the years. One such priority is the security of the homeland and of communist rule within the homeland. Another is the security of the empire. In the view of the leadership, the question of communist rule and dominance in Eastern Europe is an internal Soviet problem. This of course does not mean that some Soviet actions do not in fact bring about dangers as unintended consequences (such as the consequences in Eastern Europe of Khrushchev's secret speech in 1956); it means only that in the calculus of foreign policy-making, the leadership's sensitivity to such dangers has been extraordinarily high.

There is a second group of priorities that carries variable weight in foreign policy-making. One is the goal of enhancing international influence, which is reflected in attempts to establish strong ties with individual countries, and to support and encourage governments friendly to the Soviet Union. These efforts are partly defensive in nature, directed at achieving the retreat and isolation of recognized hostile powers or unfriendly competitors for influence, and partly offensive, aimed at establishing a solid base of support in particular areas of the world. The offensive aims explain the presence of Cuban proxy troops in Angola, the Soviet and Cuban presence in Ethiopia, efforts to gain influence on Syrian policy, economic and military aid to North Yemen, and the delivery of weapons from communist countries to revolutionaries in Central America.

Another priority is economic: to promote the inflow of technology from industrialized capitalist countries, to secure agricultural imports, and to obtain credits from and cooperative economic arrangements with the West. In the last decade this goal has acquired a great deal of importance, becoming a condition for maintaining the desired rate of growth of economic and industrial productivity without resorting to internal economic reforms.

Promoting revolution abroad, fostering and helping Communist takeovers, probably ranks low on the list. Here of course the degree of control that the Soviets hope or expect to have over the regimes that would emerge from such takeovers and the strategic importance of the countries themselves make an important difference in the extent of Soviet interest. Khrushchev awarded the highest Soviet military decoration, the Golden Star of Hero of the Soviet Union, to the Egyptian leader Gamal Abdel Nasser at a time when he had outlawed Egypt's Communist Party and jailed its members. Yet in other places and in other times the aim of helping to sustain foreign communist movements and of trying to keep actual or at least symbolic control of these movements, still retains an important place among the priorities of foreign policy.

The "natural" relationship between doctrine, ideology, nationalism is one of mutual reinforcement. When an incongruity or conflict between those elements occurs, however, pure power interests and nationalism almost invariably win out. It was Lenin's pragmatism and not Trotsky's idealism that decided the issue of the Brest-Litovsk peace treaty with Germany in 1918. The causes of republican Spain in 1936 and the communist insurrections in Greece after the Second World War were quickly abandoned when they conflicted with Soviet power requirements. The American bombing of Haiphong did not lead to the cancellation of President Richard Nixon's visit to Moscow. And it was the "ideological" Soviet Union, not the "pragmatic" European democracies, that made peace with Nazi Germany in 1939. (Perhaps, therefore, Western European fears about a U.S.-Soviet condominium are not groundless.)

The Soviet belief system does not provide a detailed blueprint for the decision-makers. It has served to create perceptions, inclinations, and predispositions that are frequently inconsistent among themselves and that rarely have unambiguous implications for action. Throughout its history, the Soviet Union has adapted its international behavior to the changing circumstances of world politics and to its own domestic conditions and requirements.

For all the variations and tactical adjustments, however, there are some constant factors in Soviet foreign policies. Three are worth noting: fears, hopes, and the adjustment of foreign policy thinking.

When the Soviet Union reached strategic parity with the United States, its sensitivity to its own security did not diminish. The buildup of forces did not stop. It is sometimes asserted that this buildup proceeded in the 1970s by the force of inertia, supervised and pushed by the military. This view is probably correct, but the military thrust was accepted without question by the civilian leadership. The views and policies of the military were in perfect harmony with those of the political establishment. The backlash in the West against this buildup created conditions for the reemergence of Soviet insecurities and new attempts to alleviate them. The self-fulfilling pattern in Soviet foreign and military policy reasserted itself once more. Western analysts sometimes ask whether actions such as the military buildup of the 1970s and the invasion of Afghanistan in 1979 were defensive or offensive steps from the Soviet point of view. The Politburo's decision to invade Afghanistan was surely dictated by the goal of preserving a communist regime in that country. Yet the question misses the point. Soviet policies may have had a defensive purpose, a defensive intention. But the consequences were clearly offensive, in the one case providing a force to intimidate Western Europe, in the other improving their strategic position in the sensitive Persian Gulf area.

Moreover, the Soviet concept of security itself has changed in the last decades. In addition to the expansion of global involvement and influence, security increasingly includes the preservation of Soviet status. With this status comes the right to intervene in any civil war or regional conflict, to be present in military terms or through proxies far away from Soviet borders, and to be represented in negotiations of any significant international problem.

The redefinition of Soviet security interests makes the concept broader and involves the nation in its defense. But other countries upon whose power and interests such a broadening impinges, respond through their own buildups and growing anti-Sovietism in their foreign policies. This is turn heightens Soviet insecurity.

The Soviet leaders see the world as a permanent battleground between nations and classes, political systems, and ideologies, in which they hope gradually and systematically to attain new positions of power, new beachheads. Given what has happened since 1917, there is no logical reason for foreign policy-makers to be dissatisfied with what they have accomplished. The appetite for greater international influence and power is fed by increasing capabilities. Far from being a sated power, the Soviet Union has only recently entered a truly global phase of expansionist ambitions. The elite cannot imagine an end to the worldwide, multidimensional conflict and is not committed to strive for such an end. It thinks that the laws of history are stronger than any agreements reached by opposing states. To put it simply, the Soviet Union is the only major power that is not committed to the status quo and that considers gradual change and sociopolitical and economic evolution in the non-Soviet world as no substitute for violent change, revolutions, civil wars, and regional military conflicts. It is to those forms of change that Moscow is committed, and it is on those forms that the leadership rests its hopes for expansion and influence.

The United States is a status quo power in the Third World in two senses: it prefers an existing condition to revolutionary changes, and it wants countries that by themselves or with Soviet assistance have established leftist revolutionary regimes to revert to a nonrevolutionary status.

The Soviet adjustments in foreign policy are directly related to the realities of a nuclear world. Coexistence of countries with differing and opposing social, economic, and political systems was understood both by Lenin and Stalin as a *peredyshka,* a breathing spell, between the violent battles to be fought between the major powers representing the opposing systems. Even in his last writings, *The Economic Problems of Socialism in the USSR,* published less than a year before his death, Stalin insisted on the inevitability of war between the two world blocs. It is also worth recalling the conversation with Stalin just after the end of World War II reported by Milovan Djilas, in which Stalin said, "We shall recover in fifteen or twenty years, and then we'll have another go at it."

After Stalin's death, the attitude towards a major war between the two systems changed radically. The Soviet Union began to recognize and publicly acknowledge the new realities nuclear weapons had created. Beginning with Khrushchev's declaration that wars were no longer inevitable, and continuing with the statements of his successors about the suicidal consequences of a nuclear clash for both sides, the Soviet Union became committed consciously and deliberately to the prevention of nuclear war. Moreover, the Soviets believe that any major military clash with the United States will tempt the enemy to use nuclear weapons. They also feel that it would be almost impossible to contain a limited nuclear war. Therefore, in Soviet thinking, it is important to avoid a direct military confrontation with the United States at almost any price. They are determined to achieve their global goals without such a clash.

Hence, the thrust of Soviet foreign policy can be best expressed as neither war nor peace. It is a formula that still stresses the security of the homeland and its empire as the uppermost priority of foreign and military policy. The leaders are still committed to the expansion of influence and power, and to a global definition of what they consider legitimate interests. At the same time, they are determined to prevent a nuclear war for any reason whatsoever, and to avoid dangerous confrontations with the United States. The formula of neither war nor peace is fundamental and will remain so in the foreseeable future. In the meantime, Soviet international fears and hopes are directly dependent on the resources available to further the goals of influence and power without provoking a nuclear war.

14

Foreign Policy Resources

The general foreign policy orientation of the Soviet Union does not determine its strategies and day-to-day tactics. These are more influenced by Soviet capabilities, by the resources that it can employ in the international arena, and by opportunities to use them.

These capabilities include economic strength, technological development, military potential and actual expenditures, allocations for foreign assistance, the contributions of allies, and the degree of dependence on international cooperative arrangements and on foreign trade.

This group of factors is the best known and most extensively studied in the West. It encompasses measurable physical facts and more or less testable predictions. It constitutes a major focus of the great debate about the extent of the Soviet danger.

However, there are two aspects of Soviet capabilities that have to be understood first: the role of nuclear weapons, and the imbalance of foreign policy resources.

The nuclear revolution in weaponry and warfare and its military, political, and psychological effects place the Soviet Union in a more favorable middle-range position than the United States to achieve its international goals without a nuclear war.

Nuclear weaponry acts as a great equalizer of the actual, conventional military potential of the Western and Soviet alliances and therefore as a guarantor of the security of the Soviet Union. Far from being an equal, the Warsaw Pact countries are well behind the Western alliance in conventional military-economic potential.

The difference in GNP between the Western and Soviet blocs has more than doubled in the last twenty-five years from less than $2 trillion to well over $4 trillion dollars. Recent studies have shown that this lopsided superiority in technological advancement is at least as pronounced today as it was in 1953. Nuclear weapons provided a degree of security to the Soviet Union that it never enjoyed in the past. Further, they enhance the psychological effectiveness of the threat from Soviet conventional forces and their projection abroad—a military posture that was never entirely credible in the past.

TABLE 13   MILITARY-ECONOMIC POTENTIAL OF SOVIET AND CAPITALIST DEMOCRACIES

	US, OECD, Japan & Canada	USSR & East European Bloc
Population (in millions)	646.3	380.4
GNP in 1982 (in billion $)	6,741.0	2,430.0
Absolute Difference (in billion $)	4,311.0	—
GNP in 1960 (in billion $)	2,980.0	1,090.0
Absolute Difference (in billion $)	1,890.0	—

The nuclear revolution also led to the establishment of an American security umbrella over Western Europe, which in turn led to much lower levels of conventional military spending by the industrial democracies than at any time in the twentieth century. It led, too, to American preoccupation with the nuclear balance, which has encouraged the decline or lack of growth of U.S. conventional forces and military-industrial plant. This happened at a time when the increase in Soviet nuclear and conventional weapons was steady and substantial. The resulting ratio of mobilized conventional forces has provided the Soviet Union with increased freedom of military action below the level of nuclear war, with regional conventional superiorities, and the politically attractive commitment to no-first-use of nuclear weapons.

The Soviet system further secures for its leadership a high degree of independence from public pressure in formulating its policies and in calibrating its use of military threats towards its opponents. The leadership is therefore free to manipulate the legitimate fears of the peoples of the industrial democracies about nuclear weapons.

Regardless of how one looks at the realities of nuclear parity between the two superpowers, and of the danger implicit in nuclear confrontation, their existence favors the Soviets. It is the Soviet Union that would really suffer in the military, political, and psychological sense if nuclear weapons were abolished or decisively reduced in number. This is one of the fundamental reasons why the abolition or destruction of all nuclear weapons, or even their deep numerical reduction, is not a feasible goal.

Soviet views on international relations assume the decisive importance of military power. The slogan "power grows from the barrel of the gun" was not invented by Mao Zedong. The emphasis is reinforced by the resources that the Soviet Union has at its disposal.

The military character of Moscow's foreign policy resources defines both the most dangerous and disquieting aspects of the attempted expansion of Soviet power and the intrinsic weakness of this policy. Military force dictates the method by which the Soviet Union grabs for greater international power and influence. Moreover, it compels the United States to meet the Soviet challenge on its own military terms. It is difficult to counteract Soviet military assistance including Soviet or proxy troops with American economic aid or political influence. At the same time, however, Soviet foreign policy resources prevent the Soviets from becoming a dominant global power.

Ideological resources, at one time among the strongest components of its power, have largely been exhausted. The Soviet Union has ceased to be the symbol of radical social transformation. As a leftist revolutionary power it could not compete initially with the aggressively anticapitalist China and more recently with extremist terrorist movements. As a model and symbol of social progress for the leftist intelligentsia in industrialized societies, it has been irrevocably compromised because of its suppression of human rights, its oppression of nonconformist intellectuals, its subjugation of Eastern Europe, and its anti-Semitism. In the case of the leftist intelligentsia of the Third World, this process is less advanced but is moving in the same direction.

Third World revolutionary regimes are attracted to the Soviet Union not by ideology and even less by practice, but by expediency. A typical example is the peculiar flirtation of Libya with the Soviet Union. The Libyan Muslim revolution cannot be pleasing to the Russians, while the atheistic Soviet system certainly does not attract Libya. Yet the two find common ground in opposing moderate Arab states and the American presence in the Middle East, and in trying to destabilize such countries as Sudan and Chad.

In Stalin's day true believers could and did excuse and accept the cruelty, viciousness, and oppressiveness of the Soviet construction of socialism as long as they believed that it represented the extreme and unique birth pangs of a better world, of a genuinely progressive system. Today they cannot accept the much more limited cruelty and dull oppressiveness of the system because they don't think that a better world is being created in the Soviet Union, or that it bears any relation to the vision of the good society that had inspired the revolutionaries of old. For the radical intellectual especially, the dilemma in the past was often expressed and rationalized as a trade-off between intellectual freedom and the luxury of "formal" democracy for the relatively few, and the value for the many of abolishing hunger and exploitation. Soviet communist intellectuals still cling to the distinction between formal and real democracy. As one of them said to me: "Your American formal freedoms are advantageous to intellectuals, and in this sense I envy you. But our freedoms are those of secured employment, social mobility, and egalitarianism, and they are more important than formal freedoms and intellectual interests." Hunger in the Soviet Union has been abolished, but intellectual freedom has not been restored even to the levels of the 1920s, when it co-existed with deprivation and economic hardships. The rationalization of a necessary exchange of one valued item for another no longer makes sense.

The cultural assets of a country—whether language, educational tradition, mass cultural patterns, or what can generally be described as the attractiveness and impressiveness of a way of life—can be of great importance in furthering its influence. Soviet culture is not appealing. Far from being the carrier of a culture that enhances their efforts to gain influence, the Soviet people are tremendously attracted to American style and Western culture. Soviet cultural behavior exhibits an attitude of superiority in relations with the poor and backward, and a sense of inferiority in their relations with the West.

The sheer size of the economy and especially of the industrial plant, coupled with centralized control over resources, provides the Soviet Union with considerable economic potential in support of its foreign policy. Yet there can be little doubt that this potential is sharply constrained in practice. Soviet involvement in the world economy is not commensurate with its status as a global power.

Political resources are significant and impressive. The government has ended its sectarian and isolationist approach to non-Soviet forces abroad. The greatest foreign policy asset is the attitude towards change and particularly towards revolutionary and nationalistic aspirations in the non-Communist world. The Soviets have almost blindly underwritten any movement or tendency that undermines the status quo. It makes them a natural ally of the nations and movements that aspire to change things. The costs have been relatively small. Yet the Soviet alliance system is ultimately upheld by force of arms rather than by common political goals. Efforts to transform it from the undisguised empire of Stalin's days into a stable commonwealth are counteracted by popular and elite irredentism in Eastern Europe and by social and economic instability.

The situation is quite different with regard to military assets. The Soviets can offer a vast array of weapons covering the needs of any nation at almost any level of technology. In addition to weapons, they can deliver the entire range of military aid, from advisers through the deployment of the troops of its client surrogates to the massive use of its own military forces as in Afghanistan. As a result, Soviet policies are a factor in most every important area of global conflict. The willingness to commit military assets abroad in a growing number of areas strongly suggests a partial redefinition of what constitutes a risk. One of the main tendencies of Soviet behavior is the attempt to translate military assets into political influence. The fact that this policy has in the past brought some conspicuous failures and that its present successes are far from assured should not obscure the fact that the tendency is growing.

The weakness of alternative foreign policy resources and the preponderance of military assets means that the Soviet desire to spread its influence can be realized primarily when the military factor plays an important role. The Soviet Union is therefore interested in fomenting conflicts, escalating them, maintaining them at a high level of intensity, and exploiting them. Its interests are less likely to be served by peaceful resolution.

The imbalance in foreign policy resources contains obvious dangers, and also inherent weaknesses and long-range costs. The stress on the military and its uses does not affect the central power relationship. Here the Soviet Union must resort to détente if it wishes to alleviate its main fear—confrontation with the United States and the danger of war. Extensive reliance on the military factor has already created an American backlash that, through an unavoidable linkage, will make direct and indirect Soviet intervention in the Third World much more risky now than in the 1970s.

What comes from the barrel of a gun today is only short-term power, not long-range influence—unless it is used as it has been in Eastern Europe. When military resources support regimes that are ideologically alien to the Soviet Union, such as Syria, or Iraq, the gains are likely to be fleeting, as they were in Egypt. And in the case of ideologically more friendly regimes, where the Soviet Union hopes to gain a stronger and more permanent foothold through its military resources, it will find revolutionary leaders reacting after the crisis has passed as did the Polish leader Marshal Pilsudski, who when recounting his revolutionary youth, said, "I took the train of socialism and left at the station of independence." Little has remained, for instance, of so-called African socialism, whose leaders shifted to conventional dictatorships or have been overthrown.

After creating an empire on its own borders and failing to transform it into a commonwealth, the Soviet Union is now in the process of attempting to institute a system of client states, most of them far from its borders. Success in this endeavor is very unlikely where the Soviets cannot use direct military power. It is even less likely that they will be able to transform those client states into staunch allies: This would run counter to these states' tradition, the experience and the basic aims. One does not fight for independence simply to switch from one master to another.

The case of Mozambique is instructive. This self-proclaimed Marxist-Leninist regime torn by a civil war was unable to secure sufficient military and economic aid from Moscow. It was forced to reach agreements with South Africa. The situation in other African states, where the Soviets are not yet engaged at high levels of military commitment, may create other Mozambiques.

Considering the sorry state of the economy, a question emerges: How can the Soviets keep up with the West in preserving an up-to-date military establishment? (Some people in Washington consider the Soviet military superior to that of the West.) The answer to this question is not easy to give. There are other related questions as well: How valid are the estimates of those who assert that the Soviets are superior in armaments? And why do American analysts consistently overestimate Soviet military strength?

The calculation of the extent of Soviet mobilization directly after the Second World War and the danger that it posed to Western Europe was the initial step in the process of assessment. From the perspective of forty years it seems ridiculous to think that in the face of American forces the Soviets were capable of annexing Western Europe. At the beginning of John F. Kennedy's presidency we discovered the first "missile gap," which was later found not to exist. Today we hear about the "window of vulnerability" that provides the Soviets with a first-strike capability against the American deterrent. This vulnerability, we are instructed, has to be closed by such stopgap measures as the MX missiles (for which nobody has yet found a rational mode of deployment) and later by Midget missiles. That a numerical disproportion between Soviet and American land-based strategic missiles exists is unquestionable. Whether this difference, which should be counteracted, provides a clear and immediate danger necessitating American crash programs is questionable to say the least.

The new reduced estimates concerning the accuracy of the SS-19 missiles can only increase one's doubts about alleged Soviet strategic superiority. And we have learned only recently that CIA appraisals of Soviet military spending since 1976 were faulty and that it was probably only half of the presented percentage of GNP. It is to the credit of our democratic system that the revisions were made by the CIA itself and have been published. Yet how can one forget that the initial estimates provided an important factor in spurring requests for defense appropriations over a number of years. They created a seemingly solid factual basis for a public mood receptive to the need to rearm America.

On the other hand, there is sufficient evidence of Soviet military, particularly strategic, growth in the 1970s which had no counterpart in post-Vietnam, post-Watergate United States. Americans were skeptical about the claims of their own government. The military buildup process which started under Jimmy Carter and accelerated under Ronald Reagan was necessary and positive in proclaiming the country's determination and political ability to deny the Soviets any chance of gaining a military edge. Without accepting all the military programs that were initiated and without supporting the overall sum of military expenditures, I think the Carter and Reagan programs were right in principle and necessary to convince the Russians that America was not helpless, as the Soviets may have believed at times in the 1970s.

It is sometimes asked what difference it really makes whether either superpower has a preponderance in atomic weapons and accurate means of their delivery when a small percentage of their arsenals can destroy the world many times over. The answer most often given is that it may make a difference in two respects: First, one superpower acquires the capacity to "take out" most of the accurate missiles of the other side and is ready to consider losses small in proportion to the weapons deployed to be acceptable; second, if the nominal preponderance of one power's nuclear weapons (nominal in the sense that neither side really contemplates their use) generates a psychological climate that intimidates the other superpower, and especially the smaller powers and the nonaligned nations, thus reducing their resistance to the increasingly bolder demands of the "strong" superpower.

But there is no sign that either scenario is valid. Unless one thinks of Soviet or American leaders as maniacs, losses which the superpower under attack can inflict on the attacker are prohibitive to the nth degree. As far as the psychological factor is concerned, the roots of the successful Soviet offensive stance of the 1970s are to be found more in the U.S. government's paralysis than in the Soviet buildup of nuclear weapons. Once the level of mutual assured destruction (MAD) has been reached a further offensive buildup makes no military sense. To the extent that there has been a perception of a nuclear balance in our disfavor, it was the United States with its unending declarations of an alleged Soviet superiority that created a climate of denigrating itself and making the Russians seem so powerful. The Soviet Union has never claimed strategic superiority over the United States.

One hears and reads, however, that the Soviet military juggernaut has achieved a technological edge in addition to its quantitative lead over the United States in a broad spectrum of weapons and weapons systems. These assessments, which originate primarily from the defense secretary's office, have been regarded by many analysts with skepticism. Detailed analyses from other Defense Department branches have stated that out of the twenty categories of military technology which were assessed, the United States clearly led in nineteen and was more or less similar in one. This report has not been rebutted or challenged.

Why does the American government consistently and continuously overestimate the military strength of its adversary? There are a number of reasons. First, power is evaluated on the basis of worst-case scenarios. (This attitude surely also prevails within the Soviet military.) On the basis of what we know about the Second World War, such a bias is probably preferable to the reverse. Perhaps the military has to operate on such premises. There is no valid reason, however, for the intelligence community to adopt this approach, or for the political establishment to act in such a way in its appropriation and executive roles.

The intelligence community and the analysts are partially victims of paranoid Soviet secretiveness. Without access to some fundamental data about the Soviet military and its equipment, they often have to translate fragmentary information into American items. The example that comes immediately into mind is the ratio between throwweight and yield. Physicists and seismologists at Columbia University have pointed out that the American ratio of throwweight to yield is routinely used to define the yield of Soviet strategic weapons. These scientists are engaged in research, however, which tends toward the conclusion that the Soviet coefficient of yield per weight is much lower than our own. This assumed similarity between the systems must have played a major role in our national estimates of Soviet strength.

A much more mundane reason accounts for the consistent overvaluation of Soviet mobilized military strength. The only way in which the American military can get increased appropriations is by convincing the people and the Congress of Soviet advances in the modernization of their forces and of the subsequent danger to the United States. But in the 1970s the American military was scandalously underpaid, underequipped and generally put on a starvation diet. The increased attention it received in Carter's last year and Reagan's first term was necessary to keep the nation strong, although the amount of budgetary growth was probably excessive.

But it seems perfectly natural for the consumer of military goods to exaggerate the effectiveness and scope of the other side's actual performance. Khrushchev's memoirs make exactly the same point about Soviet military leaders: "Who in our own country is in a position to intimidate the leadership? It is the military. . . . The military is prone to engage in irresponsible day-dreaming and bragging. Given a chance, some elements within the military might try to force a militarist policy on the Government. Therefore the Government must always keep a bit between the teeth of the military."* There is no way to rid ourselves of this element in the evaluation of Soviet forces.

Yet still another element of exaggeration has to do with the asymmetry not only of America's respective strategic tasks and doctrines, but also of the actual mix of its forces. For various reasons having to do with historical departure points, past decisions, technological capabilities, the evaluation of costs and the role of cost factors in development, and even political preferences, the Soviet Union has an advantage over the United States in some military areas and lags behind in others. Thus the Soviets have more and larger land-based intercontinental missiles, while the Americans have a preponderance of nuclear submarines and submarine-launched missiles, especially of the advanced Trident class. Thus American political and military leaders, if they are so inclined, can always point to instances of Soviet preponderance, just as Soviet military leaders have been able to frighten their political leadership by pointing to American strengths in the strategic balance.

Two facts, however, remain indisputable: First, in the 1970s when American military expenditures were flat, Soviet expenditures grew by approximately 4 percent a year until 1976, after which the growth slowed to about 2 percent and procurement expenditures remained almost stationary. Second, the Soviet Union is an awesome, modern military power, and the relatively backward nature of its overall economy must in some manner have found an exception in its military sector. It is certainly plain that until recently the Soviet military sector could be modern precisely because the civilian economy remained backward.

Simply put, the entire economy works for the military forces. The figure of 12 to 15 percent of GNP devoted to the military conceals more than it reveals. Disputes about the relative weight of the military-industrial complex in overall Soviet fixed capital, or about the scale of the growth of military expenditures are highly controversial and need not be discussed here. While presenting different evaluations of Soviet military strength, most of these controversies are largely irrelevant to an explanation of the indisputable fact of Soviet military strength.

Four characteristics are important to understand the strength of the Soviet military-industrial complex as compared to the civilian economy:

* *Khrushchev Remembers: The Last Testament.* Translated and edited by Strobe Talbott. With a foreword by Edward Crankshaw. (Boston: Little, Brown and Co., 1974), pp. 540–541.

- the acceptance of military strength as an overriding concern by the political leaders;
- the military-industrial sector's priority in acquiring supplies;
- the military's superior and constant claim on the best available manpower and brainpower;
- the cardinal differences in the design and procurement process in the military economy as compared to the civilian sector.

In the first postrevolutionary decades the Bolshevik Party was a small urban organization in a sea of alien elements—the old bourgeoisie, the old intelligentsia, but, most importantly, the peasants, whose alienation from the Bolsheviks was probably even greater in the late 1920s (*before* collectivization started) than at the time of the original Bolshevik Revolution. By 1921, as the civil war against the Whites was coming to a close, Russia was at the beginning of a mass peasant rebellion against the Bolsheviks. "War Communism" had been based on the confiscation of all produce above a peasant's own minimal needs. The peasants, without waiting for Bolshevik direction, and more often than not without their help, had divided the landowners' land among themselves and became en masse what the Bolsheviks called middle peasants, or *petit bourgeoisie*. They had no sympathy for the Party's program. Officially, the land did not belong to the peasants; it had been nationalized by the Bolsheviks, who established a high rural tax. There was, in the Party's view, however, no other way to gain firm control over the peasantry than to conduct what Stalin later described to Winston Churchill as the second civil war—the forced collectivization. Military power was the key instrument through which the Bolsheviks remained in power and promoted social change. What was true concerning the peasantry was as true concerning the southern belt of non-Russian nations, where military actions continued well into the 1930s. Without the sustained use of military power, the Bolsheviks could not have seized and held power in Russia.

Military power was also important because of the international isolation of the Soviet Union. Marx and the Bolsheviks had expected the socialist revolution to spread throughout the industrialized world. But the dreaded capitalist encirclement became a major fact of life. There was never any doubt in their minds that sooner or later a coalition of capitalist countries would attack with the intention of destroying their system. The experience of the Civil War of 1918–21 reinforced this belief. The reality of this so-called capitalist intervention was far from the "crusade of fourteen nations" presented in Soviet history books. Yet Germany occupied the Ukraine; Britain and France did supply materiel to the White generals Denikin and Wrangel; Pilsudski's Poland did attack the Bolsheviks in 1920; Japan did occupy Soviet territory in the Far

East until 1922, Czech prisoners of war did fight the Bolsheviks, and even the United States landed a battalion of soldiers in the northern port of Arkhangelsk. From the time of the war scare of 1928, created by Stalin as part of his struggle against his rightist opponents within the Party, and throughout the whole pre-World War II period, an attack was a constant preoccupation of the leaders and dictated their policy of forced industrialization and collectivization, as well as the mass mobilization of the population. The fact that the prophecy was eventually fulfilled, and perhaps all the more so since the invasion came from the only great power with which the Soviets had a nonaggression pact (in reality, more of a friendship treaty), has formed the postwar and contemporary Soviet image of what can be expected from "world capitalism," even when the realities of the nuclear age have made such fears nothing short of paranoia.

Military power has been central to the creation and continuation of the Eastern European empire. These nations were compelled to join the empire primarily by the force of Soviet arms or the credible threat of its use. The realism of Soviet leaders in questions of power politics has certainly convinced them that the perpetuation of the empire has the same basis. The Soviet troops stationed in most of these countries are not there to defend them from NATO but to ensure that they will remain in the Soviet imperial orbit.

Another factor is once again an amalgam of Marxist and Leninist dogmas, the "realism" of practical politicians, and an assessment of the way in which great powers behave. The Marxist-Leninist inheritance embedded in the Soviet consciousness is a belief in the role of violence, force, the military factor as the "midwife of history." From Marx's insistence on violent revolutions as the "locomotives of history," through Lenin's teachings of imperialist war as the inevitable course of capitalism, to Stalin's ideas of the transformation of domestic class struggle into an international clash of socialist and capitalist forces, Soviet leaders came to recognize military power as the central factor of contemporary history, which would decide the outcome of the communist-capitalist competition.

During the Khrushchev era there was a period of high hopes about the revolutionary process in Third World countries. The Brezhnev regime determined that the real chance for Soviet gains lay in the strength of their arms and the ability to project them far from their borders. (This evaluation, in addition to strategic parity with the United States and the Soviet interpretation of détente, may help answer Professor Myron Rush's question as to why the Soviets under Brezhnev sacrificed part of their investment program for an accelerated military buildup. It supports Rush's proposition that "The arms buildup appears to have resulted from a reevaluation by the Brezhnev leadership of the place of military means in the attainment of Soviet objectives.")*

During the Brezhnev era the continuous and large-scale Soviet armament effort was not the result of pressure from the professional military on the political leadership, but rather of a convergence of goals on the part of political and military leaders. The military and political points of view could differ on many specific questions concerning particular weapons systems and the exact amount of military appropriations necessary. Yet, there was an unshakable consensus that military might is an absolute priority both with regard to the survival of the regime and its empire and with regard to furthering Soviet ambition, power, and influence abroad.

The need for military power led, not surprisingly, to the promotion of the military sector of the economy over other branches, and an extreme sensitivity to its needs. It remains the top-priority recipient of materials in short supply. Moreover, its standards for performance are much higher than those in civilian activity. There is a Soviet saying that, in an imperfect translation, conveys the difference between these standards: "For light industry [not fulfilling the plan] they hit you lightly, for heavy industry they hit you heavily, for military industry they take off your head."

The Soviet economy has always operated with shortages of natural resources and manufactured goods, which are therefore the objects of competition among the various economic branches. The needs of military production determine the pool of resources available to the civilian sector. The Ministry of Medium Machine Building, which manufactures nuclear weapons, has always fulfilled its plan and has a claim on the primary and manufactured products necessary for the implementation of its goals. The attention given to the military goes far beyond the priority of supplies to the *nomernye zavody,* "numbered factories." (Unlike factories producing predominantly for civilians, which bear a trademark name, almost all military plants are recognized only by their number.) As important is the fact that enterprises allocated small or large supply tasks for the military sector are directed to consider these tasks their first priority. In America, this condition would be equivalent to imposing enormous financial penalties on military subcontractors.

The military sector also has a priority claim on manpower. It employs the best-qualified workers, and its pay scales, housing, and fringe benefits are better than in civilian industry. The fact that they work for the military makes infractions of discipline and absenteeism less frequent because the punishments for such behavior are much harsher. There are

* Myron Rush, "Guns over Growth in Soviet Policy," *International Security,* Winter 1982/83, Vol. 7, No. 3, p. 177.

indications also that the turnover of personnel, an important problem in civilian industry, is much lower in the military sector. Apparently, the personnel employed in military factories sign long-term work contracts and have no right to change jobs without the permission of the directors, and probably of the KGB or military counterintelligence units that exist in every "numbered factory."

Military industry has a claim on the best engineers and scientists, whose rewards are also substantially greater than in the civilian sector. Aside from the personnel who work in the factories themselves, many engineering schools and institutes work entirely for the military as do major research institutes in fields of theoretical or applied science. As we now know from various sources, including Solzhenitsyn's novel *The First Circle,* many engineers and scientists arrested during Stalin's purges were not sent to ordinary concentration camps but were employed in so-called *sharashki*—prison research institutes. The greatest incentive for their devotion to their task was the prospect of having their sentences commuted. Many major inventions and improvements in Soviet weaponry took place in the *sharashki.* Some of the best-known engineers and scientists made their basic professional contributions while in these special prisons. They include the Tupolevs, the designers of bombers and civilian jets, and Ilyushin, who designed the first Soviet dive bomber and produced the standard long-range jet for the Soviet airline Aeroflot.

As William Odom, a well-known Sovietologist and intelligence specialist, once remarked:

> Almost unnoticed by Western observers, an enormous military-educational complex is emerging in the Soviet Union today. It holds a commanding position in graduate education as well as in undergraduate training; it permeates the civil secondary-school system and ties up more than one-fourth of the population in voluntary work in support of military skill training; and it touches every Soviet citizen by entangling him in a nationwide civil defense structure.*

In the mid-1970s there were 161 military institutions of higher education—at the college, graduate, and postgraduate levels, constituting about one-seventh of the total higher education establishment. They account for more than 30 percent of the educational establishment at the graduate and postgraduate level. These institutions have a higher faculty-student ratio than civilian schools. They employ top faculty and have very demanding entrance and graduation requirements. They place great emphasis on the study of technology and coexist with special research institutes working entirely for the military.

* William Odom, "The Militarization of Soviet Society," *Problems of Communism,* Vol. XXV, No. 5 (September–October 1976), p. 34.

In all probability the most important differences between the military and civilian sectors have to do with quality control and methods of procurement. While in the civilian sector the producer is dominant, in the military, the "consumer" retains sovereignty. In contrast to the civilian sector, where quality control belongs to the supervisory ministry or organization, in the military, quality control is fully in the hands of the professionals. During all phases of production there are officers, sometimes even generals, in residence, who are on the Defense Ministry payroll and who are responsible to their own ministry for the quality of production. They are rotated regularly so that they do not become too familiar with the management of any single enterprise. The level of rejection of the intermediate and final products, the so-called *brak,* is much higher than in civilian industry. Final acceptance of end products remains a prerogative of a special committee formed by the Defense Ministry.

The military procurement process, and especially the selection of product design and methods of production, has no counterpart in the civilian sector. Its most important characteristic is competition. Each new military product of importance is simultaneously designed with regard to its end use, maintenance specifications, production method, and costs by several design bureaus that are parallel but independent of each other. Their projections and prototypes are examined and tested by special commissions, who submit recommendations to the Council of Ministers, the Military Council or the Politburo. Given the existence of this system and the fact that over 80 percent of American weapons procurements have a single source or bidder, it may be suggested, not entirely in jest, that the model for Soviet military industry is the American civilian economy while for the American military industry the model is the Soviet civilian economy.

The mutual isolation and differing standards of the military and civilian sectors has been and basically remains the prevailing picture of the Soviet economy in the writings of Western analysts. The consequences of this separation were not entirely understood when applied to the Soviet past. Moreover, it is increasingly evident that the military-civilian borderlines are becoming less sharply etched, and that the interaction of these fields, running in both directions, is tending to increase.

The significant lowering of the CIA evaluation of Soviet military expenditures and the lack of growth of military procurement since 1976 may reflect new dimensions and trends in the relationship between the two sectors. The experience of the last decade suggests some tentative new conclusions: The importance of the military priority in Soviet economic planning may have declined and may continue to do so; the efficiency and effectiveness of the military sector as compared to the civilian may have been exaggerated; the general malaise that engulfs the economy may reach beyond civilian production and rub off on military industry.

In Stalin's time, it was widely believed that if human and material costs did not matter, then the military sector was equal to almost any task. That was obviously untrue of Soviet preparations for the Second World War. But it was true in another sense: Neither the Soviet ability to mobilize resources for the military, nor the technological level of its military production can be properly assessed based on the general level and state of the economy. Nor are Western standards of resource mobilization proper comparisons. The Soviets were mobilized for military goals in a period of peace (1939–41) to a higher degree than the Nazi economy was throughout the war, with the exception of the year 1944, when Albert Speer became virtual dictator of the German economy. Of course the level of military mobilization after June 1941 has no parallel in modern history. One figure mentioned by Nikolai Voznesensky, the chief Soviet planner during the war, tells the story: In 1941–45 consumption accounted for only 40 percent of national income.

The argument that the military sector has to be measured by different criteria than its civilian counterpart, and that the Soviets possess an unquestionably superior ability to mobilize for security purposes, is still used today by them. By doing so, they are trying to counteract the image that they are unable to respond adequately to Ronald Reagan's plans to rearm America.

Yet even in Stalin's time, the idea that almost anything in the military sphere was possible and that "costs are costless" was untrue. Ironically, in today's different and much more powerful Soviet Union, the idea of costless costs is even more erroneous than in Stalin's day. The level of military expenditures has an immense impact in terms of opportunity costs—that is to say, in draining civilian resources for military purposes, on economic growth and even on future military capabilities. The military priority has not only physical but also technological limits when the state of the entire economy is taken into consideration. Moreover, the question of costs clearly influences the scale of overall military production and preparedness. The interconnections between the military and civilian sectors have grown and will continue to do so. Raising the priority of military projects at the expense of the civilian economy will have a negative influence on military preparedness itself.

Given the present slowdown of Soviet economic growth, military spending increases will harm the Soviet economy in a number of ways. The most obvious effect has already taken place: a decline in investments in order to continue the rate of military growth and to prevent a short-term decline in the standard of living. As Henry W. Schaefer of the U.S. Arms Control and Disarmament Agency convincingly argues:

"What is required for Soviet military growth rates to be maintained because of favorable production possibilities as overall growth slows, however, is that PPPFs [Power Production-Possibilities Frontiers] increasingly favor military production at higher income levels."* As I understand this proposition, it means that the productive effort of the military sector, which is more efficient and rewarding, will influence the existing overall level of Soviet productivity only if increasing increments of input go to the military. But such increased inputs will have different short- and long-range consequences for the economy as a whole and even for the military sector. To quote Schaefer again:

For many years the Soviets have devoted considerably more of their resources to military production than most countries. This has been reflected in the structure of the economy, particularly the lack of consumer goods and housing. An *a priori* case can be made that a command economy will in the short run be best prepared to produce more of what it has accorded top priority; given the level and particularly the quality of military production capacity, there may well be increasing returns if military production is raised in the near term.

However, these same circumstances suggest that the opposite may be true in the long run. Because so much stress has been placed on military production, many sectors of the economy have been neglected and are very inefficient by world standards (e.g., materials handling). A good case can be made that the transfer to the civilian sector of certain resources now utilized in military R & D and military investment would yield good returns.†

What all this means is that the Soviets' ability to run two parallel economies and to isolate military production from general economic trends has declined in the last ten years, and will continue to decline if the economic system is not transformed. That is, the civilian sector will drag the military sector down with it.

With the economy's present level of development and the military-technological challenges that the Soviets face, the flow of influence between the military and civilian sectors has increased sharply. This flow has consequences not only for the society as a whole but also directly and indirectly for the military sector and military potential. The mutual interconnections and influences include:

• The range of priorities that are essential to economic expansion through intensive growth, which remains the only possible method, are much broader than they were in the past. Solid and stable increments of production that can be attained only by increased productivity require the introduction of new technology in the civilian economy almost as much as in the military sector.

* Henry W. Schaefer, "Soviet Power and Intentions: Military-Economic Choices," in *Soviet Economy in a Time of Change*, pp. 343–344.
† Ibid., p. 345.

• With the abolition of terror, with the shortage of labor and cheap natural resources, with the growth of consumption, the social and ultimately the political stability of the system, an important factor of military strength, require continuous growth in the standard of living. Such growth is unattainable without productivity increases based on new technology.

• The performance of the military sector is more and more inhibited by the underdevelopment of the industrial infrastructure and the bottlenecks that this creates. The development of railway and highway networks, and their effective exploitation, is almost as important to the progress of the military as it is to the civilian sector. The same is true of bottlenecks in the extraction of raw materials and energy. Increased productivity in the economy as a whole is improbable without higher wages, incentives, and an uninterrupted flow of food and consumer goods. This is true in both the civilian and military economies. Greater military spending, however, creates an obstacle to increased productivity incentives in the economy as a whole.

• The military depends extensively on the production of items that have both military and civilian uses. Difficulties in the civilian sector that provides such dual-use goods will affect the military.

• The necessity of limiting expenditures on education will have an impact on the quality of draftees into the armed forces. Civilian economic problems will also influence the morale of Soviet soldiers.

• The military sector will be forced to assume greater responsibility for the production of civilian goods. This will first occur through the production of such goods in military factories. We can also expect from Gorbachev a flow of managers from military industries into the civilian sector, and greater cooperation and exchanges of experience between military and civilian management.

• *Stroyevye otriady,* "military construction troops," will be increasingly employed at civilian construction sites, which will limit their training and employment for military purposes.

• Military research and development activities, which together with procurement account for about 60 percent of military expenditures, will more and more depend on the scope and results of civilian research and development. American, West European, Japanese, and Chinese military experts are convinced that contemporary military research and development will inevitably be curtailed by a narrow and shallow base of civilian R. & D. There is no evidence to suggest that the Soviet Union will be an exception to this rule.

Such interconnections between the military and civilian sectors of the economy still provide the best explanation for the limitations imposed on military growth and the curtailment of investments in the last decade.

"If Soviet priorities have become more complex," argues David Holloway, "so, it seems, has the relationship between the defense sector and the rest of the economy. . . . [This] argues against the idea that the Soviet leaders can insulate the defense sector from the economy at large and undermines the thesis that the Soviet Union has a dual economy." Of course, Holloway's proposition concerns the recent decade and not the more distant past. His statement also appears a bit too categorical. A degree of duality in the Soviet economy is and will be preserved; it is clearly on the decline.

What is the outlook in the 1980s for the growth of Soviet military resources and of the economic base that supports them?

It is doubtful that the economic slowdown can be reversed in the 1980s, although it may be arrested at a level low in comparison with that of the 1970s, perhaps at about 2 percent real GNP growth a year. The level of economic development and growth in the last decade did provide a sufficient base for the maintenance of a strong military posture, highly competitive with the levels of Western military expenditures. It has to be remembered, however, that American military spending in the 1970s did not grow at all.

If the growth of U.S. military spending continues at the rate projected by Ronald Reagan, or even at a somewhat lower level, the Soviet Union will find it much more difficult and more costly to keep up. This will be especially true if the other NATO countries and Japan also increase their military spending, as they have agreed to do. It will be hard to maintain the level of increase of Soviet military spending, even at the rate of 1976–80. This level could be barely competitive with American military spending of the early 1980s. Low economic growth and inferior quality of industrial output, investment of very large sums in the infrastructure, in energy, and in new or renovated machine stock, and raising incentives for the working force if labor productivity is to grow, are all obstacles to Soviet military ambitions. (However, the Soviet leadership will not attempt to match every item in American expenditures, but rather will concentrate on weapons systems which may effect the most urgent or desirable change.)

Soviet ability to devote whatever is considered necessary to national defense and to change the military balance in its favor will decline (but not disappear) in the 1980s. Past neglect is finally catching up with the leaders and planners. The question is not one of guns versus butter, but of guns versus investments. By cutting investments to keep military spending high, the Soviets are mortgaging their future and making economic reforms more difficult. Throughout the 1980s and 1990s, Soviet attempts to devote a high percentage of its GNP to the military will put pressure on economic performance and therefore on domestic stability.

From the incomplete data at our disposal, it appears that in the last year of Brezhnev's rule and during the Andropov/Chernenko interregnum, military expenditures did not increase faster than in the post-1976 period. New generations of weapons and weapons systems may be entering long-run production, however, and thus could signal a new jump in military expenditures that the leadership will have to accept. (Judging from the particular weapons procurement mix of the last several years the emphasis of new expenditures may be on theater nuclear weapons and on conventional forces, particularly helicopter transports and gunships and antitank devices.) Such a trend can only be reinforced by the recent rise in American military spending.

It is generally agreed in the West that in the 1970s Soviet military expenditures accounted for about 12 to 14 percent of GNP. There is no evidence that this figure has grown in the early 1980s. Since then, defense increases have not outstripped the general growth of the Soviet GNP. The extent of the defense burden as measured in percentage of GNP—although often twice as large as in the industrial democracies—still does not convey its real pressure on the economy, particularly civilian investments and consumption. In addition, military research and development does not find its way into the civilian sector as happens in the United States.

Given the trade-off between defense expenditures and civilian investments, civilian consumption and overall GNP growth, the leadership faces a limited number of options. Unless a major change occurs in the tense international situation or a decisive breakthrough is achieved in the arms control negotiations, the following scenario, which assumes a medium growth rate of about 2 percent for the Soviet economy as a whole is likely:

• The growth of the defense sector will constitute the point of departure of Soviet planning and will be decided primarily on the basis of security needs, but with greater consideration than before given to economic factors.

• It is highly unlikely, however, that the rise in military expenditures will approach the 3 to 4 percent in real terms typical of the early 1970s. It is more likely that they will stay at the 2 percent level of the late 1970s.

• During the 1980s, any larger growth of military expenditures will raise the size of military outlays as a percentage of GNP.

• In the short run, any increase in military expenditures beyond the growth of the GNP as a whole will require cutbacks in civilian investments and a leveling of civilian consumption.

• In the intermediate term, the slackening of civilian investments will be more pronounced and consumption will probably stagnate in absolute terms and decline per capita.

• The leadership will probably seek to counteract the unfavorable trend in economic development, and the rising socioeconomic costs of military spending, by the traditional method of social mobilization and political appeals to patriotism combined with tighter domestic controls. Yet economic problems are very different from those in the past, and the economy will probably respond in a sluggish way to the leadership's prodding.

• A radical economic reform could reverse the present trend. There are, however, no signs that such a change is contemplated. Moreover, in the shorter run, even a major reform would not resolve the dilemma posed by the trade-off between defense spending, consumption, and investment. A precondition of such a reform is substantial investment in productivity, which cannot be made without lowering the most unproductive expenditure, that of the military.

• Spending in support of foreign policy will probably also be curtailed, with the possible exception of direct military aid and, of course, cash sale of weapons. It is already clear that the Soviet Union has decided to cut its subsidies to Eastern Europe, Cuba, and Vietnam. In a time of declining growth and, simultaneously, rising claims on the increase of investment funds, the approximately 5 percent of GNP spent by the Soviets on their empire and in support of their foreign policy will represent a much greater burden than in the 1970s.

• The leadership may develop an interest in arms limitation and control that is dictated or reinforced by economic determinants.

• If the West can coordinate its trade, credit, and technology-export policies with respect to the Soviet Union, the chances of its effectiveness in influencing Russia's policies, while still limited, will be higher than in the 1970s.

In a difficult economic situation, where quick fixes would be hard to find, the new leadership might conceivably be tempted to resort to the classic method of regimes in domestic trouble, and engage in foreign adventurism to distract the attention of its weary population. But this is not at all likely. The factors that weigh against it are strong.

If the Soviet leaders decide to pursue foreign adventure (and only a major attempt would likely be effective), they have to be prepared for a confrontation with either the United States, China, or both. Yet traditionally, both before it gained strategic parity with the West and after, the Soviet Union has taken a low-risk approach in its foreign policy even when it expanded abroad. It is remotely possible that the new leaders will have a different set of attitudes. But the roots of a low-risk posture remain in force: the knowledge of Soviet weaknesses and of the relative superiority of the West; the fear that in order to gain some advantages abroad, all might be lost; the apprehension that the leadership could lose control over events, a terrible prospect with their deep-seated fear of spontaneity.

Moreover, the leadership will also have its hands full in the Eastern European empire. Patriotism can be mobilized in defense of the Soviet Union. Soviet citizens are not, however, attracted to offensive adventures in faraway places—as witness the government's difficulties in trying to explain the Afghanistan invasion. The low-key treatment of Afghanistan in the home media tells us much about popular attitudes. Further, a major adventure would endanger Soviet–Western European relations that are essential for economic growth. (On the other hand, nothing short of an expansionist move or invasion of an Eastern European country could change Western Europe's determination to preserve détente, particularly economic détente.)

The leadership can attain a high degree of nationalistic political mobilization at home without resorting to foreign adventures. The propaganda machine can whip up chauvinistic emotions to a high pitch and effectively promote a siege mentality in the country. So the Kremlin is not likely to make a foreign thrust unless compelled to do so by overwhelming strategic and foreign policy reasons and not simply for domestic purposes.

15

The Politics of Foreign Policy

Our knowledge of how domestic political forces shape Soviet foreign policy is limited. There is little available data. The analyst relies heavily on historical evidence, on contacts and exchanges with Soviet experts and officials, and finally on his experience in studying the system. He must build his case based on indirect and circumstantial evidence that would be considered insignificant when writing about policy-making in democratic societies.

Foreign policy as a factor in Soviet policy-making increased significantly in the 1970s and early 1980s. There is greater emphasis on international issues in the deliberations of the Politburo and symbolic bodies like the Supreme Soviet. Important domestic issues are more closely connected with foreign policy concerns. The recognition of the consequence of foreign policy in ideological and theoretical literature is expanding.

Soviet foreign policy and its successes abroad legitimize the leadership and the regime. Détente in the early 1970s provided such legitimacy by giving visible proof that the Soviet Union had arrived, that it was recognized as a superpower alongside the United States. The other extreme— abuse, toughness, and increased military competition with the United States—also provides a sort of legitimacy by permitting the leadership to exploit patriotism, and by promoting a siege mentality to reinforce the unity of the leaders with the Party and of the Party with the public.

The making of foreign policy has become more institutionalized and regularized than at any previous time. Both the Party and the government have expanded and upgraded the foreign policy apparatus. So the process is no longer dependent primarily on one individual, as it was under Stalin, or on highly improvised procedures, as was the case during the Khrushchev era.

Almost to the end of Khrushchev's rule, foreign policy-making depended on the civilian and military intelligence services and on the officials of the foreign ministry. Yet Khrushchev did expand the foreign policy establishment. He created or enlarged departments in the Central Committee Secretariat that dealt with foreign communist movements and Eastern European affairs. He formed an advisory body similar to the American National Security Council, although much less formal or powerful and less security-oriented.

Now the information about foreign countries and international issues that reaches the leaders and their associates is much greater, and its quality has considerably improved since Khrushchev's time. There is now a large group of specialized experts outside the Foreign Ministry in the numerous research institutes under the auspices of the Academy of Sciences. These institutes often function as auxiliary institutions of the Central Committee Secretariat. Aside from the American Institute, led by Georgi Arbatov, they include IMEMO (the Institute of World Economy and International Relations), headed for many years by Nikolai Inozemtsev, an alternate member of the Central Committee, and after his death in 1982 by Central Committee member A. N. Yakovlev (whom Gorbachev in 1985 appointed to run the Party's Propaganda Department); the Oriental Institute, led by Yevgenii Primakov, and the African Institute, directed by Andrei Gromyko's son Anatolii.

The role of these institutes in foreign policy-making is a subject of contention in the American academic and political community. They are not simply propaganda outlets to the West. They perform an important staff function for the leadership. They contribute to the Central Committee's evaluations of international events and trends. At the same time they provide an unofficial channel of communication to foreign political and scholarly communities.

The institutes have large research staffs with access to foreign publications. Their personnel often visit the countries of their specialization and maintain wide contacts with Western political and academic figures. Of course the quality of their analysis is uneven, but generally speaking their knowledge of foreign countries is impressive and detailed. With notable exceptions, the same cannot be said of their *understanding* of foreign nations. And the quality of their writings is even lower because of the requirements of ideological conformity and censorship. The real difficulty comes, however, in how accurately they report what they learn to the leadership, and to what extent their differences of opinion reflect differences in the leadership.

The accuracy of their reports, of course, depends on the individual who researches them and on the leaders to whom he is responsible. We are probably unable to deduce the range and substance of the leadership's views on the basis of what scholars write. Unfortunately, but unavoidably too, much of Western literature on Soviet foreign and security policy-making is based on the writing of the *institutchiki* (members of the institutes) and thus may be misleading.

Despite the key roles of Brezhnev, Andropov, and Gromyko in formulation of recent Soviet foreign policy, the process has begun to place more emphasis on consensus than in the past. Efforts are made to achieve unanimity at the Politburo level and to take into consideration the interests of various groups. From the summer of 1983 until early 1985 it was Gromyko who played the decisive role in formulating foreign policy and who held a virtual veto over Politburo decisions. This situation was far from normal and did not last. Gromyko could monopolize Soviet foreign policy decisions not only because of the makeup of the Politburo, but also because there was an apparent consensus of its members in favor of an unyielding posture toward the United States. Moreover, by all indications, this line was supported in its extreme forms by the most authoritative Politburo member of the Chernenko period, Defense Minister Dimitrii Ustinov, and the Soviet military high command.

The diminished compartmentalization of foreign and domestic policy issues and the resulting tendency toward the greater participation and access of diverse political entities seems to have resulted in a situation in which no one institutional group has achieved preponderant influence. While the leadership still possesses greater freedom of action in foreign policy than, say, the U.S. executive, its autonomy is more limited than in the past by the wishes of various interest groups. While the Soviets lacked a strong leader, the need for compromise solutions at home made flexibility abroad somewhat restricted and compromises in dealing with foreign powers somewhat limited. It is probable that this will no longer be the case under Gorbachev.

There is some evidence even in published materials to suggest the existence within the leadership and among important groups of important differences of opinion, if not about the general course of foreign policy, then about particular steps. Some divergences can be traced to the particular interests of bureaucratic organizations and some to predispositions or orientations that cut across organizational lines. There is opposition among mid-level party officials to economic reforms in times of international danger and their supposed predilection for a hard foreign policy line. And there are differences over the distribution of investment funds between the military-industrial complex and agriculture.

The streamlining of the process has not led to the establishment of a foreign policy line that is clear-cut and consistent. As a matter of fact the policies in Brezhnev's last years and after his death were characterized by many inconsistencies, ambiguities, and drift. A recent example was the Soviet invitation to President Reagan in August of 1984 to start negotiations in Vienna on the question of the militarization of outer space, and the withdrawal of this invitation only a short time later. The invitation itself dealt a blow to the campaign of Walter Mondale, who had insisted that the Russians would not negotiate with the Reagan Administration. So the leadership undercut its goal of helping President Reagan's opponent. The decision by Gromyko during his trip to the United Nations in October 1984 to see Reagan showed that the ambiguity in the Soviet position had been resolved. The Politburo had come to the conclusion that Reagan would win the election and decided that from a political and public relations point of view it was better to meet him in advance.

Domestic factors propel Soviet foreign policy in diverse directions. The economic situation, the concern for internal stability, together with the leadership's preoccupation with security, and its recognition and fear of the dangers inherent in great power confrontations, all strongly militate against an unrestricted arms race and for the development of control in strategic arms deployment and development.

On the other hand, the attainment of strategic parity with the United States and the acquisition and expansion of elements of global military capacity inspire the Soviets toward a search for more influence abroad.

But domestic economic difficulties, in conjunction with the unwillingness of the leadership to engage in a basic restructuring of the system, motivate the authorities to develop cooperative arrangements with democratic industrial societies, especially those that secure advanced technology and grain.

The relationship between domestic politics and the formation of foreign policy in the post-Brezhnev era raises two particularly relevant issues: the role of the military and the impact of succession.

Zbigniew Brzezinski has suggested that the accession of Andropov to the top leadership position was the result of an alliance of the KGB and the military. Reagan in his 1984 New Year interview for Time magazine stated his worries about the possibility that the Soviet military "have become a power on their own."

There is no doubt that the military as a whole constitutes an important interest group in the Soviet Union. Under Andropov their influence became more visible. It is also clear that the military and the KGB are the only two institutions strong enough to provide an alternative to the bureaucracy's predominance and rule. The KGB, however, has no claim to national legitimacy. In addition, its strength can be neutralized by the military, which is the only institution that has as valid a claim to national legitimacy as the Party bureaucracy. It is highly respected, it serves the national interest, it is responsible for the great victory in the Second World War, and it is recognized as the foremost Soviet accomplishment and the most efficient of all Soviet organizations. Moreover, it is doubtful whether a military bid for power could be neutralized by the KGB.

All of this notwithstanding, there is still a tendency among Western analysts to exaggerate the role of the military in politics, and particularly in the making of foreign policy. While one should heed Khrushchev's warning about the policy-making ambitions of some elements within the military establishment, the entire Soviet tradition of Party-military relations and of the political significance of the military weighs against exaggeration of its political strength and in favor of civilian control. It is even likely that as military power grows, the Party leadership becomes more sensitive to its political potential and more determined to preserve its control.

In the modern history of Russia there has been only one minor example of a military elite opposing the civil order, the Decembrist Conspiracy in the early nineteenth century. If anything this civilian tradition has been reinforced by the Soviet Party-state. The way in which the Red Army was created and the experience of the Russian Civil War (in addition to the tradition inherited from tsarist Russia) led to the separation of the army and the Party, and to an especially pronounced control over the armed forces. The Party's vigilance toward its army also came from the leadership's knowledge of the French Revolution and the fear that the phenomenon of Bonapartism might emerge in the Russian Revolution.

In the newly established Red Army almost half of the commanders were initially former tsarist officers who were totally alien to Bolshevik ideas. The Party instituted a dual system of command. Commissars were attached to every unit to control the loyalty of the commanders and were given the right to overrule commanders' decisions. While the core of the soldiers were mobilized workers, most of the troops were drafted peasants whose loyalty to the Bolsheviks was also questionable. The rate of desertion from the army was very high. Treason was widespread, both among rank-and-file soldiers and, particularly, among commanders, including the highest command.

In the early period of Stalin's rule, the Red Army became a true professional force, but Party and secret police controls remained very strong. The function of the political commissar in the armed forces remained intact. The institution of the Osobyi Otdel, the Special Department, composed of secret police and counterintelligence personnel with a separate chain of command, remained intact throughout Stalin's rule.

(During the war they were called SMERSH and subsequently were immortalized in the James Bond novels.) Yet Stalin apparently believed that he did not have a sufficient control over the armed forces. When the Great Purge of 1936–38 commenced, its most destructive blow fell on the military. The purge, in fact, liquidated the overwhelming majority of the middle and upper levels of both the professional military command and the staff personnel, as well as the commissars and special department people. In Germany Hitler took command of the existing armed forces, but in the Soviet Union, Stalin crushed them.

Stalin needed a new breed of high-level commanders to conduct and win the Second World War. During the Battle of Stalingrad in 1942, the position of commissar was abolished and single-command responsibility was vested in the professional commanders. Yet the network of political officers, representatives of the Party who acted as deputy commanders, remained in the armed forces and continues even today. Even during the anti-Stalin campaign of 1955–64, the KGB acted as a separate counterintelligence unit and checked political loyalty within the armed forces. Today it continues to do so, although in a much less visible and less formally organized manner.

Stalin recognized that to win the war he not only needed the full cooperation and confidence of the new commanders whose talent and ability emerged during the struggle against the Nazis, but also that he had to allow them more freedom of action than he had been willing to permit before the war. General staff leaders, such as Shaposhnikov, Zhukov, Vasilevskii, Shtemenko, Voronov, and field commanders such as Rokossovskii, Konev, Malinovskii, Yeremenko—in contrast to military figures of the prewar period like Voroshilov, Kulik, and Budenny, none of whom had progressed beyond their Civil War experience—received grudging respect from Stalin, who was willing to listen to their opinions. Their respect for his authority was unquestionable, not so much as a military leader, but as the man who, with enormous willpower and brutality, organized Soviet resources and mobilized the country for victory.

With the end of the war, what emerged was a situation closely resembling the 1931–41 period. On the lower level of command the return to normalcy, the conversion from war to peace, brought with it the "purge of the heroes," which sent to concentration camps tens of thousands of frontline commanders who thought that their wartime sacrifices and loyalty had earned them the rights that had been destroyed by the Great Purge. The man more responsible than anyone for the Soviet victory, Marshal Georgi Zhukov, was sent to an obscure military district in Siberia. The Soviet command, at the moment of its greatest victory, became a puppet of Stalin. One sign of his contempt for and domination of his professional commanders was the appointment of the former head of the state bank, a political marshal, Nikolai A. Bulganin, to head the Ministry of Defense.

As in most areas, Stalin's death reopened the issue of civil-military relations in the USSR. Zhukov was almost immediately recalled from Siberia and appointed Minister of Defense. The armed forces played an important role in the elimination of the secret police chief Lavrenti Beria. On the order of the Politburo, the Moscow garrison was mobilized to prevent Beria's use of his own forces, and selected marshals were ordered to arrest Beria at a meeting in the Kremlin.

Yet the chief service performed for the armed forces by the eventual new leader, Khrushchev, was the restoration of their honor. The Great Purge was declared unjust and the result of Stalin's paranoia, and the names of the legendary commanders of the civil war who were shot in 1937–38 were rehabilitated with full honors. The role of armed forces commanders in winning the war against Germany was celebrated, as was the contribution of Party leaders who were commissars on the front. Stalin himself was primarily associated with the major strategic errors of the first year and a half of the war.

But the armed forces did not gain under Khrushchev a significant role in internal politics or a decisive influence in the formulation of military, let alone foreign, policies. The subordinate role of the commanders, and the directing role of the Party, was quickly underscored by Zhukov's forced retirement in the fall of 1957. For five months he had sat on the Politburo, the first professional military man to become a member of that body. Zhukov represented the desire of the military leaders for a freer hand in organizing their internal affairs, and with his dismissal, the supremacy of the Party was established beyond doubt.

When Khrushchev was ousted in October 1964, and Brezhnev succeeded him, the military gained additional privileges. If Khrushchev reestablished the armed forces' honor, Brezhnev sponsored its professional pride and autonomy. Concerning strategic doctrine, operational principles, the structure of the forces, and their armament and deployment, the military leaders enjoyed a freedom of decision that they had lacked under Khrushchev. Yet exactly because the professional autonomy of the commanders was established under Brezhnev, it was also made very clear that the internal political control of the armed forces would in no circumstances be relinquished by the Party, and that the central role of the politician in deciding military policy, the allocation of resources to the military, and foreign policy would be retained.

Under Brezhnev, the military advised the leadership, but the hand on the gun, so to speak, belonged to the professional politician. It has been asserted that the armed forces received everything they requested in terms of allocations. This is largely true. However, the reason for this was not the political influence of the armed forces, but rather the agreement of the Brezhnev leadership and the commanders on the question of military buildup. Under Andropov an attempt was made to strengthen the political supremacy over the armed forces.

In analyzing the politics of the Soviet military it is important to separate three aspects of its role. The first concerns the long-range trend in the role of the military and what it influences. The second involves the role of the military in the recent series of Soviet successions. The third deals with the generational question.

People often confuse the role of the military *factor* in Soviet policy-making and the role of the military *sector* in Soviet politics. The military factor, the importance and growth of military power, has been, is today, and will probably remain the central focus of domestic and foreign policy-making. At the same time the military sector, that is, the military establishment, was not in the past and is not today a central actor on the political stage.

The political leaders are determined to keep the military under strict Party control—as an instrument rather than a partner of the Party. It is true that in the internal Party struggles in the post-Stalin era the military played a role. Yet its importance in Khrushchev's victory over Molotov, Malenkov, Kaganovich, and others in 1957 is grossly exaggerated. There is also no evidence that it was a leading factor in the ouster of Khrushchev and Brezhnev's victory in 1964.

After Stalin, Khrushchev would allegedly have been unable to defeat the anti-Party group if he had not had the wholehearted support of the military led by Zhukov. As a decisive piece of evidence, it is alleged that the use of military planes which brought the members of the Central Committee of the Party to Moscow in June 1957 was crucial in Khrushchev's victory. But the victory was already secure before the Central Committee meeting. Using intimidation and political bribery, Khrushchev was able to switch the division within the Politburo from a mathematical majority for his opponents to a political majority for himself. Yet the events of 1957, taken in context, do not support the case for the importance of the military in Soviet politics. Only a few months after the defeat of the anti-Party group, Khrushchev was able, without a murmur of dissent, to dismiss and retire Zhukov, the greatest and most popular war hero in the country and the paragon of professionalism in the armed forces.

It is similarly alleged that the military played a central role in the ouster of Khrushchev in 1964. The first secretary is supposed to have alienated the military services, first by significantly reducing the size of the ground forces, and second by pressing for the deployment of IRBMs in Cuba and later agreeing under humiliating circumstances to withdraw them. These actions are said to have created enormous dissatisfaction within the military and led to the participation of its leaders in the coup. The line of argument, however, is less than convincing. Not only the armed forces but, more important, most of his colleagues in the Politburo were dissatisfied with Khrushchev's military policies and with his behavior in the Cuban missile crisis. The coup was accomplished within the Politburo during Khrushchev's absence and later rubber-stamped by the Central Committee. The head of the Soviet military, Marshal Rodion Malinovskii, was not even a candidate member of the Politburo at that time, and the fact that he was not subsequently elevated to the Politburo also argues strongly against his active participation in the overthrow. The success of the plot depended more on the acquiescence of the secret police to keep Khrushchev in the dark. The head of the KGB was V. E. Semichastny, a close protégé of A. N. Shelepin, an important partner of Brezhnev and his clique in organizing the plot against Khrushchev.

It is true that with the selection of Marshal Grechko to full membership in the Politburo in April 1973, the Soviet military had a spokesman there for the first time since the short interlude of Zhukov in 1957. Yet, after Grechko's death, Central Committee Party Secretary Dimitrii Ustinov, a civilian, though one with long and close ties to the military, was appointed minister of defense and full member of the Politburo. The choice of Ustinov was a setback for the political role of the professional military leaders since he was the first civilian head of the ministry in the post-Stalin era. Grechko's ascent to the Politburo appeared to be more a reward to a close companion of Brezhnev (they fought together in the war) than the recognition of the political weight of the military.

Still, with the international position of the Soviet Union different now from what it was in the past, with the enormous role of the military in implementing global plans, with its visibility as the main achievement of Soviet power, might not the military leaders play a more significant role today than in the past?

In making military policy, that is, in selecting and developing weapons systems, shaping strategic doctrine and operational plans, deploying the Soviet armed forces, influencing the general approach to arms control, and calculating the pros and cons of specific proposals, the role of the Soviet military increased substantially in the Brezhnev era and will certainly remain important. The lack of a meaningful group of Soviet civilian strategists and experts, the decline of leadership expertise in strictly military matters (none of the present Politburo members has any experience of high service position during or after World War II), the growing intricacies of military questions have given the high command a dominant role in formulating defense policies.

Foreign policy-making, however, is a tightly guarded prerogative of the core of the Politburo and the direct role of the military is quite limited. Yet defense questions play an increasingly significant role in foreign policy-making, especially since resources are so important. The indirect influence of the military on foreign policy has increased and will probably continue to remain significant.

Evidence of such influence on domestic policies is much more ambiguous. It is probably limited. The Party leadership restricts professional military membership in its decision-making and executive bodies, and controls the military establishment from within through political officers and departments and by nonmilitary counterintelligence, neither of which follows the military chain of command but is directly responsible to the Party. The traditional aversion of the leadership to political statements made by military leaders remains strong, as does the suspicion of and resistance to military leaders engaging in domestic intra-Party politicking.

The military had an interesting role in the recent succession process. As mentioned, Andropov seemingly wished to achieve greater control over the services. Yet in his last months in office and during the transitional leadership of Chernenko, the military seemed to have acquired not only greater visibility but also greater power through the preeminence of Ustinov and the strength of its claims on resources. Its increased power appeared to be a function of the tense international situation and prospect of a new arms race and confrontation with America, and of the weakness of the transitional leadership. As one official expressed it privately in 1984: "Who in the Politburo, or for that matter outside it, will in the present dangerous situation dare to refuse any military demand having to do with strengthening Soviet national security?"

These factors appear to be declining significantly with Gorbachev's rapid consolidation of power. It is again becoming clear that a united and rejuvenated leadership considers it important to reestablish a firm grip over the military regardless of the international situation. The authority of Ustinov, on matters of national security was unique and is not likely to be repeated soon.

At one point in appeared probable that with Ustinov's death or retirement a military professional, specifically Marshal Nikolai Ogarkov—the chief of the general staff and a brilliant, hard-headed, outspoken and authoritative figure—would become the next minister of defense, perhaps with a seat on the Politburo. In September 1984, however, Ogarkov was suddenly fired. We do not know the immediate reasons for this unexpected decision, which apparently was supported by Ustinov. What we do know, however, is that in a number of instances Ogarkov advocated policies that were not in line with the preferences of the Politburo.

His article in a Soviet journal in April 1984 advocated that the defense of the Soviet Union required and will require greater expenditures, that the question of strategic weapons and strategic balance with America should not be exaggerated, and that the technological revolution in conventional weapons in the West posed a major challenge to which too little attention was being paid. Ogarkov seemed to be putting pressure on the political leadership for much greater military allocations, and to be opposed to the views of the Politburo about the crucial nature of strategic weapons and the need for their increased deployment because of the American challenge. (From earlier writings of Ogarkov and Ustinov, it also seems that there may have been differences between the military and political leadership over the distribution of resources within the military budget. The military appeared to be pressing for larger direct military spending, while the political leadership wanted a balance between direct military spending and investments in military industrial plant.) Firing Ogarkov was the Politburo's response to the growing visibility and probably ambitions for greater political influence among the military leadership. It was a timely reminder that even in a time of weak and fragmented political leadership, the principle of Party control over the military remains uncontestable.

Only a few months after the removal of Ogarkov, Ustinov died, creating a dilemma for the leadership: whether to appoint in his place a younger professional who would not, however, become a member of the Politburo, or a younger political leader from within the Politburo. Characteristically, the leadership again chose an intermediate solution. Ustinov's vacancy was filled by a professional soldier, Marshal Sergei Sokolov, who because of his age (seventy-three) was clearly a transitional appointee.

The new Politburo is without a professional or civilian military representative. Sokolov was given only alternate Politburo membership. The man who succeeded Ogarkov as the chief of the general staff, the sixty-one-year-old Marshal Sergei Akhromeyev, will need a long time to establish himself as an authoritative figure with the political leadership, and, one can be sure, he will remember the fate of his predecessor.

In his consolidation of power, Gorbachev's key priorities have been control over the Politburo and over the party's Central Secretariat. In the summer of 1985, however, the goal was extended to include personnel crucial to Soviet military and foreign policy-making. Ogarkov had not been retired and disgraced. At the beginning of 1985, it was announced that he was inspecting Soviet forces in East Germany, and his picture with the East German Party boss, Erich Honecker, appeared in the East German Party paper. In July 1985, Western journalists in Moscow reported that just as unexpectedly as he had been removed the previous year, Ogarkov had been appointed to be the commander of the Warsaw Pact Forces, a position that carries with it the title of first deputy minister of defense. (In light of Ogarkov's known views that the technological revolution in conventional weaponry requires an urgent Soviet response and reorganization of the troops facing NATO, his new command would seem a rational decision of Gorbachev's.)

In the summer of 1985 Gorbachev decided to assert his leadership over the armed forces. After a July 10 meeting with top field and staff commanders, a whole series of personnel changes took place. In most cases old commanders were replaced by younger people. Gorbachev was certainly eager to have the key people in the high command personally beholden to him for their positions.

These military changes have been accompanied by newspaper articles and a propaganda campaign within the armed forces stressing the leadership role of the Party over the military. One way or another, luck (e.g., Ustinov's death) and political astuteness combined to put Gorbachev in a strong position vis-à-vis the military during his first year in office. He is already an authoritative voice on questions of military allocations and arms control negotiations and he will not need to defer constantly to the opinions and biases of the high command.

Finally, an important new element relating to the political role of the military concerns generations. The present and future general officers belong to the post–World War II generation. They do not have the same prestige and experience as the heroes of the Great Patriotic War. They resemble managers rather than the generals who led the sons of Russia into battle. Their ties with Party leaders are purely professional.

The generation of war commissars is quickly disappearing politically, and the process of replacement inside the military is progressing somewhat more quickly than in the Party itself. However, this difference will vanish in the near future and both the army and the Party leadership will again belong to the same generation. It seems likely that the relatively young military and Party leaders will not be particularly impressed by each other's pasts and, at the same time, they will not have special personal ties to each other. In such a situation, the Party's preeminence in the Soviet political system may even be reinforced. The old maxim, "You don't ask a general whether a place should be bombed, but only how," may be followed even more strictly than in the past.

Past Soviet successions have left a greater mark on domestic politics than on international affairs. Foreign policy has generally reflected international capabilities. The continuity of foreign policy from one succession to another has been more striking than its discontinuities. The present succession has the potential to be different in this respect, but in all probability it will not be.

In the past if the new leader wanted to put his mark on foreign policy he had to gain control over the policy-making apparatus. In this respect Gorbachev's luck and astuteness are spectacular. His consolidation of control over foreign policy seems to be more rapid and complete than that of any of his predecessors.

One should remember that Dimitrii Shepilov, Khrushchev's choice to replace his adversary Vyacheslav Molotov as Minister of Foreign Affairs in 1956, joined Molotov in 1957 in an attempt to oust Khrushchev. In the Brezhnev era, Mikhail Suslov, the chief Party ideologue, was until his death in 1982 a recognized and respected force in foreign policy-making. Yet Gorbachev's control is already beyond question.

During Andropov's critical illness and Chernenko's short leadership, Andrei Gromyko and his ministry were in full charge of foreign policy. It was the first time in Soviet history that the foreign minister actually shaped international policy. By all accounts, Gromyko fought a rear-guard battle during Chernenko's last months, together with Prime Minister Tikhonov and Moscow Party Secretary Grishin, to block the succession of Gorbachev. Then, when it became clear that Gorbachev could not be stopped, Gromyko manipulated himself into the position of being the one to nominate the new leader before the special meeting of the Central Committee.

But on July 2, 1985, Gromyko was kicked upstairs to the largely honorific position of chairman of the Supreme Soviet, the titular head of the state. This way-station to his full retirement ended an era in the conduct of Soviet foreign policy. The appointment of Eduard Shevardnadze to succeed Gromyko was surprising. Shevardnadze, who was little known even in the Soviet Union, has his power base in Georgia. His entire life and career had been spent in Georgia, where he was a Communist Youth League functionary, a Party official, minister of the interior (that is to say chief of the police), and finally, from 1972, the first party secretary. In his new position in Moscow, therefore, he is entirely dependent on Gorbachev's good will and support and on Gorbachev's further accumulation of power. Policy will be made by Gorbachev and his associates. Moreover, to the best of our knowledge, Shevardnadze lacks experience or expertise in international relations or security affairs. This will increase his dependence on Gorbachev and his Politburo colleagues.

In addition, Shevardnadze owes nothing to the Gromyko protégés who run the Ministry. He will be sensitive to any attempts they might make to shape policies directed from above while implementing them. Finally, the decline of the Foreign Ministry bureaucracy, which now lacks a powerful sponsor in the Politburo, will be paralleled by an increase in the importance of the foreign policy specialists on the Central Committee staff and the high-level experts in the academic institutes, such as Georgii Arbatov.

While Gorbachev puts his own imprint on Soviet foreign policy, his priorities are unquestionably domestic. The leadership is fully aware that the internal situation will drastically affect international aspirations. But the Soviet Union's international situation, the revitalization of America's world role, and the arms control negotiations in Geneva do not leave Gorbachev the luxury of letting things drift.

There is an additional reason why Gorbachev felt compelled to establish a dominant position in foreign policy-making and to be perceived at home as being in control of international relations. Except for short periods in the succession process, leadership in the Soviet Union is indivisible. In order to be considered a strong leader by the elite and the population as a whole, no major area of responsibility can be seen to be outside one's control.

Aside from the question of who is in control of foreign and military policy, the succession process also influences the substance of international relations. New leaders have always wished to insulate the domestic political process and their own still shaky positions from external challenges and international crisis situations. A major tendency of Soviet foreign policy during the internal transfer of power is to project an image of solidity, determination, and unity. Another is an effort to cut international losses and attempt seriously to reverse unsuccessful policies and approaches of the departed leader. Thus, after Stalin's death the leadership was instrumental in reaching a quick end to the stalemated Korean War and solving the issue of Austria. After Khrushchev's ouster the Kremlin embarked on a policy to promote European stability and to end the crises over the status of West Berlin. Nor can a new leader afford to respond indecisively to foreign challenges. During the consolidation of his power, a show of weakness in the face of an external crisis would compromise his standing among his colleagues and provide ammunition for his detractors.

A small group of men at the apex of the hierarchy, served by a large staff of advisers and officials, monopolizes decision making in foreign policy. The overwhelming majority of the political elite, including the Central Committee, is isolated from this process. The leaders inform the Central Committee of the policies to be adopted, rather than asking what the policies should be. In the Secretariat of the Central Committee, the general secretary alone is involved in the conduct and direction of foreign policy. No other secretary is responsible for or specializes in foreign policy per se. (Boris Ponomarev of the Central Committee is responsible for ties with nonruling communist and leftist movements and such "progressive" countries as Angola and Ethiopia. Another, at present Konstantin Rusakov, deals with relations with Eastern Europe, Cuba, and Vietnam.)

Gorbachev took control of foreign and military policies in odd circumstances. He inherited awesome military power. He is the first leader to begin his rule in a position of strategic parity with the United States. Yet he also inherits a recent legacy of passive or reactive policies. His country has lost the international initiative. He and his associates are faced with military-political decisions of even greater importance than those confronted by Khrushchev or Brezhnev at the beginning of their rule. Gorbachev's task is nothing less than to regain initiative at a time when the domestic situation provides limited foreign policy resources and American is both resurgent and confident. Whether conciliatory or aggressive tendencies prevail depends to a large degree on Western policies and on the extent to which both the Soviet and American leaderships have learned the lessons of their recent relations.

16

Détente and the Legacy
of the 1970s

Toward the end of the 1960s, it became clear that the United States and the Soviet Union were moving toward nuclear parity. In the early 1970s, both nations acknowledged publicly that a state of parity existed between their respective strategic forces. Parity meant that each country, if attacked, would still be able to destroy the other. Both possessed a second strike capability sufficient for mutual assured destruction (MAD).

Détente, or, as the Russians call it, *razryadka,* was the response of both superpowers, but especially the United States, to the state of strategic parity. It was an acknowledgment of the absolute necessity of managing and regulating the international conflict so as to avoid the dangers that the growing number of nuclear weapons posed. To most Western analysts in that period, détente meant that both superpowers would negotiate for arms control agreements that limit the number and categories of nuclear weapons on both sides and by so doing make the attainment of superiority impossible, promoting instead balance and stability. They would try to develop confidence-building measures between the two superpowers and alliance systems, such as prior notification of troop movements and maneuvers. There would be regular communication between the two governments and consultation on regional conflicts and on the resolution of international tensions having the potential to involve the two countries in an undesired confrontation. And they would create a web of mutual relations in such areas as trade, credit, civilian technology exchanges, and cultural and scientific exchanges, which would gradually increase mutually beneficial peaceful relations and counteract their basic differences in values, ideologies, and political aims.

Détente emerged from the domestic and international circumstances of both superpowers in the early 1970s. The years 1965–75 were the best economic decade in Soviet history. Socially and politically it was a time of unparalleled stability. From the military point of view, those years marked a key breakthrough—parity with Western adversaries and, for all practical purposes and for the first time in Russian and Soviet history, security from attack from abroad. It was also a period of growing Soviet awareness of its international position and seeming potential for ever greater influence. With the exception of relations with China, it was probably the apogee of Soviet international influence. And while the Sino-Soviet conflict escalated, China was in the throes of its Cultural Revolution, and therefore weak and unstable. After the abortive Czech attempt to break its imperial chains, Eastern Europe was relatively prosperous and at peace with its rulers. Soviet involvement in the Middle East was at its peak, with Egypt and Iraq as allies and Iran a peaceful neighbor. The alliance with India looked strong and stable. The commitment of Western European countries to good relations with Eastern Europe and the Soviet Union, which started with the West German *Ostpolitik,* resulted in the growing transfer to the Eastern bloc of Western credits and technology, in Western European and particularly West German acceptance of the division of Europe, and a lack of interest in—or a decision to ignore—Soviet activities outside Europe.

The realization of the dream of a stable, prosperous and secure Soviet Union that would be dominant internationally seemed to be within reach. To cap its achievement of strategic parity with the United States, the leadership required Western and American recognition of the spheres of influence in Europe and of U.S.-Soviet equality as global powers. The Soviets also wanted to minimize frictions and dangers with the United States through arms control agreements that, while leaving the Soviet Union enough leeway to develop its military strength, would nevertheless secure strategic parity with America. The arrangement would help to translate nuclear parity into growing international power and influence. The new situation with the United States would prevent a Sino-American alliance and deflect China's growing international activism, particularly in its relations with Western nations and Japan. The Soviet Union would increase trade, credit, and technology transfers, and scientific exchanges with the West.

For the United States, the late 1960s and early 1970s were a time of trial and doubt, both internationally and domestically. Internationally, American economic and political dominance was already past its peak. Most importantly, the United States was committed to an increasingly costly war in Vietnam. On the domestic front it was plagued by the civil

violence and unrest and the divisiveness and other negative consequences of the Vietnam War.

The war divided America as had no other event in the twentieth century, and sharpened generational, class, and regional fissures. The way in
which the war was pursued financially weakened the economy, spurring
inflationary trends and depleting U.S. military power outside Southeast
Asia. Watergate, which came shortly after the beginning of détente, was
a historic crisis of the institution of the presidency, and coming on top of
the other events, deepened the problems of social and political life,
creating an unprecedented degree of self-doubt and self-questioning that
almost paralyzed U.S. foreign policy.

A comparison of the Soviet and American situations in the early 1970s
clearly reveals the two superpowers' different points of departure for
détente. Regardless of how much stronger the United States was potentially in almost every respect, because of an unusual confluence of circumstances the Soviets began the new relationship from a position of
strength. This uncharacteristic temporary situation produced unrealistic
expectations on both sides, and probably predetermined the failure of
détente.

By the mid-1970s the Soviets were convinced that the American decline would not be reversed and that the awesome American economic,
technological, and military potential would not be harnessed effectively
for the goals of U.S. foreign policy. American shapers of détente underestimated the seriousness of the nation's malady. They hoped unreal-
istically that agreements with the Soviet Union not backed by actual
American power, strength of will, and ability to act would restrain the
Soviets and moderate their policies.

This unrealism was strengthened by one of the first major documents
of détente, the "Basic Principles of Mutual Relations Between the
United States of America and the Union of Soviet Socialist Republics."
The high-sounding language was precise in inverse ratio to the importance of the subjects it covered. Key issues between the two, such as the
military buildup beyond the SALT I and ABM agreements, and the use
of military force, directly or by proxy, against countries outside the two
alliance systems, were alluded to only in the most general terms. There
was much room for interpretation. At least in part, the ambiguity of the
1972 Nixon-Brezhnev declaration on the rules of behavior was due to
the fact that the United States expected Soviet help in ending the Vietnam War and was therefore anxious to have a document establishing
this cooperation, however vaguely.

The agreements were supposed to benefit both sides equally, but they
did not always do so. A case in point is the exchanges of scholars and
officials. The Soviets who came to the United States had broad access

both to politically or economically important elites and to the media, through which they could and did present their views. Their American counterparts had nothing even approaching this access and influence in the Soviet Union.

Such practical disparities, however, were not directly the result of Soviet ill-will but simply reflected the differences between an open and a closed society—and, after all, détente did not imply that either nation would change its system. Détente was accepted by both as a necessity not because of a convergence of the American and Soviet systems and policies, but precisely because of the divergence of the two systems, which meant that their relationship had to be monitored, and insulated by a web of agreements to minimize the possibility of a nuclear war. Détente in this relatively narrow but overwhelmingly important sense is still and will remain in the years to come necessary for human survival. What went wrong with détente resulted from the unwritten hopes and expectations—the obligations and opportunities—associated with its spirit. The unwritten American obligations of détente, which the Soviets expected would be honored, were consultation and negotiation on major military issues and on regional conflicts; the recognition of the Soviet Union as a legitimate global power; cooperation in scientific and technological areas; the granting of Most Favored Nation status in trade relations; a long-range commitment to sell grain to the Russians, and the provision of assistance to the Soviet Union in the areas where it was visibly lagging. In exchange for such commitments America expected Soviet restraint in the area of its only strength—military power, a scaling down of the military buildup and restraint in the use of force in the international arena.

What America expected at détente's inception was first and foremost that the Soviet Union would help in bringing an honorable end to the war in Vietnam. According to Henry Kissinger's memoirs, détente was also to buy time for the United States while it tried to rebuild its nuclear and conventional forces to a level necessary to contain Soviet expansion.

The Soviets had quite a different view of their obligations, aside from those spelled out in the written agreements. They would tone down their anti-American propaganda, treat their dissident movement more liberally and with greater caution, accept the necessity of allowing a large number of Jews and Volga Germans to emigrate, and make a few other such concessions that were marginal to their international ambitions and domestic concerns. The opportunities Soviet leaders saw for their country in détente were probably also limited at first. Expectations of one-sided advantages seemed primarily a product not of the initial agreements themselves but rather of internal American developments, which changed the Soviet perception of détente and its potential benefits.

Détente created exaggerated hopes in the United States for better relations with the Soviet Union. In part, these were a function of the popular desire to eliminate the prospect of nuclear war. They were also a product of the Nixon Administration's style in the conduct of foreign relations, its flamboyant and optimistic pronouncements picked up uncritically by the media. And, finally, they were a consequence of the Watergate affair, to which President Nixon responded by glorifying his international achievements.

America's situation, however, precluded the management of Soviet-American relations so as to fulfill these expectations. On the contrary, it laid the groundwork for a Soviet thrust in military and foreign policies. The post-Vietnam syndrome made impossible even indirect American intervention in foreign conflicts where the Soviet Union or its proxies became engaged. (As for example, Angola, where Congress rejected Henry Kissinger's request for at least indirect help for the anti-Soviet Unita.) Watergate paralyzed the executive branch of the government and created a built-in resistance in Congress to an active stance in foreign relations, a tendency reinforced by the critical attitude towards American policies in the media, a key force shaping public opinion.

The paralysis combined with Soviet eagerness to exploit the situation created a détente which in practice favored the Soviet Union. Once the reality of the post-Vietnam syndrome and of the internal crises created by Watergate was recognized by the Soviets, the leadership interpreted détente in a way which permitted an effort to improve the Soviet Union's international and military position.

Détente is blamed today for many actual and imagined sins. Despite the SALT process it did not stop the Soviet arms buildup. There was a major effort to strengthen Soviet strategic nuclear forces and theater nuclear weapons. The simultaneous buildup and modernization of conventional forces tipped the balance of military power in Europe and on the Chinese border in Soviet favor. The construction of a blue water navy and logistical capabilities transformed the Soviet Union into a truly global power. Under the umbrella of strategic parity and in the face of American inaction, the Soviet Union alone, or in combination with the proxy forces of its Cuban allies and its East German satellite, entered southern Africa and, by exploiting regional conflicts, established its partial control over Ethiopia and its influence over a number of north and central Africa states, like Mozambique and Angola.

Soviet actions were, in the American view, imcompatible with the spirit of détente. But on what basis can one say that without détente and the agreements of the early 1970s the Soviets would not have developed their military forces, tried to improve their strategic and theater positions, and engaged in expansion in the Third World? On the contrary, without détente, Soviet actions probably would have been even less re-stricted and more adventurous. The ascension of the Soviet Union, and the demise of détente resulted not so much from what the Soviets did in the 1970s, as from what the Americans did not do. An increase in American and Western European military expenditures did not take place. The incursions into Angola and Ethiopia, and Soviet support of socialist-oriented states in Africa, were similarly not confronted by America.

The real sin of détente was that it created false illusions among the American people that reinforced the effects of the post-Vietnam and Watergate syndromes. Part of the American public understood détente as nullifying the Soviet-American rivalry, especially in the military field. Détente added justification for American military and foreign policy passivity. It made more difficult the mobilization of American public opinion for an active reaction to Soviet expansion.

The destruction of détente was sealed by the Soviet invasion of Afghanistan in 1979, by the 1981 internal invasion of Poland, and by the Vietnamese occupation of Kampuchea.

Controversy surrounds the invasion of Afghanistan. The circum-stances are quite clear—a communist government established in Af-ghanistan in 1978 without protest from the West was in major trouble. The invasion was certainly a defensive move, undertaken to prevent the fall of the government and to preserve the country's status as a client buffer state. The American-Chinese relationship, the sharp conflict be-tween China and the Soviet ally Vietnam, the Sino-Japanese pact, and the increase in Japanese military spending, the rise of an unpredictable fundamentalist Islamic regime in Iran, the virtual end of the Soviet-Iraqi pact of cooperation, the stalemate in Poland, and the potential instabil-ity of Eastern Europe, all created in the minds of Soviet leaders the fear of a new encirclement and pushed them to restore stable communist rule in Afghanistan.

Yet the consequences—intended or unintended—were clearly offen-sive. The invasion positioned Soviet forces for possible future expansion to the south; it secured the rear in the event of such an expansion; and it reasserted Soviet power and determination on the borders of the Middle East, where the Soviet presence was at its lowest point in the post-Stalin period.

Most important, however, was the symbolic meaning of the invasion. It was the first massive move of Soviet military forces since post–World War II beyond the established and recognized sphere of influence in Eastern Europe. While largely ignored by the Europeans, the invasion signified to American policy-makers both in the Carter and Reagan ad-ministrations a mood of new Soviet confidence, recklessness, and contempt for the "spirit of détente." Carter withdrew the SALT II agreement from consideration by the Senate because it had no chance whatsoever of passing. This in reality was the end of détente.

In the 1970s, the United States and the Soviet Union were out of phase in their basic attitudes toward the international system, in their fears and ambitions, and in their ability to mobilize internal resources for international purposes. The Soviet Union was still in a rising phase as an international power. Having only recently acquired its global status, it was still flexing its muscles, eager to translate its military status into international influence. In America détente found fertile soil and was understood as a promise of peace and noninvolvement to be attained, so to speak, on the cheap. For the Soviet Union, détente proffered temptations to grasp the opportunities of the moment.

The two countries entered into détente because they both recognized the dangers of a possible nuclear confrontation and opted for the chance of a controlled relationship. Yet détente did not abolish all conflict between them. No agreement can nullify the pursuit of American and Soviet interests and the promotion in the international arena of their respective values and priorities. Thus, the Soviet advances and American losses cannot be blamed entirely on the policy of détente. The most important conclusion is that in the 1970s, no American policy would have worked. However, a détente with much lower expectations and with America in a position of strength could have resulted in a different outcome.

The decline and then the demise of détente led to general evaluations that are of limited validity. To Americans, détente began to look increasingly like a fraud perpetuated by the Soviets. To the Soviets their actions were simply evidence of a change in "the correlation of forces," reflecting the irreversible trends of American decline and Soviet ascendancy. Throughout the 1970s détente came to be increasingly understood by the Politburo as an instance of the expected and justified shift in Soviet favor. It was this understanding of détente that stood behind Moscow's repeated assertions that the process was irreversible.

It took Soviet leaders a long time to understand the devastating impact of the Vietnam War and the Watergate crisis on America. Once they understood, however, they underestimated the basic soundness of the American system—its ability to bounce back. So they were late again in recognizing the return to a new confidence, renewed commitment to leadership of the free world, military strength, and increased international activism. They clearly overestimated their ability to influence or intimidate the Western Europeans and split them from U. S. positions. Only in the middle of Reagan's first term did they wake up to the new realities, of which American ability to deploy new missiles in Europe was a fundamental part.

The American-European plan for the deployment of INF (Intermediate-Range Nuclear Forces) was a basic test of will between the Western alliance and the Soviet Union. The West regarded INF as a response to the unwarranted (and exaggerated) deployment of Soviet SS-20s. The Soviets saw it as a question of whether the strategic balance based on American and European weakness in the 1970s could be changed by NATO. INF was less a military issue than a political one. It was a test of whether the Soviet Union could veto NATO's military policies. The successful deployment of INF was a major Soviet defeat, which showed that the limits imposed on America by the "correlation of forces" in the 1970s no longer applied.

The 1970s demonstrated that agreements reached with the Soviet Union from positions of weakness will never stick. It also conclusively proved that no Soviet-American agreements will eliminate the basis of their conflict—different values pursued globally as national interests. Yet the two basic premises that led to détente have not been invalidated—the need for arms control as a result of strategic parity, and the need to manage relations so as to avoid a disastrous military confrontation. The initial goals of détente that derive from these premises remain valid. The description of relations in the late 1940s and in the 1950s, during the Cold War, as "neither war nor peace" is still accurate today and will remain so. The situation of the 1970s, which changed the balance of power temporarily in the Soviets' favor, is unlikely to be repeated. Soviet economic difficulties, and recognition of the resurgence of American power, make unlikely another underestimation of the resilience and vitality of American power.

In the 1970s, the Soviet Union tried to exploit U.S. domestic troubles to gain advantage, thus helping to change American attitudes and leading to the demise of détente. It is likely that future Soviet historians will consider this policy as the greatest mistake of Brezhnev's leadership.

American weaknesses and illusions and Soviet strengths and greed assured a U.S. backlash once the illusions became too obvious and the weaknesses proved temporary. And as at other times in American history, national reaction swung from one extreme to the other. The exaggerated optimistic expectations about détente were replaced by exaggerated pessimism about what can be achieved through arms control and crisis management in Soviet-American relations.

17

Russia and Reagan

Ronald Reagan entered office proposing to reverse what he saw as an unfavorable trend of U.S.-Soviet relations and to stand up to the Russians. His first administration tried to translate into policy the basic ideas its members brought into office. These ideas have remained unchanged despite pressures that inevitably affect every president. The foreign policies of the Reagan Administration, like his presidential campaign, have continued to display some characteristics of an ideological crusade.

Reagan has connected almost all foreign policy decisions to the East-West conflict. Yet his conduct toward the Soviet Union is guided less by a comprehensive and consistent long-range policy than by an ideological orientation. All American presidents in the 1970s pursued a two-track policy toward the Soviet Union, one of rivalry and cooperation at the same time. Reagan, at least until the 1984 election, stressed the first element over the second. Soviet-American relations deteriorated further and the tension between the two nations increased.

The president's concentration on the Russian danger as the fundamental issue in world politics is matched in intensity by the Soviet preoccupation with Reaganism as a menace to its international authority. If anything, Soviet attention to America's words and actions has become even more acute during the transition to new leaders. In deciding the future course of Soviet policy toward the United States, those leaders are building upon the views of their American analysts—analysts whose assessments of the Reagan Administration, with due allowances for differences of language and approach, are strikingly similar to those of American and Western European liberal critics of Reagan's Soviet policy. In Soviet eyes, the most significant element of the Reagan approach is what they regard as its attempt to alter the balance of military power. Particularly striking in this regard, many Russians feel, is Reagan's willingness to sacrifice social welfare spending to support the cost of a larger military budget—something that would have seemed unthinkable only a few years ago. Reagan, they believe, has shown the will and the political capacity to rearm America.

Like their American counterparts, of course, the Soviets appreciate the difficulties involved in the Reagan program. The Administration's military commitments—to the MX strategic missile, the Trident submarine, the B-1 bomber, the Rapid Deployment Force, improved command and communications structure—read like a shopping list with no clear priorities. Years will elapse before these programs actually affect the military balance, and ultimate success will also depend upon Reagan's ability to pass similar budgets in the future. While unconvinced that the U.S. military budget seriously threatens them as yet, the Russians do believe that the United States aims in the next few years to change the present strategic balance, which, in their view, is one of parity. What they fear most is any effort to realize one repeated theme of Reagan's election campaign—strategic superiority.

If in material terms the Reagan military program does not yet affect the actual Soviet-American power balance, the Soviets recognize that its psychological and political effects are immediate and important. They have been warned that their unceasing military buildup will at least be matched should Reagan have his way. Although he may not yet have persuaded them he will succeed, the prospect that American resolve to engage in a military buildup would continue into Reagan's second term brought home to Soviet leaders the unintended consequences of their own military development and expansionist policies. It also promises them a new arms race, the cost of which would probably exceed that of the past two decades.

The second element of Reagan's policy, the Russians feel, is his effort to wage economic warfare by exploiting their dependence on Western imports. If, in the early days of détente, trade with America failed to expand as expected, economic relations with Western Europe have become important for their plans to improve industry. Directly or indirectly, Western technology influences the Soviets' ability to continue modernizing their military forces, and the impact of these imports is maximized because they are concentrated on key projects of the five-year plans. But since Soviet-American trade in industrial items scarcely exists, Reagan's attempt at economic warfare consists primarily of pressing allies to limit their trade and especially to abolish their favorable credit arrangements.

Here, the Soviet propaganda line proclaims Reagan's policy to be a fiasco. When one probes deeper, however, it seems that the Russians see it as neither an unqualified success nor a total failure. America's lack of success in trying to stop the Soviet-European trade in modern technology clearly demonstrates the alliance's difficulty in pursuing a coordinated and effective policy in this respect. It is now evident that this policy will not bring the Soviets to their knees. Yet tightening the rules of trade, broadening the embargo list, and pressuring American allies do restrict trade, make Soviet planning more difficult, and are of more than nuisance value in the Soviet-American rivalry.

The third element of Reagan's policies, in the Soviet analysis, is an effort to redefine the very atmosphere of Soviet-Western relations and, particularly, public attitudes in the United States. Reagan's strident anti-Soviet rhetoric was, the Soviets believe, addressed primarily to the American public, in order to ensure its acceptance of reduced social programs together with substantial growth in military spending. The rhetoric also aimed to persuade Western Europeans that the period of détente was over, and that if they wanted to retain their various ties with the United States, they would have to be more in step with the American policy. Only finally was the rhetoric addressed to the Russians themselves, who were put on notice that the U.S. would not engage in business as usual with them.

From the Soviet perspective, the fourth element of Reagan's policy concerned the timing of U.S.-Soviet negotiations. The Soviets recognized that before Reagan the American government tried to use incentives and disincentives simultaneously. Now, in the Soviet view, they are used sequentially. Sticks come first with the carrots held in reserve. Serious negotiations on arms limitations and reductions, on commercial relations and credits, on compromise solutions to regional conflicts and imbalances, can be undertaken only when Soviet leaders understand that the mood of the American people and the government has really changed and that the trend of the Soviet-American military power balance has been reversed. This position was clear to the Soviets from the speeches of former Secretary of State Alexander Haig and they have been continued under Secretary George Shultz.

The fifth element of Reagan's policy in the Soviet view is his approach to regional conflicts and civil wars in the Third World and to regional security arrangements. The Reagan Administration appears to look at Third World issues primarily through the prism of American-Soviet relations. They say Reagan regards Soviet policies as either the direct cause of instability in the Third World or at least as the decisive obstacle to the resolution of regional problems in line with American preferences and interests. There is, for example, the rigid American position toward Cuba, a country that, in the view of the Reagan Administration, shares with its Soviet patron the blame for the civil war in El Salvador; or, to take another example, the American attempt (since abandoned) to arrange a "strategic consensus" in the Middle East expressly in order to neutralize the threat of Soviet expansionism.

On all these points, dismay has replaced the complacency with which Soviet specialists on the United States first responded to the election of President Reagan. During the 1980 election campaign, it appeared that the majority of Soviet leaders and commentators on the American political scene preferred the election of Reagan, his anti-Soviet rhetoric notwithstanding, to what they saw as the unpredictability, ambiguity, and indecisiveness of the Carter Administration. Even after Reagan chose his new associates, the Soviets were not unhappy about Carter's defeat. They expected that the process of governing would inevitably drive Reagan's policies toward the center, and they remembered that conservative Republicans have found it easier than liberal Democrats to make agreements with the Soviet Union. To put it simply, the hope of Soviet leaders was to see another Richard Nixon in the White House.

During Reagan's first year, many Soviet specialists regarded his administration as "Carterism without Carter," that is, as a continuation and intensification of policies pursued during Carter's last year in office. By the end of 1982 there was scarcely a Soviet official or expert who continued to subscribe to this view. They saw Reaganism as a major break with the past despite important continuities in policy. They came to recognize that Reagan's team included people who were different from the leading administration figures of the 1970s and who served different constituencies. They felt that the president and his team would behave differently in crisis situations, partly because their image of the world is much more conservative and partly because there is much more popular support in the United States for activism and hard-line policies. Finally, whatever the elements of continuity, the Soviets suspected that Reagan pursues different, more ambitious, and—for the Soviet Union— more dangerous aims than did his predecessors.

Soviet analysts do see differences and divisions within the Reagan Administration, although they ascribed little importance to them initially. They distinguish, for example, what may be termed the anti-Soviet position of former Secretary Haig and more generally of the State Department from the anti-Soviet and anti-communist position of the Defense Department and the White House. The former are said to espouse policies designed to counteract the expansion of Soviet power by means of realpolitik. The latter go beyond this position to call for a crusade against the Soviet Union, its clients, and communism in general, through the rhetoric and instruments of the Cold War. The first group, the Soviets believe, would make American policy dependent on Soviet behavior with regard to specific issues, such as Poland or Afghanistan.

The latter would pursue an intransigent cold war policy regardless of any adjustments, compromises, or changes in Soviet policy on specific issues believing that any accommodation would prove an illusion because the Soviet Union is incapable of altering its behavior.

While Soviet specialists broadly agree on Reagan's policies, they disagree over the nature and sources of Reaganism. The two main views have important implications for policy planning.

According to one school of thought, Reaganism represents a significant if temporary departure from the policy in the direction of accommodation. In this view, Reagan, his associates, and his principal supporters constitute only one tendency within America's ruling circles. They are primarily responsible for the present harsh direction of American policy and mood of American opinion. The United States bears the overwhelming responsibility for the failure of détente, although it is admitted that certain Soviet actions, such as the invasion of Afghanistan which were "forced" on the Soviet Union by circumstances, did contribute to the deterioration of Soviet-American relations.

According to this view, there are other forces in America that are more realistic and pragmatic, and whose time will come. Reaganism may pass after the 1988 election. Soviet patience will eventually find its reward in a changed American political climate and in a new administration that will once again choose regulated competition and compromise solutions over confrontation.

This new administration will not go so far as to restore the détente of the early 1970s. Such an outcome, according to one analyst, might be all for the better, so that neither side harbors unwarranted illusions or exaggerated expectations of what détente can accomplish. Yet sooner or later the United States will recognize that Soviet-American relations must be regulated in ways that acknowledge the vital interests of both parties and avert potentially dangerous conflicts.

There are other Soviets who argue that the change in American direction came not with Reagan but with détente. The situation in the early 1970s, this view holds, was unusual. The shock of Soviet-American strategic parity, in addition to American domestic and international trends, created pressures for change in American foreign policy. Détente was temporary and moved against the tradition of American policy in the postwar period. According to this view, Reaganism has deeper roots in the American sociopolitical structure. It represents not a temporary aberration in America's policy but rather the mainstream thinking of the country's ruling circles.

The bases of the Reaganite trend in foreign policy are the malleability of the American public and the extent to which anti-Sovietism and anticommunism have become firmly rooted in popular attitudes; the expression and exploitation of frustration among America's ruling circles and public over the decline of U.S. power; and the traditionally moralistic character of American foreign policy, with its aversion to Kissinger-style realpolitik. The failure of détente was entirely the fault of the Americans, who wish to deny the Soviet Union the equal role in international relations that it deserves.

This view argues that the tendency represented by Reaganism will not pass quickly from the American scene. Even should the Democrats achieve victory in the 1988 elections, the entire spectrum of American politics and policies has moved toward the right, and the pendulum may not swing back during the present generation. In any case, the Soviet leadership cannot base its long-range plans on the assumption that the present trend of American policy is a passing phenomenon.

Important as the differences between these views are, their similarities should also be recognized. It is often asserted in the United States that two distinct orientations toward the West characterize the Soviet foreign policy-makers. "America-firsters" are said to assert the absolute centrality of Soviet-American relations and hope for improvement in these relations. "Europe-firsters" are thought to see the greater opportunities in relations with Western Europe. Such a distinction, however, exaggerates the differences within the foreign policy establishment, which as a whole attaches central importance to Soviet-American relations—more than ever in the 1980s. It believes that the United States alone stands between the Soviet Union and its dominant international role.

The Soviet foreign policy elite does tend to divide on strategic and tactical objectives concerning Western Europe, especially in periods when relations with the United States are unlikely to improve. Then the Soviets advocate a very active policy toward Western Europe. Here the two Soviet evaluations of Reaganism suggest two distinct lines of foreign policy. The first school would court Western Europe mainly in order to realize the potential for influencing American policies toward the Soviet Union through European pressure. The second would advocate improving relations with Western Europe primarily to weaken the Western alliance and increase the cost of American confrontational policies.

Despite these differences, however, there are no illusions about how much can be gained from the West Europeans and how far differences between the United States and its allies can be exploited in the near future, especially on crucial questions of military policy.

The foreign policy elite are all hard-liners publicly on Soviet-American relations. For some, these views no doubt express real convictions; for others, they compensate for the earlier soft line toward the United States.

In the early spring of 1984, after Chernenko's death, unofficial Russia's fear and official Russia's anger dominated the atmosphere in Moscow. The urban population had been affected by the war scare fueled by incessant, agitated and strident vilification of the United States. The Party and government elite had been deeply stirred to hostility by the combination of perceived American insults and pressure, which were made all the more bitter by the Soviets' recognition of political vulnerability in their Eastern European empire and economic weakness at home.

Most striking was the intensity with which officials, and their aides and experts, responded personally to real or imagined slights generated in Washington. Westerners—Ronald Reagan foremost—are accustomed to viewing Soviet leaders and their advisers, regardless of ideological baggage, as pragmatic traffickers in power, as prudent calculators of risks and costs in international relations. This sanguine evaluation is in some measure belied by the sensitivity and emotion with which leaders and elites, who even at the height of détente remained publicly committed to ideological warfare, respond to strong doses of their own medicine from the American side. Part of their response was obviously calculated to mobilize Soviet public opinion for times of internal hardship and external pressure. In part, however, the anger of the leadership seemed to be genuine.

Reagan's rhetoric injured the self-esteem and patriotic pride of the political elites. His moralistic tone and his characterization of what the Soviets regard as achievements as crimes by international outlaws from an "evil empire," were impossible for the leaders and elites to swallow, especially as they followed so suddenly upon a decade of civility. The political culture of Soviet Russia, not to speak of its historical tradition, places great emphasis on words. Among the highly ideologized elites, words are taken very seriously. Rhetoric conveys existing attitudes and policy orientations. No less is expected of the adversary's rhetoric. For Soviet leaders and elites Reagan's rhetoric was and is political fact and policy pronouncement. The Soviets became convinced that far from mere posturing, Reagan's words reflected actual beliefs that heralded still tougher policies if the Soviet Union allowed itself to be pushed around. Thus even the subsequent muting of the administration's attacks, and the president's speeches in 1984 stressing the need for serious Soviet-American negotiations on arms control did not ease their alarm.

High Soviet officials believe that Reagan is determined to deny their nation nothing less than its international legitimacy, indeed its status as a global power. These objectives had supposedly been conceded once and for all by Reagan's predecessors, not to speak of America's allies. A rekindled sense of insecurity fires an angry and defiant response, a desire to lash out, to reassert self-esteem, to restore the diminished respect of others.

Without detailed information or profound understanding, Soviet officials often resort to ideology's simplistic formulas and to superficial comparisons with times past in explaining Reaganism. Reagan then becomes the spokesman of aggressive new business interests in the western and southwestern United States and of the military-industrial complex, which has reemerged to overcome post-Vietnam caution to seek new conquests and huge profits. The historical analogy used and probably believed in official circles is, ironically, the same that underpins the analysis of some in the West—the 1930s. Reagan's America is seen as an aggressive force plotting, if not to attack the Soviet Union, then to roll back the Eastern European empire, to isolate the Soviets, and to deny them equality as a superpower. Reagan's military budgets are seen as proof of his determination to alter the balance of European nuclear power and of global strategic forces. His refusal to accept a nuclear no-first-use declaration is said to reflect his willingness to contemplate nuclear war. The lesson of the 1930s—the Western policies towards Nazi Germany—is as obvious to Soviet leaders and their advisers as it is to Reagan: "Appeasement" can only bring disaster.

The intensification of suspicion in an already paranoid regime is not difficult to imagine. Mistrust of Reagan and his policies is profound and total. A high Soviet official harangued me for twenty minutes on American culpability in the Korean Air Lines disaster. It was, he insisted, deliberately engineered by Reagan's people so that the Soviets would be forced to shoot down a passenger plane, thereby exposing them to international condemnation and loss of stature. From all appearances, he believed what he was saying.

The Soviets contemplate present and future relations with America soberly. They expect only the worst from Reagan and are preparing for it—an accelerated arms race, efforts to destabilize Eastern Europe, closer military cooperation with the Chinese and so on. At formal and informal meetings with Americans they speak more earnestly and aggressively than in the recent past. Like their American counterparts, they no longer harbor illusions about the prospects for cordial relations over the long term.

The Soviets expected that Congress and the media would act to moderate the President's policies. Instead they were stunned by Reagan's masterful maneuvering of increased military budgets through Congress during a recession, reduced social expenditures, and controversial programs like the MX missile and the B-1 bomber. They were amazed as the media deferred more to Reagan and criticized him less than any president since Kennedy.

Soviet expectations that Reagan would fail were disappointed. They hoped the Democratic Party would battle energetically against Reagan's policies. Instead they saw only lethargy and the absence of any coherent and imaginative alternative. They expected that European public opinion would constrain Reagan and prevent deployment of medium-range weapons in Europe. But they suffered a major defeat as the INF deployment commenced. The Soviets believed that the post-Vietnam syndrome would restrict American activism abroad. Instead they had to watch the invasion of Grenada to the accompaniment of public applause, the covert war in Nicaragua, and the dispatch of American marines and a large naval task force to Lebanon. The Soviets thought that Reagan would moderate Israel's policies. Now they see American support for Israel as a strategic asset in the Soviet-American competition in the Middle East. The Soviets feel that during the period of détente they underestimated the strength of anti-Soviet feeling in America. They accuse Reagan of skillfully exciting popular fears of Soviet world domination.

Starting from the end of 1983, a new tone and a new trend in the President's Soviet policy has been recognized and commented on by both Americans and Western Europeans. The sharp decline in hostile and offensive language about the Soviet Union and its leaders, the return to a two-track policy, the resumption of arms negotiations, numerous signals to the Soviets to encourage a more moderate perception of Reagan's policies and plans for the future—all these changes have been noticed by observers and reported to the leadership. It appears, however, that the dominant Soviet view of the "new" Reagan is not very different. They have not been impressed by the shifting attitudes of the administration. What did change was their view of the immediacy of the danger Reagan presents. The alarmist predictions were toned down somewhat.

This new view continues to be entirely negative about Reagan, but recognizes the necessity and wisdom of negotiating with him. It sees a tactical change and a strategic continuity. The sources of the tactical change have been the pressure from Congress, the American people, and especially America's European allies. In contrast to Reagan's first term, the Soviets now pay serious attention to the obvious split in the administration and consider the influence of moderates like George Shultz and Robert McFarlane to be partly responsible for the shift. Yet they are convinced that even if Reagan's mind is with the moderates, his heart is with the hard-liners like Caspar Weinberger and Richard Perle.

Soviet analysts point to a number of factors as indicators of strategic continuity. Reagan's basic goals and attitudes, in their opinion, have not changed. He still stands for the destruction of the Soviet system, its international isolation, the denial of its legitimate rights as a global power equal to the United States. His first-term policy of radically changing the balance of military power has been reinforced by what appears to be a national commitment to the Strategic Defense Initiative, "Star Wars," which Reagan does not seem to consider a negotiable issue. Star Wars is uniformly judged by the Soviets as an attempt to achieve American strategic superiority, that is, a first-strike capability. The Soviets see no change in Reagan's position on East-West trade, which they regard as economic warfare. Despite the generally toned-down rhetoric, Moscow points to a number of official, semiofficial and private statements on issues of special sensitivity to the Russians, including the validity of the Yalta agreements, which touch upon the very legitimacy of their Eastern European empire.

The Soviets have gotten accustomed to Reagan. They are much less panicky and apprehensive as to where his policies will lead. The end of the prolonged leadership succession and the high hopes for their new leader have contributed to the feeling that the tide may be turning and that ways can be found to deal with America.

An example of the sophisticated and moderate view of the "new" Reagan can be glimpsed from a paper by a prominent Soviet specialist on America. A view of this sort does not often find its way into Soviet publications. While describing various tendencies in American foreign policy, the author defines Reaganism as a right-wing internationalism and describes its major characteristics as follows:

1. America's vital interests are global in nature. A *sine qua non* for economic prosperity, social stability and "survival of democracy" in the US is creation of a global order which would be more favorable to US political and economic activities abroad.

2. Creation of such an order means providing maximum freedom to international movement of private capital, and strengthening military-political structures designed to secure that freedom. The military-political measures to that end include: achievement of US military superiority over the Soviet Union; a tightening of the American alliance system; a stepped-up use of force, both open and covert, against revolutionary movements in the Third World; policies of economic warfare; an ideological offensive against socialist countries under the slogan "democracy v. totalitarianism."

3. The domestic components of this policy are: an expansion of the economy's military sector at the expense of the civilian economy and social policy; freer and more advantageous conditions for entrepreneurial activities inside the US (deregulation, lower taxes, government-corporate pressure on the unions to curb their power); a strengthening of the presidency; a general toughening of the political regime, including limitations on the news media.

The effects of Reagan's foreign policy, which the author defines as Cold War II, on the American domestic situation are analyzed thus:

> By raising the specter of nuclear war and the prospects for direct US military involvement abroad, Cold War II policies have sown discord in American society on questions of nuclear weapons, arms control and interventionism.
>
> Finally, the Cold War–induced measures to curb "excesses of democracy" and increase overall regimentation of the society's political and spiritual life provoke a whole range of acute and deep conflicts, rubbing upon some of the most sensitive spots in American consciousness.

The new Reagan of the second term is explained in the following way:

> Right-wing "internationalism" had clearly exposed its flaws by the end of President Reagan's first term, and in 1983–84 the administration took steps to broaden its approach on both flanks. On the one hand, it cultivated more actively nationalist trends, represented in the Republican coalition by the New Right. The invasion of Grenada, Star Wars, a number of protectionist measures, and a good deal of bombastic "America Is Back" rhetoric significantly galvanized Reagan's support not only with the right wing, but also in broader "isolationist" segments of the population.
>
> On the other hand, the administration made a nod toward liberal "internationalism," agreeing to start new arms control talks with the Soviet Union and modifying its Cold War rhetoric with a few pro-détente statements.
>
> Conceivably, it may look to some like a broader, more balanced approach—in the sense that the administration may appeal, depending on the situation at hand, either to those who keep faith in a "long twilight struggle against Communism," or to those to whom a good foreign policy is "rapid and resolute action" without big losses and tangled commitments to foreigners, or to those who are mostly concerned about the danger of nuclear war and the rising international tensions.
>
> The "balanced" approach did make the intended impression on the voters and secured Reagan's reelection, but it in no way looks like a ready and thought-out policy. The core of the approach remains the same old Cold War model, which is clearly as much of a lemon as the ill-fated Edsel.

The author rests his hopes on the development of what he calls radical reformism, which, as he sees it, was represented in the 1984 election by Jesse Jackson. He characterizes it as follows:

> Radical reformism appeals mainly to those groups in American society which have suffered from conservative policies—that is, to the poor and a considerable part of "the middle class," Blacks and Hispanics, working women, students, and some other groups. Attention of radical reformers is focused primarily on America's social and economic problems, and they tie prospects for their solution with the goals of curbing corporate power, a fairer distribution of national

wealth, a broadening of public services, and an overall democratization of the American political system. . . . Their active search for a democratic alternative to the reigning bipartisan conservatism may sooner or later create on the left flank of American politics a new catalyst of political process, similar to what was done in the 1970s by the New Right on the opposite side.*

By the late summer of 1984, well before the election campaign was over, the Soviets knew that they would have to deal with Reagan. The Andropov statement of September 1983, that Russia would not negotiate with America if the new INF missiles were deployed in Europe, has been abandoned. The INF issue became a subject of the Geneva talks without any preconditions, as did the START arms negotiations. The repeatedly used Soviet official phrase, that "we can wait out Reagan until America comes to its senses" has faded away. As the Russians have often discovered in the past—starting with their 1950 UN walkout on the Korean War issue—withdrawals and public displays of hurt feelings ultimately do not pay in relations between superpowers. Yet, as Strobe Talbott warns us, congratulations may be premature:

> It may turn out that the Soviet leadership has allowed itself to be lured back into active diplomacy with the U.S. not so much with much hope of transacting *cooperative* business in Geneva and elsewhere as with the intention of conducting more effectively the *competitive* aspects of the relationship across the board.†

The combination of the Reagan challenge and the recognition of their own vulnerability reinforces caution in Soviet international conduct only in the short run. In the long run it may lead to high-risk behavior by fueling anger, obduracy, and defiance. Soviet leaders are frustrated by the unexpected difficulties and dangers that they have encountered in translating their military might into international political and economic gains. They expect respect from their adversaries and the uncommitted world. What they cannot tolerate is not being taken seriously.

There is domestic pressure in Russia for national assertion. Public opinion of a kind does exist in the Soviet Union and does affect policy. The unrelenting media attack on the United States has created an atmosphere in which the public expects its leaders to act forcefully. In this sense the leadership has become a captive of its own rhetoric and may well be caught in a cycle of self-fulfilling prophecy. The allegiance of the political public and especially the elites cannot be manipulated as completely as in Stalin's day. Nor does the leadership enjoy that unlimited flexibility that in the past allowed Soviet diplomats to call Hitler a mad

* From unpublished papers presented at a conference titled "The Psychology of U.S.-Soviet Relations," Spring 1985.

† Ibid.

dog one day and a few months later send him friendly telegrams. So relations between the Soviet Union and the United States will remain tense even as arms negotiations proceed.

Until the beginning of Reagan's second term and the selection of Gorbachev as general secretary, there was no coherent and active Soviet policy that looked beyond tactical goals toward a discernible middle-range strategy. When Gorbachev took charge of Soviet foreign and security policies this became one of his very urgent tasks.

18

Gorbachev and the Dilemmas
of Foreign Policy

It is sometimes said that in U.S.-Soviet relations there is always one constant and one variable: The constant is provided by Soviet foreign policy, the variable by American foreign policy. This view is neither entirely right nor entirely wrong. American policy towards the Soviet Union has changed since World War II. Yet there does exist a line of continuity, combining two ever-present strands: a desire to avoid a nuclear clash or confrontation, and a determination to contain Soviet external expansion.

As for Soviet foreign policy, it is true that they have pursued an uninterrupted growth of nuclear and conventional power. It is also true that Soviet ambition and ideology reinforce each other and fuel a drive for expansion. Yet, the Soviets do adapt to changing circumstances and, given the realities of the nuclear era, combine their driving ambition to translate military power into international influence and dominance with the wish, not much different from the West's, to avoid nuclear war. The problems with Soviet foreign policy are its exaggerated expectation of how military might can be translated into concrete power, and the conflict between a policy of expansion and the desire to prevent nuclear war.

Soviet foreign policy at any given moment is primarily determined by tactical goals, opportunities, and temptations. Such a policy does not differ much from that of other great powers in the past or from the United States. The characterization of American policy as pragmatic and Soviet policy as ideological confuses the question of means and ends. Both Soviet and American policies are highly ideological, although of course subscribing to different ideologies. Both are more or less pragmatic, al-

though often far from successful in their evaluation of what means will
achieve which goals.

The cycles of Soviet foreign policy may be described in terms of an
ebb and flow of international activism, with offensive, expansionist periods alternating with defensive, consolidating ones. Under Stalin from
1934 to 1939, a defensive foreign policy was preoccupied with breaking
international isolation in the face of the Nazi and Japanese threat. Stalin's postwar foreign policy offensive halted with the stalemate in Korea
in 1951. Under Khrushchev the years 1957–62 saw a foreign policy offensive, while in 1962 and 1964 there was a retrenchment. So while the
general tendency of Soviet foreign policy is dynamic, assertive, and ambitious in the long run, its tactics in the short run oscillate between expansion and retrenchment. At the present juncture, the policy can best
be described as a holding operation, a response to both international and
domestic circumstances.

The Soviets are afraid of overextension internationally and have become more cautious in deploying their relatively scarce resources. They
are afraid of troubles in their Eastern European empire and particularly
in Poland, where the precarious stalemate still threatens to explode.
They are eager to preserve détente with Western Europe, for its economic benefits, its potential moderating influence on America, and its
potential for driving a wedge into the Western alliance. They have been
pushed by the unprecedented succession process in Moscow toward domestic political preoccupations and away from new foreign involve-
ments. Finally, they were and still are searching for a good alternative to
the centerpiece of their policy in the 1970s—the détente with the United
States.

Gorbachev's mark on foreign policy could already be seen when
Chernenko was still alive though not active. In a speech to party leaders,
he tried to define the problem of relations with America from a long-
range point of view. He advised the leadership not to get bogged down
by problems in these relations; the Soviets should avoid becoming preoccupied with tactics on one or another issue and should think instead in
strategic terms. In the months following Gorbachev's assumption of
power, the style of his foreign policy-making started to emerge. He toned
down the alarmist, sometimes even panicky, reaction to American foreign policy steps, and introduced a calmer attitude. He has paid much
greater attention to the public relations side of foreign policy, and seems
determined to utilize and manipulate the Western media to get the Soviet point of view packaged in the most attractive ways. He has dealt
with foreign policy problems in a much more systematic and consistent
way. He has tried to turn foreign policy away from its reactive and
negative pattern, to take the initiative and propose positive steps

and programs instead of only criticizing Reagan and American positions. And he has projected a confident and dignified image to the outside world and to his own people.

Gorbachev swiftly and significantly changed policy-making staff and took control over their activities. But the context of policy has not changed with his assumption of power. He will have to deal with serious issues and dilemmas inherited from the past Soviet international activity.

There are four principal problems that affect the conduct of Soviet foreign policy in the 1980s. The first is the most important and most difficult to resolve, the internal material and spiritual decline. Soviet ambitions require a large commitment of resources that can be employed in support of a dynamic foreign policy. Yet such a commitment will deepen the internal crisis. Growth of the military at a rate faster than in the last decade, or even at about the same rate, will not only lead to the stagnation or even decline of consumer spending, but will also cut the growth of investments that are crucial for the increase in labor productivity. For the first time in the post-Stalin years, then, the growth of military spending has become an insurmountable barrier to the rise in consumer spending and investment. Expansionism is no solution to internal difficulties, as it had been for many previous empires, but rather an added burden.

The Soviet Union must decide whether to concentrate on its domestic problems and those of its empire while moderating its foreign policies and international ambitions, or to continue on a course that combines efforts to restore internal dynamism with the pursuit and expansion of its ambitions as a global power. Of course, such choices never amount to clear-cut either/or propositions, but instead involve changes in emphasis, in intensity of commitment, in degree of preference. Yet it is exactly such a change in degree—sometimes dismissed as merely marginal—that can reverse a trend and make possible compromises between the Soviet Union and the West that were impossible before. How Soviet leaders resolve their conflicting policy priorities will sharply influence the international situation in the years ahead.

The second problem—the incongruity between a managed rivalry with the United States and foreign expansion—has come into sharp focus through the détente experience. Military, political, and to some extent economic relations with the United States constitute the heart of foreign and security policies. Experience has shown, however, that stable and beneficial relations cannot be reconciled with the pursuit of expansionism, and an unrelenting buildup of military power. On the one hand, the necessity of accommodation with the United States presses the leaders to be cautious and limited in their pursuit of "peripheral" expansion;

on the other, turmoil in the Third World creates opportunities for aggrandizement that they are tempted to exploit, opportunities that may not recur if allowed to pass. In recent years the leadership learned that détente is not divisible; a linkage between the various responsibilities of détente and the benefits it offers is unavoidable, given the domestic political realities of the United States. It might be argued that in the areas where Soviet-American relations are not a zero-sum game, and where the interests of the two sides overlap (such as in arms control), accord ought to be reached regardless of confrontation on other issues. But the experience of the 1970s demonstrates that this is simply not possible.

The Soviets are reaching the conclusion that they cannot have their cake and eat it too. They have learned that by pursuing marginal advantages in Africa, the Persian Gulf, and the Middle East they damage their relationship with the United States. Regardless of the internal American political situation, a continuation of the pattern of Soviet behavior of 1975–79 will preclude the restoration of even a semblance of détente even on arms control questions where compromise is possible and plausible.

At the same time, while détente with Western Europe survived the break with the United States, Soviet policies in Eastern Europe nevertheless have weakened the Western European commitment to accommodation and the leaders are becoming aware of that. Furthermore, events like the successful installation of the intermediate-range missiles and the electoral success of conservatives in Britain and West Germany have shown the Soviet Union cannot count on a weakening of the American-Western European-Japanese relationship if it pursues aggressive policies. The Soviets have also found that détente with Western Europe, while highly gratifying and economically profitable, is not a substitute for stable relations with the United States.

Here again the leadership faces a difficult choice: between sacrificing the American relationship in order to gain advantages in the Third World and adjusting military and foreign policies in such a way as to restore that relationship—for example, agreeing to a solution in Angola that would lead to the withdrawal of Cuban troops.

The third problem concerns Soviet activities in the Third World. After Stalin's death, the leadership recognized that the world beyond Soviet borders, and especially the non-Western world, was an arena of opportunity. They began to court the Third World. But as every great power has learned, to translate pure military strength into status and influence is not a simple task. At first, under Khrushchev and in the early years of Brezhnev's rule, the Soviets proved naive about what they could accomplish, underwriting any and all aspirations of Third World countries. The results of Soviet efforts are not very impressive, even though they should not be dismissed out of hand: Their major exploit, domination of Egypt, proved temporary; the communist movements of Third World countries either rejected Soviet domination or the Soviets were out-flanked on the left; expenditures were no match for Western aid and trade, and did not seriously influence the politics of the recipient states or the character of their political systems; the term Marxist-Leninist as used by many of the newly created Third World states proved meaning-less, in most cases simply serving as a cover for personal dictatorship and the greed of the leader; the so-called noncapitalist path of development in the Third World, for which the Soviet Union was to act as instructor and protector, proved to be nothing more than a slogan; and Third World instability has shown itself to be not only a condition for Soviet involvement and influence but also a barrier to the continuation of such influence.

Well into Brezhnev's tenure, the leaders came at least partly to recog-nize the temporary nature of the profits from their investments in the Third World, and the rising costs. Their conclusion, it seems, was to opt wherever possible for actual power rather than for mere influence. While the Soviets did not abandon efforts to achieve low-cost influence over Third World regimes, they probably decided that long-lasting power over those countries could be attained only through a visible and serious military presence of their own or allied forces. This fact partly explains the pattern of military intervention in such places as Afghanistan, Ethio-pia, and Angola.

In the years to come, Moscow's foreign policy resources will be even more skewed toward the military than in the past. The Soviets will con-tinue to put a premium on situations where Third World instabilities escalate into armed conflicts or civil wars, so that arms and military in-tervention count for a great deal. Yet this lack of balance will under-mine—sooner rather than later—the efficacy of Soviet aid, and the extent and durability of the control over Third World regimes.

This manner of acquiring power through military intervention may in the long run prove disappointing. The Soviet Union has little to offer except its own and Cuban military forces. Efforts by Third World coun-tries to achieve economic viability can hardly be satisfied through ties with the Soviet Union and Eastern Europe. Yet the danger that military intervention will still be repeated in the 1980s is quite high.

If in the 1970s the Soviet leaders could engage in foreign military ad-ventures without recognizing what effect they would have on the United States, today there can no longer be any doubt in their minds about the danger of repeating the pattern. A decision to do so, then, will not only be premeditated and carefully considered, but will also signify a major reordering of foreign policy priorities, an evaluation that relations with the United States cannot improve in the foreseeable future, and a willingness to take much higher risks than before.

The leadership must also confront the cost of interventionist policies. Already, subsidies to Eastern Europe and Cuba are being cut. Yet Soviet policy-makers have only one alternative to military intervention: to do nothing. While doing nothing is unattractive, military intervention can be very dangerous because of worse relations with the United States or an outright confrontation, and exorbitant costs.

The third problem may be identified as that of anticolonialism versus hegemonism. When the Soviets' presence in the Third World was virtually nonexistent, it was easy for them to act as a champion of anticolonialism. Today, Third World states expect not only vocal support from their Soviet friends, but major economic aid with no strings attached, and a willingness to take political-military risks. The Soviet Union is perceived by the Third World as an industrial power that has the responsibility of responding actively, as the Western democracies also should, to demands for global redistribution of wealth. Rejection of any claim on a share of its national wealth sometimes places the USSR on an equal footing with the Western states.

Furthermore, Soviet military presence in the Third World creates either an enmity among some Third World countries—aid to Ethiopia, for instance, alienated Somalia—or at least a feeling of unease. It is a reminder of the colonial experience, complete with unpleasant overtones of white supremacy. China's unimpeachable revolutionary credentials have led some Third World leaders to consider seriously Chinese accusations that the Soviet Union is a hegemonic power striving to replace past colonial dependency with something remarkably similar. The Soviet Union has unconditionally supported so-called national liberation struggles in the Third World. These struggles were invariably directed against Western powers and regimes sympathetic to the West. The sign of the changing times is that the Soviets and regimes sympathetic to them are themselves targets of national liberation struggles—in Angola, Mozambique, Yemen, Afghanistan, Cambodia, Nicaragua and Ethiopia.

If one accepts this image of the Soviet situation vis-à-vis the Third World, as many in Moscow do, then the leadership must carefully weigh its desire for expansion against the dangers of such expansion, its uncertain long- or intermediate-range results, and its increasing costs. Decisions on these issues will be difficult to make and at the same time important to the cast of international relations in the coming decades.

In response to these dilemmas the Soviets will probably concentrate selectively the expenditure of their foreign policy resources on much fewer but more important targets of opportunity in the Third World, but they will commit more resources to these targets.

The fourth foreign policy problem stems from its connection to the internal legitimization of Soviet power. The legitimacy of the regime in the eyes of its people and elites is much stronger than many Western analysts assume. Yet it is shakier than in the industrialized democracies or even in some traditional authoritarian systems. Legitimacy founded on acceptance of existing legal rights is obviously relatively weak in the Soviet Union. By contrast, in the post-Stalin period legitimacy based on performance increased markedly. Yet the mainstay of popular legitimacy was and is provided not by communist ideas and the communist system, but by traditional Russian nationalism disguised as Soviet patriotism. (Communist ideas and the communist system still seem to play a major role in legitimizing the regime within the elite.)

The legitimization of Soviet power through performance has visibly declined in recent years and it will in all probability decline even further in the next decade. Where can the leadership find further reserves of legitimacy for its regime? It is doubtful that military growth alone is such a source. The authority of the armed forces among the youth seems to have lowered sharply. Moreover, the new middle class and the middle generations of the working population are by now fully cognizant of the effect that military spending has on their standard of living. For military growth to provide a reinforcement of the regime's legitimacy it has to have a recognizable purpose acceptable to the population.

It is doubtful whether foreign policy achievements could become a more important factor of legitimization than they were in the 1970s. As mentioned above, the pursuit of expansion abroad will carry with it greater risks and will be much more costly than earlier, thus further weakening the regime's legitimacy based on domestic performance. There is little doubt that Soviet rule in Eastern Europe has the support of the elites and at least the Russian population if not necessarily the non-Russian peoples. The security of the country, its defense against possible aggressors from both East and West, also provides a legitimizing function for the Soviet regime.

It does not appear, however, that adventurism in distant lands is equally attractive to the home population, or even to certain parts of the elite. This apparently does not evoke legitimizing support—at least the leaders do not believe it does, judging by the minimal media coverage the Soviets have given their actions in Angola, Ethiopia, and Afghanistan. There exists a widespread resentment of the costs of those enterprises. There is similar dissatisfaction about subsidies to Eastern Europe, Cuba, and Vietnam. (In both cases the public exaggerates the size of Soviet expenditures.)

So the surprising and ironic conclusion is that, at a time when domestic performance is declining and foreign expansion by military means is becoming risky and quite costly, a cold war provides a way to strengthen the legitimacy of the regime. A new cold war fulfills all the requirements necessary for popular support: for the Soviets it is a defensive enterprise; it appeals to Russian patriotism and justifies the sacrifices necessary for the growth of military expenditures; it establishes a siege mentality that fosters an atmosphere conducive to the strengthening of the conservative themes of unity, law, and order.

This is not to say that, given a cost-free choice between détente with the United States and a cold war, the Soviet Union would pick the latter. After all, détente also provides legitimacy. But a cold war, despite all the risks and difficulties that it would arguably create, may ease domestic political difficulties. The best situation for the West would be neither a return to cold war nor détente but rather a combination of some elements of détente (such as arms control) and of containment (such as heightening the risks of expansionism), with confrontation as a policy course when the credibility of the West requires it. But, if the leaders cannot have détente, they may for domestic reasons prefer a cold war to the hybrid preferred by the West.

It is still too early to say how Gorbachev and his closest associates will deal with the dilemmas of Soviet foreign policy. In the light of domestic and international circumstances his maneuvering room is limited. His natural inclination to pursue a highly activist foreign policy must be tempered by the recognition of Soviet weaknesses and domestic goals. Nevertheless, an outline of Gorbachev's foreign and security policies is already emerging and its main directions can be identified.

He is attempting to reestablish his country's international image as a superpower that is strong, decisive, and determined to pursue a global role of equality with the United States. He will find opportunities to damage the image of the United States in the international arena. He will intensify significantly the effort to weaken the American alliance system. And he will try to obtain an arms control agreement that will permit him to concentrate on more pressing domestic economic and social problems.

In pursuing the improvement of the Soviet image, Gorbachev seems determined to maintain Soviet control over traditional or relatively new areas of influence or dominance. The Soviet Union, in Gorbachev's eyes, may be too weak to show weakness.

A principal example of this saber-rattling is the emerging hard line towards the Eastern European allies. Eastern Europe is as hard-pressed economically as the Soviet Union, but it cannot expect significant help from Moscow. Favorable economic performance in Eastern Europe depends primarily on close economic relations with the capitalist, industrial democracies of the West. Eastern European social stability, which requires close relations with the West, and the political orthodoxy of these regimes, which requires limitations on Western contacts, cannot easily be reconciled. Gorbachev appears to be unequivocally in favor of political orthodoxy.

The crackdown on liberals in Eastern Europe is meant to prevent political unrest and the drift of the region from tight Soviet control. The policy is not sympathetic to the desires of the leaders of most of these countries for closer ties with the West. It demands a greater contribution from Eastern Europe to the development of Soviet natural resources while trying at the same time to impose higher prices for Soviet exports and lower prices and better quality for Soviet imports. It is a policy directed against political and economic innovations.

Another example of the hard line is in Gorbachev's Afghanistan policy. Soviet military pressure in the Afghan civil war has increased, while efforts to close the lifeline of anticommunist guerrillas from Pakistan have dramatically intensified. The scorched earth policy—indiscriminate air attacks on mountain villages—intended to destroy the guerrillas' infrastructure, has become more ruthless. Whatever frustrations the Soviets may have endured in their prolonged Afghan adventure, there is no sign the new leadership will settle for anything less than a secure communist government in Kabul.

In Africa Gorbachev does not seem to be pursuing the policies that were characteristic of the 1970s. The Soviets do not intend to pour good money after the bad that they invested in such marginal areas as Mozambique. Yet they seem determined to continue commitments where their prestige and credibility are already involved. Their commitment to Ethiopia, the African state that comes closest to being a Leninist regime and that has an important strategic location, is undiminished.

In Angola, where the Soviets have underwritten the presence of 32,000 Cuban troops, their commitment to the survival of the present regime is likely to remain firm. Angola is a country where the Soviets have to show their determination and their staying power. Any increase in South African or American assistance to the insurgent UNITA forces is certain to be counteracted by greater Soviet commitments. Angola is also the Soviet outpost in the coming struggle of the black continent against South Africa. The new Soviet leadership will continue its commitment even if the issue of Namibia should be resolved to the satisfaction of the West; that is to say, even if South African intrusions into Angola diminish. But it is highly unlikely that the next few years will see the Soviet Union engaged in a broad international offensive along the lines of its 1976–79 activism in Africa and Asia. What is more likely is a combination of further retrenchment in the positions they already hold, and active opposition to American policies.

Gorbachev's attempts to tarnish the current international image of the United States stem from the new image of America as a strong and decisive global power. He will try to undermine the impression of American strength by exposing and exploiting U.S. weaknesses.

There are a number of worrisome situations in the world where, by choice or necessity, American interests are engaged. Although the problems of these trouble spots are domestic and regional, and although they were not created by the Soviets, the Soviets can and probably will destabilize and exploit them.

One example is Pakistan, which is the most likely area of Soviet-American confrontation. The internal stability of Pakistan is questionable, and Soviet help to opponents of the present regime could be effective.

Pakistan may soon be able to produce nuclear weapons which might well invite a preemptive Indian attack against its nuclear facilities. The country is under much-increased Soviet pressures to terminate its role as a haven for Afghan refugees and a training base for Afghan guerrillas. Soviet attacks against Pakistani territory bordering Afghanistan have increased significantly. America's ability to provide effective military support to the Pakistani is limited. All these factors make the situation there potentially explosive.

Another area ripe for Soviet exploitation is Central America, particularly Nicaragua. The Soviets are pleased with the American preoccupation with Central America. They may be particularly gratified that the Reagan administration has devoted so much attention to Nicaragua, guaranteeing that the survival of the Sandinista government there will be seen as an American defeat.

Nicaraguan President Daniel Ortega Saavedra's 1985 meeting with Gorbachev in Moscow signified an increased Soviet interest in Central America and an upgrading of the commitment to provide military and economic aid to Nicaragua. The Soviets have little to lose in Central America. Their aid to revolutionary forces is indirect and on a scale that precludes a Soviet-American confrontation of the Cuban missile crisis magnitude.

What they want is to place the United States in a no-win situation. Even if Congress relaxes its restraints on American aid to the Nicaraguan rebels, Soviet and Cuban help is probably sufficient to ensure the survival of the Sandinista regime short of an American invasion. After the Reagan administration's talk about the strategic significance of Nicaragua, the Sandinistas will stand as a glaring example of American impotence. On the other hand, an invasion would brand the United States as an imperialist power throughout the Third World and also among American allies in Europe.

The situation in the Philippines resembles that of Iran in the late 1970s. The main difference is that the primary anti-Marcos forces are not Muslim fundamentalists but leftist revolutionaries. In the future, Soviet aid to the Filipino insurrectionists would appear to offer too attractive an opportunity to diminish American stature to pass up.

The United States may have no attractive options in the Philippines. A policy of all-out support for Marcos is doomed to failure. The Philippine military services are too closely connected with Marcos to offer even a temporary alternative. Democratic forces are disjointed and weak.

There are many other areas where the Soviets can try to harass the United States—the potentially unstable situation on the Korean peninsula, or the Middle East, particularly Egypt, which has severe domestic problems. Under Gorbachev's consolidated leadership, the relative passivity of Soviet foreign policy may come to an end. The capacity to make bad things worse for American interests may be utilized more energetically.

Gorbachev will seek to drive a wedge within the Atlantic alliance by trying to aggravate differences between America and its allies. Actually, this was probably the core of Soviet foreign policy in the early 1980s, and it was not very successful. Despite differences between America and Western Europe on economic questions, on trade with Russia, on military spending, on arms control strategy, and despite their diverse perspectives on Soviet behavior, the alliance has remained relatively united. In 1983, the Soviets launched a campaign against the installation of American intermediate-range missiles in Western Europe that was second in intensity only to their drive against West German participation in NATO thirty years ago. The failure of this campaign constituted one of their major defeats of the postwar era. Yet most of the issues that divide the alliance remain unresolved. There is potential for greater success in a new round of the anti-American campaign if Gorbachev can show more imagination and skill than his predecessors.

Basic differences remain between the United States and Europe on the issue of East-West trade and credits, and these differences may grow in importance unless there is a change in the American position. European economic recovery has been slow. The decline of Europe as an innovative technological power is visible. Economic competition between Europe, America and Japan will intensify. The importance of the Soviet and Eastern European markets will thus increase at a time when the Soviets will be launching a major effort to import Western technology. American efforts to restrict its allies' trade with Russia may create resentment.

Western Europe, in NATO and in the Common Market, is divided against itself. The progress of decades toward a unified Western Europe has been reversed. Economic interests and simple old-fashioned nationalism divide European powers. The idea of Western Europe as a political entity unified by a parliament has been laid to rest. (In the last election, less than one-third of the voters participated.) A divided Europe is a much easier target for Soviet courting. Moreover, experience has shown that the dissonance between Europe and the United States is greater when the continent is divided.

The domestic political situations in Britain and West Germany are significant for Euro-American and Euro-Soviet relations. Although different, both countries share a potentially disruptive characteristic—the main opposition parties have moved to the left, and threaten to unravel the basic consensus on military and foreign policies toward the Soviet Union and Eastern Europe. Both Americans and Europeans have responded to this shift complacently, believing that the swing left would ensure conservative rule for at least the next decade. But in the late 1980s the electorate could turn out the Tories and the Christian Democrats, not because of their foreign policies, but because of the failure of their economic programs. How far the Labour Party and the SPD would moderate their views on foreign and military policy if elected is an open question. What is almost certain is that both parties will have major differences with American economic, political, and military policy toward the Soviets. If the Soviet Union does not ineptly intervene in British and German politics, as Gromyko did in the 1983 German elections, it could contribute significantly to the victory of the British and German left.

West Germany, the key European country in the Atlantic alliance, occupies a special place in Soviet policy toward the West. There are opportunities for the Soviets to sow discord: The current German recovery is progressing slowly. The postwar economic miracle is over. With its political-economic tradition (Germany after all is the place where the welfare state came into being), high unemployment and inflation, and the cost of transition to a high-tech economy are probably unacceptable to the population and will carry a great political cost for the Christian Democrats. Hence Eastern markets will be of growing importance.

The Social Democrats have significantly moved left in foreign policy and military issues. We are witnessing the rebirth of German nationalism, this time on the left. The SPD is no longer the party of Helmut Schmidt. Acclaimed by a national poll as the most respected and admired man in West Germany, he received only one-third of the votes among SPD people polled. The majority of his party objects to most American policies in the Third World and to Ronald Reagan's Soviet policy. The SPD voted against the installation of the INF, and on arms control issues it stands closer to the Soviet Union than to the United

States. It supports such Soviet initiatives as nuclear freeze and the no-first-use commitment unequivocally, so it provides a good target for anti-American initiatives.

There is also the issue of German unification, or at least improvement in West/East German relations. This issue has reentered politics and the public consciousness in Germany. In 1970 it was a question for the distant future; today it is a central issue for the present. Some Germans entertain illusions of making a deal with the Russians that will lead to a process of gradual unification. The price for such an agreement is obviously withdrawal from NATO. But even the majority places the emotional issue of relations between West and East Germany high on the list of priorities. To put it simply, the West Germans feel responsible as never before for the fate of their fellow Germans in the East. The Soviet Union holds 20 million East Germans as hostages, through whom it can influence West German politics and policies.

Finally there is the increasingly complex question of arms control. The Western Europeans' attitude toward Soviet-American negotiations on arms is close to being schizophrenic. They do not want tension or confrontations between America and Russia and they press the United States to make arms control agreements. But Western Europeans are also apprehensive about accords that go too far. They are afraid that such deals could leave Western Europe out in the cold. They are sensitive to a Soviet-American condominium, which they are sure is of interest at least to the Soviets. They have limited faith in American security guarantees. (A French defense official once said: "If we were in your place we would never seriously entertain such guarantees.") Reagan's Strategic Defense Initiative may increase European doubts about American commitments. A program that is intended to ensure American invulnerability, and is certain to be adopted by the Russians as well, can only leave the Europeans to fend for themselves.

The most important goal of Gorbachev's emerging foreign policy is his deep interest in avoiding a new cycle of the arms race. Gorbachev appears to understand the uniqueness of the present moment, with both superpowers poised to cross new thresholds of arms competition with consequences that are difficult to predict. We are at the point where the momentum of major technological advances threatens to take charge of our nuclear strategies and long-range security policies. We are reaching a stage in the development of new weapons, particularly space-based, and land mobile systems, and cruise missiles, at which the essential requirement for an agreement—verifiability—may become extremely difficult if not impossible to fulfill.

The extremely sophisticated technology involved in America's proposed SDI program will put the Soviet Union at a clear disadvantage and require heroic efforts to compete. Gorbachev's concerns therefore provide an important reason for his genuine interest in a breakthrough in arms control negotiations. They provide an opportunity for the United States to press the Soviets for concessions with regard to offensive weapons that will make the superpower military balance more equitable and stable.

The various elements of Gorbachev's policies may be well orchestrated to serve his primary goals. Yet they do not resolve the dilemmas that plagued his predecessors. Even in the short run Gorbachev's goals may not be compatible with one another. The pursuit of both an arms control agreement and an aggressive foreign policy is reminiscent of the policies that ultimately brought an end to détente.

Gorbachev may believe he needs to demonstrate strength in order to drive a successful bargain with the United States. That view may be a tragic misunderstanding of how America regards the Soviet Union. If Gorbachev succeeds only in arousing American distrust, will he be able to back away from an aggressive policy in order to pursue arms control? Or will he then decide that moderating an aggressive policy will be a fatal sign of weakness?

Gorbachev's leadership is still very young, but his speeches and writings and those of his associates already provide a rich source of clues as to the directions in which he is moving. One position stands out clearly. It will probably become the prime distinction between Brezhnev and Gorbachev. Under Brezhnev consensus was the most valued characteristic of policymaking. His foreign policy was a hostage to his colleagues in the Politburo. His Politburo, however, was a heterogeneous group whose members differed on many foreign policy issues. These differences were tolerated, and the consensual politics were a product of compromises between the different views. It appears that such variety will not be tolerated in Gorbachev's Politburo. Foreign policy will more closely reflect his views and therefore have fewer internal inconsistencies and ambiguities than that of Brezhnev.

Gorbachev's positions are becoming clear and are in many respects different from the attitudes and preferences of his predecessors. His position on the issue of reconciling domestic decline with foreign policy aspirations is unequivocal. Domestic problems have priority over foreign policy goals, and they are a necessary precondition of improving Soviet international status. In many speeches Gorbachev has criticized Brezhnev, implicitly and explicitly, for not recognizing that foreign and international security aims have to be based on domestic strength if they are to be successful in the long run. This position is not isolationist, and does not mean withdrawal from foreign positions already achieved. Also, a central goal of Gorbachev's effort to get the Soviet Union moving again is precisely internationalist—to make Russia a dominant world power.

The dilemma of Soviet foreign policy finds a response from Gorbachev that is different from Brezhnev's and quite original. Military expansion in the Third World is not high on his list of priorities. In light of limited Soviet resources and other, higher priorities, expansion in the Third World is less important to Gorbachev than it was to Brezhnev. Yet it seems that Gorbachev does not believe that restraint in that part of the world will be sufficient to establish better and more durable relations with the United States. The importance of relations with America concerning arms control is fully recognized; the necessity of making a deal in this respect is very strong. But Gorbachev does not seem to expect any agreement to be on terms satisfactory to the Soviet Union. Most critically he sees limited opportunities for improvement in overall Soviet-American relations. In arms control negotiations, as noted before, Gorbachev appears to be willing to make major concessions concerning strategic offensive weapons, verification methods that would include some on-site inspections, and acceptance of research on Star Wars systems if tied to a moratorium on testing and development. His position seems to indicate a belief, however, that this will not be enough to satisfy Ronald Reagan.

Gorbachev apparently places his hopes for avoiding a new arms race and preserving the existing balance of forces not so much on negotiations as on skillful, continuous manipulation of Western European and American public opinion. Regardless of whether an acceptable arms reduction agreement can be reached, his basic attitude seems to be that the Soviet Union can gain very little from America politically and economically. In all his speeches, articles, and interviews the idea of restoring détente with the United States seems to lack conviction. If these impressions are true, there is little need for Gorbachev to make concessions to America aside from arms control, since there is almost no expectation that the tensions in Soviet-American relations will subside in the foreseeable future.

Although Gorbachev assigns lower priority to direct expansion in the Third World, he remains committed to the preservation of such important investments as Angola, Ethiopia, and Afghanistan. This position grows logically from his sense of priorities with domestic revitalization at the top of the list, but may very well be temporary. One can characterize it as a decision by Soviet leaders to postpone, but not to abandon, the next round of major intrusions into regional conflicts and instability. There is no difference between Gorbachev and his predecessors regarding the centrality of Soviet military power in gaining international power and influence.

Gorbachev believes that domestic dynamism, social discipline, technological progress, and better living standards are crucial for the country's sociopolitical stability. The legitimization of the regime through performance, however, also has a foreign and security policy dimension that is a constant theme in Gorbachev's public statements. The danger from abroad, the necessity of discipline and hard work in the defense of Mother Russia, the sacrifices needed to make the Soviet Union strong, the patriotic duty of selfless work all figure prominently in the Party's communications to the population. In a situation in which material incentives have to be limited, and promises of the good life have to be delayed, the patriotic theme, the siege mentality stressed so much by Yuri Andropov, continue to be Gorbachev's main stimulus for the population to regain the system's dynamism.

Philip Stewart identifies three types of foreign policy orientations among Soviet leaders. He calls the first accommodationist and campaign-oriented. It is centered on America and is characteristic of Brezhnev. The second is Leninist-internationalist, and was represented by Suslov. The third is simply nationalist. Obviously his typology presents "ideal type" abstractions—no Soviet leader fits fully into a single category. Yet the distinction is valid in the sense that individual leaders do tend to approximate one or another of the three positions. Gorbachev is representative of the third, nationalist type.

In his analysis of the change in the Kremlin, Stewart reaches the following conclusion. The shift to Gorbachev

may be characterized as movement from the moderate, outward and western orientation of the Brezhnev era to a tough, uncompromising, predominantly inward, nationalist or isolationist perspective, . . . over the next period, Soviet behavior may be determined to a far greater extent than during the seventies by internal Soviet priorities and self-reinforcing nationalist perspectives on foreign policy than by any policies or actions of the United States.*

Stewart may exaggerate the present trend in Moscow, especially when he calls it "isolationist." Moreover, it is still too early to tell whether these conclusions are valid in the longer run. What is valid beyond doubt, however, is that America now faces a leader who differs from his predecessors in orientation and sophistication. To be ready for his challenge, accurate assumptions and perceptions of the Soviet Union are necessary.

* Philip D. Stewart, "Toward Nationalist Self-Assertion: Soviet Policy After Brezhnev," forthcoming in *Political Science Quarterly* (Winter 1986).

19

Assumptions and Perceptions

The psychological factor in Soviet-American relations, the different national characters of the two antagonists, their images of each other, and the predispositions of their leaderships, all influence their behavior. The least studied aspect of the conflict, it is an important determinant of its direction and intensity. It cuts across all the other dimensions and makes the rational management of the conflict even more difficult.

The picture that will emerge from the following analysis will be one-sided and incomplete. The analysis will slight the assumptions each has about the other that are correct and the patterns of behavior that serve to further each country's goals, and will minimize the danger of nuclear escalation. The principal preoccupation here is with the Soviet Union—the nature of its system, of its leadership, its ideology and so on. These views will be presented against the mirror of American perceptions of Russia.

From the many psychological aspects of the Soviet-American conflict I have selected one to consider—the perceptions that the leaderships and the political publics of the two superpowers have of each other. These perceptions are often faulty, but they nevertheless provide many assumptions on which the preferences of the elites and the policies of the superpowers are based.

The assumptions are as important as military capabilities. The nuclear relationship is not simply a matter of the number, accuracy, and destructiveness of the weapons systems that both sides possess, but also of the attitudes of their political and military leaders. It is not purely nuclear military capability that will determine the future, but the intentions, and the intended or unintended consequences of the actions, of the Soviet and American leaders who control those weapons. To paraphrase McGeorge Bundy, the problem between America and the Soviet Union is not only one of warheads but of heads.

Even as both the Soviet and the American leadership are determined to achieve as many of their international goals as possible, they are also both subject to a strong, self-generated pressure to control their actions rationally, to regulate their competition. Any such cooperation requires that the opponents understand each other's moves and motives. An important determinant of one state's interpretation of another's specific actions is the first's image of the second. Both Soviet and American leaderships often misperceive each other, and these misperceptions deeply affect the nature and evolution of their conflict. The conflict is not primarily a consequence of misperceptions; its roots are extensive and concern the values and interests of the superpowers. The misperceptions, however, make the conflict more difficult to manage in the dangerous nuclear era.

Current false assumptions about the Soviet Union span the whole range of the American political spectrum. The misperceptions of liberals and the left now appear less substantial than they did before the late 1970s. The Soviet treatment of dissidents, as well as foreign military adventures, has done much to reshape the views of the American liberal left. The misperceptions of the right, on the other hand, have been reinforced during the Reagan Administration.

Among these, the comparison of the contemporary Soviet Union with Nazi Germany holds pride of place. There was justification for such a comparison in Stalin's day. Yet even then it stretched the evidence. When one contrasts Stalinism and Nazism, the question is not whether the Stalinist regime was better or worse than the Nazis, but whether, given its worst excesses, it was very different. But now, the correlation has very little validity, either as a description of contemporary Soviet reality or as a policy guide for America.

The Soviet Union today is significantly different from Nazi Germany in the mechanism of rule, the economic system, the ideology of the people and the elite, the existence and management of a multiethnic internal and external empire, the prevailing culture, the use of coercion, the level of politicization of everyday life, and the role and social place of the military. In general, the Soviet Union has come to resemble the type of highly authoritarian system well known from the Russian past.

The most important difference between the contemporary Soviet Union and Nazi Germany lies in the two countries' international behavior. Unlike the Nazis, the Soviets do not want war with their adversaries. They do not propagandize or glorify offensive military action as the means by which to achieve their international goals. The foreign adventures they undertake are in fact low-risk and low-cost affairs, and not the "go-for-broke" gambles of the Nazis.

The immorality, the oppressiveness, and the brutality of the Soviet system are not in question here. Soviet international behavior, however, differs from that of the Nazis in its pragmatism, gradualism, and caution. The Nazi regime was a racist and extraordinarily uninhibited personal dictatorship with an enormous nationalistic appetite for conquest, whereas the Soviet Union is an oligarchical system that takes advantage of the weak, is fearful of the strong, and is averse to taking risks in situations where it may lose everything. This was true even before the advent of nuclear weapons.

The political vocabulary of many American leaders and their mental image of the Soviet Union are sometimes rooted in the period between the world wars. Deals with the Soviets are said to be impossible or extremely fragile; Soviet signals for mutual agreements are dismissed as propaganda; there are implicit suggestions of the inevitability of a military clash; any search for greater stability of the superpower relationship through mutual compromise is deemed an immoral appeasement of the forces of evil. This approach, insofar as it reflects the belief that the Soviet Union of today is fundamentally similar to the Nazi Germany of yesterday, is mistaken.

Americans also tend to misperceive the current phase of the Soviet Union's international activity and its approach to order and disorder. The view that still predominates within part of the American liberal establishment identifies the Soviet Union as a status quo power, incorrectly equating its international goals with its domestic character.

No analyst of the Soviet domestic system would describe it as anything but highly conservative. Yet in the minds of leaders and elites the internal system, with its emphasis on the cult of national unity, law and order, and its condemnation of individuals and groups who threaten to impair it, goes hand-in-hand with an openly revolutionary attitude toward the international system. The Soviet Union is very far from being an international status quo power.

Of course one may argue, as some do, that Soviet leaders have lost their zest for foreign adventures and do not assign top priority to revolutions abroad (which is partly true), and that when necessary, they do not hesitate to betray their followers and the revolutionaries abroad (which is entirely true). Yet it would be quite erroneous to conclude that the leaders are not intensely committed to promoting change in the existing international order, and to supporting by any means at their disposal the emergence of left-oriented "follower" states abroad that would increase their circle of satellites and clients.

The Soviets' willingness to betray their followers and leftist revolutionaries when expedient does not signify any decline in their commitment to accelerating and exploiting the breakup of the international status quo. The ideological justification for such conduct was laid down long ago by Stalin, whose definition of international rules of behavior can be reduced to two circular propositions: 1) The interests of world revolution and those of the Soviet state are indivisible; 2) Only groups which support, uphold, and promote Soviet international interests can be considered revolutionary.

The Soviets' deeply ingrained and fundamental opposition to the international status quo has many negative consequences. In the long run it puts the Soviet Union and the United States on a collision course. It also calls into question the stability of any Soviet-American agreements about the Third World whenever the "correlation of forces" changes, or whenever the American will to deny the Soviet Union the advantages that may accrue from revolutionary change recedes. There is, however, one positive consequence. The United States may be able to raise the risks and costs of supporting revolutionary developments beyond the level that the Soviets would consider compatible with their overall interests.

A further misperception concerns the process of Soviet foreign policy-making. There is a view that the Soviet leaders follow a master plan for world conquest, and that almost every major step in their foreign policy is part of such a program and even proceeds according to a timetable. Nothing of the sort can be deduced either from the international policies of the Soviet leaders, or even from the writings of Marx, Engels, Lenin, and Stalin—the Soviet Union's holy writ.

The view of the leaders and elites on the direction and evolution of world history is of course deterministic. They expect the final victory of communism. But their formulation of short- and middle-range foreign policy is not so different from that of any nation-state. Soviet foreign policy stresses what is possible and prudent. It is derived from careful evaluation of both the temptations and opportunities to maximize international influence, and the dangers and obstacles to such influence, which dictate restraint and caution. Not that Soviet international behavior consists simply of a reflexive reaction to external stimuli. Over the long run, the leaders display an almost pathological peoccupation with the security of their own system that is coupled with a powerful ambition to expand their influence. Without doubt, they also believe that in the long run they are on history's side. But even under Stalin, and especially under his successors, the goal of worldwide communization has not been the operating principle of Soviet foreign policy. The joke that the goal of communism can be compared to the horizon—the closer you come to it the further it moves away—better portrays the Soviet view of the world's future than does the concept of some master plan.

There is also the opposite belief, that all Soviet foreign policy, particularly Soviet-American relations, can be explained by a vicious circle in which American action generates Soviet reaction, which in turn leads to American counteraction.

Such a view is doubly satisfying. It carries the comfortable assumption that a change in foreign policy toward the Soviet Union will be reciprocated. And it assumes that the Soviets' international behavior would be basically identical to that of industrial democracies if only Western, and particularly American, foreign and military policies would leave them the option of cooperation instead of forcing them into conflict.

This view is naive and faulty because it neglects the divergence of Soviet and Western interests, values, and stages of development. Western revisionism of the origins and history of the Cold War, which assigns equal blame to the two protagonists (or even places the larger blame on the United States), may be correct in particular instances, but suffers from myopia and misreads or neglects the domestic pressures that determine Soviet behavior.

Aggressive international behavior, both after the Second World War and in the 1970s, was not primarily the result of Western actions and Soviet reactions, but of Kremlin drive independent of Western behavior. The task for American leadership is not to treat the Soviet Union gingerly so as to bring out the best human traits in the Kremlin, but to regulate the conflict and competition with an inherently aggressive Soviet Union. Washington's goal should not be détente for its own sake, but rather curbing Soviet expansionism while avoiding a nuclear confrontation.

Americans of all political persuasions misperceive the people who shape Soviet foreign policy. One could only wish the various misperceptions were accurate. If the present Soviet leaders were doctrinaire fanatics, then their foreign policies would be so far out of touch with the reality of the contemporary world that their defeat would be assured. If they were simply cynics, they could be bought off by their wealthier adversaries.

The Soviets are neither fanatics nor cynics. True, any doctrinaire belief in the tenets of Marxism-Leninism has long since burned out. But top Soviet politicians are probably not much more cynical than their European counterparts, although they have a greater opportunity to conceal their attitudes from their own people. Like politicians the world over, they have constantly to reconcile their beliefs and values with the exigencies of existing situations, and with the quest for effectiveness and success.

Soviet intolerance of internal dissent is dictated by mundane considerations: preserving their power and hold over their own population. Yet at the same time their apparent cynicism, in whatever form and degree it exists, should not be mistaken for a lack of strongly held beliefs. To conclude that because the leaders' hypocrisy can be so easily detected—as well as their immorality, and Byzantine politics, and scheming—they are therefore bereft of any code of beliefs and behavior, would contradict what we know about all types of political leaders and political psychology. Not unlike Americans, the Soviet leaders do subscribe to beliefs, though of course entirely different ones.

The Soviet leaders are highly nationalistic, believing in the spiritual strength of Russia and its people, and often suspicious of anything foreign. At the same time they are very proud of the changes that their party has wrought in the Soviet Union. The certainty that history is on their side is associated with a view of historical development according to which ends justify means and revolutionary change becomes the basic form of progress. They hold a deeply ingrained belief in the instrumental values of science and technology and in modernization as a fundamental goal. They are economic determinists, but they put great stress on the need for order and discipline and on the interest of the collective as opposed to the individual. They see military power not only as the key instrument of their security but also as a way to international stature.

American perception of the nature and character of the Soviet policy makers carries with it one especially pernicious consequence, which has to do with matters of form. Even if one accepted, as many Americans do, that the Politburo is nothing but a group of Mafiosi with the *capo di capi,* the general secretary, at its head, the question of form in relations with such people would still be of importance. Sociological studies of the Mafia show beyond any doubt that this organization developed an intricate and strict code of relations both internally and with the outside world. Probably at the core of this code is the concept of "respect," as it is also at the center of Soviet sensitivities.

There is a Russian proverb that expresses the Soviet attention to form, especially in public actions between governments very well: "Do what you have to do, but do it according to the accepted form." This form is very close to the Oriental value of saving face. It goes beyond the use of personalized abusive rhetoric in interaction with foreign leaders, though the rhetoric is important. (The written and spoken words of "responsible" officials have a much greater weight in Soviet society than in democratic countries.) It also includes the question of continuity of agreements reached by the two superpowers and restraint from unilateral actions embarrassing to the adversary. The argument that the Soviet Union itself may not conduct its business according to this code does not change the fact that its leaders are extremely sensitive to American behavior that does not take this code into account. It may be very tempting to give the Russians a taste of their own rhetorical medicine, especially when it is so often appropriate, but by doing so we may undermine our own interests.

With regard to the importance of style and form in dealing with the Soviets, separate incidents are less important than the more general attitude. It concerns the inability of some American officials to resist the temptation to demonstrate publicly their "toughness" towards the Soviets and their pleasure in making the Russians squirm. Such an attitude is counterproductive. By introducing an unnecessary emotional factor, it is less likely to make the Russian leaders crawl than to stand up and fight for respect. It is necessary to cage the bear, but there is no need to jab him with a pitchfork through the bars of the cage.

The view of Soviet leaders as fanatics or cynics brings us directly to yet another misconception of the Soviet Union held by influential American political groups. How often do we hear the question from well-intentioned people who are shocked and frightened by the direction in which Soviet-American relations are moving: "Why can't we reach an agreement with the Soviets that will avert the danger of nuclear war? After all, they are people just like us, and if we only could explain to them our sincere desire for peace we can reach agreement." Of course the Russians are people: They love and hate, feel pain and fear, are loyal or treacherous, ambitious or stolid, amiable or rude, clever or stupid. Those who have had the opportunity to know Russia well are constantly amazed by the intensity of Russian friendship. But to those who think that Soviet leaders, officials, and experts are people like us, let me say that if I have learned anything from my study of the Soviet Union, it is that the Soviets are not like us. They have a different prism through which they see the world, a different set of priorities that they impose on their society, and a different way of appraising domestic and international affairs.

We are divided not only by our dissimilar interests as great powers, but also, and more importantly, by different values and beliefs to which we subscribe, by a different historical experience, and by devotion to different systems and rules of behavior that are based on contrasting principles and priorities of human existence, human values, and political beliefs. To understand each other is not easy. And understanding each other as far as possible does not eliminate the problem but leads only to its reemergence on the rational level. If there are to be successful negotiations with the Soviets on issues in which both sides are vitally interested and to which both are committed, if there is to be an effort to decelerate the conflict and to move the world away from nuclear confrontation, the first thing that American leaders must understand is that their Soviet counterparts are individuals with beliefs that do not correspond to their own. However alien, unnatural, illogical, and unacceptable the Soviet beliefs may seem to Americans, this is exactly how American beliefs look to the Soviets.

Many in the West have pronounced the death of Soviet ideology. Despite their corruption and cynicism, however, official Russia still subscribes to and believes in an ideology that is a mixture of simplified Marxism-Leninism, the Russian tradition, and the experience of postrevolutionary Russia. The best way to understand it is not as a doctrine but as a culture that dominates the socialization and politicization of the Soviet leadership and permeates its thinking and its values. The Soviets do believe that their system is better for Russia than is Western democracy. They are convinced that history will vindicate them. And, looking back at the not so distant past, they have a sense of accomplishment in how far, in material terms, they have moved and pushed Russia.

However difficult it is for Americans to come to terms with the realities of official Russia, understanding them will not be sufficient to break the escalating conflict and arms spiral. What divides the two countries are truly opposed interests, which divergent beliefs or ideologies endow with symbolic weight. Yet if America understands and takes seriously Russian beliefs, and works to help the Russians understand the reality and the depth of the United States' commitment to its beliefs, then the strength of common international interests, and the catastrophic seriousness of the potential nuclear danger, might promote a better adaptation of both ideological orientations to the realities of the nuclear world. It would not be the first time in history that external (or for that matter internal) stimuli led to a reorientation of Soviet beliefs and actions. In the 1920s the Soviets switched from revolutionary, internationalist priorities to "socialism in one country." In the post-Stalin era they moved away from isolationism and autarky.

Another attitude in the West is well known in the history of conflicts. It is the dehumanization of adversaries, the view that all good resides in one's own nation, while all evil is attributed to another.

The dislike of democratic citizens of the authoritarian Soviet system, the aversion to past crimes and brutalities and present harshness, is natural, inescapable, and positive. To trust in the Soviets' good will when one is weak is sheer folly; to believe in assurances of good will when one enters into an agreement with them without verification is to close one's eyes to reality. But it is wrong to dehumanize the complex experience, thoughts, and fears of the Soviet people, and demonize the Soviet leaders, denying any validity to their fear of war, their legitimate security concerns, and their recognition of the imperative need to create some sort of *modus vivendi* with the other nuclear powers.

The *modus vivendi* that the Soviets have in mind may be very different from what Americans wish. The United States should fight for those agreements that bring closer the ideal of the world order to which it subscribes. But Americans nevertheless should seek agreements with the Soviet leaders. They can despise those leaders, deplore their actions, and have not the slightest trust in their promises; but both nations have to deal with the realities of the nuclear age. Whatever beliefs and goals the current Soviet leaders represent, they and their people are as fearful of nuclear war as are Americans, and are eager to find a way to minimize this danger and establish a means of coexistence with the United States.

Another assumption about the Soviet Union stems from the attempt to analyze its political scene in terms derived from American politics: the division into "hawks" and "doves." It is often argued that American policies toward the Soviet Union should be tailored to strengthen the position of the "doves" within the Soviet leadership. But there is no convincing evidence of such a division.

Even if it exists, it would be futile for the United States to aim its policies to try to influence Soviet leadership politics. Not enough is known about the personal, political, or ideological divisions in the Politburo for outsiders to hope to be able to manipulate it. The best course for the United States is to pursue its interests regardless of who presides in the Kremlin or what the momentary configurations of leadership politics in the Soviet Union may be.

Finally, there is an assumption of particular importance. It holds that Western policy generally and American policy in particular have the capacity to affect the Soviet Union's international behavior principally by exerting influence on its internal developments. This is wrong, and worse, dangerous. It spawns exaggerated and unrealistic objectives. It has its origins in the truism that the deepest sources of the foreign policy of any nation are rooted in domestic politics. In this respect the Soviet Union is not different from other states; the sources of its international conduct derive from the ambitions of leaders and elites, their expansionist impulses, and their messianic Marxist-Leninist ideology, which encourages them to see the Soviet power as the instrument of an inevitable historical process.

The logic of this argument moves with some justification to the observation that during the entire post–World War II period, American policy could significantly modify neither Soviet foreign policy nor Soviet tendencies toward expansion, regardless of whether it used sticks or carrots. Some draw the conclusion that the only way, short of an all-out war, for

Western policies to shape Soviet international behavior is to speed up the process of change in and decline of the Soviet system. Richard Pipes of Harvard University (and in 1981–82 Director of Eastern European and Soviet Affairs at the National Security Council) has made this case. In his book *Survival Is Not Enough* he concludes:

Experience has repeatedly shown that attempts to restrain Soviet aggressiveness by a mixture of punishments and rewards fail in their purpose because they address the symptoms of the problem, namely aggression, rather than the cause, which is a political and economic system that induces aggressive behavior.*

In an endorsement of Professor Pipes's book, Ambassador Max M. Kampelman writes: "His message that the Soviet Union can be a partner in peace with us only when and if it makes peace with its own people is particularly worthy of serious attention in the face of the unrealistic illusions which permeate so much of Western political dialogue today." This case leads to the attempt to affect the domestic roots of Soviet international behavior rather than to deal with Soviet policy as the consequence of domestic pressures and tendencies beyond our control.

But the ability of the West to effect change within Soviet Russia, let alone rapid change, is severely limited. Even if the West were able to impose extreme economic choices, the system would not crumble, the political structures would not disintegrate, the economy would not go bankrupt, the leadership would not lose its will to rule internally or to be a global power.

The origins of the belief in U.S. leverage over domestic Russian affairs are not difficult to identify. They lie in the perceptible deterioration of the Soviet economy, the expectation that this will lead to political disintegration or radical change, and the idea that a policy of unrelenting pressure can accelerate the process. There is no shortage of literature about the "coming revolution in Russia," the "revolt of the nationalities," the widening dissident movement that will "engulf the Soviet intelligentsia," and, in an ironic reversion to dogmatic Marxist analysis, the expectation that an economic breakdown will lead to a political collapse. All of these expectations rely on worst-case interpretations of the abundant evidence that in the 1980s the political and social stability of the Soviet Union will be severely tried; that the economic situation will be more difficult than at any time since Stalin's death; and that the empire has probably peaked and has already slipped into a period of decline.

Economic stress provoking political failure is conceivable in the next

* Richard Pipes, *Survival Is Not Enough: Soviet Realities and America's Future* (New York: Simon and Schuster, 1984), pp. 13–14.

decade, but it is very unlikely. What generations have wrought with so much sacrifice, cruelty, and conviction will not change radically under pressure of economic decline or leadership instability. The system is not now nor will it be at any time in the next decade in the throes of a true crisis of survival. It boasts enormous, unused reserves of political and social stability that will enable it to weather deep difficulties. The economy may stagnate, it may even experience a slide for a year or two; but, like the political system, it will not collapse.

As for the related goal of inhibiting Soviet military growth by ensuring that the drastic escalation of costs in a new arms race exerts intolerable pressures on the economy, this too is unrealistic. Aside from the fact that the United States alone does not have sufficient leverage to impose such costs on the Soviet Union without the cooperation of Western Europe and Japan, it cannot prevent Soviet leaders from engaging in a military buildup should those leaders deem it essential to their security. If threatened by the prospect of a radical shift in the present balance of military power, the Soviets will certainly redeploy their economic resources, restrict civilian consumption, enforce internal discipline, and, under the slogans of a siege mentality and unbridled nationalism, arm and arm regardless of the cost. This much is confirmed by Brezhnev's last speech, and echoed in Gorbachev's speeches.

Another flaw in such an effort to affect Soviet foreign policy stems from the weakness of Western options, given the political and economic realities in the United States and the Western alliance. While lecturing the West Europeans on the need for economic sanctions against the Soviet Union, the Reagan Administration was unable to sustain the American grain embargo. Moreover, the Western allies are not likely, as the gas pipeline affair of 1982–83 demonstrated, to be willing to curtail trade with the Russians.

The costs and limits of efforts to influence Soviet policy pose important questions. There is without doubt a general recognition in the United States that greater military strength is required to counter the Soviet challenge. There is, further, a realization that the détente that permitted the Russians a military buildup at home and expansion abroad was misguided. But the decline of inflation and the economic recovery have hidden the vulnerability of an American economy saddled with high interest rates and huge budgetary deficits. Without the resources a healthy economic base provides, the United States may well be unwilling to bear the kind of foreign policy burdens that are currently contemplated.

While the roots of Soviet foreign policy are to be found in the domestic system, the extent to which foreign policy is able to be expansionist depends very largely upon international factors: on the temptations and opportunities that the international environment offers; on the risks and costs of exploiting those opportunities. Here the potential of the West for increasing the risks and costs of expansion has a significant influence on Soviet behavior. It is not within the West's power to bring about significant change in the Soviet system or to redirect radically the leadership's preoccupations from international to domestic concerns. But it is possible to frustrate those Soviet global ambitions that are most threatening.

Although the essential outlines of the Soviet global drive are defined by the nature of the Soviet system, the range of possibilities that can fit within those outlines is very broad. Soviet foreign policy may involve military engagement in regional conflicts and civil wars or outright invasion of neighboring countries; but it may also concern ideological and political attempts to gain influence over the policies of other countries. There are differences among the various forms of Soviet expansionism, between competition with and without dangerous confrontation, and also between a Western policy of containment that increases the danger of war and one that can succeed without such dangers.

By making clear that the objective of American policies is not to work for the radical change of the Soviet system or its collapse, American policy could be much more effective in mobilizing the West, influencing the course of specific policies, and diminishing Soviet international aggression. Those objectives fall far short of what we may wish, but they are realistic and attainable.

The two extremes of recent American policy with regard to East-West relations, that is, the détente of the 1970s, and the approach of the 1980s—have characteristics in common. Both assumed that changes in Soviet behavior could be achieved in a short time; détente sought to influence Soviet internal and international attitudes through positive and negative linkages, recent policies through continuous and increased pressures. Both sought to avoid facing the long-term Soviet challenge: Détente overestimated the effects of combining incentives and disincentives on Soviet behavior, and the harder line of the 1980s exaggerated the political consequences of Soviet economic and social difficulties.

The Reagan Administration's policies enjoyed some success because they coincided with Soviet overextension, with leadership succession, and with a phase of retrenchment in foreign policy. Yet, in the longer run, the United States will fail unless its goals and expectations regarding the evolution of the Soviet system are significantly readjusted and the policy instruments used to influence its foreign policy appreciably broadened.

Difficulties between the superpowers are multiplied by Soviet misconceptions of America and of Western democracies that are at least as great and harmful. The Soviets believe in American economic determinism, whereby changes in American policies and internal differences among policy-makers are explained by the effect of shifts in the domestic economic situation on the relative power of various economic "power groups." They are convinced that American beliefs in democracy, liberty, and human rights are hypocritical and counterfeit, and that U.S. leaders are cynics who manipulate these concepts in their struggle against the Soviet Union. They do not understand that American foreign policy-makers have a high degree of autonomy from business pressures. They subscribe to the notion that U.S. military policies and the arms race per se are primarily the result of the power and effectiveness of the American military-industrial complex. They misunderstand the ways in which the U.S. system functions—particularly the linkage between its policies towards the Soviet Union and the movement of elite and public opinion, that is, the influence of public opinion on American policies; they display an extraordinary lack of sensitivity to the impact of Soviet actions and policies on the policies and actions of the United States. They believe that the American media are not only tools of the economic establishment, but also malleable instruments of the political power holders. They exaggerate the ability of the American government to influence the policies of its allies and clients. They assume that the United States is aiming at a first strike capability and will not hesitate to strike first if the circumstances are right. And finally they believe that, despite many differences in form from traditional imperialism, the United States is propelled by the same urge for domination and exploitation as the imperialist powers of old.

Here is an excerpt from a paper by a Soviet expert on America, one of the most enlightened and astute Soviet students of international relations:

[Since the end of the Soviet-American wartime alliance] and up till now U.S. international behavior, as seen from Moscow, could be for the most part described by just one word—outrageous. The most pronounced components of that behavior are the following:

Striving for Pax Americana,

Struggle for military supremacy,

Expansion in the Third World,

Attempts to impose the "American model," American schemes and yardsticks on the rest of humanity,

Disregard for international law, international agreements and gentlemen's understandings,

Continuous moral lecturing of others without being appointed, elected, or asked to be the world's preacher or judge.

As regards the dominant foreign policy style, it is erratic and bellicose.

These are the impressions about the main characteristics of American foreign policies since the end of the Second World War that are shared by the Soviet layman and the expert on the United States. The differences between their viewpoints that might exist are just nuances, resulting from the amount of information and of time devoted to pondering the problem.

This is the author's preamble about the motives and nature of postwar American foreign policy. The remainder of his lengthy paper elucidates the particular points of his general statement. This was not an article published in the Soviet Union but a paper presented at a small Soviet-American conference, where the author had freedom to express his own views. The following is typical of some of his statements:

I believe for instance that the main reason why American leaders cling so much to the NATO mechanism is not because they really believe NATO to be the prime force against the Soviet Union, but because it is the sole instrument left in their hands to continue U.S. domination over Western Europe, at least to the extent of influencing foreign policies of West European countries. And throughout the world Washington clings wherever it can to the vestiges of Pax Americana. And that is one of the main obstacles to ensuring a stable peace on this planet.

Having defined NATO as an American instrument for subjugating Western Europe, he then evaluates the American concept of deterrence in a truly fantastic way:

The fact is that whatever the past or current definitions of convenience of the term "deterrence" are, from the very moment of its appearance in American military usage it had nothing to do with the defense of the United States or its allies. It was purely an offensive, aggressive concept. A somewhat vague and forgotten English word was found to denote a total strategy, a world military offensive if necessary, or optimally, global military pressure to achieve Pax Americana. It was a syncretic, all-embracing concept.

The Soviet author turns to American attitudes toward nuclear arms control.

From the beginning of the atomic age the U.S. has been trying to pursue a double-track strategy: either the adversary capitulates through negotiations and a resulting international accord fixing his inferiority, or he will be forced to become inferior through an arms race, forced upon him, if not through actual employment of military forces. As an example of the first type of approach one may refer to the Baruch plan of 1946 for the so-called international control of atomic energy. The aim of this plan was crystal clear—to perpetuate the American monopoly over the atom bomb under the guise of international guardianship over peaceful uses of atomic energy. Another example of the same tactics—the START negotiations of 1982–84, during which the aim of the United States was to contractually freeze the USSR into a permanent position of inferiority.

After arms control, he provides an evaluation of what he calls American expansion in the Third World: "The attitude of official Washington to developing countries [is to see them] as America's natural vassals."

The author then explains why his country is engaged in a military buildup.

As the U.S. invasion of Grenada and the America war by proxies against Nicaragua show, Washington is still not averse to using "fire and sword" to impose the American "model" on other peoples.

The only thing, it seems, that is able to stop the U.S. in this endeavor is countervailing power. When confronted with equal power that it has to respect, Washington so far has stopped short of military action and restrained itself to preaching the virtues of the U.S. "model"—as the case of the U.S.-Soviet relationship shows. That explains why the Soviet Union has to keep up with the United States militarily—otherwise we and our allies would have probably long ago experienced the "reforming intrusion" of U.S. power.

That is the problem we have to face constantly, though it is not our conscious choice to race with the U.S. in arms buildups. But even when favorable conditions arise for deals to stabilize the Soviet-American military balance on the principle of equality and equal security and to cut armaments we again have to face incessant U.S. pressure to force on us the American model, American approaches and solutions.

Under the heading of "The Bellicose Style of U.S. Foreign Policy" the author's analysis includes the following statement:

After the collapse of the U.S. military intervention in Indo-China, when Washington for a number of reasons chose the course of détente, American leaders and foreign policy theorists seemed to recognize the limited usefulness of military power. There were well known pronouncements that military power cannot be automatically transferred into political influence, that truly strategic goals in the new multipolar world cannot be achieved through the application of raw military power, that the road to these goals ought to be political, not military.

But these realistic voices were soon lost in the roar of a new conservative wave—in the demands for a new foreign policy assertiveness, through the demonstration and use of military force. The military buildup, the creation of the Rapid Deployment Force for "express service" to remote regions of the world, increased military threats and finally, the Grenada invasion and SDI were concrete manifestations of this new American thinking.

It was hardly a grass-roots impetus as some U.S. theorists of military solutions and of arms buildups try to assert. It was more the mentality of venture capitalists who broke into the corridors of power in the country.

The author ends his paper by evaluating the roots of détente ("grass roots pressures on the American leadership") and then makes the following statement about Soviet behavior during that period.

We welcomed those developments, we helped them (to the extent we were responsible) to materialize, we looked forward to continuing to work hand in glove with the United States to alleviate tensions in the world, to promote stability, security and good-neighborly relations among all nations.

Regrettably, as the present situation shows, the Soviet-American détente of the 1970s happened not to be irreversible, despite the basic feelings of the people everywhere for it.*

The author of these random quotes is an honest man in the sense that he believes in what he is saying. In his entire paper, however, there was not a single reference to Afghanistan, Angola, Ethiopia, Poland in 1980, Hungary in 1956, dissidents and so on.

Soviet misconceptions about America and the West are played out against the background of a general approach to international relations that holds that relations between nations with different systems are basically antagonistic. As ideologues have endlessly repeated, even at the height of détente, no international agreement, no element of accommodation between East and West can nullify the "law of class struggle." Moreover, in the long term, the march of history favors the expansion of communism in its Soviet incarnation and the growth of its relative strength in the international arena vis-à-vis capitalist adversaries.

Knowledge of the United States among Soviet experts has grown immensely in the last fifteen years. Yet it is doubtful whether understanding has kept pace with the accumulation of factual knowledge. It is almost unavoidable that in the bureaucratic and oligarchic Soviet system, the expertise and advice of American specialists is adjusted to the views that the leaders want to hear. In the process of trickling up from the professional expert to the policy-maker, the nuances, subtleties, uncertainties, and ambiguities are probably lost.

It should be stressed again that misperceptions are not the core of the Soviet-American conflict. Even if the superpowers' views of each other were correct, as they often are, the conflict under any leadership would be sharp and dangerous. Psychologizing away the conflict is an imprudent exercise.

Some misperceptions, however, add virulence to the conflict and make

* From an unpublished paper presented at a conference titled "The Psychology of U.S.-Soviet Relations," Spring 1985.

negotiations much more difficult. Others divert the policy-maker from the realities of the dispute and create unwarranted illusions about the adversary. In the final analysis they produce a backlash that makes the hostility more dangerous. Misperceptions and false analogies account for at least part of the stalemate and spirit of confrontation that have dominated Soviet-American relations in the 1980s.

20

From the Past to the Future

Although both the Soviets and Americans recognize the need to manage their conflict, both have had difficulty in doing so. Many Americans consider the relationship with the Soviet Union during the 1980s as normal. This "normality" has been accompanied, however, by high tension. If steps are not taken on both sides to redefine what is normal, the tensions will multiply. Better management of the conflict depends heavily on learning the proper lessons from the recent history of Soviet-American relations.

Those who see the tensions of Soviet-American relations in the last five to six years as normal may be unnecessarily gloomy. But those who look back longingly to the artificial glow of the heyday of détente in the early 1970s should not expect the exceptional circumstances that led to it to reoccur. In the light of past experience, what both superpowers can expect at most in the coming years is a *military* détente, to stabilize the arms race, combined with more regular and substantive communications with the Soviet Union on political issues, which will however take place in the shadow of intense competition in the Third World.

Nuclear deterrence has prevented a direct Soviet-American military confrontation. Neither today nor in the past decades did we really face the danger of a nuclear war or even limited employment of nuclear weapons. The conclusion is clear: Nuclear deterrence is effective.

The American and Soviet leaderships have proved to be determined and able to avoid nuclear war. There is no reason to believe that this sanity will somehow evaporate. Its fundamental base is the recognition by both sides of the reality of nuclear deterrence. In this sense, deterrence will remain the only rational nuclear strategy.

The present size and level of destructiveness of the nuclear arsenal of both superpowers however, has moved, and continues to move, far beyond the necessities of rational deterrence. The pressure on both superpowers is growing to reverse the arms race and move in the direction of a finite deterrence. Negotiations may present the last chance in this century to agree on such finite deterrence, which would be minimal in size and destructiveness, balanced despite the differences in advantages and the geopolitical situation of the two superpowers, and most importantly, stable in denying to either side a first-strike capability.

In military questions long-term cooperation between the two superpowers is possible only if both sides are committed to parity rather than superiority. The desire to attain superiority is not only impossible to fulfill, it is counterproductive. It makes stabilizing the arms race and preventing nuclear confrontation more difficult.

In political and military relations, the two countries are caught in a bind. At the center of the conflict are political issues, that is, questions of intentions much more than of capabilities. Only if compromise can be reached on these issues, and a modicum of respect, trust, and civility created and preserved, are military agreements possible.

West German President Richard von Weizsäcker recently and rightly observed: "Experience teaches that it is not disarmament that points the way to peace, but rather that peaceful relations open the door to disarmament."

On the other hand, the political issues that divide the superpowers are very complex, and their positions are very far apart. They include the question of human rights in communist states, Soviet dominance over Eastern Europe and their pressure for political orthodoxy in these countries, the export of communist revolution as in Afghanistan and Angola, American support of democratic and/or nationalistic counterrevolutions, and restrictions on East-West trade. The only area where the superpowers' interests really overlap and produce the potential for agreement concerns arms control. Negotiations and agreements here will probably bear the entire burden of Soviet-American relations. There is no easy solution to this dilemma. The rational solution would require simultaneous effort and progress in both political and military sectors. If this proves impossible, however, the obvious priority belongs to military negotiations whenever the chances of progress and success seem plausible.

While the 1972 agreements on rules of behavior between the United States and the Soviet Union are ambiguous, both superpowers believe in prudence, which has prevented the escalation of their various conflicts to the danger point.

Since the time when the Soviet Union achieved strategic parity with the United States, there have been a number of occasions when matters could have gone out of control. In each case, however, the danger was defused by the judicious behavior of both superpowers. In the early days of détente the 1973 Arab-Israeli War provided an example of such behavior. The Soviet threat to intervene on the side of Egypt, implicit in the high-level alert of the armed forces, was abandoned quickly because of the strong American response. But the total destruction of the Egyptian military in the Sinai by Israeli forces was prevented by strong American pressure on its ally.

The latest example of good judgment came in Lebanon in 1984. In 1983 the Syrian air force suffered a disastrous defeat by Israel during its invasion of Lebanon. In response, Moscow deployed SAM-5 and SS-21 missiles operated by Soviet personnel in Syria, its last and only ally in the Middle East. In 1984 the United States, in trying to resolve the Lebanese civil war peacefully, brought two naval and air task forces to the shores of Lebanon and deployed a contingent of marines in Beirut itself. The Soviet and American forces were separated from each other by less than 150 miles. The potential danger of the situation was defused on the Soviets' side by their assurance that they would employ their forces only in case of an Israeli attack on Damascus, and on the American side by the withdrawal of forces when a face-saving opportunity arose.

From the experience of Soviet-American relations in the postwar era it is possible to define the "rules of prudence" that both sides have observed and, it is to be hoped, will observe in the future.

They avoid extreme behavior, and especially direct military intervention in each other's declared or recognized spheres of influence. Examples are American actions with regard to the Hungarian revolution of 1956 and in Poland during 1979–81, and the strictly limited Soviet engagement in Central America. While America does not now accept, and should never accept, the existence of the Eastern European empire as an irreversible fact, American policy in this regard excludes military options. Soviet support for the Sandinista regime in Nicaragua is low enough to avoid a confrontation there.

They act with restraint where vital interests of either superpower are involved (as with Soviet caution in their activity in the Persian Gulf, and American discretion in developing military cooperation with China).

They avoid direct confrontation or contact of military forces and are eager to disengage when such confrontation or contact seems probable, as in Lebanon in 1984.

They are willing not to corner the other side without a means of saving face when a direct confrontation does occur. The Cuban missile crisis started because Khrushchev broke the rules of prudence, but both sides showed judgment in ending the crisis.

They do not inflict a catastrophic defeat on a superpower's ally and therefore humiliate the superpower itself, as in the outcome of the 1973 Arab-Israeli War.

They refrain from even the most limited, that is tactical, use of nuclear weapons.

They consult privately about areas or issues of potential confrontation even at times of highly strained relations, as in Lebanon in 1984 and Iran in 1984–85.

Except for short intervals, the continuity of arms control negotiations goes on even in the face of great difficulties in general political relations.

They formulate explicit agreements to create mechanisms which contribute to the avoidance of confrontations. A prime example of such a mechanism is the Incident at Sea agreement. Each superpower closely monitors the actions of its adversary's fleets—incidents and complaints arising from this practice are the subject of regular meetings of high-level naval personnel from both countries. Another example is the "hot line" connecting the White House and the Kremlin, which can be used on very short notice by the leaders of both nations.

The rules of prudence have been tacitly observed with rare exceptions, because they served the self-interests of each superpower. Self-interest provides the strongest reason for the two to continue to observe such rules. Some of them, in times of improved relations, may even become more explicit and institutionalized. There might, for instance, be an agreement not to intervene directly with their own or proxy forces in regional conflicts. With notable exceptions, moreover, the tacit rules of prudence were also associated with tacit rules of mutual respect where harsh rhetoric was toned down and the legitimacy of global interests of the two superpowers mutually recognized. It is quite probable that these rules of mutual respect will again be adhered to. It may also be hoped that regular summit meetings, as a tool to reinforce the rules of prudence and respect, will become a norm in superpower relations.

For either superpower to be too quick to take advantage of its opponent whenever the correlation of forces moves in its own favor would be unwise and counterproductive. The change in the balance may be temporary and can quickly be reversed.

Soviet-American relations in the 1970s and 1980s went through two cycles—détente and the period of high tensions and very limited negotiations and communications. Both carry important lessons. In the first period the Soviet Union tried to take advantage of America by exploiting its period of weakness. Moscow's harsh and dominating attitude provoked surely and predictably a reaction that went beyond wise and calibrated response.

It was not long in coming. The rhetoric emanating from the Reagan

Administration was unnecessarily humiliating to the Soviet leadership. When combined with the announcement of the SDI as a non-negotiable national goal, it was perceived by the Soviets as an attempt to gain strategic superiority. In addition, most of the agreements reached in the 1970s were allowed to lapse. With regard to the American side, however, the most important action in the 1980s was inaction. The two-track position of competing with Russia in defense of America's security and against Soviet expansion, while at the same time negotiating on the key issue of arms control, was abandoned. The American position was in part a justified response to Soviet behavior in the 1970s. However, it also has to be seen from the point of view of opportunity costs, of what could have happened in arms negotiations but did not. Precious years were lost by the isolation of each country from the other.

Conscious of its grave domestic and imperial problems, Russia's defiant response to America was to stonewall even Reagan's concessionary offers and attitudes. The Soviets seemed ready to respond to any and all military initiatives to strengthen America by their own programs of similar magnitudes. Those who entertain the idea that they will be unable to match America's effort have learned nothing from past experience.

Both Americans and Russians are locked in their proclaimed positions, are unprepared to rescind their past actions, and are slow to suggest new and more equitable negotiating positions. Domestic circumstances, anger, pride, and suspiciousness have made both leaderships inflexible and unwilling to take major steps toward deceleration. The lesson of this experience is clear: Do not be inflexible and dogmatic about military, or even political questions when you think that the other side is weaker. The situation may soon reverse. Temporary satisfaction and gains are not worth it.

In the 1980s the trend in the international correlation of forces has shifted in favor of the West and particularly of the United States. It would now be wise for Washington to present to the Soviets negotiating offers which, in Arnold Horelick's words,

will require Moscow to make concessions to relieve pressing US strategic concerns that accumulated in the 1970s. But such an offer must also be sensitive to Soviet strategic anxieties, which are growing; it must promise Moscow a more acceptable outcome in the mid-term than the Soviets could expect from a totally unregulated strategic competition. It should communicate US determination to shape an international environment that is increasingly less hospitable to Soviet aggrandizement, but that is not so implacably hostile as to signal that Soviet self-restraint would remain unreciprocated.*

* Arnold Horelick, "U.S.-Soviet Relations: The Return of Arms Control," in *Foreign Affairs*, Vol. 63, No. 3 (1985), p. 537.

The main risk of a dangerous Soviet-American incident stems not from a direct clash in Europe, but rather from conflicts elsewhere. In Europe both sides are extremely cautious, are in direct control of the situation, and have recognized and assimilated the truth that for the foreseeable future military actions across the demarcation line are out of the question. In regions outside Europe, where the interests of the superpowers collide, Soviet and American commitments may escalate out of control, influenced by local allies over whom the superpowers may have only limited authority.

They should continue to understand that demands for basic changes in the military balance in Europe and for redrawing the political demarcation lines are the surest way to a war-threatening confrontation. They should, however, also be aware of the danger of being manipulated by their allies outside of Europe. From this point of view, for example, a Soviet temptation to destabilize South Korea through its North Korean ally or deliver large quantities of offensive weapons to Nicaragua, or an American temptation to rearm China in a significant way or to encourage Sino-Vietnamese military clashes would be risky and could create points of tension that could escalate into Soviet-American confrontation.

The age of ideological crusades, with their high level of emotionalism and self-righteousness, is over, at least for the great powers. In the nuclear era it is necessary to break the connection between ideological predispositions and actual foreign policies. If there was ever a time in the history of mankind to have the most powerful states conduct a realpolitik, that time is now.

Neither superpower will suddenly abandon its ideology. The United States will not give up its commitment to human rights in communist countries whatever its future relations with the Soviet Union might be. The Soviet Union will not abandon its support for leftist revolutionary movements even if its relations with America improve. Russia cannot secure U.S. acquiescence in its violations of human rights with a more moderate military policy. America cannot buy off Russian global aspirations through economic incentives.

To return to the title of Richard Pipes's book, *Survival Is Not Enough,* he is absolutely right. However, this is only the beginning of the problem. The central question for America and Russia is "How much beyond survival is enough?" If what is "enough" for the Soviets is not much less than the destruction of the American democratic system, of their allies and of America's vital international interests, then there will not be survival. If what is enough for the Americans is not much less than the destruction of the Soviet system and its empire, then there will once again be no survival. In the prenuclear age ideology was often not satisfied by anything less than categorical answers. In the nuclear age the superpowers must be satisfied with answers that show greater flexibility. In calculating the preservation of principles one must also consider the price that is to be paid for tactical inflexibility under conditions of strategic consistency.

The issues at stake are interconnected. Soviet behavior that affects American policy on one issue influences the American response across the whole gamut of Soviet-American relations. In America this interconnectedness is provided by shifts in public and elite opinion. It is rarely recognized that in the Soviet Union this tendency towards linkage, while much weaker than in the United States, does nevertheless exist. It is the leaders themselves who tend to connect various aspects of American policy. A simple example is the relationship between the status of Soviet-American relations and Soviet emigration policies. The end of détente was accompanied by the virtual termination of Jewish emigration from Russia.

The imperatives for both superpowers should be defined as follows: The price of any important international action or policy should be calculated not only according to the expected response of the other superpower in that same area, but also across the whole range of Soviet-American relations. What happens to Andrei Sakharov cannot be isolated from Soviet-American relations in general, nor can the question of Most Favored Nation status for the Soviet Union.

Soviet-American relations in virtually every field are stalemated. Both sides have contributed to this situation. They have pushed themselves into corners from which they are trying to escape. It is possible that they will be able to reverse the trend of their relations. But the alternative to stalemate is not necessarily détente. Whatever the policy, it must serve what should be America's main goals in its relations with the Soviet Union: the preservation of an equitable and stable balance of strategic power; the prevention of nuclear escalation and decline in the chances of employment of nuclear weapons; the curbing of Soviet expansionism, particularly by military means, into areas of vital Western interests.

Détente became a symbol of America's lack of will and of the failure of the Western alliance to preserve its unity and to influence Soviet conduct constructively. It was identified with American weakness at home and abroad, and with an aggressive Soviet push for global power and influence. Finally it did not stop the arms race and did not stabilize the balance of power. Détente acquired a negative connotation going well beyond the actual assumptions on which it rested.

The alternative to the stalemate and slide towards a cold war is to stop and reverse the existing trend. This can simply be called normalization. It is a situation in which elements of competition and cooperation are better balanced. Yet even in the longer run cold war and détente are not the only alternatives. A cold war carries with it the dangers of an arms race and unmanaged conflict. Détente may bring the danger of demobilization of the Western alliance, of low-risk, low-cost Soviet expansionism, of tilting of the military balance in favor of the Soviet Union. We should aim at a type of relationship that can be defined as competitive coexistence or managed rivalry.

The three kinds of relations—cold war, détente, and competitive coexistence—have major areas of overlap. They can be understood as trends. Also, to use Hugh Seton-Watson's phrase, they all describe a situation of "neither peace nor war." Yet at their cores they differ significantly from one another.

Cold war describes a relationship where cooperative elements are almost entirely absent; where direct communication between the two superpowers is reduced to a minimum; where actual conflict is not managed at all; where there is a constant danger of their confrontation; where almost no rules of the game are observed except the avoidance of direct military attack; where the danger of a clash of proxy forces is always present; where the arms race in all categories is unrestricted; and where attempts to moderate each other's foreign policy consist entirely of threats and preventive actions, and what moderation there is comes simply from the specter of nuclear disaster.

Détente aims at gradually making the cooperative elements dominant over the conflicting aspects of the two superpowers; where each side tries to moderate and restrain the other's behavior by developing a web of mutual economic, cultural, and political relations and explicit or tacit agreements; where a system of incentives and disincentives is developed to achieve trade-offs between the major or even marginal concerns of the two superpowers; where the arms race, and particularly the strategic balance, is the central subject of negotiation; where these negotiations are continuous and are aimed at gradually reducing and ultimately stabilizing strategic and theater forces and preventing their introduction into new geographic areas and new technological frontiers; where communications are well developed and systematic; where military confidence-building measures are introduced and expanded; where each acknowledges the other's vital interests; where declaratory rules of interaction are agreed upon, initially in ambiguous terms that are developed gradually into a more specific code of behavior; where the level of ideological discourse is lowered and internal and external propaganda muted; where regional conflicts are to be an object of consultations prior to their explosion.

Competitive coexistence recognizes that intense rivalry will, for the foreseeable future, dominate Soviet-American relations. To avoid the dangers of nuclear escalation, elements of cooperation should be encouraged, nourished and developed; yet however urgent and necessary they are, they will in all probability remain secondary to the competitive political, ideological, and military relations. The aim of Western policies toward the Soviet Union should be neither the illusory hope of destruction nor the equally illusory hope of Soviet internal transformation.

Whatever American policies toward the Soviet Union are, they will not effect a change in its domestic system nor a shift in foreign policies. Americans have both to compete and cooperate with the Soviet Union, even if the prospects of radical domestic or international change in Soviet attitudes are very slim. This is the only realistic approach to Soviet-American relations.

What Americans can and should try to influence is the content of the Soviets' specific military and foreign policies and their readiness to exploit international opportunities. Both superpowers should recognize the state of strategic parity as a basic and unchangeable fact of their long-range military relations, and accept the level of insecurity that strategic parity implies. The United States should reconcile itself to strategic parity and abandon illusions that its technological advantages can produce strategic superiority and attain a level of security available in the past but no longer possible in the nuclear age, especially when facing such a determined and powerful opponent. The Soviet Union will have to resist exploiting temporary weaknesses of the West to engage in unilateral military buildups and recognize that such actions will inevitably evoke an American response, and will simply lead to a further escalation of the arms race.

The arms race has now reached a new stage. The destructiveness, accuracy, and number of offensive strategic weapons deployed, under development, and planned, have reached a level that makes imperative their radical limitation by channels other than the slow and very limited SALT-type negotiations. In the words of McGeorge Bundy, "we can and should come to understand, citizens and government alike, that at levels of nuclear armaments long since achieved on both sides, there is no significance, political or military, in the words *ahead* or *behind.*"* The intensified testing and development of antisatellite weapons increases each side's potential for a preemptive strike. Ronald Reagan's introduction of the Strategic Defense Initiative puts the fundamental strategic-philosophical question of deterrence versus defense on the arms control agenda for the first time. The increased mobility of strategic and theater weapons and the rapid development of cruise missiles

* McGeorge Bundy, "The Nuclear Arms Race: Can Thinking Straight Help Slow It Down?," John G. Palfery Memorial Lecture, Columbia University School of Law, October 30, 1984.

create new conditions and put new urgency to the vital question of verification.

Regardless of what position one advocates with regard to these developments, it is probable that a time of fundamental decisions with regard to arms control has been reached, a time that may only last a few years. It would be naive to entertain hopes that a comprehensive arms agreement, which would systematically tackle the central aspects of the arms race, could be achieved in anything but prolonged negotiations that would gradually build up the framework of a stable military balance. Yet the key decisions that could provide the point of departure for such a process must be made.

The central decision has to be enacted by the United States. The U.S. has two options for enhancing its security. The first is to press for mutual, verifiable, and equitable reductions of offensive weapons. The second is to press forward with unilateral plans of missile defense—the Strategic Defense Initiative. These cannot be reconciled. The first option seems better suited to achieve the goals of arms control—to deny either power the capability to launch a first strike, to build stability into the strategic balance, and to establish a new balance based on finite deterrence, that is, the minimum forces necessary to deter the other side from attacking.

A commitment to the SDI as a national goal will both intensify the arms race and preclude terrestrial arms reduction. The process of testing and deploying the space weapons system, the road from "here" to "there," carries with it an unavoidably dangerous destabilization of the nuclear balance and an almost certain end of the gradual arms control process.

SDI is presented by its supporters as a defensive effort that, while breaking the ABM treaty with the Russians, does not alter the basic premise of parity: the inability of either superpower to strike the other at a low cost of retaliation. But one need only think about how American political and military leaders would react to the initiation of an identical Soviet program.

The assumption is that no American president would ever order a strategic first strike against the Soviet Union. The Soviet leaders are not convinced of this. One superpower's strategic buildup will once again be repeated by the other superpower. Moreover, in this case, the buildup will involve not only ABMs but a large-scale expansion of "offensive" ICBMs as well—the cheapest and surest strategy against an ABM system through overloading its capacity. There can be no doubt that the Russians will commence such a buildup in offensive strategic weapons. The United States, without its complex ABM systems yet in place, will probably choose to respond with its own offensive buildup.

The incentive for the Soviets to avoid a new arms race and to be serious and forthcoming in negotiations on drastic arms cuts is much greater than in the past. Yet Washington is divided into two groups, drawing different conclusions from their similar diagnoses. One faction advocates imposing on the Soviet Union the harsh conditions of a new arms race in outer space, for which the Russians are economically and technologically much less prepared than America. The increased burden is intended to destabilize Russia internally and impose severe limitations on its activities abroad. The other faction wants to use the opportunity to achieve the sort of comprehensive and radical offensive arms control deal that would have been unthinkable ten years ago. It also wants to squeeze the Russians, but with a different goal and rationale in mind.

With one reservation, my sympathies are with the second group. The reservation concerns the time limits that should be imposed on the Russians. An arms control deal will require two preconditions. The United States should agree that if it receives a suitable offer from the Russians on offensive weapons, which can serve as the point of departure for serious negotiations, it will declare a moratorium on the testing and development of SDI components. The Russians should present such an offer in a reasonably short time. American willingness to instigate an SDI moratorium should have a clear time limit, and its continuation should be dependent on progress in the negotiations.

There is a real opportunity to cash in on Soviet weaknesses for mutual benefit. Before America rejects that option it should at least patiently explore the extent of concessions that Gorbachev would be willing to make to avoid a new arms race.

Soviet-American political relations must be normalized. To this end a number of institutions and procedures should be established: open lines of emergency communications and established sequence of emergency behavior which at each level of escalation would introduce firebreaks and provide the opportunity for pause and deescalation; systematic, intensive private communications that could reduce the ambiguities and misperceptions of each of the superpowers' positions; regular consultations on regional conflicts and civil wars in the Third World; summit meetings, which should be convened regularly even if they do not result in specific agreements but contribute only to a better understanding of each other's positions and improve atmospherics, which are extremely important to the Soviet rulers; precise definitions of what both sides consider to be their vital interests in specific geographic areas and on particular issues; resistance to the temptation of making the other side squirm in difficult situations and a commitment to preserve its "face" if agreement on substance can be achieved; nongovernmental meetings and exchanges on a strict basis of reciprocity.

A policy of competitive coexistence would both recognize the utility of trade-offs and be clear about their limits. Trade-offs are especially necessary in arms control negotiations. Unilateral U.S. concessions are both unacceptable for American and West European security, and counterproductive, considering the nature of the Soviet system and its leadership. At the same time, the United States cannot expect unilateral concessions from the Soviet Union, and therefore should present the Soviets with proposals that take into consideration their fears and interests. Another trade-off would be improvement in Soviet policies on human rights and emigration tied tacitly (but not through an act of Congress) to American readiness to grant the Soviets Most Favored Nation status. This privilege is important as an expression of equality.

Yet one should also emphasize the limits of trade-offs and the slim likelihood of their effectiveness as a central tool of American policy. The U.S. should reject an economic war if for no other reason than its ineffectiveness when other industrial democracies fail to curtail their trade with Russia. But at the same time America should have no interest in economically strengthening the Soviet Union by providing technological know-how or investment credits.

It is highly unlikely that, even in Moscow's difficult economic situation, the leadership will be ready to make military-economic trade-offs, or abandon its international ambitions. Through its economic policy the United States can have no more than marginal influence on Soviet foreign and military policy; it is impossible to buy peace. Experience shows that military power can be neutralized only by military power, and military action by military counteraction.

Managed rivalry presumes that Soviet military engagement in areas vital to Western interest will be met by American intervention. The knowledge that America will use its military power if its interests are endangered by interventions will in itself act as a restraint on the Soviet use of military power. The Soviet Union for a considerable time entertained the idea that under conditions of strategic parity its immense conventional power could be used at relatively low cost and risk to gain not only influence, but also control over selected targets of opportunity in the Third World. The United States should try to increase the costs and risks of such adventures. The Soviets should realize that the global transformation of military into political power is both more dangerous and difficult and more damaging to overall relations than they thought in the past.

It should dawn on the Soviets, as it has been recognized by Americans, that military power cannot always be used effectively in the service of political goals. As a matter of fact, despite the immensity of American military power, its deployment is relatively more difficult than it was in the past. It is not the absolute size or growth of military power that counts most, but the risks that are involved in its use. The magnitude of those risks are expressed in the might of the other superpower, the importance of the area to the other side, and the commitment of the superpower to use force if necessary to prevent its rival from gaining an important advantage.

The Soviet Union by now understands that the paralysis in U.S. foreign policy is largely over, as America has surely learned the necessity of restraint in interventionist policy, the key lesson of Vietnam. If the Soviet-American conflict is to be managed at all, both sides have to rule out direct or proxy application of military power in areas of regional conflicts and civil wars.

At present it is unclear how U.S. policy toward the Soviet Union fits into an overall scheme. There still is a tendency to treat most international developments first and foremost as an aspect of the Soviet-American conflict. It is an attitude that leads to undesirable consequences. It heats up Soviet-American relations because every civil war, regional conflict, or confrontation is interpreted as being primarily of Soviet doing. And it makes more difficult and sometimes precludes a realistic and positive American approach toward the resolution or deescalation of such conflicts. Moreover, it ignores the necessity to develop a complex of preventive political, social, economic, and military measures to counteract the proclivity of many Third World countries to become embroiled—with or without Soviet intervention—in unmanageable conflicts.

Americans need not imitate or respond in shrill rhetoric to exaggerated Soviet propaganda. There can be no doubt that ideologically the United States enjoys an enormous and insurmountable superiority over the Soviets. The time when the Soviet model was attractive to other nations is gone. Precisely because the Soviets are on the defensive in this respect, they make up in volume and intensity what they lack in substance.

A managed rivalry constitutes a separate and distinctive type of relationship. Yet in public discourse, the terms that are most often used and counterposed to each other as mutually exclusive options of American policy toward the Soviet Union, are détente, containment, and confrontation. This triad is important, not because of its intellectual or analytical force, but because it reflects the public view of the Soviet-American conflict. It reinforces the model of regulated rivalry as the most rational option of Soviet-American relations.

It is probable that détente, containment, and confrontation will all characterize international relations in the 1980s. No one of these approaches will dominate. Indeed, the three should be present as deliberate and coordinated policies of the Western alliance, and their particular mix will depend not only on Soviet conduct but also on differing attitudes within the alliance.

Under the conditions of the nuclear revolution, strategic parity, and mutually assured destruction, détente between West and East in one form or another is simply unavoidable. The scope, intensity and forms may vary over time, but it is necessary to avoid a runaway arms race and the potentially destabilizing and unpredictable consequences of conflict, as well as to promote cooperation in areas where interests overlap.

The main area for restoring détente is in military relations. The instruments for attaining and preserving it were developed in the 1970s but in practice they did not work. *But in the 1970s no policy towards the Soviet Union would have worked.* American paralysis denied credibility to any coherent policy. The situation in the 1980s is quite different.

Avoidance of nuclear war, however, does not exhaust the goals of the Western alliance. These also include the prevention of Soviet global expansion, the survival of independent and democratic systems in the West, and orderly and evolutionary change in Third World countries. A major dilemma is how to arrest Soviet expansion while at the same time minimizing the chances of nuclear escalation. If the policy of détente renders the competition more stable and thereby less dangerous, the policy of containing the Soviet Union is no less necessary. Indeed, détente makes sense when it contains the expansion of Soviet power. The policy of containment and its limitations are subject to various interpretations within the Western alliance. Implemented with determination and skill, it is essential.

Soviet power can be contained successfully only by substantially increasing the costs and risks of the kind of international conduct it pursued from 1975 to 1979. The Soviets will continue to exploit targets of opportunity in the Third World. The Western alliance has no choice but to make known its vital interests outside Europe and to prepare a credible response whenever those vital interests are threatened. For this response to be effective, the United States and Western Europe must be prepared for political, economic, and military confrontation with the Soviet Union or its satellites. The containment of Soviet power can be achieved only if the threat of East-West confrontation is credible.

The teaching of history, or, for that matter, political science and sociology, is almost without exception the distillation of the past. Yet the application of the lessons of the past to the present and the future cannot be abstract. Those who apply them have to consider the social, political,

and economic realities of political systems, as they exist today. This jux-
taposition of the abstract past and the specific present creates problems
for the policy-makers who try to shape the present and the future. These
represent among other things the disparity between what leaders want to
do and what they can do. Leaving aside the question whether politicians
are inclined to learn from the past, these dilemmas represent the knowledge of what should be done and what is possible and likely in the system which the policy-makers inherited: one which has been shaped and
defined in its key parameters by the past.

As was mentioned before, the nuclear revolution requires a redefinition of many concepts that were adopted in the prenuclear era. The
famous Clausewitzian formula "War is the continuation of politics by
different means" is one such concept. For this formula to sound rational
today, it has to be rephrased to read "Politics is the avoidance of nuclear
war without surrendering one's core values and interests." The difficulties of an American policy that would pursue the dual goals of the above
formula have become particularly obvious in the last decade.

Whether a carefully managed policy toward the Soviet Union, with
limited, realistic aims, can be conducted over time under the American
system, or whether the shifting moods of the electorate and the media
will again lurch from one extreme to the other, is not clear. It certainly
should be understood, however, that American leaders in both parties
have a duty to present to the public the grim reality of a prolonged conflict and the need for flexibility in the use of foreign policy resources in
the decades to come. To the end of this century and probably even beyond, democratic nations have no choice but to face the conflict with the
Soviet Union while at the same time striving to cooperate in areas of
mutual interest. There is no precedent in human history for the type of
danger now being faced, or for the complexity of the issues that must be
resolved. For Americans, knowledge of both the adversary and themselves is an indispensable factor in the search of an effective and safe
policy toward the Soviet Union.

In his survey of the forty years of troubled Soviet-American coexistence, Adam Ulam's analysis of the past and his prescription for the future are wise and accurate:

... an effective foreign policy, at least for a democracy, does not depend only on
the skill of the experts. Both the American public and its government ought to
be mindful of the past. The 1940s and early 1950s teach us how vital it is to cor-
rectly assess strengths and vulnerabilities, both our own and those of the USSR.
The Khrushchev era shows how important it is to penetrate the rhetoric of Soviet policies and discern their real aims and fears. The late 1960s and the 1970s
warn against allowing democracy's internal turmoil to affect unduly its foreign
stance. And the current emotionalism in which the debate about subjects like

nuclear arms control and international terrorism is swathed makes it all the more important for the American public to develop that combination of sophistication and patience, qualities which in turn enable the policymakers to combine tenacity of purpose with a flexibility of tactics—the necessary prerequisites for a viable U.S. policy toward the Soviet Union.*

* Adam Ulam, "Forty Years of Troubled Coexistence," *Foreign Affairs*, Vol. 64, No. 1 (Fall 1985), p. 52.

Bibliographical Essay

I

The following primary sources are of central importance in gathering statistical data on the Soviet Union: (1) *Narodnoe khoziaistvo SSSR; SSSR v tsifrakh;* and *Sel'skoe khoziaistvo SSSR.* The *Handbook of Economic Statistics* (1983) published by the Central Intelligence Agency is also an important source of data on the Communist world in general. For additional statistical data, also see J. Scherer, *USSR: Facts and Figures Annual.*

From the studies prepared for the Joint Economic Committee of the United States Congress, the following publications are especially relevant: (1) *USSR: Measures of Economic Growth and Development: 1950–1980* (December 1982); (2) *The Soviet Economy in a Time of Change* (2 volumes, October 1979); and (3) *The Soviet Economy in the 1980s: Problems and Prospects* (Parts I and II, 1982).

For those who do not read Russian, access to the contents of the Soviet press is provided by the *Current Digest of the Soviet Press,* which publishes each week a translated selection of relevant materials. Documentary records of the party congresses, beginning with the 19th Congress in 1952, are published by the *Current Digest of the Soviet Press* under the title *Current Soviet Policies.* The most recent issue is Volume VII, which records the speeches and proceedings of the 26th Congress, held in 1981.

On the issue of the stability of the Soviet regime, see the extended discussion of this topic in Seweryn Bialer, *Stalin's Successors* (1980). For the importance of political culture, see Archie Brown, ed., *Political Culture and Communist Studies* (1984), as well as Tibor Szamuely, *The Russian Tradition* (1974). Also of considerable interest is the article by Zbigniew K. Brzezinski, "Soviet Politics: From the Future to the Past?" in Paul Cocks, Robert V. Daniels, and Nancy Heer, eds., *The Dynamics of Soviet Politics* (1976).

The following works are of importance to any general understanding of Soviet stability and the policy process: Robert C. Tucker, *The Soviet Political Mind: Stalinism and Post-Stalin Change* (1971); Stephen Cohen, Alexander Rabinowitch, and Robert Sharlet, eds., *The Soviet Union Since Stalin* (1980); Tucker, ed., *Stalinism: Essays in Historical Interpretation* (1977); Brown and Michael Kaser, eds., *The Soviet Union Since the Fall of Khrushchev* (1975); Brown and Kaser, eds., *Soviet Policy for the 1980s* (1982); Karl Ryavec, ed.,

Soviet Society and the Communist Party (1978); Donald Kelly, ed., *Soviet Politics in the* *Brezhnev Era* (1980); John Strong, ed., *The Soviet Union Under Brezhnev and Kosygin* (1971); Jerry Hough, *The Soviet Union and Social Science Theory* (1977); Chalmers Johnson, ed., *Change in Communist Systems* (1970); and Erik P. Hoffmann, ed., *The Soviet Union in the 1980s* (1984).

The problems confronting the Soviet regime in the areas of technological development and diffusion are examined in the following works: Loren Graham, "Science and Computers in Soviet Society," in Hoffmann, ed., *The Soviet Union in the 1980s* (1984); Frederick J. Fleron, Jr., ed., *Technology and Communist Culture* (1977); and Ronald Amann and Julian Cooper, eds., *Industrial Innovation in the Soviet Union* (1982). The interaction between politics and technological performance from a broad historical perspective is analyzed by Bruce Parrott in his excellent study *Politics and Technology in the Soviet Union* (1983). A narrower focus of attention is employed by Hoffmann and Robbin Laird in *The Scientific-Technological Revolution and Soviet Foreign Policy* (1982). Concentrating primarily on the Brezhnev period, they examine the extent to which the Soviet leadership is willing to rely on the West for technology.

An outstanding overview of the structural defects inherent in the Soviet "command economy" is provided by Charles Lindblom in Part VI of his *Politics and Markets: The World's Political Economic Systems* (1977). The deep social and economic problems facing the present Soviet leadership are analyzed in the following works as well: Abram Bergson and Herbert S. Levine, eds., *The Soviet Economy: Toward the Year 2000* (1983); Marshall Goldman, *The USSR in Crisis: The Failure of an Economic System* (1983); Konstantin Simis, *USSR: The Corrupt Society* (1982); Morris Bornstein, ed., *The Soviet Economy: Continuity and Change* (1981); George Feiwal, *The Soviet Quest for Economic Efficiency* (1972); Holland Hunter, ed., *The Future of the Soviet Economy, 1978-1985* (1978); and Karl-Eugen Wadekin, "Soviet Agriculture's Dependence on the West" in *Foreign Affairs* (Spring 1982).

Useful analyses of contemporary Soviet society from a radical socialist perspective are contained in the works of Tony Cliff, especially his *State Capitalism in Russia* (1974), and of Milovan Djilas, *The Unperfect Society: Beyond the New Class* (1969). Also see *The Unfinished Revolution* (1967) by Isaac Deutscher.

A first-rate introduction to the issue of reform in the Soviet Union is presented by Stephen F. Cohen in his "The Friends and Foes of Change: Reformism and Conservatism in the Soviet Union" in Cohen et al., eds., *The Soviet Union Since Stalin* (1980). Also see Cohen's "Toward a Moscow Spring?" in Cohen, ed., *An End to Silence* (1982). Of equal interest are the following studies, which assess the pressures for and against economic reform: Abraham Katz, *The Politics of Economic Reform in the Soviet Union* (1972); Bruce Parrott, *Politics and Technology in the Soviet Union* (1983); Moshe Lewin, *Political Undercurrents in Soviet Economic Debates* (1974); Joseph Berliner, "Managing the USSR Economy: Alternative Models" in *Problems of Communism* (January–February 1983); Bornstein, "Improving the Soviet Economic Mechanism" in *Soviet Studies* (January 1985); Gertrude Schroeder, "The Soviet Economy on a 'Treadmill' of Reforms" in *Soviet Economy in a Time of Change* (1977).

On agricultural reform and rural policy in general, see Thane Gustafson, *Reform in Soviet Politics: The Lessons of Recent Policies on Land and Water* (1981) as well as Werner Hahn, *The Politics of Soviet Agriculture* (1972). Also see Alexander Yanov, *The Drama of the Soviet 1960s: A Lost Reform* (1984).

The role of the professional stratum in the policy-making process is the subject of *Social Scientists and Policy-Making in the USSR,* edited by Richard Remneck (1977).

On the subject of political succession, the following works are of particular interest: Bialer, *Stalin's Successors* (1980), Part II; "Succession and Turnover of Soviet Elites,"

Journal of International Affairs, Special Issue on Leadership Succession in Communist States (Fall/Winter 1978); Grey Hodnett, "Succession Contingencies in the Soviet Union," in *Problems of Communism* (March–April 1975); Donna Bahry, "Politics, Succession, and Public Policy in Communist Systems: A Review Article," in *Soviet Studies* (April 1983); George Breslauer, *Khrushchev and Brezhnev as Leaders: Building Authority in Soviet Politics* (1982); and Myron Rush, *Political Succession in the USSR,* 2nd ed. (1969). For a general discussion of succession in modern nation-states, see Dankwart Rustow, "Succession in the Twentieth Century," *Journal of International Affairs* (1964).

For the personalities and issues involved in the post-Brezhnev accessions to power, see Jerry Hough, "Andropov's First Year" in *Problems of Communism* (November–December 1983); Mark Zlotnik, "Chernenko Succeeds," *Problems of Communism* (March–April 1984); and Brown, "Gorbachev: New Man in the Kremlin," *Problems of Communism* (May–June 1985).

II

Regarding Soviet doctrine on revolution, one can find official documents of the Comintern period in Jane Degras, ed., *The Communist International, 1919–1943,* 3 vols. (1956–65). For an examination of the shifting tactical doctrines of the Comintern, see Kermit E. McKenzie, *Comintern and World Revolution, 1928–1943: The Shaping of Doctrine* (1964). V. G. Afanasyev, *Fundamentals of Scientific Communism,* trans. David Skvirsky (Moscow: Progress, 1977), presents *inter alia* the contemporary Soviet view of the appropriate methods for achieving socialist revolution, including a review of the conditions that allow for "peaceful" or "armed" revolution in developed and developing countries. See also Iurii Andreevich Krasin, *Sociology of Revolution: A Marxist View,* trans. Jim Riordan (Moscow: Progress, 1972).

On the actual conquest of Eastern Europe, see the classic study by Brzezinski, *The Soviet Bloc: Unity and Conflict* (2nd ed., 1967). Wlodzimierz Brus, "Stalnism and the 'People's Democracies'," in Tucker, ed., *Stalinism: Essays in Historical Interpretation* (1977), deals with the question of whether Stalinism was an inevitable stage in the development of Communist East Europe or the result of a conscious Soviet policy to remake these countries in its own image. For a Soviet view of these events, see the chapter on the formation of the "world socialist system" in *Soviet Foreign Policy, 1917–1980:* Vol. 2, *1945–1980,* under the general editorship of A. A. Gromyko and B. N. Ponomarev (Moscow: Progress, 1981). For the view of a former foreign Communist party leader, see Fernando Claudin, *The Communist Movement: From Comintern to Cominform* (2 vols., 1975). See also Djilas, *Conversations with Stalin* (1962).

On general Soviet relations with East Europe today, be sure to see Sarah Terry, ed., *Soviet Policy in Eastern Europe* (1985). Jan Vanous, "East European Economic Slowdown," *Problems of Communism* (July–August 1982), examines the nature of the region's economic difficulties as well as possible future trends. For details on the sort of burden Eastern Europe places on the Soviet economy, see Michael Marrese and Vanous, *Soviet Subsidization of Trade with Eastern Europe: A Soviet Perspective* (1983).

A great deal of information on the general economic situation in Eastern Europe can be found in *East European Economic Assessment* (2 vols., 1981), papers presented to the Joint Economic Committee, United States Congress, and also in NATO Economics and Information Directorates, *Economic Reforms in Eastern Europe and Prospects for the 1980s* (1980). Egon Neuberger and Laura D'Andrea Tyson, eds., *The Impact of International Economic Disturbances on the Soviet Union and Eastern Europe* (1980) and Bornstein, Zvi

Gitelman, and William Zimmerman, eds., *East-West Relations and the Future of Eastern Europe* (1981), deal with the effect of world economic conditions and of East-West relations on Eastern Europe and, in the latter case, with the effect of these factors and East Europe's own domestic policies and foreign relations on the region's relationship with Moscow.

Jacques Rupnik, "The Politics of Economic Crisis in Eastern Europe," *Problems of Communism* (July–August 1982), takes issue with the notion that East Europe's economic problems stem from its greater openness to the West in the 1970s and stresses the importance of considering the political contribution to and consequences of economic problems. Antonin J. Liehm, "East Central Europe and the Soviet Model," *Problems of Communism* (September–October 1981), assesses the basic situation in Eastern Europe in terms of a Soviet-style system that has been "grafted" onto foreign political cultures and that those cultures repeatedly strive to reject. Jan Triska and Charles Gati, eds., *Blue-Collar Workers in Eastern Europe* (1981), focuses on the growing assertiveness of the East European industrial working class.

Christopher D. Jones, *Soviet Influence in Eastern Europe: Political Autonomy and the Warsaw Pact* (1981), examines the Warsaw Treaty Organization as an instrument of Soviet control within the Eastern bloc. For a view of the same organization's utility as a forum for settling intrabloc disputes, see Robin Alison Remington's *The Warsaw Pact: Case Studies in Communist Conflict Resolution* (1971) and "Politics of Accommodation: Redefining Soviet–East European Relations," in Roger E. Kanet, ed., *Soviet Foreign Policy in the 1980s* (1982).

On Poland, Abraham Brumberg, ed., *Poland: Genesis of a Revolution* (1983), offers the best available study of the underlying causes of the social upheaval in 1980–81, with analytic articles focusing on specific institutions and sectors of society and translations of primary materials. Other documents on the strikes of 1980 and the origins of Solidarity can be found in Oliver MacDonald, ed., *Polish August: Documents from the Beginnings of the Polish Workers' Rebellion, Gdansk, August 1980* (1981). *Poland Today: The State of the Republic* (1981), compiled by the "Experience and Future" Discussion Group, is a study written by a group of Polish intellectuals, just months before the strikes of 1980, which argues Poland's need for fundamental reform if it is to avoid a "social eruption." David E. Paul and Maurice D. Simon, "Poland Today and Czechoslovakia 1968," *Problems of Communism* (September–October, 1981), draws attention to Polish society's success in confronting their government with the sort of united social front that the Czechs were never able to achieve in 1968.

Martin Malia, "Poland: The Winter War," *New York Review of Books* (March 18, 1982), offers what is perhaps the best concise exposition of why the Polish experiment was destined to fail. Solidarity, although it sought to conduct a "self-limiting revolution" and to avoid challenging the Soviets, socialism, or state power, by its very existence created a "dual power," denied "the Lie" of the system, and thereby threatened to undermine the communist regime's legitimacy.

Richard D. Anderson, Jr., "Soviet Decision-making and Poland," *Problems of Communism* (March–April 1982), analyzes the political process behind the apparent wavering within the Soviet leadership concerning direct military intervention in Poland. For a view giving the United States partial credit for deterring Soviet intervention, see Brzezinski, *Power and Principle: Memoirs of the National Security Advisor, 1977–1981* (1983). See also Alexander M. Haig, Jr., *Caveat: Realism, Reagan and Foreign Policy* (1984).

Zbigniew M. Fallenbuchl, "Poland's Economic Crisis," *Problems of Communism* (March–April 1982), outlines the history and nature of Poland's economic crisis and explains how the imposition of martial law could further exacerbate the situation. For a view of General Jaruzelski as a potential Polish Kadar, see Gati, "Polish Futures, Western Options," *Foreign Affairs* (Winter 1982–83).

Implications of martial law in Poland for U.S. policy are discussed in Dimitri K. Simes, "Clash over Poland," *Foreign Policy* (Spring 1982). For a journalistic history of the events in Poland in 1980–81, see Timothy Garton Ash, *The Polish Revolution: Solidarity* (1983). A Soviet view of (at best) uneven sophistication can be found in Igor Medvedev et al., *Who Pushed Poland to the Brink?,* which includes discussion of such topics as "the tactics of 'quiet' counterrevolution."

On China, Kenneth G. Lieberthal, *Sino-Soviet Conflict in the 1970s: Its Evolution and Implications for the Strategic Triangle,* Rand Report #R-2342-NA (July 1978), provides background and argues that the United States has little ability to manipulate the conflict, but also that the likely "no rapprochement/no war" situation should not be unfavorable for U.S. policy. Donald S. Zagoria, "The Moscow-Beijing Detente," *Foreign Affairs* (Spring 1983) and William E. Griffith, "Sino-Soviet Rapprochement?," *Problems of Communism* (March–April 1983), examines the interest that the Chinese and the Soviets have displayed recently in improving their relations, but both authors, while finding the interest real, also find that there are substantial limits concerning the extent to which each side is willing to go. See also Zagoria, ed., *Soviet Policy in East Asia* (1982). Implications for U.S. policy are discussed in Richard H. Solomon, ed., *The China Factor: Sino-American Relations and the Global Scene* (1981).

Harry Harding, "Change and Continuity in Chinese Foreign Policy," *Problems of Communism* (March–April 1983), argues that despite the major changes in the nature, degree, and direction of Chinese involvement in world affairs over the past three decades, Chinese policy has shown a number of "strategic continuities," including concern with strategic independence, economic self-reliance, and opposition to hegemonism. On Chinese strategic considerations, also see Jonathan D. Pollack, "Chinese Global Strategy and Soviet Power," *Problems of Communism* (January–February 1981). Herbert J. Ellison, ed., *The Sino-Soviet Conflict: A Global Perspective* (1982), examines not only the various aspects of bilateral Sino-Soviet relations—political, security, economic—but also the impact of their dispute on international politics in general and on a number of specific regions.

Zagoria, "China's Quiet Revolution," *Foreign Affairs* (Spring 1984), provides background on the extensive domestic economic and political reforms of the post-Mao era, as well as some of the obstacles yet to be overcome. Perhaps the best book available on the Chinese economy is A. Doak Barnett, *China's Economy in Global Perspective* (1981).

For a discussion of the current state of U.S. scholarship on Chinese foreign policy, see Samuel S. Kim, "China's Place in World Politics," *Problems of Communism* (March–April 1982). Those with a knowledge of Russian can find a Soviet view of China by a highly regarded analyst in Fedor Burlatskii, *Mao Tszedun i evo nasledniki* [Mao Zedong and His Heirs] (Moscow: Mezhdunarodnye Otnosheniia, 1979).

III

A large number of studies concerning the sources and nature of Soviet international policy have been collected in Hoffmann and Fleron, eds., *The Conduct of Soviet Foreign Policy,* 2nd ed. (1980). An evaluation of the domestic determinants of foreign policy, such as capabilities, political beliefs, and political processes, can be found in Morton Schwartz, *The Foreign Policy of the USSR: Domestic Factors* (1975).

Robert Legvold, "The Nature of Soviet Power," *Foreign Affairs* (October 1977), evaluates the various resources available to Soviet foreign policy against the backdrop of a continuously evolving international setting. Christopher Bertram, ed., *Prospects of Soviet Power in the 1980s,* Two Parts, Adelphi Papers Nos. 151 and 152 (Summer–Autumn 1979), presents papers from an International Institute for Strategic Studies conference on the international interests and power of the Soviet Union from the Soviet perspective. An extensive study of the use of military force by the Soviet Union, making use of both aggregate analysis and individual case studies, is Stephen S. Kaplan et al., *Diplomacy of Power: Soviet Armed Forces as a Political Instrument* (1981). Probably the best available analysis of civil-military relations nd their evolution within the Soviet Union is to be found in Timothy J. Colton, *Commissars, Commanders, and Civilian Authority: The Structure of Soviet Military Politics* (1979). For a recent study stressing the importance of the professional military leadership in determining the technical aspect—and influencing the political aspect—of Soviet military doctrine, see Kenneth Currie, "Soviet General Staff's New Role,"*Problems of Communism* (March–April 1984). Dan L. Strode and Rebecca V. Strode, "Diplomacy and Defense in Soviet National Security Policy," *International Security* (Fall 1983), outlines a current policy dispute between those who advocate the use of diplomacy in order to influence the policies of opponents and those who favor heavier "unilateralist" reliance on the USSR's own defense potential.

Just how much the Soviet Union actually spends on its military has been a matter of controversy. In addition to Rush's article, "Guns over Growth in Soviet Policy," listed in Part I, see Franklyn D. Holzman, "Soviet Military Spending: Assessing the Numbers Game," *International Security* (Spring 1982), as well as William Zimmerman and Glenn Palmer, "Words and Deeds in Soviet Foreign Policy: The Case of Soviet Military Expenditures," *The American Political Science Review* (June 1983). A comparison of the divergent estimates presented by the Central Intelligence Agency and the Defense Intelligence Agency can be found in Richard F. Kaufman, *Soviet Defense Trends* (1983), a study prepared for the Subcommittee on International Trade, Finance and Security Economics of the Joint Economic Committee, United States Congress.

The policy known as détente has become quite controversial within the American political arena and the debate concerning its relative merits has yet to die down. For an authoritative exposition of American intentions in détente, see Henry A. Kissinger's 1974 statement to the Senate Foreign Relations Committee, reprinted as "The Process of Détente" in Kissinger, *American Foreign Policy* (3rd ed., 1977); also see his *White House Years* (1979). For a view of détente as a Soviet tactic for improving its position vis-à-vis the West, see "Détente: Moscow's View," in Richard Pipes, *U.S.-Soviet Relations in the Era of Detente* (1981). John Lewis Gaddis, "The Rise, Fall and Future of Detente," *Foreign Affairs* (Winter 1983/84), views détente as a form of containment policy, which, given greater discrimination, consistency, and central direction, could still be made workable. For more on this, see Gaddis, *Strategies of Containment: A Critical Appraisal of Postwar American National Security Policy* (1982). On the relationship between détente and Soviet domestic politics, see Peter M. E. Volten, *Brezhnev's Peace Program: A Study of Soviet Domestic Political Process and Power* (1982) and Harry Gelman, *The Brezhnev Politburo and the Decline of Détente* (1981).

Two of the central issues in East-West relations during the détente period concern arms control and superpower rivalry in the Third World. The history of the arms control process can be followed through John Newhouse, *Cold Dawn: The Story of SALT* (1973) and Strobe Talbott's *Endgame: The Inside Story of SALT II* (1980) and *Deadly Gambits: The Reagan Administration and the Stalemate in Nuclear Arms Control* (1984). For an analysis of the political and strategic impact of the arms control process on East-West relations and on national security decision-making in the United States and the Soviet Union, see Thomas W. Wolfe, *The SALT Experience* (1979). For a view on how the prevailing character of East-West political relations affects the outcome of arms control negotiations, see Marshall D. Shulman, "U.S.-Soviet Relations and the Control of Nuclear Weapons," in Barry M. Blechman, ed., *Rethinking the U.S. Strategic Posture: A Report from the Aspen Consortium on Arms Control and Security Issues* (1982). For background on the Soviet weapons procurement process, see Arthur J. Alexander, *Decision-making in Soviet Weapons Procurement*, Adelphi Paper Nos. 147/148 (Winter 1978–79). See also Shulman, "SALT and the Soviet Union," in Mason Willrich and John B. Rhinelander, eds., *SALT: The Moscow Agreements and Beyond* (1974).

For further information on current arms control questions, see the series of reports entitled *Challenges for U.S. National Security*, prepared by the staff of the Carnegie Panel on U.S. Security and the Future of Arms Control (various dates). For an analysis of the impact nuclear weapons have had on the nature of international relations in general, see Michael Mandelbaum, *The Nuclear Revolution: International Politics Before and After Hiroshima* (1981).

On Soviet policy and superpower rivalry in the Third World, see Zagoria, "Into the Breach: New Soviet Alliances in the Third World," and Legvold, "The Super Rivals: Conflict in the Third World," both in *Foreign Affairs* (Spring 1979). The evolution of Soviet economic policy toward developing countries is analyzed in Elizabeth K. Valkenier, *The Soviet Union and the Third World: An Economic Bind* (1983). For military aspects of the Soviet Union's interest in the Third World, see Stephen T. Hosmer and Wolfe, *Soviet Policy and Practice Toward Third World Conflicts* (1981) and Mark N. Katz, *The Third World in Soviet Military Thought* (1982). Evaluations of the effectiveness of the Soviet Union's Third World policies are presented in Robert H. Donaldson, ed., *The Soviet Union in the Third World: Successes and Failures* (1981). For a Soviet point of view, see Henry Trofimenko, "The Third World and U.S.-Soviet Competition," *Foreign Affairs* (Spring 1981).

Another aspect of détente, and one of particular interest to the Soviets, concerns economic relations. On this, see in particular Philip Hanson, *Trade and Technology in Soviet-Western Relations* (1981). The European dimension of Soviet economic relations is highlighted in Angela E. Stent, *From Embargo to Ostpolitik: The Political Economy of West German–Soviet Relations, 1955–1980* (1981). Economic relations with the Soviet Union have also been controversial in the United States. See Ellen L. Frost and Stent, "NATO's Troubles with East-West Trade," *International Security* (Summer 1983) and Gustafson, *Selling the Russians the Rope? Soviet Technology Policy and U.S. Export Controls*, RAND Study No. R-2649-ARPA (1981). On the role of foreign economic relations in Soviet development and domestic politics, see Parrott, *Politics and Technology in the Soviet Union* (1983) and Hoffmann and Laird, *"The Scientific-Technological Revolution" and Soviet Foreign Policy* (1982).

For an overall analysis of Ronald Reagan's policy toward the Soviet Union, see Alexander Dallin and Gail Lapidus, "Reagan and the Russians: United States Policy Toward the Soviet Union and Eastern Europe," in Kenneth A. Oye, Robert J. Lieber, and Donald Rothschild, eds., *Eagle Defiant: United States Foreign Policy in the 1980s* (1983). An analysis of Reagan's defense policy as going beyond traditional containment concerns to a global offense-dominated strategy is found in Barry R. Posen and Stephen Van Evera, "Defense Policy and the Reagan Administration: Departure from Containment," printed in the same book as well as in *International Security* (Summer 1983). See also Robert Jervis, *The Illogic of American Nuclear Strategy* (1984).

A number of studies have been devoted to explaining Soviet perspectives on the United States. For their view of the workings of the U.S. domestic political system, see Schwartz, *Soviet Perceptions of the United States* (1978). Concerning foreign policy, see John Lenczowski, *Soviet Perceptions of U.S. Foreign Policy: A Study of Ideology, Power and*

Consensus (1982). An analysis of the Soviet Union's surprise at the Reagan Administration's policies and the Soviet response to them can be found in Lawrence T. Caldwell and Legvold, "Reagan Through Soviet Eyes," *Foreign Policy* (Fall 1983). See also the analysis and documents in Talbott, *The Russians and Reagan,* with a foreword by Cyrus R. Vance (1984).

A seminal work on the application of cognitive science to international affairs is Jervis, *Perception and Misperception in International Politics* (1976). With special reference to East-West strategic relations, see Jervis, "Deterrence and Perception," *International Security* (Winter 1982/83). See also Arthur A. Stein, "When Misperception Matters," *World Politics (July 1982). One might also want to look at the chapters on information processing and decision-making in Glenn H. Snyder and Paul Diesing, Conflict Among Nations: Bargaining, Decision Making, and System Structure in International Crises* (1977).

On the subject of future alternatives for restructuring East-West relations, two important recent books are Stanley Hoffmann, *Dead Ends: American Foreign Policy in the New Cold War* (1983) and Aaron Wildavsky et al., *Beyond Containment: Alternative American Policies Toward the Soviet Union* (1983). See also the statements by Stanley Hoffmann and Cyrus Vance in *Building the Peace: U.S. Foreign Policy for the Next Decade* (1982), No. 5 in the series *Alternatives for the 1980s.*

Caldwell and Diebold, *Soviet-American Relations in the 1980s: Superpower Politics and East-West Trade* (1981), present two lengthy essays—one on general Soviet-American relations and one on the position of the Soviet Union and East Europe in the world economy—which focus on ways in which East-West relations can be remodeled along more cooperative lines. See Legvold, "Containment Without Confrontation," *Foreign Policy* (Spring 1984), on the need for a two-track Soviet policy that sacrifices neither firmness nor cooperation. Joseph S. Nye, Jr., "Can America Manage Its Soviet Policy?," *Foreign Affairs* (Spring 1984), discusses the difficulties that the American political system puts in the way of coherent and consistent policy-making and proposes a way to fit policy to the system rather than trying to overcome it. On this, see also Nye, ed., *The Making of America's Soviet Policy* (1984).

On the need and means for avoiding superpower crises, see Alexander L. George, ed., *Managing U.S.-Soviet Rivalry: Problems of Crisis Prevention* (1983) and also Arthur Macy Cox, *Russian Roulette: The Superpower Game* (1982), with a Soviet commentary by Georgii Arbatov. On the subject of why some crises are resolved while others lead to war, see Richard Ned Lebow, *Between Peace and War: The Nature of International Crisis* (1981).

Index

A NOTE ABOUT THE AUTHOR

Seweryn Bialer is Ruggles Professor of Political Science and Director of the Research Institute on International Change at Columbia University, and a member of the Executive Committee of Columbia's W. Averell Harriman Institute for the Advanced Study of the Soviet Union. He was born in Berlin, Germany, in 1926 and was educated at the Institute of Social Sciences in Warsaw, Poland, where he received a doctorate in political economy in 1955, and at Columbia University, where he received a second doctorate, in political science, in 1966. In 1983 Prof. Bialer became the first Sovietologist to receive a MacArthur Fellowship. He is the author of several books, including *Stalin's Successors* (1980).

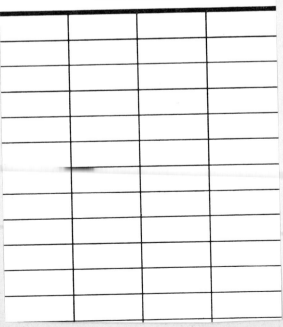

DATE DUE